PRENTICE HALL MATHEMATICS

COURSE 3

All-In-One Student Workbook

Version A

Boston, Massachusetts
Upper Saddle River, New Jersey

ISBN 0-13-201395-9

2 3 4 5 6 7 8 9 10 10 09 08 07 06

Daily Notetaking Guide

Daily Notetaking Guide (continued)

Practice, Guided Problem Solving, Vocabulary

Chapter 1: Integers and Algebraic Expressions

Chapter 2: Rational Numbers

Chapter 3: Real Numbers and the Coordinate Plane

Chapter 4: Applications of Proportions

Chapter 5: Applications of Percent

Chapter 6: Equations and Inequalities

Chapter 7: Geometry

Chapter 8: Measurement

Chapter 9: Using Graphs to Analyze Data

Chapter 10: Probability

Chapter 11: Functions

Chapter 12: Polynomials and Properties of Exponents

A Note to the Student:

This section of your workbook contains notetaking pages for each lesson in your student edition. They are structured to help you take effective notes in class. They will also serve as a study guide as you prepare for tests and quizzes.

Name ______________________ Class ______________ Date ______________

Lesson 1-1

Algebraic Expressions and the Order of Operations

Lesson Objective To write algebraic expressions and evaluate them using the order of operations	**NAEP 2005 Strand:** Number Operations, Algebra **Topic:** Properties of Number and Operations; Variables, Expressions, and Operations **Local Standards:** ______________

Vocabulary and Key Concepts

Order of Operations

1. Work inside [ ] symbols.
2. [ ] and [ ] in order from left to right.
3. [ ] and [ ] in order from left to right.

A variable is ______________________________

An algebraic expression is ______________________________

____

To simplify is ______________________________

____

To evaluate is ______________________________

____

Example

1 Writing an Expression A student earns $5 an hour babysitting. The hours vary from week to week. Define a variable. Write an algebraic expression for how much the student earns in a week.

Words [$5 an hour] times [number of hours spent babysitting]

Let h = number of hours spent babysitting.

Expression [ ] · [ ]

The algebraic expression [ ] represents the student's weekly earnings.

Quick Check

1. At a ballpark, team hats are sold for $15 each. Write an algebraic expression for the cost of any number n of team hats.

[ ]

Name ______________________ Class ______________ Date ______________

Examples

2 Using the Order of Operations Evaluate $t + (12 - t) \div 2$ for $t = 6$.

$t + (12 - t) \div 2 = \square + (12 - \square) \div 2$ ← **Substitute $\square$ for *t*.**

$= 6 + \square \div 2$ ← **Work within parentheses.**

$= 6 + \square$ ← **Divide.**

$= \square$ ← **Add.**

3 Internet Access An Internet provider charges \$25 for a connection fee and \$16 per month.

Find the cost for 5 months of Internet access.

Make a table to show the pattern of costs by month.

Number of Months	Connection Fee	Monthly Cost	Total
1	25	$16(\square)$	$25 + 16(\square)$
2	25	$16(\square)$	$25 + 16(\square)$
3	25	$16(\square)$	$25 + 16(\square)$
4	25	$16(\square)$	$25 + 16(\square)$
m	25	$16(\square)$	$25 + 16(\square)$

Use *m* to represent any number of months. → (row *m*) ← **total for *m* months**

The expression $25 + 16(\square)$ models the total cost.

$25 + 16(\square) = 25 + 16(\square)$ ← **Substitute $\square$ for *m* to evaluate for 5 months.**

$= 25 + \square$ ← **Multiply.**

$= \square$ ← **Add.**

The total cost for 5 months is $\square$.

Quick Check

2. Evaluate $3x + x \div 3$ for $x = 12$.

$\square$

3. The monthly cost increases to \$21. Write an expression to model the total cost. Find the total cost for 12 months of Internet access.

$\square$

Name ______________________ Class ______________ Date ______________

Lesson 1-2

Integers and Absolute Value

Lesson Objective	NAEP 2005 Strand: Number Properties and Operations
To find the absolute values of integers and to use absolute value to compare integers	**Topics:** Number Sense; Properties of Number and Operations **Local Standards:** ______________

Vocabulary

Two numbers are opposites if ______________________

Integers are ______________________

Absolute value is ______________________

Examples

1 Finding Absolute Value Find $|-2|$.

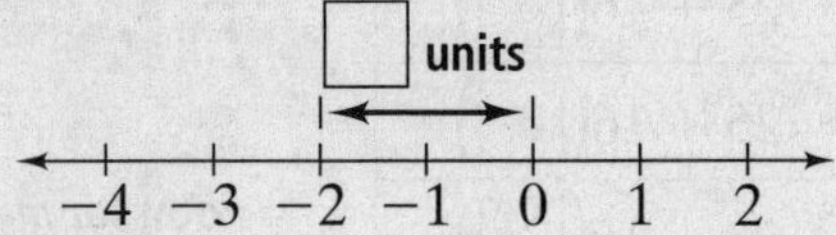

On the number line, −2 is ☐ units from 0. This means $|-2| =$ ☐.

2 Comparing and Ordering Integers Order –7, 5, and –4 from least to greatest.

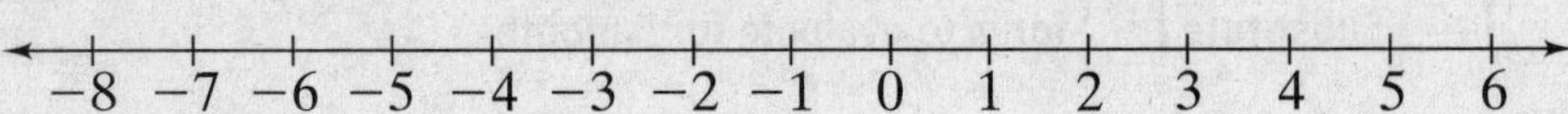

The numbers from left to right are ☐, ☐, and ☐.

Name ______________________ Class ______________ Date ______________

❸ Absolute Value in Algebraic Expressions Evaluate $|6a| - 10$ for $a = -7$.

$|6a| - 10 = |6(\square)| - 10$ ← **Substitute** $\square$ **for *a*.**

$= |\square| - 10$ ← **Work within grouping symbols first. Multiply.**

$= \square - 10$ ← **Find the absolute value.**

$= \square$ ← **Subtract.**

Quick Check

1. Find each absolute value.

a. $|-7|$ $\square$ **b.** $|7|$ $\square$

2. Order 0, −5, and 4 from least to greatest.

$\square$

3. Evaluate $3|s|$ for $s = -5$.

$\square$

Name ______________________ Class ______________ Date ______________

Lesson 1-3

Adding and Subtracting Integers

Lesson Objective	**NAEP 2005 Strand:** Number Properties and Operations
To add and subtract integers and to solve problems involving integers	**Topic:** Number Operations **Local Standards:** ______________

Vocabulary and Key Concepts

Adding Integers

Same Sign The sum of two positive integers is ______. The sum of two negative integers is ______.

Different Signs Find the absolute value of each integer. Subtract the lesser absolute value from the greater. The sum has the sign of the integer with the ______ absolute value.

Subtracting Integers

To subtract an integer, add its ______.

Arithmetic	**Algebra**
$5 - 7 = 5 + (\square)$	$a - b = a + (-b)$
$5 - (-7) = 5 + \square$	

Two numbers are additive inverses if ______________________

Examples

1 Adding Integers Simplify $-7 + (-17)$.

$-7 + (-17) = \square$ ← **Both −7 and −17 are ______, so their sum is ______.**

2 Subtracting Integers Simplify the expression $10 - 17$.

$10 - 17 = 10 + (\square)$ ← **Add the opposite of 17, which is ______.**

$= \square$ ← **Simplify.**

❸ A scuba diver descends from the surface of a lake and swims to 43 m below the surface to observe a fish. She then swims 79 m farther down to reach the bottom. What is the depth of the bottom of the lake?

$-43 - \square = \square + \square$ ← **Add the opposite of 79, which is** $\square$

$= \square$ ← **Use the rule for adding integers with the same sign.**

The depth of the bottom is $\square$ m, or $\square$ m below the surface.

Quick Check

1. Simplify each expression.

a. $-12 + 30$ $\square$

b. $-12 + (-3)$ $\square$

2. Simplify each expression.

a. $8 - (-4)$ $\square$

b. $-23 - (-11)$ $\square$

c. $-140 - 60$ $\square$

3. Diving A scuba diver goes 94 ft below the surface of the ocean and then descends 87 ft farther. What is the diver's depth?

Name ____________________ Class ____________ Date ____________

Lesson 1-4

Multiplying and Dividing Integers

Lesson Objective	**NAEP 2005 Strand:** Number Properties and Operations
To multiply and divide integers and to solve problems involving integers	**Topic:** Number Operations **Local Standards:** ____________

Vocabulary and Key Concepts

Multiplying Two Integers

The product of two integers with the same sign is ______.

Examples $8 \cdot 3 =$ ______ $-8 \cdot (-3) =$ ______

The product of two integers with different signs is ______.

Examples $8 \cdot (-3) =$ ______ $-8 \cdot 3 =$ ______

Dividing Two Integers

The quotient of two integers with the same sign is ______.

Examples $\frac{8}{2} =$ ______ $\frac{-8}{-2} =$ ______

The quotient of two integers with different signs is ______.

Examples $\frac{-8}{2} =$ ______ $\frac{8}{-2} =$ ______

Inverse operations are ____________________

Example

1 Multiplying Integers Simplify $-11 \cdot 2 \cdot (-1)$.

$-11 \cdot 2 \cdot (-1) = (\ \_\_\_\_\ )(-1)$ ← **−11 and 2 have different signs, so the product is ______.**

$=$ ______ ← **−22 and −1 have the same sign, so the product is ______.**

Quick Check

1. Simplify $-9 \cdot 8 \cdot (-2)$.

____

Examples

2 Dividing Integers A diver descends 80 ft in 4 minutes. What is the diver's rate of descent?

Let ☐ represent a descent of 80 feet. Then divide the descent by the number of minutes to find the change in elevation per minute.

feet → ☐ / ☐ = ☐ ← **The quotient of two integers with** ☐
minutes → **signs is** ☐.

The diver descends an average of ☐ feet per minute.

3 Evaluating an Algebraic Expression Evaluate $y \div (x - y) - zy$ for $x = 6$, $y = 9$, and $z = -2$.

$y \div (x - y) - zy = \square \div (\square - \square) - (\square)(\square)$ ← **Substitute ☐ for *x*, ☐ for *y*, and ☐ for *z*.**

$= 9 \div (\square) - (-2)(9)$ ← **Simplify 6 − 9 first.**

$= \square - (\square)$ ← **Multiply and divide.**

$= \square$ ← **Subtract.**

Quick Check

2. **Diving** A diver descends 90 feet in 5 minutes. What is the diver's change in depth per minute?

3. Evaluate $2x + xy \div z - 3$ for $x = -9$, $y = -5$, and $z = -3$.

Name ______________________ Class ______________ Date ______________

Lesson 1-5

Properties of Numbers

Lesson Objective	**NAEP 2005 Strand:** Number Properties and Operations
To identify the properties of numbers and use the properties to solve problems	**Topic:** Properties of Number and Operations **Local Standards:** ____________

Key Concepts

Commutative Properties of Addition and Multiplication

Arithmetic	Algebra
$7 + 12 = \square + \square$	$a + b = \square + \square$
$7 \cdot 12 = \square \cdot \square$	$a \cdot b = \square \cdot \square$

Associative Properties of Addition and Multiplication

Arithmetic	Algebra
$(4 + 7) + 3 = \square + (7 + \square)$	$(a + b) + c = \square + (b + \square)$
$(4 \cdot 7) \cdot 3 = \square \cdot (7 \cdot \square)$	$(a \cdot b) \cdot c = \square \cdot (b \cdot \square)$

Identity Properties

Arithmetic	Algebra
$6 + 0 = 0 + 6 = \square$	$a + 0 = 0 + a = \square$
$6 \cdot 1 = 1 \cdot 6 = \square$	$a \cdot 1 = 1 \cdot a = \square$

Distributive Property

Arithmetic	Algebra
$3(2 + 7) = 3 \cdot \square + 3 \cdot \square$	$a(b + c) = a\square + a\square$
$(2 + 7)3 = 2 \cdot \square + 7 \cdot \square$	$(b + c)a = b\square + c\square$
$5(8 - 2) = \square \cdot 8 - \square \cdot 2$	$a(b - c) = a\square - \square c$
$(8 - 2)5 = \square \cdot 5 - \square \cdot 5$	$(b - c)a = \square a - \square a$

Examples

1 Using Mental Math Use mental math to simplify 3.8 + 17 + 6.2.

What you think

Look for numbers that are easy to add. The sum of 3.8 and 6.2 is ____.

The sum of ____ and 17 is ____. So, 3.8 + 17 + 6.2 = ____.

Why it works

3.8 + 17 + 6.2 = 3.8 + ____ + ____ ← ____ **Property of Addition.**

= ____ + ____ ← **Order of operations.**

= ____ ← **Simplify.**

2 Using the Distributive Property Find $(d + 23)(-4)$.

$(d + 23)(-4)$ = ____(-4) + ____(-4) ← ____ **Property.**

= ____ + (____) ← **Simplify.**

= ____ − ____ ← **Rewrite as a subtraction expression.**

3 Entertainment A student buys 11 CDs. Each CD costs $6.10. What is the total cost?

11(6.1) = 11(____ + ____) ← **Replace 6.1 with** ____ + ____.

= 11(____) + 11(____) ← ____ **Property**

= ____ + ____ ← **Multiply.**

= ____ ← **Add.**

The total cost is ____.

Quick Check

1. Use mental math to simplify each expression.

   a. $26 + (-12) + 34$ ____

   b. $46 - 92$ ____

   c. $-4 \cdot 121 \cdot (-5)$ ____

2. Find $6(m + 3)$.

   ____

3. A large art kit costs $8.10. What is the cost of 20 large kits?

   ____

Name ______________________ Class ______________ Date ______________

Lesson 1-6

Solving Equations by Adding and Subtracting

Lesson Objective To write and solve equations using addition and subtraction	**NAEP 2005 Strand:** Algebra **Topic:** Equations and Inequalities **Local Standards:** ____________

Key Concepts

Properties of Equality

Addition Property of Equality

If you add the same number to each side of an equation, the two sides remain equal.

Arithmetic	Algebra
$10 = 5(2)$, so $10 + 3 = 5(2) + \square$	If $a = b$, then $a + c = b + \square$

Subtraction Property of Equality

If you subtract the same number from each side of an equation, the two sides remain equal.

Arithmetic	Algebra
$10 = 5(2)$, so $10 - 3 = 5(2) - \square$	If $a = b$, then $a - c = b - \square$

An equation is ______________________

A solution to an equation is ______________________

To isolate the variable is to ______________________

Inverse operations are ______________________

Name ______________________ Class ______________ Date ______________

Examples

1 Solving Equations Solve $-2 + m = -10$.

$-2 + m = -10$

$-2 + m + \square = -10 + \square$ ← **Isolate the variable. Use the Addition Property of Equality.**

$m = \square$ ← **Simplify.**

Check $-2 + m = -10$

$-2 + \square \stackrel{?}{=} -10$ ← **Substitute** $\square$ **for** ***m*****.**

$\square = -10$ ← **Simplify.**

2 Temperature The temperature inside a house decreases 22°F. The temperature is then 65°F. What was the original temperature inside the house?

Words $\square$ minus $\square$ = $\square$

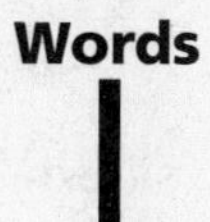

Let t = original temperature.

Equation t − $\square$ = 65

$t - 22 = 65$

$t - 22 + \square = 65 + \square$ ← **Isolate the variable. Use the Addition Property of Equality.**

$t = \square$ ← **Simplify.**

The temperature was 87°F before it decreased.

Quick Check

1. Solve $x - 7 = -10$.

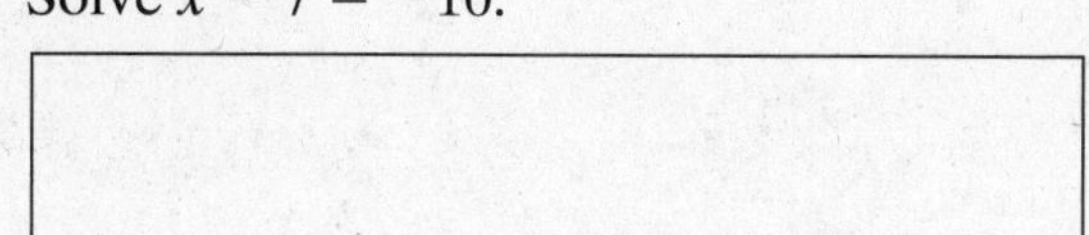

2. Yesterday an official mailed some notices for a meeting. Today she mailed 8 more notices. She mailed 52 notices in all. Write and solve an equation to find the number of notices she mailed yesterday.

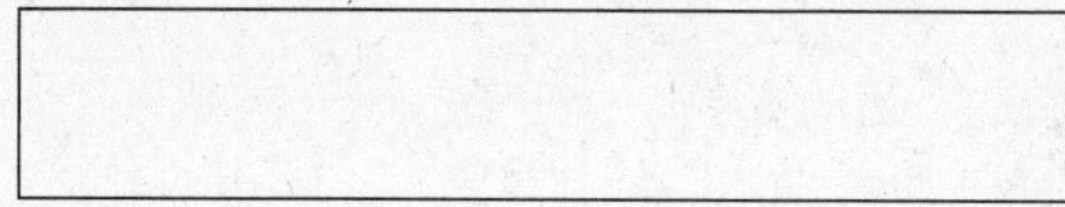

Name ______________________ Class ______________ Date ______________

Lesson 1-7

Solving Equations by Multiplying and Dividing

Lesson Objective	**NAEP 2005 Strand:** Algebra
To write and solve equations using multiplication and division	**Topic:** Equations and Inequalities **Local Standards:** ____________________

Key Concepts

Properties of Equality

Multiplication Property of Equality

If you multiply each side of an equation by the same number, the two sides ☐.

Arithmetic

$20 = \frac{40}{2}$, so $2(20) = \square$

Algebra

If $a = b$, then $ac = b\square$

Division Property of Equality

If you divide each side of an equation by the same ☐, the two sides remain equal.

Arithmetic

$30 = 3(10)$, so $\frac{30}{6} = \frac{3(10)}{\square}$

Algebra

If $a = b$ and $c \neq 0$, then $\frac{a}{c} = \frac{b}{\square}$

Example

1 Solving by Multiplying Solve $\frac{y}{-3} = 14$.

$\square\left(\frac{y}{-3}\right) = \square \cdot 14$ ← **Isolate the variable. Use the Multiplication Property of Equality.**

$y = -42$ ← **Simplify.**

Quick Check

1. Solve $\frac{t}{8} = -5$.

Name ______________________ Class ______________ Date ______________

Example

❷ Solving by Dividing Solve $265 = -5x$.

$\frac{265}{\square} = \frac{-5x}{\square}$ ← **Isolate the variable. Use the Division Property of Equality.**

$\square = x$ ← **Simplify.**

Quick Check

2. Solve $3y = -12$.

Name ______________________ Class ______________ Date ______________

Lesson 2-1

Factors

Lesson Objective	**NAEP 2005 Strand:** Number Properties and Operations
To identify prime and composite numbers and to find the greatest common factor	**Topic:** Properties of Number and Operations **Local Standards:** ______________________

Vocabulary

A factor is ______________________

A number is divisible by a second number if ______________________

____

A prime number is ______________________

____

A composite number is ______________________

The prime factorization of a composite number shows ______________________

____

The greatest common factor (GCF) of two or more numbers is ______________________

____

Example

1 **Prime and Composite Numbers** Identify 3,117 as *prime* or *composite*. Explain.

The sum of the digits is ☐, which is divisible by ☐. Since 3,117 is divisible by 3 it is ☐.

Quick Check

1. Identify 15,482 as *prime* or *composite*. Explain.

Name ______________ Class ______________ Date ______________

Examples

❷ Finding Prime Factorization Use a factor tree to find the prime factorization of 588.

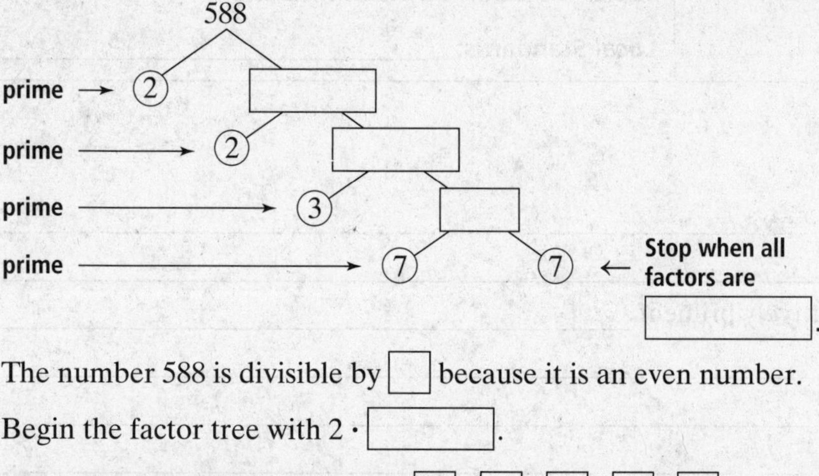

The number 588 is divisible by ☐ because it is an even number.

Begin the factor tree with 2 · ☐.

The prime factorization of 588 is ☐ · ☐ · ☐ · ☐ · ☐.

❸ Finding the GCF by Listing A band with 36 members is marching beside a 32-member band. If the two bands are to have the same number of columns, what is the greatest number of columns in which you could arrange the two bands?

Begin by finding the factors of 36 and 32.

36: ☐

32: ☐

The factors ☐, ☐, and ☐ are common to both numbers. The GCF of 36 and 32 is ☐.

So ☐ is the greatest number of columns in which you can arrange the bands.

Quick Check

2. Use a factor tree to find the prime factorization of each number.

   a. 96

   b. 240

3. Two pipes have lengths of 63 ft and 84 ft. You cut them into pieces of equal length with no leftovers. What is the greatest possible length of the pieces?

Name ______________________ Class ______________ Date ______________

Lesson 2-2

Equivalent Forms of Rational Numbers

Lesson Objective To write equivalent fractions and decimals	**NAEP 2005 Strand:** Measurement **Topic:** Measuring Physical Attributes **Local Standards:** ____________________

Vocabulary

A rational number is ______________________________

Two integers *a* and *b* are relatively prime if ______________________________

A terminating decimal is ______________________________

A repeating decimal is ______________________________

Example

1 Simplifying a Fraction Write $\frac{138}{150}$ in simplest form using the GCF.

The GCF of 138 and 150 is ☐.

$\frac{138}{150} = \frac{138 \div \square}{150 \div \square}$ ← **Divide the numerator and the denominator by the** ☐.

$= \frac{\square}{\square}$ ← **Simplify.**

Quick Check

1. Write $\frac{12}{20}$ in simplest form using the GCF.

☐

Name ____________________ Class ____________ Date ____________

Examples

2 Writing an Equivalent Decimal Find the batting average of a hitter with 28 hits in 77 times at bat.

$\frac{28}{77}$ ← **Write the batting average as a ☐.**

$0.363636... = ☐$ ← **Divide. This is a ☐ decimal.**

The player's batting average is about ☐.

3 Writing an Equivalent Fraction Write 1.24 as a mixed number in simplest form.

$1.24 = \frac{1.24}{1}$ ← **Write as a fraction with the denominator 1. Since there are ☐ digits to the right of the decimal point, multiply the numerator and the denominator by ☐.**

$= \frac{☐}{100}$

$= \frac{124 \div ☐}{100 \div ☐}$ ← **Divide the numerator and the denominator by the ☐.**

$= \frac{31}{25} = ☐\frac{☐}{☐}$ ← **Simplify. Write as a mixed number.**

Quick Check

2. Find the batting average of a hitter with 39 hits in 85 times at bat.

3. Write 1.42 as a mixed number in simplest form.

Name ______________________ Class ______________ Date ______________

Lesson 2-3

Comparing and Ordering Rational Numbers

Lesson Objective	**NAEP 2005 Strand:** Number Properties and Operations
To use least common denominators, decimals, and number lines to compare and order rational numbers	**Topic:** Number Sense **Local Standards:** ____________

Vocabulary

The least common multiple (LCM) of two or more numbers is ______________________

____

The least common denominator (LCD) of two or more numbers is ____________________

____

Example

1 Comparing Using the LCD Which is greater, $\frac{7}{18}$ or $\frac{5}{12}$?

Multiples of 18: 18, ☐

Multiples of 12: 12, ☐, ☐

List multiples of each denominator to find their LCD.

The LCM of 18 and 12 is ☐. So, the LCD of the fractions is ☐.

$\frac{7}{18} = \frac{7 \cdot \square}{18 \cdot \square}$ ← **Multiply the numerator and denominator by** ☐**.**

$= \frac{\square}{\square}$ ← **Simplify.**

$\frac{5}{12} = \frac{5 \cdot \square}{12 \cdot \square}$ ← **Multiply the numerator and denominator by** ☐**.**

$= \frac{\square}{\square}$ ← **Simplify.**

Since $\frac{15}{36} \square \frac{14}{36}$, $\frac{5}{12} \square \frac{7}{18}$.

Quick Check

1. Rewrite $\frac{1}{6}$ and $\frac{1}{9}$ using their LCD. Which fraction is greater?

Name ____________ Class ____________ Date ____________

Examples

2 Comparing Using Decimals The Eagles won 7 out of 11 games while the Seals won 8 out of 12 games. Which team has the better record?

Change each fraction to a decimal. Compare the two decimals.

Eagles: $\frac{7}{11} \approx$ ____________

Seals: $\frac{8}{12} \approx$ ____________

← **Divide. Use a calculator.**

Since 0.666 ☐ 0.636, the ____________ have a better record.

3 Ordering Rational Numbers Order $-0.175, \frac{2}{3}, -\frac{5}{8}, 1.7$, and -0.95 from least to greatest.

Write each fraction as a decimal.

$\frac{2}{3} \approx$ ____________ and $-\frac{5}{8} =$ ____________.

← **Then graph each decimal on a number line.**

The order of the points from left to right gives the order of the numbers from ____________ to ____________.

$-0.95 <$ ☐ $<$ ☐ $<$ ☐ < 1.7

So ☐ $<$ ☐ $<$ ☐ $<$ ☐ $<$ ☐.

Quick Check

2. At the local pet store, 7 out of 10 cats are male and 12 out of 17 dogs are male. Which animal has the greatest fraction of males?

3. Order $\frac{8}{5}, 1\frac{1}{2}, -.625, -\frac{7}{8}$, and 1.61 from least to greatest.

Lesson 2-4

Adding and Subtracting Rational Numbers

Lesson Objective	**NAEP 2005 Strand:** Number Properties and Operations
To add and subtract fractions and mixed numbers and to solve problems involving rational numbers	**Topic:** Number Operations **Local Standards:** ____________

Examples

1 Adding Fractions A cake recipe calls for $\frac{1}{3}$ cup of white flour and $\frac{3}{4}$ cup of wheat flour. How many total cups of flour do you need?

$\frac{1}{3} + \frac{3}{4} = \frac{1 \cdot \square}{3 \cdot \square} + \frac{3 \cdot \square}{4 \cdot \square}$ ← **Write equivalent fractions with the same denominator.**

$= \frac{\square}{12} + \frac{\square}{12}$ ← **Simplify.**

$= \frac{\square}{12}$ ← **Add the numerators. Simplify.**

You need $\frac{\square}{\square}$, or $\square\frac{\square}{\square}$, cups of flour.

2 Subtracting Fractions Find $\frac{4}{5} - \frac{1}{3}$.

The LCM of 5 and 3 is $\square$, so the LCD of $\frac{4}{5}$ and $\frac{1}{3}$ is $\square$.

$\frac{4}{5} - \frac{1}{3} = \square - \square$ ← **Write the equivalent fractions using the LCD.**

$= \frac{12 - 5}{15} = \square$ ← **Subtract the numerators.**

Quick Check

1. Find $\frac{2}{15} + \frac{1}{10}$ by using $15 \cdot 10 = 150$ as the common denominator.

2. Find $\frac{1}{10} - \frac{1}{4}$.

Name ______________________ Class ______________ Date ______________

❸ Adding Mixed Numbers Find $6\frac{3}{4} + 8\frac{2}{3}$.

Estimate $6\frac{3}{4} + 8\frac{2}{3} \approx 7 + 9 = 16$

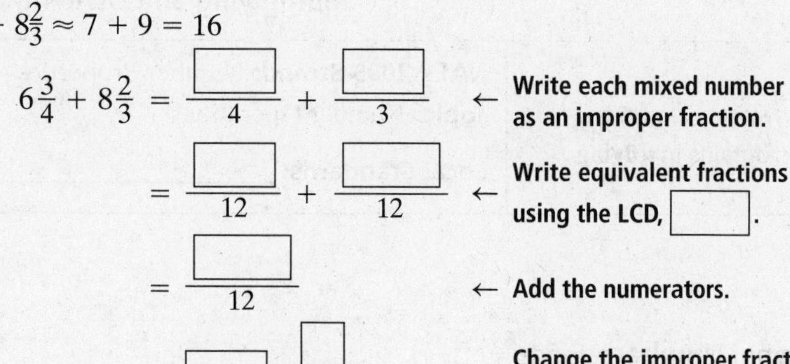

$6\frac{3}{4} + 8\frac{2}{3} = \frac{\square}{4} + \frac{\square}{3}$ ← **Write each mixed number as an improper fraction.**

$= \frac{\square}{12} + \frac{\square}{12}$ ← **Write equivalent fractions using the LCD, $\square$.**

$= \frac{\square}{12}$ ← **Add the numerators.**

$= \square\frac{\square}{\square}$ ← **Change the improper fraction to a mixed number.**

Check for Reasonableness Since $15\frac{5}{12} \approx 16$, the answer is reasonable.

❹ Subtracting Mixed Numbers On a 50-foot roll of cable, $15\frac{3}{4}$ feet are left. Which equation can be used to find how many feet of cable were used?

A. $t = 50 + 15\frac{3}{4}$ **B.** $t = 50 - 15\frac{3}{4}$

C. $t = 15\frac{3}{4} - 50$ **D.** $t = 15\frac{3}{4} + 50$

To find the amount left, you ________ the amount used from the original amount.

The answer is ____. You can find the amount left on the roll by subtracting.

$50 - 15\frac{3}{4} = 49\frac{4}{4} - 15\frac{3}{4}$ ← **Rewrite 50 as 49 + $\frac{4}{4}$, or 1.**

$= \square\frac{\square}{\square}$ ← **Subtract integers: 49 − 15. Then subtract the fractions: $\frac{4}{4} - \frac{3}{4}$.**

The amount of cable left is $\square\frac{\square}{\square}$.

Quick Check

3. Find $4\frac{1}{5} + 2\frac{3}{4}$.

4. **Weather** In 2000, a single storm dropped $20\frac{3}{10}$ in. of snow in North Carolina. The previous record was $17\frac{4}{5}$ in. in 1927. Write and solve an equation to find out how much more snow fell in 2000 than in 1927.

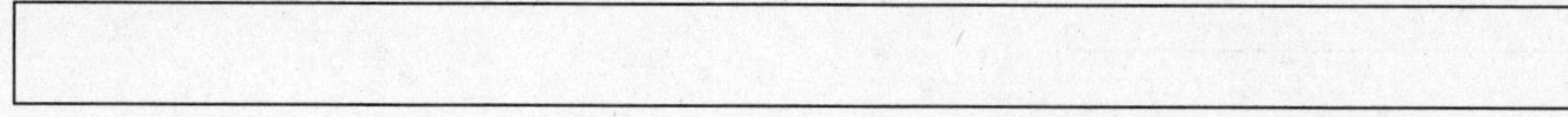

Name ______________________ Class ______________ Date ______________

Lesson 2-5

Multiplying and Dividing Rational Numbers

Lesson Objective	NAEP 2005 Strand: Number Properties and Operations
To multiply and divide fractions and mixed numbers and to solve problems involving rational numbers	**Topic:** Number Operations **Local Standards:** ____________________

Examples

1 Multiplying Rational Numbers Find $\frac{5}{12} \cdot \left(-\frac{4}{7}\right)$.

$\frac{5}{12} \cdot -\left(\frac{4}{7}\right) = -\frac{5 \cdot \square}{12 \cdot \square}$ ← **Multiply the numerators. Multiply the denominators.**

$= -\frac{5 \cdot \cancel{4}^{\square}}{\cancel{12}_{\square} \cdot 7}$ ← **Divide the numerator and denominator by their GCF, $\square$.**

$= -\frac{\square}{\square}$ ← **Simplify.**

2 Solving Equations by Multiplying Solve $\frac{3}{4}y + 2 = 2\frac{1}{8}$.

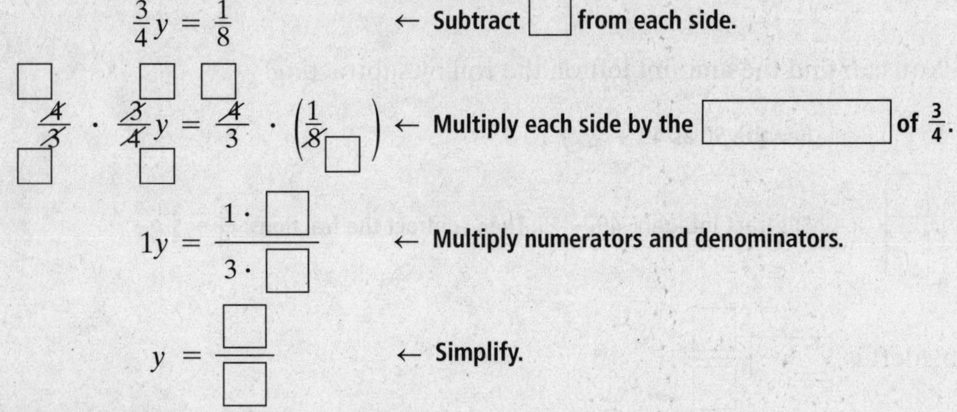

Quick Check

1. Find each product. Write the answer in simplest form.

a. $-\frac{4}{5} \cdot \left(-\frac{3}{8}\right)$

b. $2\frac{1}{10} \cdot \left(-1\frac{2}{5}\right)$

2. Solve the equation $\frac{3}{7}p + 1 = 3\frac{1}{2}$.

Name ______________________ Class ______________ Date ______________

Example

❸ **Dividing Rational Numbers** A scarf designer has $13\frac{5}{6}$ yards of fabric. Each scarf uses $2\frac{1}{6}$ yards of fabric. How many scarves can the designer make? You need to find how many $2\frac{1}{6}$-yard pieces there are in $13\frac{5}{6}$ yards. Divide $13\frac{5}{6}$ by $2\frac{1}{6}$.

$13\frac{5}{6} \div 2\frac{1}{6} = \frac{\square}{6} \div \frac{\square}{6}$ ← **Write the mixed numbers as** ☐ **fractions.**

$= \frac{83}{{}_1\not{6}} \cdot \frac{\not{6}^1}{13}$ ← **Multiply by the reciprocal of $\frac{13}{6}$.**

$= \frac{\square}{\square}$ ← **Multiply.**

$= \square\frac{\square}{\square}$ ← **Write as a mixed number.**

Since you cannot make $\frac{5}{13}$ of a scarf, the designer can make only ☐ scarves.

Check for Reasonableness Round $13\frac{5}{6}$ to 14 and $2\frac{1}{6}$ to 2. Then $14 \div 2 = 7$, which is close to 6. The answer is reasonable.

Quick Check

3. **Sewing** You have $13\frac{3}{4}$ yards of material to cut into $2\frac{1}{2}$-yard lengths. How many lengths can you cut from the material?

Name ______________________ Class ______________ Date ______________

Lesson 2-6

Formulas

Lesson Objective	**NAEP 2005 Strand:** Algebra
To use formulas to solve problems and to solve a formula for a variable	**Topic:** Equations and Inequalities **Local Standards:** ____________

Vocabulary

A formula is ____

____

Example

1 Using Formulas to Solve Problems Find the area of a trapezoid with a height of 6 cm and bases of 5.2 cm and 7.5 cm.

$A =$ ☐ ← **Use the formula for the area of a trapezoid.**

$= \frac{1}{2}$(☐)(☐) ← **Substitute.**

$= \frac{1}{2}(6.0)(12.7)$ ← **Add within the parentheses.**

$=$ ☐(12.7) ← **Multiply from left to right.**

$=$ ☐ ← **Simplify.**

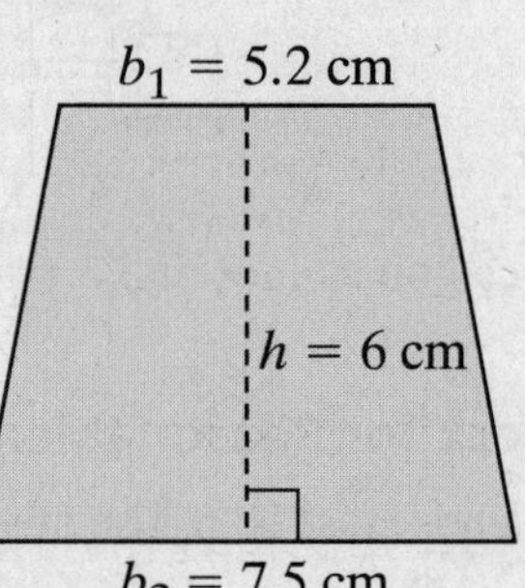

The area of the trapezoid is  cm^2.

Quick Check

1. Find the area of each figure.

   a. trapezoid: $h = 4.2$ cm, $b_1 = 1.4$ cm, $b_2 = 4.6$ cm

   b. rectangle: $\ell = \frac{2}{3}$ yd, $w = 3$ yd

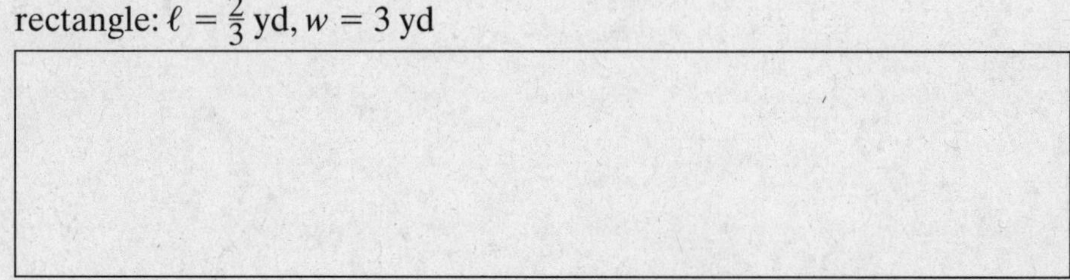

Name ______________________ Class ______________ Date ______________

Example

2 Isolating a Variable Write a formula for finding the length of each non-parallel side s of an isosceles trapezoid given the perimeter and length of the bases. Begin with the perimeter formula: $P = 2s + b_1 + b_2$.

$$P = 2s + b_1 + b_2$$ ← **Use the perimeter formula for an isosceles trapezoid.**

$$P - \square - \square = 2s + b_1 + b_2 - \square - \square$$ ← **Subtract ☐ and ☐ from each side.**

$$P - b_1 - b_2 = 2s$$ ← **Simplify.**

$$\frac{P - b_1 - b_2}{\square} = \frac{2s}{\square}$$ ← **Divide each side by ☐ to to isolate the variable *s*.**

$$\frac{P - b_1 - b_2}{2} = \square$$ ← **Simplify.**

Quick Check

2. Solve $A = w - 5$ for w.

Name ______________________ Class ______________ Date ______________

Lesson 2-7

Powers and Exponents

Lesson Objectives	**NAEP 2005 Strand:** Algebra
To write, simplify, and evaluate expressions involving exponents	**Topic:** Variables, Expressions, and Operations
	Local Standards: ____________________

Vocabulary

An exponent ______________________

A base is ______________________

A power is ______________________

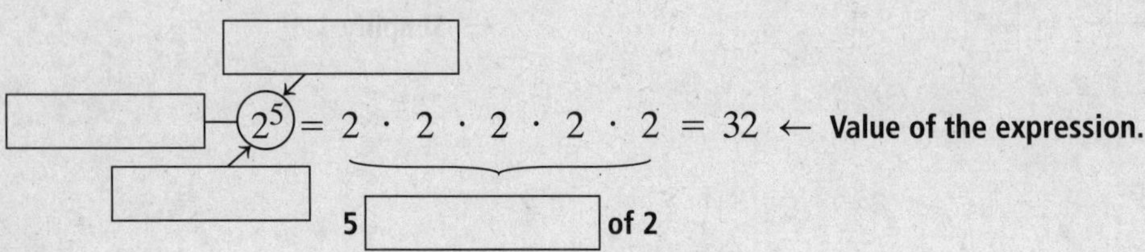

Example

1 Writing With Exponents Write using exponents.

a. $2 \cdot 2 \cdot 2 \cdot 7 \cdot 7 = 2^{\square} \cdot 7^{\square}$ ← **2 is a factor** ☐ **times, and 7 is a factor** ☐ **times.**

b. $5 \cdot 5 \cdot p \cdot q \cdot q = 5^{\square}p^{\square}q^{\square}$ or $5^{\square}pq^{\square}$ ← **5 and *q* are factors** ☐ **times each and *p* is a factor** ☐.

Quick Check

1. Write $6 \cdot 6 \cdot 7 \cdot 7 \cdot 7 \cdot 7 \cdot 7 \cdot 7$ using exponents.

☐

Name ______________________ Class ______________ Date ______________

Examples

2 Simplifying Expressions Simplify each expression.

a. $-2^6 = -(\square \cdot \square \cdot \square \cdot \square \cdot \square \cdot \square)$ ← **The base is** $\square$.

$= \square$ ← **Multiply.**

b. $(-2)^6 = (\square)(\square)(\square)(\square)(\square)(\square)$ ← **The base is** $\square$.

$= \square$ ← **Multiply.**

3 Evaluating Expressions Architecture You can find the radius of the arch in a doorway with the expression

$$\frac{s^2 + h^2}{2h}.$$

Find the radius of a doorway with dimensions $s = 6$ ft and $h = 4$ ft.

$\frac{s^2 + h^2}{2h} = \frac{\square^2 + \square^2}{2 \cdot \square}$ ← **Substitute 6 for *s* and 4 for *h*.**

$= \frac{\square + \square}{2 \cdot \square}$ ← **Simplify the powers in the numerator.**

$= \frac{\square}{\square} = \square\frac{\square}{\square}$ ← **Simplify. Then divide.**

The radius of the arch is $\square\frac{\square}{\square}$ ft.

Quick Check

2. Simplify each expression.

a. $(-7)^3$ | **b.** -7^3 | **c.** $-4 + 6 \cdot 3^2$

3. Find the radius r of a doorway with dimensions $s = 5$m and $h = 3$m.

Name ______________________ Class ______________ Date ______________

Lesson 2-8

Scientific Notation

Lesson Objective	**NAEP 2005 Strand:** Number Properties and Operations
To write numbers in both standard form and scientific notation	**Topic:** Number Sense **Local Standards:** ____________________

Key Concepts

Scientific Notation

A number is in scientific notation if ______________________________________

____

Examples 1×10^8 1.54×10^7 9.99×10^4

Example

1 Writing in Standard Form At one point, the distance from the Earth to the moon is 1.513431×10^{10} in. Write this number in standard form.

$1.513431 \times 10^{10} = 1.5134310000. \leftarrow$ **Move the decimal point** ☐ **places to the right. Insert zeros as necessary.**

$=$ ☐

At one point, the distance from the Earth to the moon is ☐ in.

Quick Check

1. Write 7.66×10^6 km^2, the area of Australia, in standard form.

☐

Name ______________________ Class ______________ Date ____________

Examples

2 Writing in Scientific Notation The diameter of the planet Jupiter is about 142,800 km. Write this number in scientific notation.

$142{,}800 = 1.42{,}800.$ ← **Move the decimal point ☐ places to the left.**

$= \square \times 10^{\square}$ ← **Use ☐ as the exponent of 10.**

The diameter of the planet Jupiter is about ☐ km.

3 Negative Exponents Among the microscopic fossils found on Mars, the largest are less than approximately 2.45×10^{-5} cm in size. Write this number in standard form.

$2.45 \times 10^{-5} = 0.00002.45$ ← **Move the decimal point ☐ places to the ☐ to make 2.45 less than 1.**

The largest of the possible fossils found on Mars are less than about ☐ cm in size.

Quick Check

2. Write 3,476,000 m, the moon's diameter, in scientific notation.

3. Write 2.5×10^{-4} inches, the diameter of a cell, in standard form.

Name ______________________ Class ______________ Date ______________

Lesson 3-1

Exploring Square Roots and Irrational Numbers

Lesson Objective	**NAEP 2005 Strand:** Number Properties and Operations
To find and estimate square roots and to classify numbers as rational or irrational	**Topic:** Estimation **Local Standards:** ______________

Vocabulary

A perfect square is ______________________

The square root of a number is ______________________

____

Irrational numbers are ______________________

____

The real numbers are ______________________

Examples

1 Finding Square Roots of Perfect Squares Find the two square roots of each number.

a. 81

$\square \cdot \square = 81$

$\square \cdot \square = 81$

The two square roots of 81 are $\square$ and $\square$.

b. $\frac{1}{36}$

$\square \cdot \square = \frac{1}{36}$

$\square \cdot \square = \frac{1}{36}$

The two square roots of $\frac{1}{36}$ are $\square$ and $\square$.

2 Estimating a Square Root Value Estimate the value of $-\sqrt{70}$ to the nearest integer.

Since 70 is closer to 64 than it is to 81, $-\sqrt{70} \approx \square$.

$-\sqrt{81}$ $\square$ $-\sqrt{64}$

-9 -8

Quick Check

1. Find the square roots of each number.

a. 36 **b.** 1 **c.** $\frac{1}{16}$

2. Estimate the value of $\sqrt{38}$ to the nearest integer.

Name ____________ Class ____________ Date ____________

Examples

❸ **Physics** The math class drops a small ball from the top of a stairwell. The students measure the distance to the basement as 48 feet. Use the formula $d = 16t^2$, where d is distance (in feet) and t is time (in seconds), to find how long it takes the ball to fall.

$d = 16t^2$ ← **Use the formula for distance and time.**

$\square = 16t^2$ ← **Substitute $\square$ for d.**

$\frac{48}{\square} = t^2$ ← **Divide each side by $\square$ to isolate t.**

$\square = t^2$ ← **Simplify.**

$\sqrt{3} = \sqrt{t^2}$ ← **Find the positive square root of each side.**

[√] 3 [=] $\square$ ← **Use a calculator.**

$\square \approx t$ ← **Round to the nearest tenth.**

It takes about $\square$ seconds for the ball to fall 48 ft.

❹ **Classifying Real Numbers** Identify each number as *rational* or *irrational*. Explain.

a. $-9333.\overline{3}$ $\square$; the decimal repeats.

b. $4\frac{7}{9}$ $\square$; the number can be written as the ratio $\square$.

c. $\sqrt{90}$ $\square$; 90 is not a $\square$ square.

d. 6.363663666... $\square$; the decimal does not terminate or repeat.

Quick Check

3. Find the time it takes a skydiver to fall each distance using the formula in Example 3. Round to the nearest tenth of a second.

a. 480 ft **b.** 625 ft

4. Is $0.\overline{6}$ *rational* or *irrational*? Explain.

Name ______________________ Class ______________ Date ______________

Lesson 3-2

The Pythagorean Theorem

Lesson Objective	**NAEP 2005 Strand:** Geometry
To use the Pythagorean Theorem to find the length of the hypotenuse of a right triangle	**Topic:** Relationships Among Geometric Figures **Local Standards:** ____________

Vocabulary and Key Concepts

The Pythagorean Theorem

In any right triangle, the sum of the squares of the lengths of the ☐ is equal to the square of the length of the ☐.

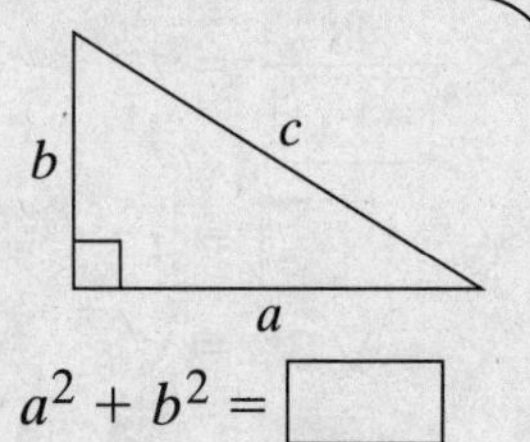

$a^2 + b^2 =$ ☐

The legs of a right triangle are ______________________

The hypotenuse of a right triangle is ______________________

Examples

1 Finding the Hypotenuse Find the length of the hypotenuse of a right triangle with legs of 6 ft and 8 ft.

☐ ← **Use the Pythagorean Theorem.**

$☐^2 + ☐^2 = c^2$ ← **Substitute ☐ for *a* and ☐ for *b***

$☐ + ☐ = c^2$ ← **Simplify.**

$☐ = c^2$ ← **Add.**

$\sqrt{☐} = \sqrt{☐}$ ← **Find the positive square root of each side.**

$☐ = c$ ← **Simplify.**

The length of the hypotenuse is ☐ ft.

Name ______________________ Class ______________ Date ______________

❷ The bottom of a ladder is 10 ft from the side of a building. The top of the ladder is 24 ft from the ground. How long is the ladder?

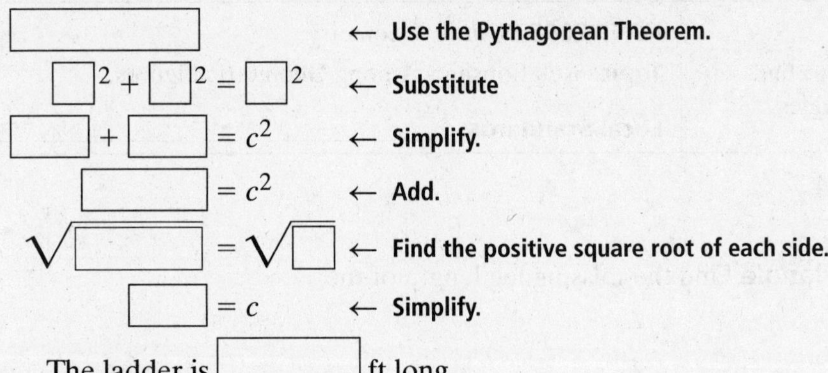

The ladder is ______ ft long.

Quick Check

1. Find the length of the hypotenuse of a right triangle with legs of 12 cm and 16 cm.

2. A bridge has 22-ft horizontal members and 25-ft vertical members. Find the length of each diagonal member to the nearest foot.

Lesson 3-3

Using the Pythagorean Theorem

Lesson Objective	NAEP 2005 Strand: Geometry
To use the Pythagorean Theorem to find the missing measurements of triangles	Topic: Relationships Among Geometric Figures Local Standards: ____________

Example

❶ **Finding a Leg of a Right Triangle** Find the missing leg length of the triangle below.

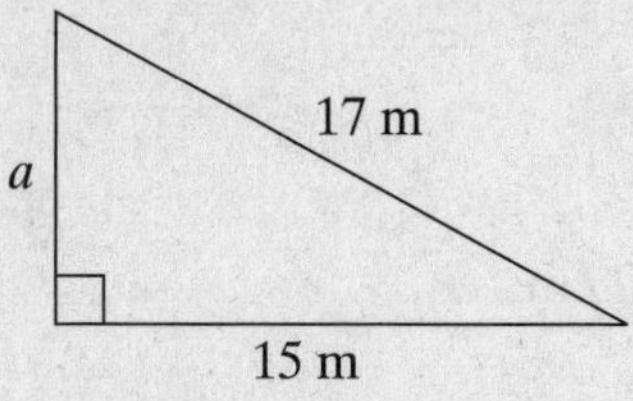

$\square$ ← **Use the Pythagorean Theorem.**

$\square^2 + \square^2 = \square^2$ ← **Substitute $\square$ for *b* and $\square$ for *c*.**

$a^2 + \square = \square$ ← **Simplify.**

$a^2 = \square$ ← **Subtract.**

$\sqrt{\square} = \sqrt{\square}$ ← **Find the positive square root of each side.**

$a = \square$ ← **Simplify.**

The length of the other leg is $\square$ m.

Quick Check

1. The hypotenuse of a right triangle is 20.2 ft long. One leg is 12.6 ft long. Find the length of the other leg to the nearest tenth.

Name ______________________ Class ______________ Date ______________

Example

2 **Multiple Choice** You are riding on a carousel. You choose a horse near the outer edge of the carousel. Your friend is standing on the ground. Before the carousel starts moving, your friend is 9 m from you and 11 m from the center of the carousel. To the nearest tenth of a meter, how far are you from the center of the carousel?

A. 5.2 m **B.** 6.3 m **C.** 7.5 m **D.** 8.8 m

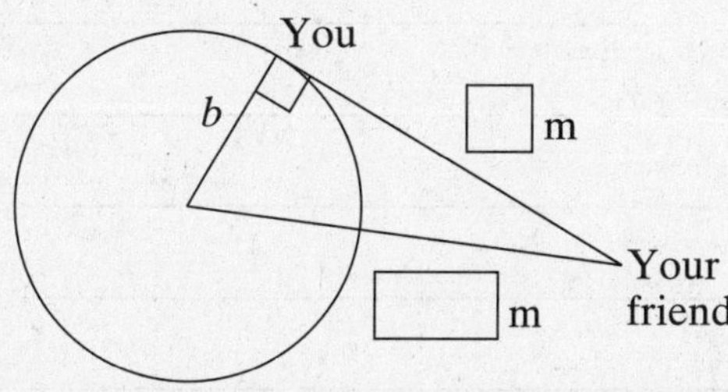

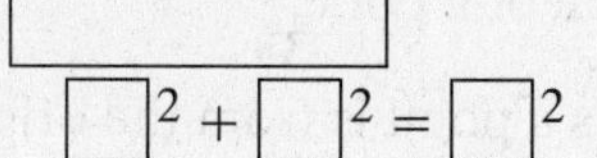

$\square$ ← **Use the Pythagorean Theorem.**

$\square^2 + \square^2 = \square^2$ ← **Substitute** $\square$ **for *a* and** $\square$ **for *c*.**

$\square + b^2 = \square$ ← **Simplify.**

$b^2 = \square$ ← **Subtract.**

$\sqrt{\square} = \sqrt{\square}$ ← **Find the positive square root of each side.**

$\square$ ← **Use a calculator.**

$b \approx \square$ ← **Simplify.**

You are about ______ m from the center of the carousel. The correct answer is choice ______.

Quick Check

2. **Construction** The bottom of an 18-ft ladder is 5 ft from the side of a house. Find the distance from the top of the ladder to the ground. Round to the nearest tenth.

Name ______________________ Class ______________ Date ______________

Lesson 3-4

Graphing in the Coodinate Plane

Lesson Objective	**NAEP 2005 Strand:** Algebra
To graph points and to use the Pythagorean Theorem to find distances in the coordinate plane	**Topic:** Algebraic Representations **Local Standards:** ____________________

Vocabulary

A coordinate plane is ______________________

The *x*-axis is ______________________

The *y*-axis is ______________________

Quadrants are ______________________

The origin is ______________________

An [ ] gives the coordinates of the location of a point.

The [ ] tells the number of horizontal units a point is from the origin.

The [ ] tells the number of vertical units a point is from the origin.

Examples

1 Graphing Points Graph point P (–3, 2) on a coordinate plane.

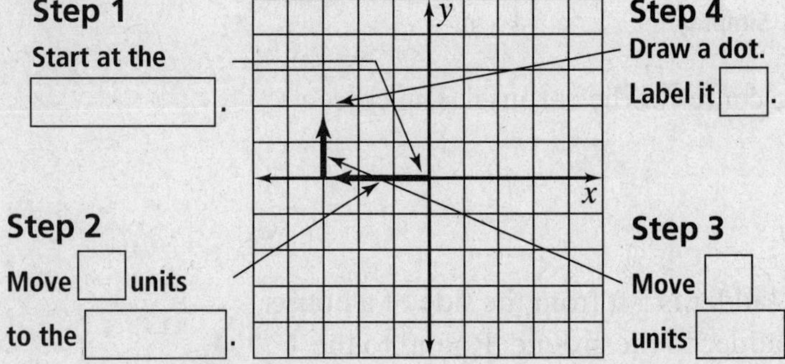

Name ______________ Class ______________ Date ______________

❷ Finding Distance on a Coordinate Plane

Multiple Choice The park is 4 kilometers west of the bus station. The grocery store is 7 kilometers south of the bus station. To the nearest kilometer, how far is the grocery store from the park?

A. 5 km **C.** 7 km

B. 6 km **D.** 8 km

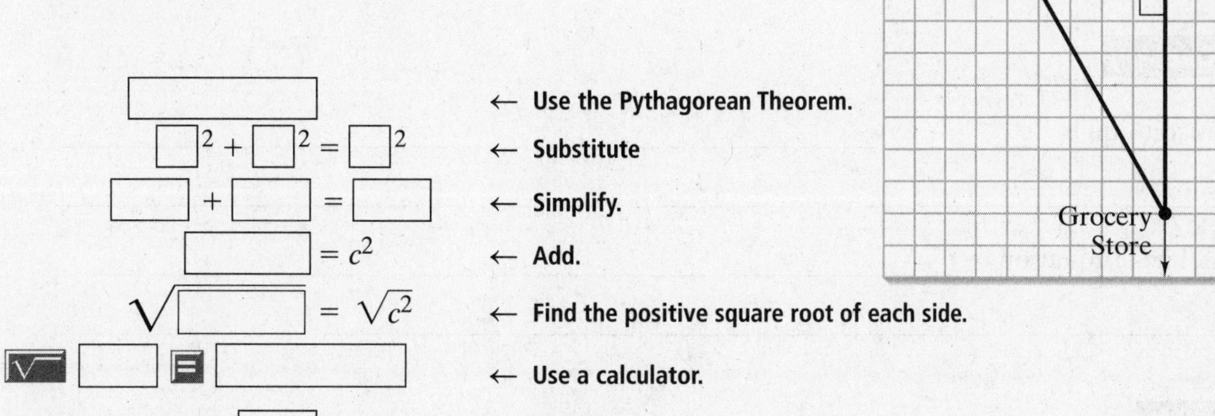

The correct answer is choice ______.

Quick Check

1. Graph $R\ (4, -2)$ and $S\ (-4, 2)$ on the same coordinate plane.

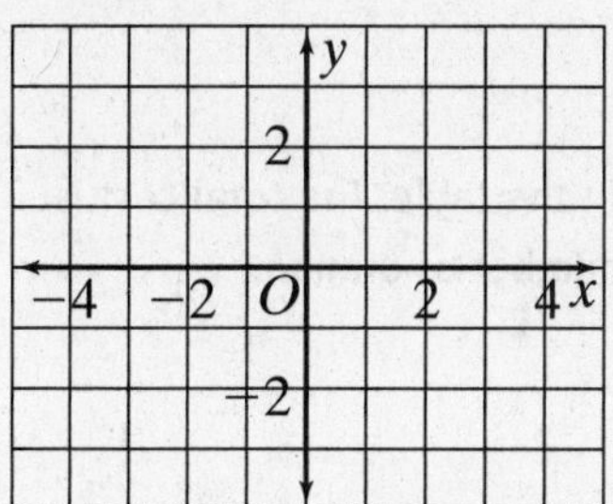

2. Your school is 3 miles south of your house. The general store is 5 miles east of your school. To the nearest mile, how far is your house from the general store?

Name ______________________ Class ______________ Date ____________

Lesson 3-5

Equations, Tables, and Graphs

Lesson Objective	NAEP 2005 Strand: Algebra
To use tables, equations, and graphs to solve problems	Topic: Algebraic Representations Local Standards: ____________

Vocabulary

A solution is ____

____

A linear equation is ____

____

Example

1 Making Tables and Writing Equations Oranges cost $0.40 each at the grocery store. Make a table and write an equation to represent the total cost of buying a given number of oranges.

Number of Oranges	Total Cost (dollars)	Expression
0		0.40(0)
	0.40	0.40(1)
2		
	1.20	
x	c	

← **Look for a pattern in the table. The total cost is ☐ times the number of oranges.**

↑ **Let x represent the number of oranges.**

↑ **Let c represent the total cost.**

The equation ☐ models the total cost.

Quick Check

1. You buy CDs from a music store. Each CD costs $15. Make a table and write an equation to represent the total cost of buying a given number of CDs. Let n represent the number of CDs. Let t represent the total cost.

0		
n	t	

The equation ☐ models the total cost.

Example

2 Graphing Linear Equations Graph the linear equation $y = -x + 3$.

Step 1 Make a table.

x	$-x + 3 = y$	(x, y)
-1	$-(\square) + 3 = \square$	$(\square, \square)$
0	$-\square + 3 = \square$	$(\square, \square)$
1	$-\square + 3 = \square$	$(\square, \square)$
2	$-\square + 3 = \square$	$(\square, \square)$
3	$-\square + 3 = \square$	$(\square, \square)$

Step 2 Graph the ordered pairs and draw a line through the points.

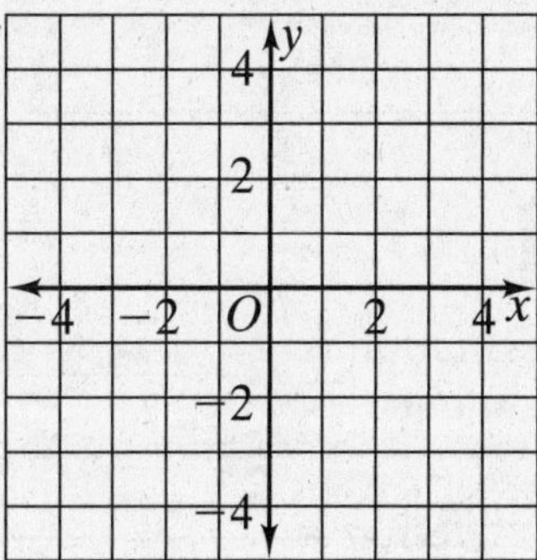

Quick Check

2. Graph the linear equation $y = 5x + 50$, where y represents the temperature in °F of a chemical solution after x minutes.

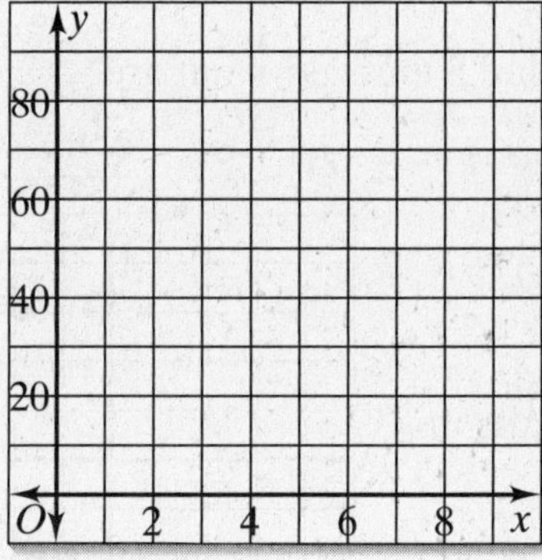

Name ______________________ Class ______________ Date ______________

Lesson 3-6

Translations

Lesson Objective To graph and describe translations in the coordinate plane	**NAEP 2005 Strand:** Geometry **Topic:** Transformation of Shapes and Preservation of Properties **Local Standards:** ____________________

Vocabulary

A transformation is ____

____

A translation is ____

____

An image is ____

____

Example

1 Graphing a Translation

Multiple Choice If $\triangle ABC$ is translated 3 units to the left and 2 units up, what are the coordinates of point A'?

A. $A'(-2, -1)$ **C.** $A'(-2, 1)$

B. $A'(2, -1)$ **D.** $A'(2, 1)$

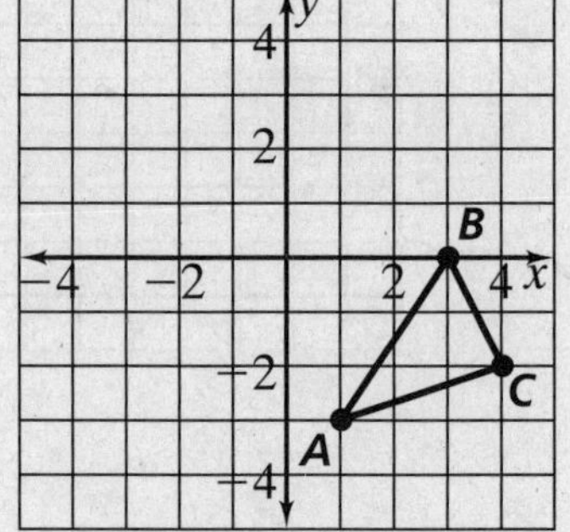

Slide each vertex ☐ units to the ☐ and ☐ units up.
Label and connect the images of the vertices.

The correct answer is choice ☐.

Quick Check

1. $\triangle JKL$ has vertices $J(0, 2)$, $K(3, 4)$, $L(5, 1)$. Translate $\triangle JKL$ 4 units to the left and 5 units up. What are the coordinates of point J'?

☐

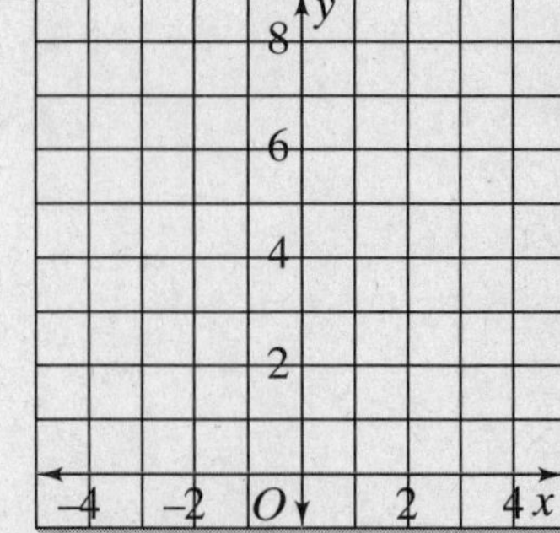

Example

❷ Describing a Translation Write a rule to describe the translation of $G(-5, 3)$ to $G'(-1, -2)$.

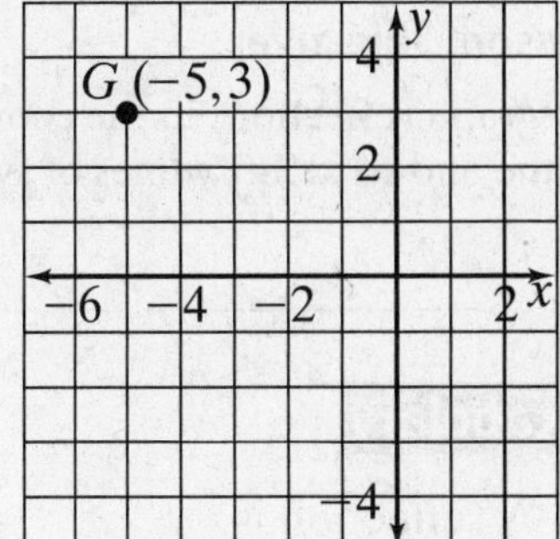

Point G moves ☐ units to the right and ☐ units down. So, the translation adds ☐ to the x-coordinate and subtracts ☐ from the y-coordinate.

The rule is ☐ → ☐.

Quick Check

2. Write a rule that describes the translation shown in the graph.

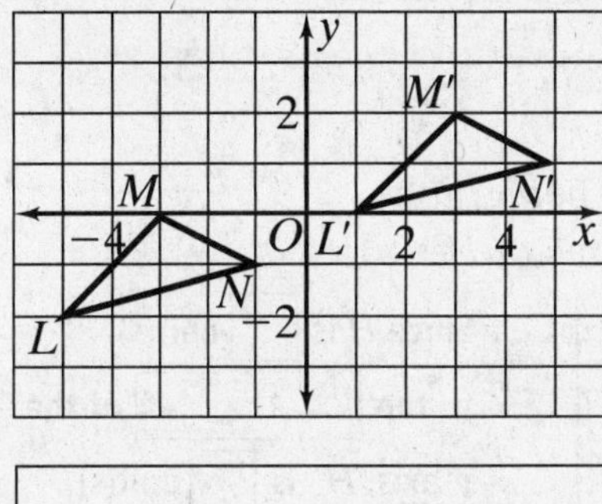

☐

Name ______________________ Class ______________ Date ______________

Lesson 3-7

Reflections and Symmetry

Lesson Objective	**NAEP 2005 Strand:** Geometry
To graph reflections in the coordinate plane and to identify lines of symmetry	**Topic:** Transformation of Shapes and Preservation of Properties **Local Standards:** ____________

Vocabulary

A reflection is ______________________

A line of reflection is ______________________

A line of symmetry is ______________________

A figure can be reflected over a line so that its image matches the original figure if it has ______________________

Example

❶ **Graphing Reflections of a Point** Graph the point $H(-4, 5)$. Then graph its image after it is reflected over the y-axis. Name the coordinates of H'.

The coordinates of H' are $(\square, \square)$.

Since *H* is ☐ unit(s) to the ☐ of the *y*-axis, *H'* is ☐ unit(s) to the ☐ of the *y*-axis.

Quick Check

1. Graph the point $D(-2, 1)$. Then graph its image after it is reflected over the y-axis. Name the coordinates of D'.

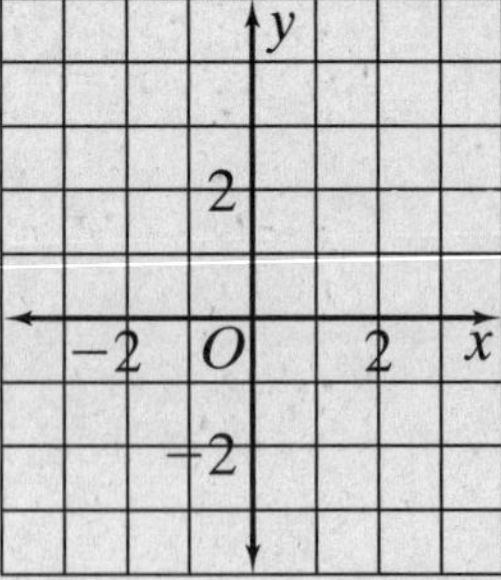

Name ________________ Class ________________ Date ________________

Example

❷ **Graphing Reflections of a Shape** $\triangle BCD$ has vertices $B(-3, 1)$, $C(-2, 5)$, and $D(-5, 4)$. Graph $\triangle BCD$ and its image after a reflection over the x-axis. Name the coordinates of the vertices of $\triangle B'C'D'$.

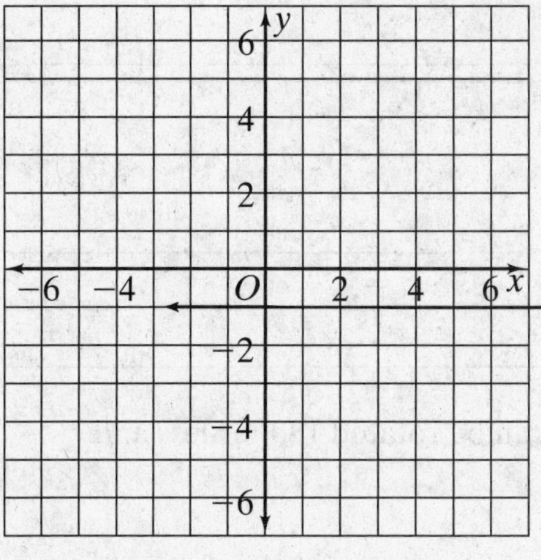

Since *B* is ☐ unit(s) ☐ the *x*-axis, *B′* is ☐ unit(s) ☐ the *x*-axis.

Reflect the other vertices.

Draw $\triangle B'C'D'$.

The coordinates of the vertices are B' (☐, ☐), C' (☐, ☐), and D' (☐, ☐).

Quick Check

2. $\triangle EFG$ has vertices $E(4, 3)$, $F(3, 1)$, and $G(1, 2)$. Graph $\triangle EFG$ and its image after a reflection over the x-axis. Name the coordinates of the vertices of $\triangle E'F'G'$.

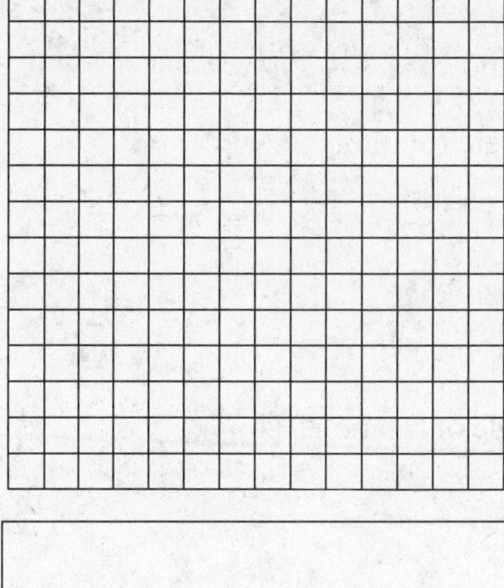

☐

Lesson 3-8

Rotations

Lesson Objective To graph rotations and identify rotational symmetry	**NAEP 2005 Strand:** Geometry **Topic:** Transformation of Shapes and Preservation of Properties **Local Standards:** ______________

Vocabulary

A rotation is ______________________________

The center of rotation is ______________________________

The angle of rotation is ______________________________

A figure has [ ] if it can be rotated 180° or less and exactly match its original figure.

Example

1 **Rotational Symmetry** Does this figure have rotational symmetry? If so, give the angle of rotation.

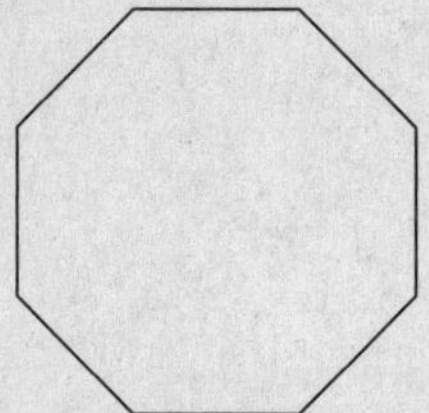

The image matches the original after [ ] of a complete rotation.

$\frac{1}{8} \cdot 360^\circ = \square^\circ$

The angle of rotation is $\square^\circ$.

Quick Check

1. If the figure below has rotational symmetry, find the angle of rotation. Write *no rotational symmetry* if it does not.

Name ______________ Class ______________ Date ______________

Example

❷ Graphing Rotations Draw the image of rectangle $ABCD$ after a rotation of 90° about the origin.

Step 1 Draw and trace.

- Draw rectangle $ABCD$ with vertices $(3, 2)$, $(-3, 2)$, $(-3, -2)$, and $(3, -2)$. Place a piece of tracing paper over your graph.
- Trace the vertices of the rectangle, the x-axis, and the y-axis.
- Place your pencil at the origin to rotate the paper.

Step 2 Rotate and mark each vertex.

- Rotate the tracing paper 90° counterclockwise. The axes should line up.
- Mark the position of each vertex by pressing your pencil through the paper.

Step 3 Complete the new figure.

- Remove the tracing paper.
- Draw the rectangle.
- Label the vertices to complete the figure.

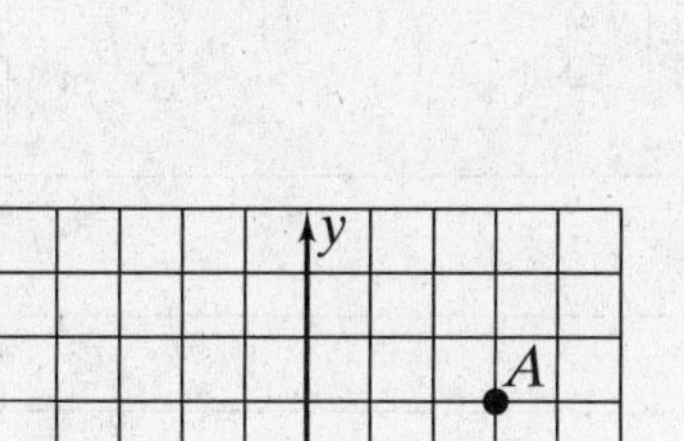

Quick Check

2. Copy $\triangle ABD$. Draw the image of $\triangle ABD$ after a rotation of the given number of degrees about the origin.

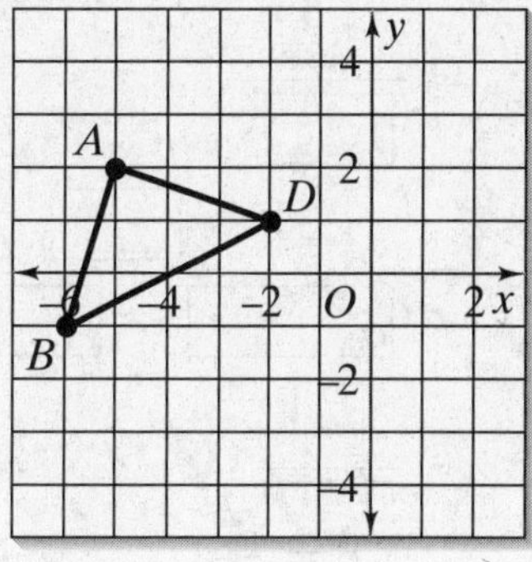

a. 180°

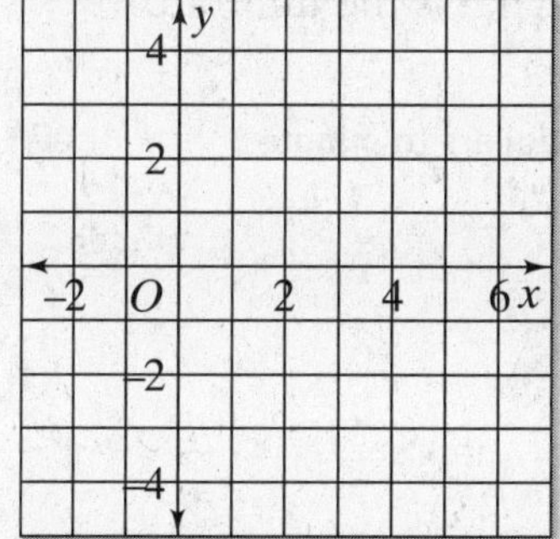

b. 270°

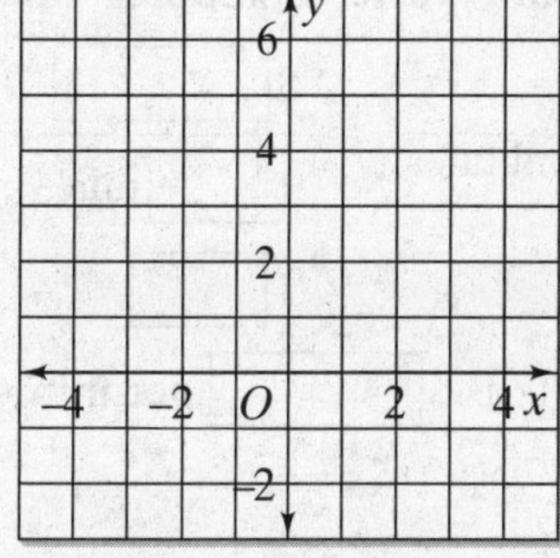

Name ____________________ Class ____________ Date ____________

Lesson 4-1

Ratios and Rates

Lesson Objective To write ratios and unit rates and to use rates to solve problems	**NAEP 2005 Strand:** Number Properties and Operations **Topic:** Ratios and Proportional Reasoning **Local Standards:** ____________________

Vocabulary and Key Concepts

Ratio

A ratio is a comparison of two quantities by division. You can write a ratio in three ways.

Arithmetic

5 to 8 $\frac{\square}{\square}$ 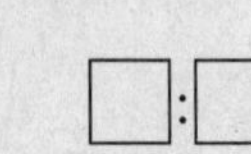

Algebra

a to b 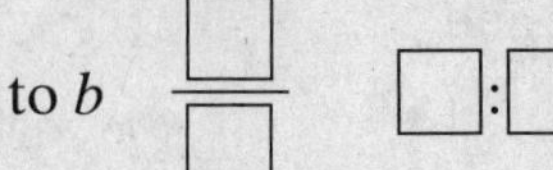

A rate is ____

____

A unit rate is ____

Examples

1 Writing a Ratio in Simplest Form Write the ratio 36 seconds to 12 minutes in simplest form.

$\frac{36\text{ s}}{12\text{ min}} = \frac{36\text{ s}}{\square\text{ s}}$ ← **Convert minutes to seconds so that both measures are in the same units. Divide the common units.**

$\frac{36}{\square} = \frac{36 \div \square}{\square \div \square}$ ← **Divide the numerator and denominator by the GCF, $\square$.**

$= \frac{\square}{\square}$ ← **Simplify.**

The ratio of 36 seconds to 12 minutes is $\square$.

2 Finding a Unit Rate Computer time costs $4.50 for 30 min. What is the unit rate?

$\frac{\text{cost}}{\text{number of minutes}} = \frac{\$\square}{\square\text{ min}}$ ← **Write a rate comparing dollars to minutes.**

$= \$\square$ ← **Divide.**

The unit rate is $\square per min.

3 Fuel Efficiency Keneesha drove her car 267 mi using 11 gal of gas. Vanessa drove her car 210 mi using 9 gal of gas. Find the unit rate for each. Which car got more miles per gallon of gas?

Keneesha		Vanessa
$\frac{\text{miles}}{\text{gallons}} = \frac{\square \text{ mi}}{\square \text{ gal}}$	← **Write the rates comparing miles to gallons.** →	$\frac{\text{miles}}{\text{gallons}} = \frac{\square \text{ mi}}{\square \text{ gal}}$
$= \square$ mi/gal	← **Divide.** →	$= \square$ mi/gal
$\approx \square$ mi/gal	← **Round to the nearest tenth.** →	$\approx \square$ mi/gal

$\square$ car got more miles per gallon.

Check for Reasonableness $\square \cdot 11 = \square$ and $\square \approx 267$. Also, $\square \cdot 9 = \square$ and $\square \approx 210$. The answers are reasonable.

Quick Check

1. Write the ratio $\frac{30 \text{ s}}{3 \text{ min}}$ in simplest form.

2. Find the unit rate for 52 deliveries in 8 hours.

3. The cost of a 20-oz box of cereal is $4.29. A 12-oz box of cereal costs $3.59. Which box of cereal is a better buy?

Name ______________________ Class ______________ Date ______________

Lesson 4-2

Converting Units

Lesson Objective	**NAEP 2005 Strand:** Measurement
To convert units within and between the customary and metric systems	**Topic:** Systems of Measurement **Local Standards:** ____________

Vocabulary

A conversion factor is ____

____

Examples

1 Converting Measurements Convert 0.7 mi to ft.

Since 5,280 ft = 1 mi, use the conversion factor $\frac{5{,}280\text{ ft}}{1\text{ mi}}$.

$0.7 = \frac{0.7\text{ mi}}{1} \cdot \frac{\square\text{ ft}}{\square\text{ mi}}$ ← **Multiply by the ______. Divide the common units.**

$= \frac{(0.7)(\square)\text{ ft}}{1}$ ← **Simplify.**

$= \square\text{ ft}$ ← **Simplify.**

There are ______ ft in 0.7 miles.

2 Rowing A rowing team completed a 2,000-m course at a rate of 6.84 m/s. Convert this rate to kilometers per minute. Round your answer to the nearest hundredth.

Multiply by the conversion factors $\frac{60\text{s}}{1\text{min}}$ and $\frac{1\text{ km}}{1{,}000\text{ m}}$.

$\frac{6.84\text{ m}}{1\text{ s}} = \frac{6.84\text{ m}}{1\text{ s}} \cdot \frac{1\text{ km}}{\square\text{ m}} \cdot \frac{\square\text{ s}}{1\text{ min}}$

$= \frac{(6.84)(1)(\square)\text{ km}}{(1)(\square)(1)\text{ min}}$ ← **Simplify.**

$= \square$ ← **Use a calculator.**

The team rowed at a rate of about ______ km/min.

Check for Reasonableness Round 6.84 to 7. Then 7 · 60 ÷ 1000 = 0.42.

The answer ______ km/min is close to the estimate ______.

The answer is reasonable.

❸ Converting Using Compatible Numbers Use compatible numbers to estimate the number of feet in 147 inches.

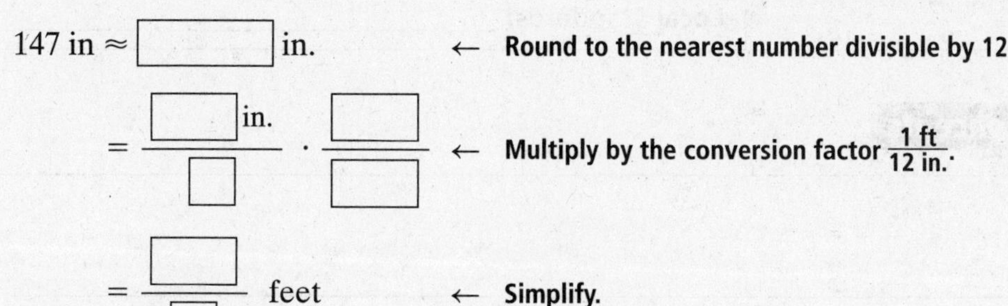

The conversion factor for changing feet to inches is $\frac{\square}{\square}$.

147 in ≈ ☐ in. ← **Round to the nearest number divisible by 12.**

$= \frac{\square \text{ in.}}{\square} \cdot \frac{\square}{\square}$ ← **Multiply by the conversion factor $\frac{1 \text{ ft}}{12 \text{ in.}}$.**

$= \frac{\square}{\square}$ feet ← **Simplify.**

= ☐ feet ← **Divide.**

There are about ☐ feet in 147 inches.

❹ Converting Between Systems Convert 5 km to miles.

$5 \text{ km} = \frac{\square}{\square} \cdot \frac{\square}{\square}$ ← **Multiply by the conversion factor $\frac{1 \text{ mi}}{1.61 \text{ km}}$.**

$= \frac{(5)(1) \text{ mi}}{1.61} \approx \square$ mi ← **Simplify. Divide using a calculator.**

There are about ☐ miles in 5 kilometers.

Quick Check

1. Convert $2\frac{1}{4}$ mi to feet.

2. You ran at a rate of 0.15 mi/min. Convert the rate to feet per second.

3. Use compatible numbers to estimate.
   a. 14,120 lb is about ☐ t.
   b. 9.8 c is about ☐ pt.

4. Convert 15 L to quarts. Round to the nearest tenth.

Name ______________________ Class ______________ Date ____________

Lesson 4-3

Solving Proportions

Lesson Objective	NAEP 2005 Strand: Number Properties and Operations
To identify and solve proportions	Topic: Ratios and Proportional Reasoning
	Local Standards: ____________________

Vocabulary and Key Concepts

Proportion

A proportion is ____

Arithmetic	Algebra
$\frac{6}{10} = \frac{9}{15}$	$\frac{a}{b} = \frac{c}{d}$, where $b \neq 0$ and $d \neq 0$

Cross Products Property

The [ ] of two ratios are found by multiplying the denominator of each ratio by the numerator of the other ratio. In a proportion, the cross products are equal.

Arithmetic	Algebra
$\frac{6}{10} = \frac{9}{15}$	$\frac{a}{b} = \frac{c}{d}$, where $b \neq 0$ and $d \neq 0$
$6 \cdot 15 = 10 \cdot 9$	$ad = bc$

Examples

1 Identifying Proportions Do $\frac{7}{12}$ and $\frac{21}{38}$ form a proportion? Explain.

$\frac{7}{12} \stackrel{?}{=} \frac{21}{38}$ ← **Write as a proportion.**

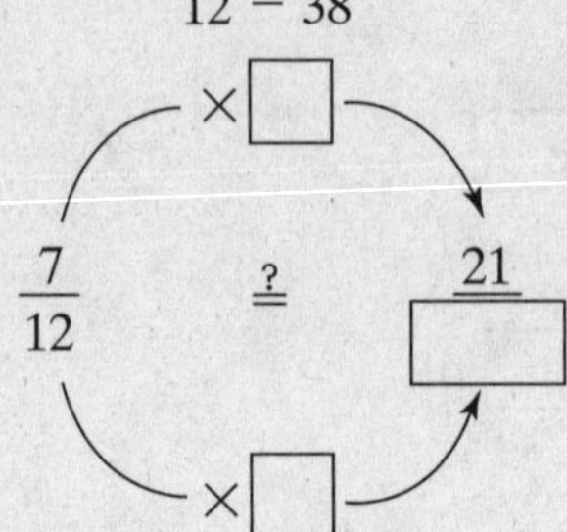

← **Use number sense to find a common multiplier.**

Since $\frac{7}{12}$ [ ] $\frac{21}{38}$, they [ ] form a proportion.

Example

2 Using Cross Products The fixed rate of conversion is 1 euro = 0.7876 Irish pounds. How many euros would you receive for 125 Irish pounds?

Let n = the number of euros.

$\frac{0.7876}{1} = \frac{\square}{n}$ ← Write the proportion 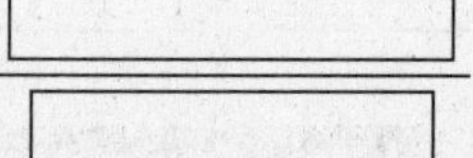.

$0.7876 \cdot n = 1 \cdot \square$ ← Write the cross products.

$\frac{0.7876n}{\square} = \frac{\square}{\square}$ ← Divide each side by $\square$.

$n = \square$ ← Use a calculator.

You would receive $\square$ euros.

Quick Check

1. Do $\frac{6}{7}$ and $\frac{23}{28}$ form a proportion? Explain.

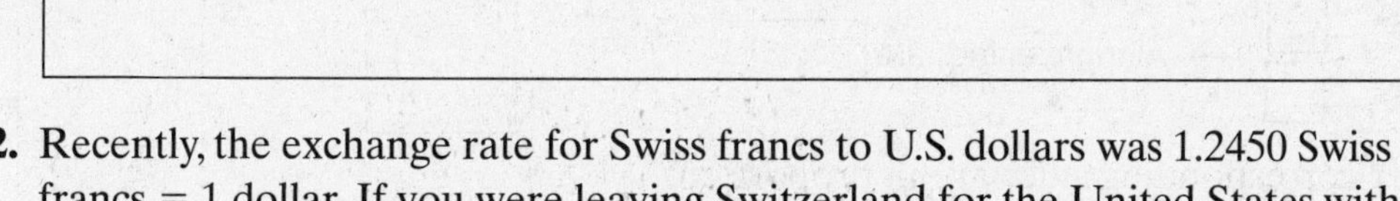

2. Recently, the exchange rate for Swiss francs to U.S. dollars was 1.2450 Swiss francs = 1 dollar. If you were leaving Switzerland for the United States with 300 francs left, how many dollars would you receive?

Name ______________________ Class ______________ Date ____________

Lesson 4-4

Similar Figures and Proportions

Lesson Objective	**NAEP 2005 Strands:** Measurement; Geometry
To identify similar figures and to use proportions to find missing measurements in similar figures	**Topics:** Systems of Measurement; Transformation of Shapes and Preservation of Properties **Local Standards:** ____________

Vocabulary and Key Concepts

Similar Polygons If two polygons are similar polygons, then

- corresponding angles are [ ] and
- lengths of corresponding sides are [ ].

Similar figures have ______________________________

Congruent angles have ______________________________

Example

1 Identifying Similar Polygons Is rectangle *ABCD* similar to rectangle *RSTU*? Explain.

First, check whether corresponding angles are congruent.

$\angle A \cong \angle$ [ ] $\angle B \cong \angle$ [ ]
$\angle C \cong \angle$ [ ] $\angle D \cong \angle$ [ ] ← **All right angles are** [ ]°.

D 3 A, 6, 6, C 3 B; U 24 R, 48, 48, T 24 S

Next, check whether corresponding sides are in proportion.

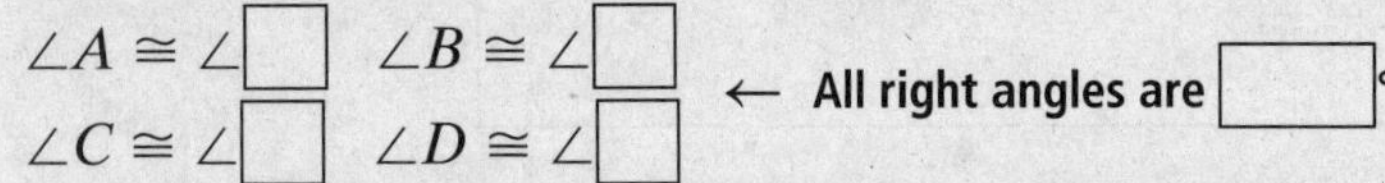
$\frac{AB}{[\ ]} \stackrel{?}{=} \frac{DA}{[\ ]}$ ← ***AB* corresponds to** [ ]. ***DA* corresponds to** [ ].

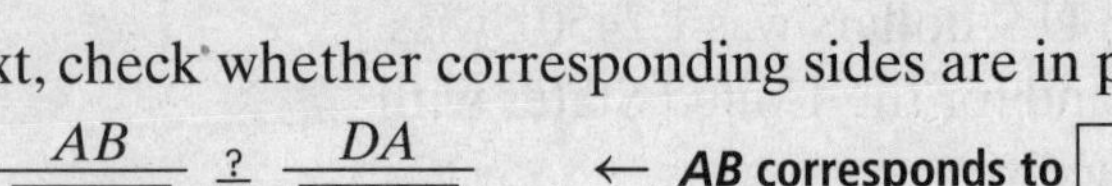
$\frac{6}{[\ ]} \stackrel{?}{=} \frac{3}{[\ ]}$ ← **Substitute.**

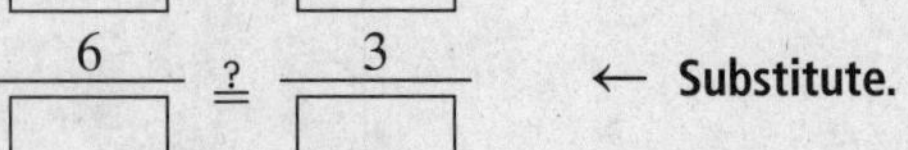
$6 \cdot [\ ] \stackrel{?}{=} [\ ] \cdot 3$ ← **Write the cross products.**

[ ] = [ ] ← **Simplify.**

The corresponding sides [ ] in proportion, so rectangle *ABCD* is [ ] to rectangle *RSTU*.

Quick Check

1. Is rectangle *EFGH* similar to rectangle *PQRS*? Explain.

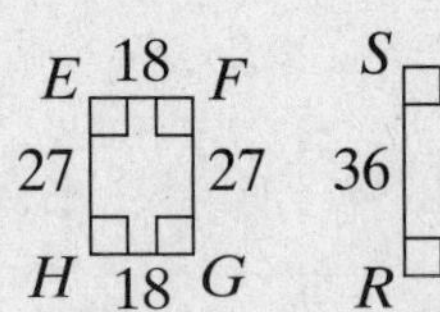

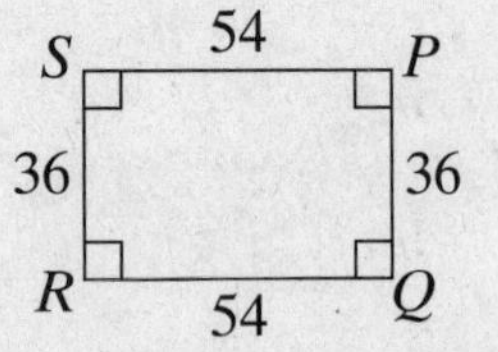

Name ______________________ Class ______________ Date ____________

Examples

2 Given that rectangle *EFGH* is similar to rectangle *WXYZ*, find *t*.

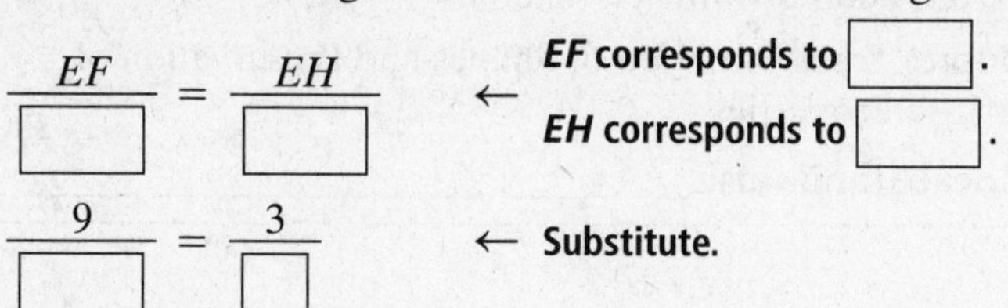

$\frac{EF}{\square} = \frac{EH}{\square}$ ← **EF corresponds to** $\square$. **EH corresponds to** $\square$.

$\frac{9}{\square} = \frac{3}{\square}$ ← **Substitute.**

$9 \cdot \square = \square \cdot 3$ ← **Write the cross products.**

$\frac{\square}{9} = \frac{\square}{9}$ ← **Simplify. Then divide each side by 9.**

$t = \square$ ← **Simplify.**

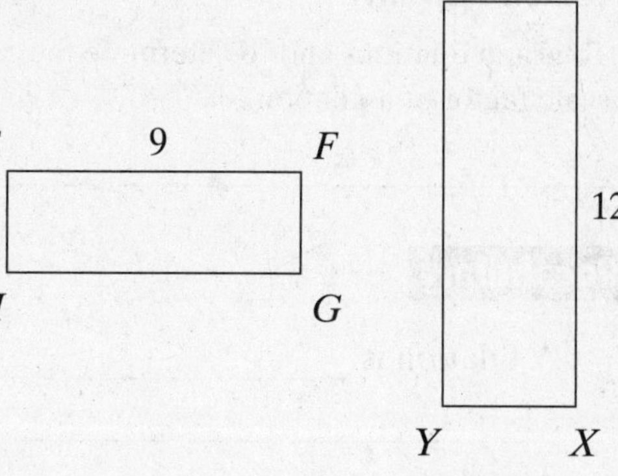

3 **Overlapping Similar Triangles** $\triangle RST \sim \triangle PSU$. Find the value of *d*.

Step 1 Separate the triangles.

Step 2 Write a proportion using corresponding sides of the triangles.

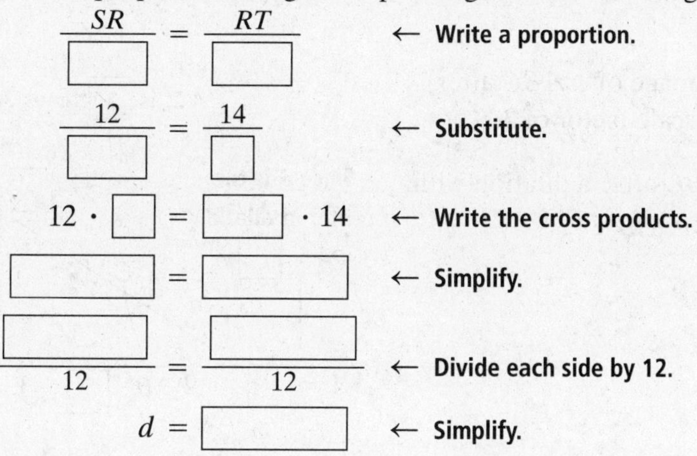

$\frac{SR}{\square} = \frac{RT}{\square}$ ← **Write a proportion.**

$\frac{12}{\square} = \frac{14}{\square}$ ← **Substitute.**

$12 \cdot \square = \square \cdot 14$ ← **Write the cross products.**

$\square = \square$ ← **Simplify.**

$\frac{\square}{12} = \frac{\square}{12}$ ← **Divide each side by 12.**

$d = \square$ ← **Simplify.**

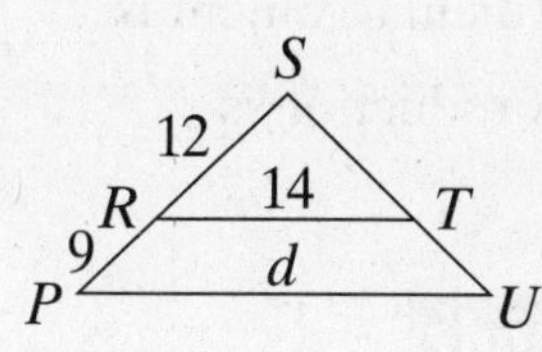

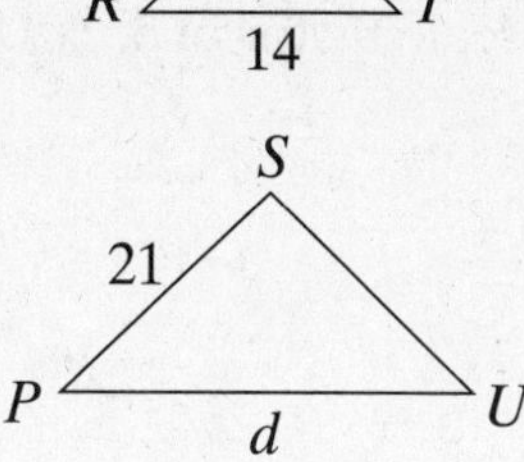

Quick Check

2. In Example 2, if the side lengths of *EFGH* are doubled, will the resulting polygon be similar to *EFGH*? Explain.

3. If *ST* is 13 ft in Example 3, what is the length of $\overline{SU}$?

Lesson 4-5

Similarity Transformations

Lesson Objective	**NAEP 2005 Strand:** Geometry
To graph dilations and to determine the scale factor of a dilation	**Topic:** Transformation of Shapes and Preservation of Properties **Local Standards:** ______________

Vocabulary

A dilation is ____

____

A scale factor is ____

____

An enlargement is ____

A reduction is ____

Example

1 Finding a Dilation Find the image of $\triangle ABC$ after a dilation with center A and a scale factor of 3.

$\triangle A'B'C'$ is the image of $\triangle ABC$ after a dilation with a scale factor of 3. $\triangle ABC$ ☐ $\triangle A'B'C'$.

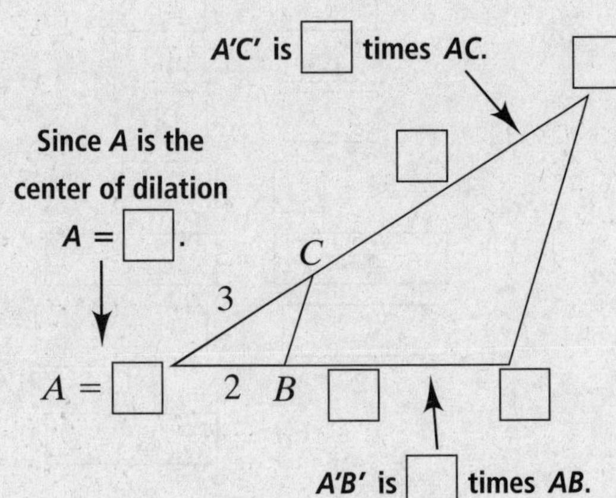

Quick Check

1. Find the image of $\triangle DEF$ with vertices $D(-2, 2)$, $E(1, -1)$, and $F(-2, -1)$ after a dilation with center D and a scale factor of 2.

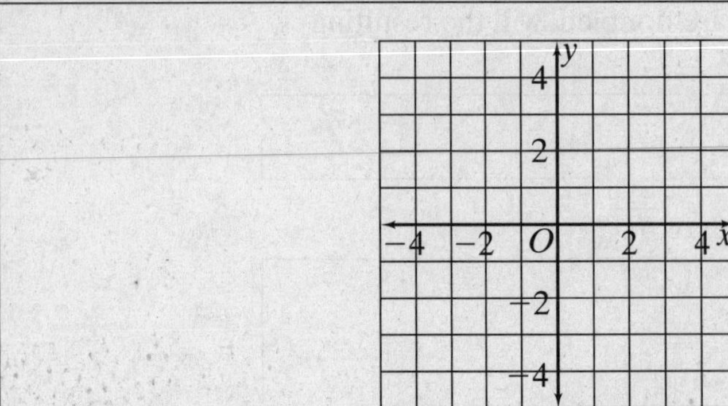

Name ______________________ Class ______________ Date ____________

❷ Graphing Dilation Images Find the coordinates of the image of quadrilateral $WXYZ$ after a dilation with center $(0, 0)$ and a scale factor of $\frac{1}{2}$.
Quadrilateral $WXYZ$ has vertices $W(-2, -1)$, $X(0, 2)$, $Y(4, 2)$, and $Z(4, -1)$.

Step 1 Multiply the x- and y-coordinates of each point by $\frac{1}{2}$.

$W(-2, -1) \rightarrow W'\left(\square, -\frac{\square}{\square}\right)$

$X(0, 2) \rightarrow X'(\square, \square)$

$Y(4, 2) \rightarrow Y'(\square, \square)$

$Z(4, -1) \rightarrow Z'\left(\square, -\frac{\square}{\square}\right)$

Step 2 Graph the image.

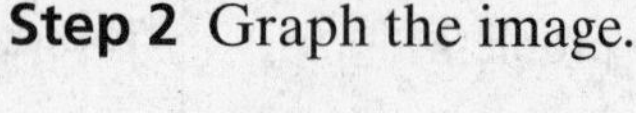

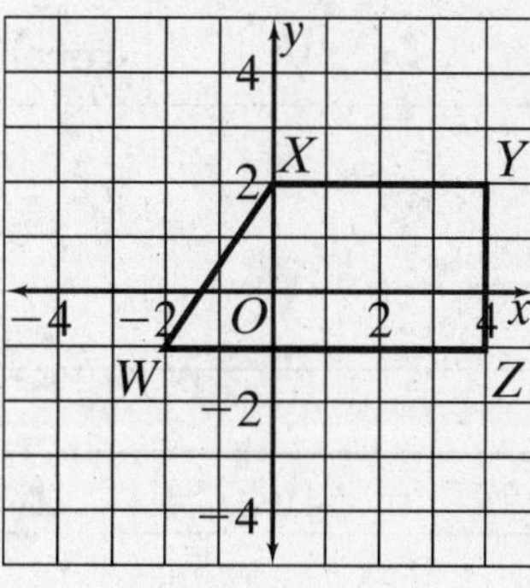

❸ Finding a Scale Factor $\triangle Q'P'R'$ is a dilation of $\triangle QPR$. Find the scale factor. Is it an enlargement or a reduction?

image → original → $\frac{Q'P'}{QP} = \frac{\square + \square}{\square} = \square$

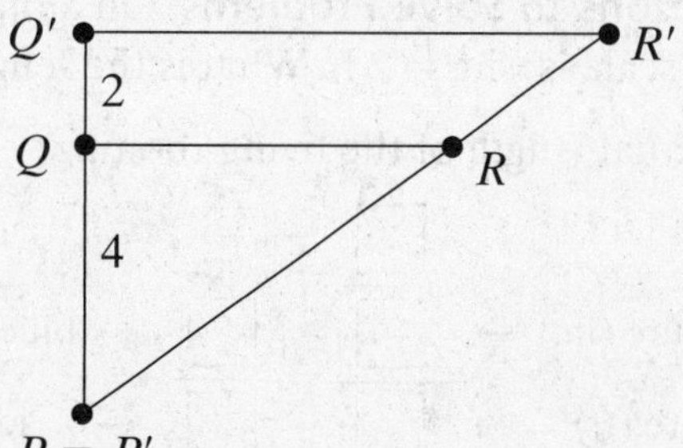

The scale factor is ______. It is ______ than 1, so the dilation is a(n) ______.

Quick Check

2. Find the coordinates of the image $ABCD$ with vertices $A(0, 0)$, $B(0, 3)$, $C(3, 3)$, and $D(3, 0)$ after a dilation with a scale factor of $\frac{4}{3}$.

____

3. Figure $EFGH$ shows the outline of a yard. Figure $E'F'G'H'$ is a doghouse. Figure $E'F'G'H'$ is a dilation of figure $EFGH$. Find the scale factor. Is it an enlargement or a reduction?

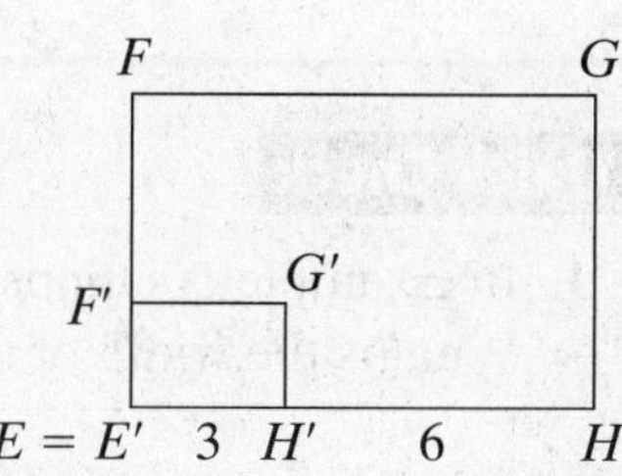

Name ____________________ Class ______________ Date ______________

Lesson 4-6

Scale Models and Maps

Lesson Objective	NAEP 2005 Strands: Measurement; Geometry
To use proportions to solve problems involving scale	**Topics:** Systems of Measurement; Transformation of Shapes and Preservations of Properties **Local Standards:** ____________

Vocabulary

A scale model is ____

____

The scale is ____

____

Example

1 Using Proportions to Solve Problems On a blueprint, the living room is 4 in. long. The scale is $\frac{1}{2}$ in. = 2 ft. What is the length of the actual living room?

Let ℓ = the actual length of the living room.

blueprint measure (in.) → $\dfrac{\frac{\square}{\square}}{\square} = \dfrac{\square}{\square}$ ← blueprint length (in.)

actual measure (ft) → ← actual length (ft)

$\frac{1}{2} \cdot \ell = \square \cdot \square$ ← **Write the cross products.**

$\frac{1}{2}\ell = \square$ ← **Simplify.**

$\frac{2}{1} \cdot \frac{1}{2}\ell = \frac{2}{1} \cdot \square$ ← **Multiply each side by $\frac{2}{1}$.**

$\ell = \square$ ← **Simplify.**

The actual length of the living room is $\square$ ft.

Quick Check

1. In Example 1, suppose the width of another room on the blueprint is 2.5 in. What is the width of the actual room?

Name ______________________ Class ______________ Date ______________

Example

2 Geography Find the map distance from Birmingham, Alabama to Montgomery, Alabama. Which is closest to the actual distance?

A. 85 mi **B.** 105

C. 95 mi **D.** 115 mi

The map distance is about $1\frac{1}{8}$ in., or 1.125 in. as a decimal.

Let d = the actual distance.

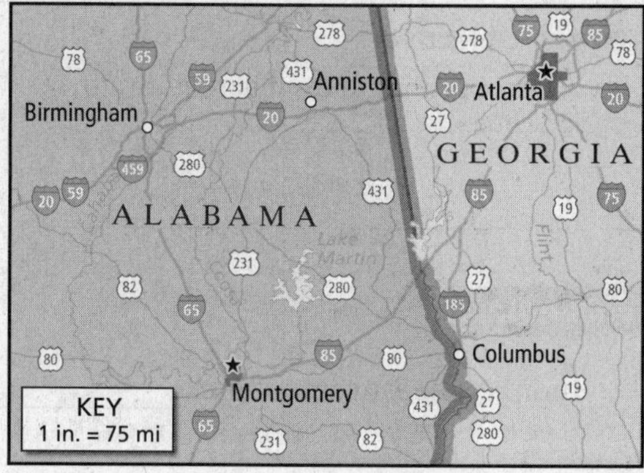

map (in.) → $\frac{\square}{\square}$ = $\frac{\square}{\square}$ ← map (in.)

actual (mi) → ← actual (mi)

$\square \cdot \square = \square \cdot \square$ ← **Write the cross products.**

$d = \square$ ← **Simplify.**

The distance from Birmingham to Montgomery is about ☐ mi.

The correct answer is choice ☐.

Quick Check

2. Use the map in Example 2 and an inch ruler. Find the actual distance from Montgomery, Alabama, to Atlanta, Georgia.

Name ______________________ Class ______________ Date ______________

Lesson 4-7

Similarity and Indirect Measurement

Lesson Objective To use proportions and similar figures to solve problems	**NAEP 2005 Strands:** Measurement; Geometry **Topics:** Measuring Physical Attributes; Transformation of Shapes and Preservation of Properties **Local Standards:** ______________

Vocabulary

Indirect measurement uses ____

____

Examples

1 **Measuring Indirectly** When a 6-ft student casts a 17-ft shadow, a flagpole casts a shadow 51 ft long. Find the height of the flagpole.

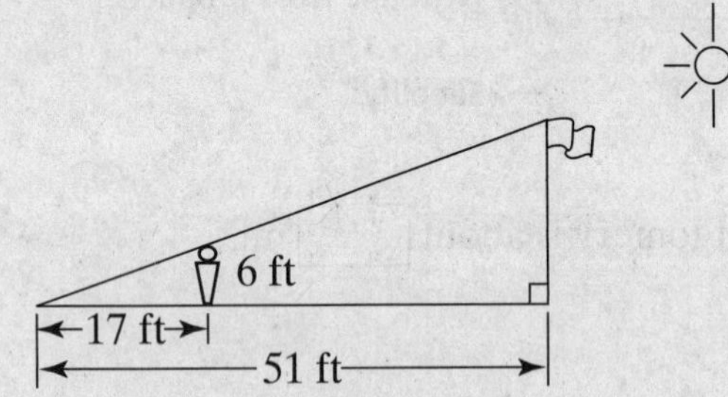

Use similar triangles to set up a proportion.

Words $\dfrac{\square \text{ height}}{\square \text{ height}} = \dfrac{\text{length of } \square \text{ shadow}}{\text{length of } \square \text{ shadow}}$

Let h = the flagpole's height.

Proportion $\dfrac{h}{\square} = \dfrac{\square}{\square}$

$\square h = \square \cdot \square$ ← **Write the cross products.**

$\square h = \square$ ← **Simplify.**

$\dfrac{\square h}{\square} = \dfrac{\square}{\square}$ ← **Divide each side by $\square$.**

$h = \square$ ← **Simplify.**

The height of the flagpole is $\square$ ft.

❷ Measuring Indirectly In the figure, $\triangle ABC \sim \triangle EDC$. Find d.

B, C, D, E, A, 312 m, 141 m, d, 416 m

Use similar triangles to set up a proportion.

$\frac{ED}{\square} = \frac{CD}{\square}$ ← $\overline{ED}$ corresponds to $\square$. $\overline{CD}$ corresponds to $\square$.

$\frac{d}{\square} = \frac{\square}{\square}$ ← Substitute.

$\square \cdot d = \square \cdot \square$ ← Write the cross products.

$312d = \square$ ← Simplify.

$\frac{312d}{312} = \frac{\square}{312}$ ← Divide each side by 312.

$\square$ ÷ $\square$ = $\square$ ← Use a calculator.

The value of d is $\square$ m.

Quick Check

1. A school 40 ft high casts a 160-ft shadow. A nearby cellular phone tower casts a 210-ft shadow. Find the height of the tower.

2. In Example 2, AC is 520 m. Find CE.

Name ______________________ Class ______________ Date ______________

Lesson 5-1

Fractions, Decimals, and Percents

Lesson Objective To convert between fractions, decimals, and percents and to order rational numbers	**NAEP 2005 Strand:** Number Properties and Operations **Topic:** Ratios and Proportional Reasoning **Local Standards:** ____________________

Vocabulary

A percent is ____

____

Examples

1 Writing a Fraction as a Percent Use mental math to write $\frac{3}{25}$ as a percent.

What you think

I can write $\frac{3}{25}$ as an equivalent fraction with a denominator of ☐.

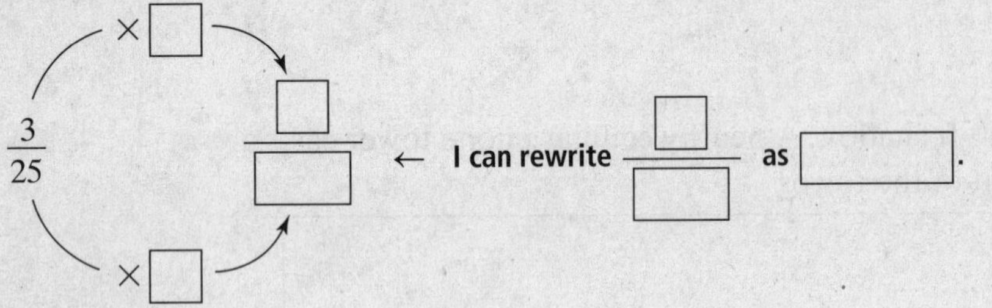

Why it works

$\frac{3}{25} = \frac{3 \times 4}{25 \times 4}$ ← **Multiply the numerator and denominator by ☐.**

$= \frac{\square}{\square}$ ← **Simplify.**

$= \square$ ← **Write the fraction as a percent.**

2 Writing a Decimal as a Percent Write 2.5 as a percent.

$2.5 = 2\frac{5}{10} = \frac{\square}{\square}$ ← **Write the decimal as a mixed number and then as a fraction.**

$= \frac{25 \cdot \square}{10 \cdot \square}$ ← **Multiply the numerator and denominator by 10.**

$= \frac{\square}{100}$ ← **Write as an equivalent fraction with a denominator of ☐.**

$= \square\%$ ← **Write the fraction as a percent.**

Name ________________ Class ________________ Date ________________

Examples

❸ Writing a Percent as a Fraction Write $62\frac{1}{2}\%$ as a fraction in simplest form.

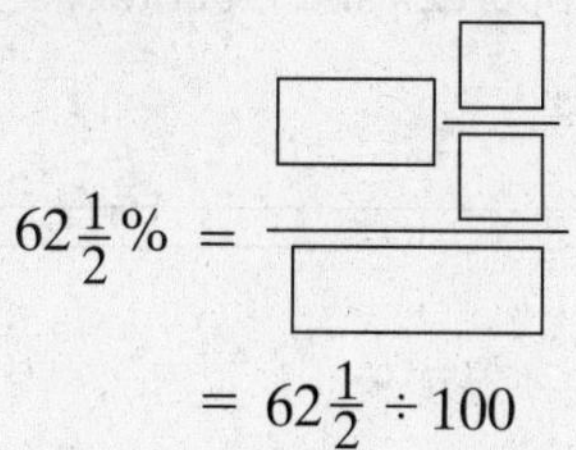

$62\frac{1}{2}\% =$ ← Write the percent as a fraction with a denominator of ▭.

$= 62\frac{1}{2} \div 100$ ← Rewrite the fraction as division.

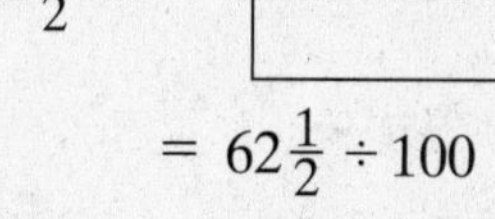

← Write the mixed number as an improper fraction.

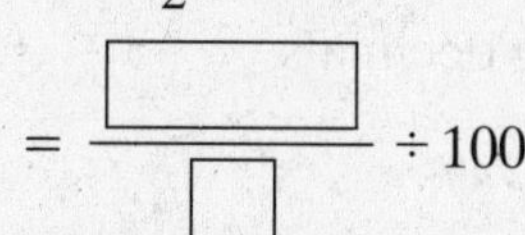

← Multiply by the reciprocal of 100.

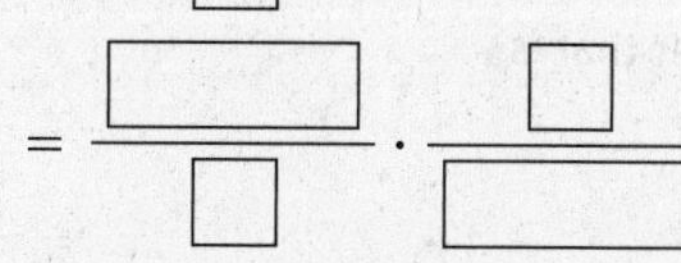

← Simplify and divide by the GCF.

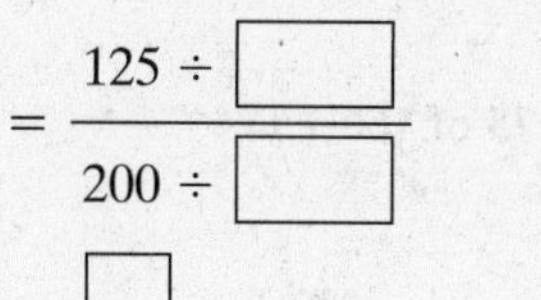

← Write the fraction in simplest form.

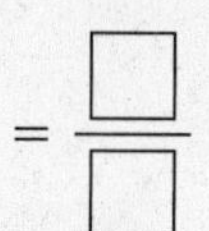

❹ Ordering Rational Numbers Order 0.31, $\frac{1}{5}$, and 27% from least to greatest.

$0.31 = 0.31 \quad \frac{1}{5} =$ ▭ $\quad 27\% =$ ▭ ← Change each number to a decimal.

Since ▭ < ▭ < ▭, ▭ < ▭ < ▭.

Quick Check

1. Use mental math to write $\frac{11}{20}$ as a percent.

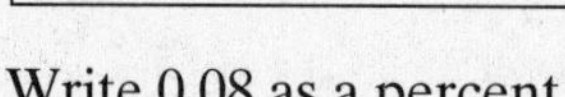

2. Write 0.08 as a percent.

3. A vitamin has 150% of the RDA of vitamin C. Write this percent as a fraction.

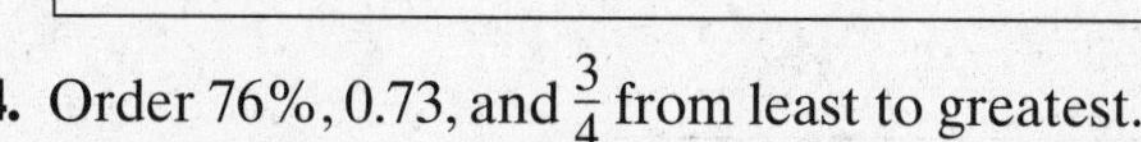

4. Order 76%, 0.73, and $\frac{3}{4}$ from least to greatest.

Name ______________________ Class ______________ Date ______________

Lesson 5-2

Estimating With Percents

Lesson Objective	**NAEP 2005 Strand:** Number Properties and Operations
To estimate percents using decimals and fractions	**Topic:** Estimation
	Local Standards: ____________

Examples

1 Estimating Percents Using Decimals Estimate 74% of 158 using decimals.

74% ≈ ☐ ← **Use a decimal that is close to 74%.**

158 ≈ ☐ ← **Round 158 to a number that is compatible with 0.75.**

74% of 158 ≈ ☐ of ☐

= ☐ · ☐ ← ☐ **to find 0.75 of 160.**

= ☐ ← **Simplify.**

2 Estimating Percents Using Fractions A video store rented 297 videos. The customers returned 19% of the videos late. Estimate, using fractions, how many videos were returned late.

$19\% \approx \frac{\square}{5}$ ← **Use a fraction that is close to 19%.**

297 ≈ ☐ ← **Round to a number that is compatible with 5.**

$19\% \text{ of } 297 \approx \frac{1}{5} \text{ of } 300$

$= \frac{1}{\cancel{5}} \cdot \frac{\cancel{300}}{1}$ ← ☐ **to find $\frac{1}{5}$ of 300.**

= ☐ ← **Simplify.**

About ☐ videos were returned late.

Quick Check

1. Use decimals to estimate 18% of 107.

2. A teacher says that about 35% of the 24 students in a class have blue eyes. Using fractions, estimate the number of blue-eyed students.

Name ______________________ Class ______________ Date ____________

Example

3 Estimating Tips Your family goes out to dinner and the total bill is \$44.87. Use mental math to estimate a 15% tip.

What you think

The bill is about \$45. I know 10% of 45 is $\frac{1}{10}$ of 45, or ☐. Then 5% of 45 is half of ☐, or ☐. A 15% tip is about \$☐ plus \$☐, or \$☐.

Why it works

15% of 45 = 0.15 · 45 ← **Rewrite 15% as 0.15.**

= (☐ + ☐)45 ← **Rewrite 0.15 as 0.10 + 0.05.**

= 0.10(45) + 0.05(45) ← **Distributive Property.**

= ☐ + ☐ ← **Simplify.**

= ☐ ← **Simplify.**

A 15% tip for a \$44.87 bill is about \$☐.

Quick Check

3. Estimate a 15% tip for a \$72.10 restaurant bill.

Name ______________________ Class ______________ Date ______________

Lesson 5-3

Percents and Proportions

Lesson Objective To use proportions to find part of a whole, a whole amount, or a percent	**NAEP 2005 Strand:** Number Properties and Operations **Topic:** Ratios and Proportional Reasoning **Local Standards:** ____________

Key Concepts

Percents and Proportions

Finding the Part
What number is 20% of 25?

$\frac{n}{\square} = \frac{\square}{100}$

Finding the Whole
5 is 20% of what number?

$\frac{\square}{w} = \frac{\square}{100}$

Finding the Percent
5 is what percent of 25?

$\frac{\square}{\square} = \frac{p}{100}$

Example

1 Finding Part of a Whole Find 32% of 240.

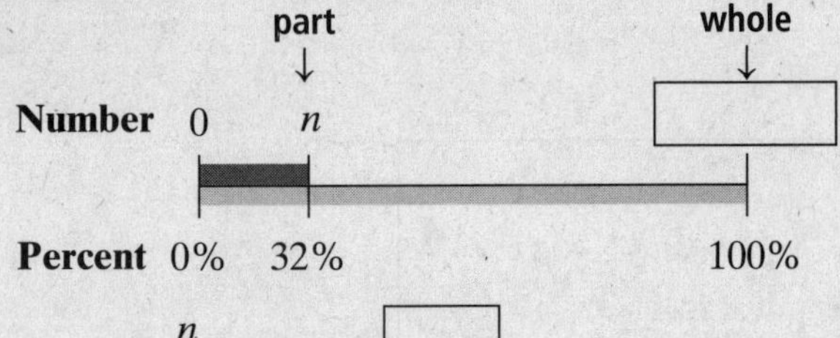

← A diagram can help you understand the problem.

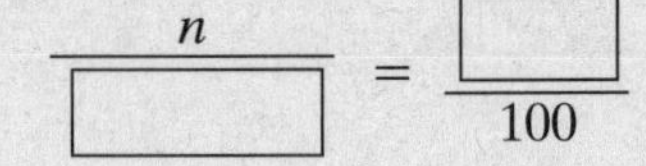

$\frac{n}{\square} = \frac{\square}{100}$ ← Write a proportion.

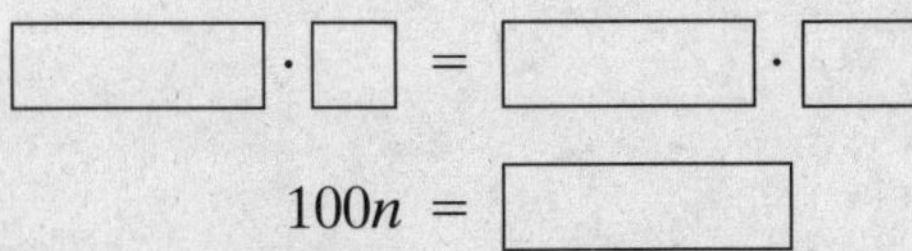

$\square \cdot \square = \square \cdot \square$ ← Write the cross products.

$100n = \square$ ← Simplify.

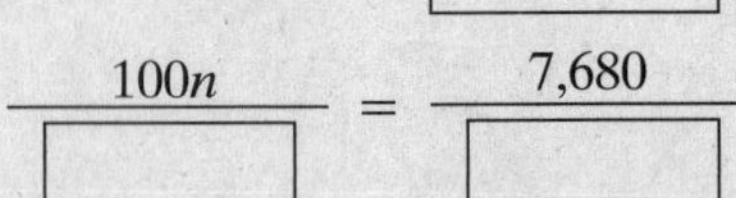

$\frac{100n}{\square} = \frac{7{,}680}{\square}$ ← Divide each side by $\square$.

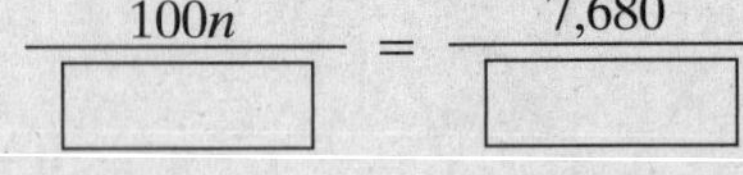

$n = \square$ ← Simplify.

Quick Check

1. Use a proportion to find 74% of 95.

$\square$

Name ________________ Class ________________ Date ________________

Examples

❷ Finding a Whole Amount Suppose 11,550 elementary students make up 14% of a city's population. What is the population of the city?

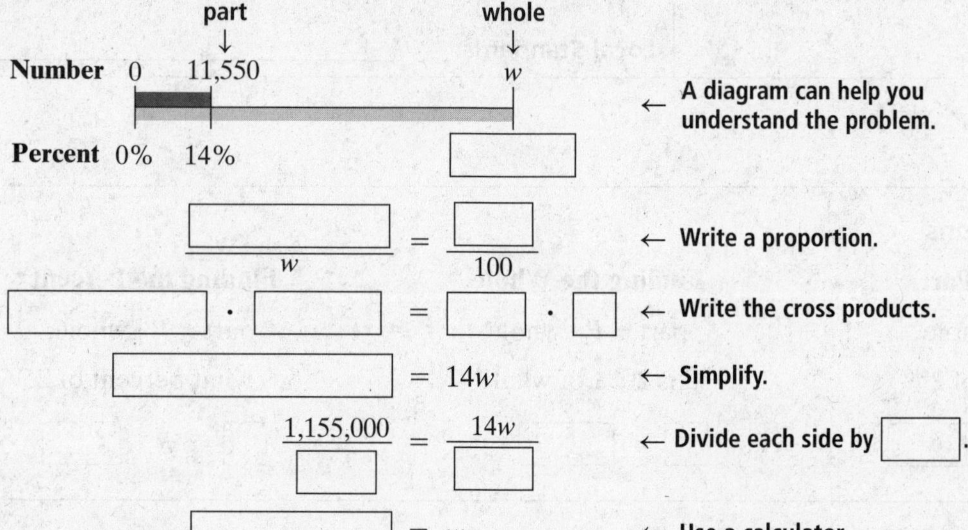

The population of the city is ______ people.

❸ Finding a Percent 26 is what percent of 80?

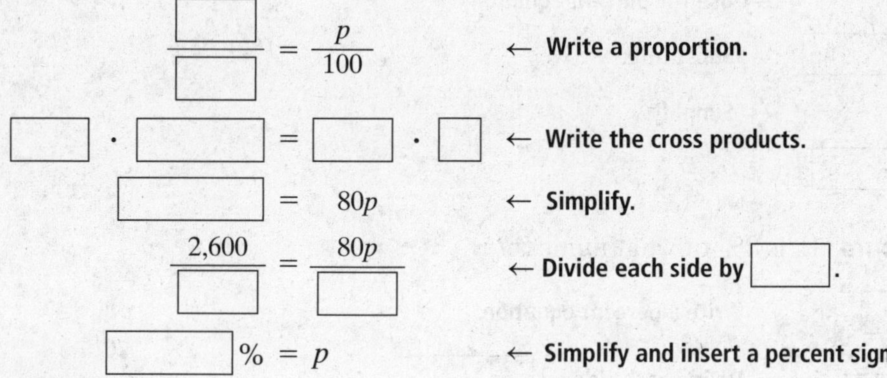

Quick Check

2. About 40% of students in a school, or 110 students, are in an after-school program. How many students are in the school?

3. 36 is what percent of 180?

Name ______________________ Class ______________ Date ______________

Lesson 5-4

Percents and Equations

Lesson Objective	NAEP 2005 Strand: Number Properties and Operations
To use equations to solve problems involving percent	**Topic:** Ratios and Proportional Reasoning
	Local Standards: ____________________

Key Concepts

Percent Equations

Finding the Part	Finding the Whole	Finding the Percent
part = $P \cdot$ whole	part = $P \cdot$ whole	part = $P \cdot$ whole
What is 20% of 25?	5 is 20% of what?	5 is what percent of 25?
$n =$ ☐ $\cdot$ ☐	☐ $=$ ☐ $\cdot\ w$	☐ $= P \cdot$ ☐

Examples

1 Finding Part of a Whole Find 23% of 234.

part = $P \cdot$ whole ← **Use the percent equation.**

$n =$ ☐ $\cdot$ ☐ ← **Substitute.**

$n =$ ☐ ← **Simplify.**

So, 23% of 234 is ☐.

2 Finding a Whole Amount 12 is 8% of what number?

☐ $=$ ☐ $\cdot\ w$ ← **Write a percent equation.**

$\frac{12}{\square} = \frac{0.08w}{\square}$ ← **Divide each side by ☐.**

☐ $= w$ ← **Simplify.**

Name ______________________ Class ______________ Date ______________

Quick Check

1. A bike costs $195.99 plus 6% sales tax. Find the amount of tax.

2. Using an equation, 18% of what number is 16.2?

Name ______________________ Class ______________ Date ______________

Lesson 5-5

Percent of Change

Lesson Objective	**NAEP 2005 Strand:** NumberProperties and Operations
To find percent of change and to solve problems involving percent of increase and percent of decrease	**Topic:** Ratios and Proportional Reasoning **Local Standards:** ____________________

Vocabulary

Percent of change is ____

____

Examples

1 **Finding Percent of Increase** Ten years ago, Max's comic book was worth \$2.50. Now it is worth \$13. Find the percent of increase in value.

amount of change = ☐ − ☐ = ☐

$P = \frac{☐}{☐}$ ← **amount of change** ← **original amount**

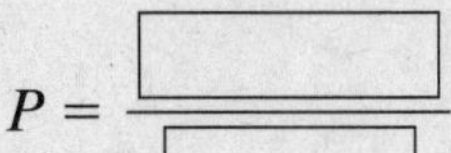

10.50 ÷ 2.50 = ☐ ← **Use a calculator to divide.**

= ☐% ← **Write the decimal as a percent.**

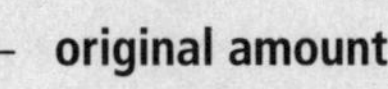

The percent of increase in value is ☐.

Check for Reasonableness 420% of 2.5 ≈ 400% of 3. Since 400% of 3 = ☐, which is close to 13, the answer is reasonable.

2 **Basketball** Andre changed the height of his basketball hoop from 8 ft 4 in. to 9 ft 2 in. Find the percent of increase.

8 ft 4 in. = 8 · ☐ + 4 = ☐ in.
9 ft 2 in. = 9 · ☐ + 2 = ☐ in. ← **Write measures in the same units.**

amount of change = ☐ − ☐ = ☐

$P = \frac{☐}{☐}$ ← **amount of change** ← **original amount**

= 0.1 ← **Simplify.**

= ☐% ← **Write the decimal as a percent.**

The height of the basketball hoop increased by ☐

Name ______________________ Class ______________ Date ____________

❸ **Finding Percent of Decrease** In 1980, the population of New Orleans was 557,927. In 1990, its population was 496,938. Find the percent of decrease. Round to the nearest tenth of a percent.

amount of change = ☐ − ☐ = ☐

$P = \dfrac{\square}{\square}$ ← **amount of change** / ← **original amount**

= ☐ ← **Use a calculator.**

≈ ☐ % ← **Write the decimal as a percent. Round to the nearest tenth of a percent.**

The population decreased by about ☐.

Quick Check

1. **Education** In 1995, about 3,748,000 students were enrolled in Texas public schools. In 2010, there will be about 4,475,000 students enrolled. Find the percent of increase to the nearest tenth.

2. A girl was 4 ft 9 in. tall last year. This year she is 5 ft tall. Find the percent of increase in her height. Round to the nearest tenth.

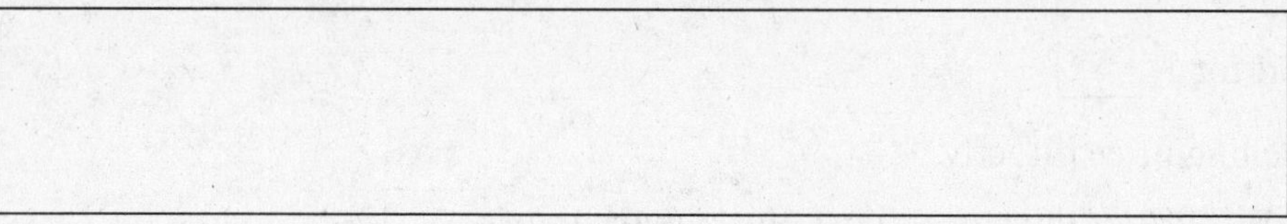

3. In 1995, the average price of a personal computer was $2,100. In 2001, the average price was $899. Find the percent of decrease in the average price. Round to the nearest tenth.

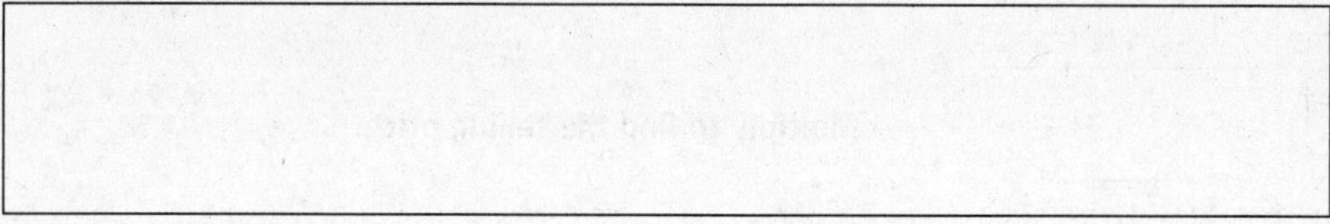

Name ________________ Class ________________ Date ________________

Lesson 5-6

Markup and Discount

Lesson Objective	**NAEP 2005 Strand:** Number Properties and Operations
To use percent of change to find markup, discount, and selling price	**Topic:** Ratios and Proportional Reasoning **Local Standards:** ________________

Vocabulary

A markup is ________________

The selling price is ________________

A discount is ________________

The sale price is ________________

Example

1 Finding Selling Price A store sells a skirt that costs the store $40 and marks up the price 25%. What is the selling price for the skirt?

Method 1 Find the markup first. Then find the selling price.

25% of $40 equals the ____.

____ · 40 = ____ ← **Multiply to find the markup.**

$40 + $____ = $____ ← **store's cost + markup =** ____

The store sells the skirt for $____.

Method 2 Find the selling price directly.

The selling price equals 100% of the store's cost plus a markup of ____%

of the store's cost. So, the selling price of the skirt is 100% + ____%, or

____%, of $____.

125% of $40 equals the ____.

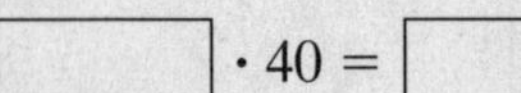 ← **Multiply to find the selling price.**

The store sells the skirt for $____.

Quick Check

1. An item costs a store $89.89. The store then marks the price up 80%. What is the selling price of the item?

Examples

❷ Finding Sale Price A shoe store advertises a 35%-off sale. What is the sale price of shoes that regularly cost $94.99?

The sale price equals 100% of the regular price minus a discount of ____ % of the regular price. The sale price is 100% − ____ %, or ____ %, of $ ____ .

65% of $94.99 equals the ____ .

$\square \cdot 94.99 \approx \square$ ← **Multiply to find the sale price.**

$= \$\square$ ← **Round to the nearest cent.**

The sale price is ____ .

❸ Finding Regular Price You buy a CD at the sale price of $6. This is 25% off the regular price. Find the regular price of the CD.

A. $4.50 **B.** $6.00 **C.** $8.00 **D.** $10.50

regular price − 25% of regular price = ____

Let r = the regular price.

$r - (\square \cdot r) = \square$ ← **Substitute. Write the percent as a decimal.**

$\square = 6$ ← **Combine like terms: $r - 0.25r$ = ____ .**

$\frac{0.75r}{\square} = \frac{6}{\square}$ ← **Divide each side by ____ .**

$r = \square$ ← **Simplify.**

The regular price of the CD is ____ . The correct answer is choice ____ .

Quick Check

2. An item that regularly sells for $182.75 is on sale for 45% off. Find the sale price to the nearest cent.

3. A stereo is on sale for $99 at 15% off. Find the regular price.

Name ______________________ Class ______________ Date ______________

Lesson 5-7

Simple Interest

Lesson Objective To find simple interest and account balances	**NAEP 2005 Strand:** Number Properties and Operations **Topic:** Ratios and Proportional Reasoning **Local Standards:** ____________________

Vocabulary and Key Concepts

Simple Interest $I = p \cdot r \cdot t$

where ☐ is the interest, ☐ is the principal,

☐ is the interest rate per year, and ☐ is the time in years.

Interest is ______________________

The interest rate is ______________________

Principal is ______________________

The balance is ______________________

Simple interest is ______________________

Example

1 Finding Simple Interest A student deposits $150 into a bank that pays 6% simple interest. Find the interest earned in 4 years.

$I =$ ☐ ← **Simple interest formula**

$=$ ☐ · ☐ · ☐ ← **Substitute.**

$=$ ☐ ← **Multiply.**

In 4 years, the interest earned is $☐.

Quick Check

1. Find the interest earned on $3,600 invested at $3\frac{1}{2}$% simple interest for 5 years.

Name ______________________ Class ______________ Date ______________

Example

❷ Finding an Account Balance You deposit $300 in an account that earns 8% simple interest. Find the balance in the account after 3 years.

Step 1 First, find the interest earned.

$I = \boxed{}$ ← **Simple interest formula**

$= \boxed{} \cdot \boxed{} \cdot \boxed{}$ ← **Substitute.**

$= \boxed{}$ ← **Multiply.**

In 3 years, the interest earned is $______.

Step 2 Find the balance in the account.
principal + earned interest = balance

$\boxed{} + \boxed{} = \text{balance}$ ← **Substitute.**

$= \boxed{}$ ← **Add.**

The final balance in the account is $______.

Quick Check

2. A teacher invests $205 in an account that earns 8% simple interest. Find the balance in the account after 10 years.

Name ______________________ Class ______________ Date ______________

Lesson 5-8

Ratios and Probability

Lesson Objective	**NAEP 2005 Strand:** Data Analysis and Probability
To find the probability and the sample space of an event	**Topic:** Probability
	Local Standards: ____________

Vocabulary and Key Concepts

Probability

The probability of an event E is given by the following formula when outcomes are equally likely:

$$P(E) = \frac{\text{number of } \boxed{} \text{ outcomes}}{\text{total number of } \boxed{} \text{ outcomes}}$$

An outcome is ______________________

An event is ______________________

The sample space is ______________________

Example

1 Finding a Probability There are 3 red, 2 green, 1 blue, and 5 yellow pens in a box. Suppose you choose one at random. Find P(yellow).

$$P(\text{yellow}) = \frac{\boxed{}}{\boxed{}}$$

← **favorable outcomes**

← **possible outcomes**

The probability of choosing a yellow marker pen is $\boxed{}$.

Quick Check

1. Using the information from Example 1, find P(green).

$$P(\text{green}) = \frac{\boxed{}}{\boxed{}}$$

Examples

❷ Probabilities and Percents In a survey, 13% of the students in a class prefer vanilla, 27% prefer chocolate, 10% prefer strawberry, and the rest chose other flavors of frozen yogurt. Find the probability that a randomly selected student from the class chose vanilla or chocolate.

A. 10% **B.** 40% **C.** 60% **D.** 90%

☐ chose vanilla, and ☐ of the students chose chocolate.

P(vanilla or chocolate) = *P*(vanilla) + *P*(chocolate)

= ☐% + ☐% ← **Substitute.**

= ☐% ← **Simplify.**

The probability that the student chose vanilla or chocolate is ☐.
The correct answer is choice ☐.

❸ Finding a Sample Space Find the probability of there being at least 1 male kitten in a litter of three kittens. Express the probability as a fraction.

Kitten 1 2 3 Sample space

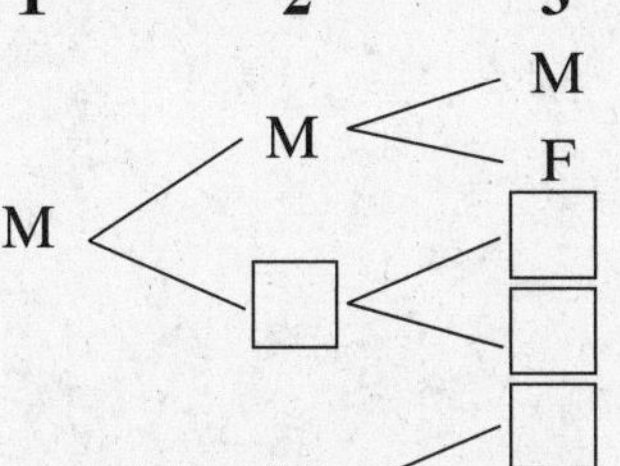

MMM
MMF
MFM
MFF
FMM
FMF
FFM
FFF

favorable outcomes: at least one male ←
There are ☐ possible outcomes.

P(at least one male) = $\frac{\text{number of outcomes with at least one male kitten}}{\text{total number of possible outcomes with three kittens}}$

= $\frac{☐}{☐}$ ← **Substitute.**

The probability of there being at least 1 male kitten is ☐.

Quick Check

2. Use the survey in Example 2 to find *P*(vanilla, chocolate, or strawberry).

3. Using the survey in Example 3, what is the probability that a litter of three kittens will have exactly two females? At least two females?

Name ______________________ Class ______________ Date ______________

Lesson 6-1

Solving Two-Step Equations

Lesson Objective	**NAEP 2005 Strand:** Algebra
To solve two-step equations and to use two-step equations to solve problems	**Topic:** Equations and Inequalities **Local Standards:** ____________

Example

1 Solving Using Subtraction and Division Solve $4p + 7 = -13$.

$4p + 7 = -13$

$4p + 7 - \square = -13 - \square$ ← **Subtract $\square$ from each side.**

$4p = \square$ ← **Simplify.**

$\frac{4p}{\square} = \frac{\square}{\square}$ ← **Divide each side by $\square$.**

$p = \square$ ← **Simplify.**

Check $4p + 7 = -13$

$4(\square) + 7 \stackrel{?}{=} -13$ ← **Substitute $\square$ for *p*.**

$\square = -13$ ✓ ← **The solution checks.**

Quick Check

1. Solve $4g + 11.6 = -23.2$. Check the solution.

Name ______________________ Class ______________ Date ____________

Example

❷ **Sharing Costs** Six people at dinner shared equally a total bill of \$180. This total included a tip of \$30. Which equation can be used to find the amount of each person's share for dinner without the tip?

A. $6s = 180$ **B.** $6s - 30 = 180$

C. $6s + 30 = 180$ **D.** $6(s + 30) = 180$

Words each person's share for dinner ☐ 6 ☐ tip is \$180

Let s = each person's share for dinner.

Equation ☐ ☐ ☐ ☐ ☐ = ☐

The equation is ☐.

The correct answer is choice ☐.

You can solve the equation to find each person's share.

$6s + 30 - \square = 180 - \square$ ← **Subtract ☐ from each side.**

$6s = \square$ ← **Simplify.**

$\frac{6s}{\square} = \frac{\square}{\square}$ ← **Divide each side by ☐.**

$s = \square$ ← **Simplify.**

Each person's share for dinner without the tip is \$ ☐.

Quick Check

2. Telephone Bill To make a long-distance call, it costs \$.50 per call and \$.85 per minute. You make a long-distance call that costs \$3.90. Write and solve an equation to find the length of the call.

Name ______________________ Class ______________ Date ______________

Lesson 6-2

Simplifying Algebraic Expressions

Lesson Objective	**NAEP 2005 Strand:** Algebra
To combine like terms and simplify algebraic expressions	**Topic:** Variables, Expressions, and Operations
	Local Standards: ____________________

Vocabulary

A term is ____

____

Like terms have ____

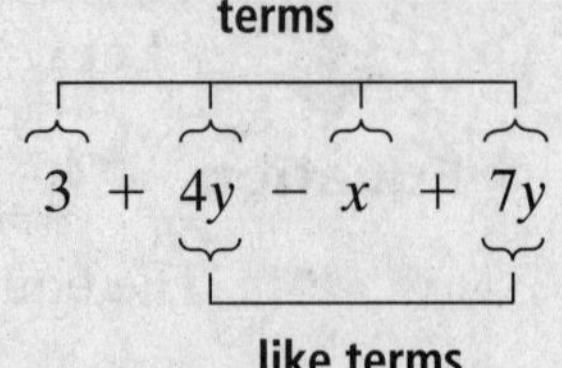

Examples

1 Combining Like Terms Combine like terms in the expression $q - 9q$.

$q - 9q = 1q - 9q$ ← **Rewrite *q* as 1*q*.**

$= (1 \square 9)q$ ← $\square$ **Property**

$= \square$ ← **Combine like terms by subtracting.**

2 Application: Shopping Karen buys 12 bottles of water and 8 cans of fruit juice for a camping trip. Monica buys 6 bottles of water and 16 cans of fruit juice. Define and use variables to represent the total cost.

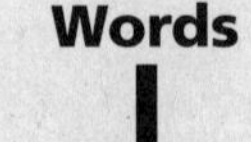

Karen: 12 bottles of water plus 8 cans of juice

Let b = the cost of a bottle of water.

Let c = the cost of a can of fruit juice.

Expression $\square b \quad \square \quad 8\square$

Words Monica: 6 bottles of water plus 16 cans of juice

$\square b \quad \square \quad 16\square$

Combined Expression $\square b \; \square \; 8\square + \square b \; \square \; 16\square$

$\square b \; \square \; 8\square + \square b \; \square \; 16\square$

$= \square b + 6b + 8\square + \square c$ ← **Commutative Property of Addition.**

$= (\square + 6)b + (8 + \square)c$ ← **Distributive Property.**

$= \square b + \square c$ ← **Simplify.**

❸ Distributing and Simplifying Simplify $4(b - 3) + 2b$.

$4(b - 3) + 2b = 4b - \square + 2b$ ← ______ **Property**

$= 4b + 2b - \square$ ← ______ **Property of Addition**

$= (\square + \square)b - 12$ ← ______ **Property**

$= \square - \square$ ← **Simplify.**

Quick Check

1. Combine like terms in the expression $2t + t - 17t$.

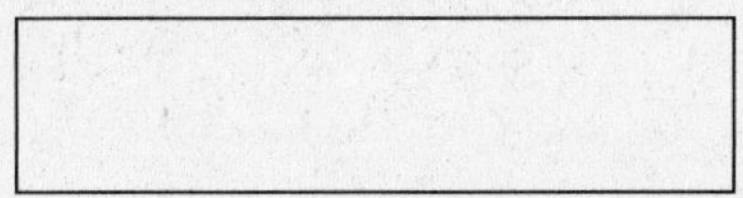

2. In one trip to a hardware store, you buy 16 boards, 2 boxes of nails, and a hammer. On a second trip, you buy 10 more boards and a box of nails. Define and use variables to represent the total cost.

Let $\square$ = ______

Let $\square$ = ______

Let $\square$ = ______

______

3. Simplify the expression $11 - 2(3b + 1)$.

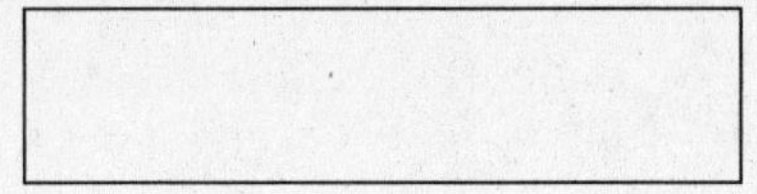

Name ____________ Class ____________ Date ____________

Lesson 6-3

Solving Multi-Step Equations

Lesson Objective To write and solve multi-step equations	**NAEP 2005 Strand:** Algebra **Topic:** Equations and Inequalities **Local Standards:** ____________

Example

1 Simplifying Before Solving an Equation Solve $2c + 2 + 3c = 12$.

$2c + 2 + 3c = 12$

$2c + 3c + 2 = 12$ ← ☐ **Property of Addition**

☐ $+ 2 = 12$ ← **Combine like terms.**

☐ $+ 2 -$ ☐ $= 12 -$ ☐ ← **Subtract ☐ from each side.**

$5c =$ ☐ ← **Simplify.**

$\frac{5c}{\square} = \frac{\square}{\square}$ ← **Divide each side by ☐.**

$c =$ ☐ ← **Simplify.**

Check $2c + 2 + 3c = 12$

$2(\square) + 2 + 3(\square) \stackrel{?}{=} 12$ ← **Substitute ☐ for c.**

☐ $= 12$ ✓ ← **The solution checks.**

Quick Check

1. Solve $-15 = 5b + 12 - 2b + 6$. Check the solution.

Example

❷ Using the Distributive Property Eight cheerleaders set a goal of selling 424 boxes of cards to raise money. After two weeks, each cheerleader has sold 28 boxes. How many more boxes must each cheerleader sell?

A. 15 **B.** 25 **C.** 50 **D.** 53

Words 8 cheerleaders · (28 boxes per cheerleader + additional boxes per cheerleader) = 424 boxes

Equation Let x = the number of additional boxes per cheerleader.

☐ · (☐ + ☐) = ☐

$8(28 + x) = 424$

☐ $+ 8x = 424$ ← ☐ **Property**

☐ − ☐ $+ 8x = 424 -$ ☐ ← **Subtract** ☐ **from each side.**

$8x = 200$ ← **Simplify.**

$\frac{8x}{☐} = \frac{200}{☐}$ ← **Divide each side by** ☐.

$x =$ ☐ ← **Simplify.**

Each cheerleader must sell ☐ more boxes. The correct answer is choice ☐.

Quick Check

2. Class Trips Your class goes to an amusement park. Admission is $10 for each student and $15 for each chaperone. The total cost is $380. There are 12 girls in your class and 6 chaperones on the trip. How many boys are in your class?

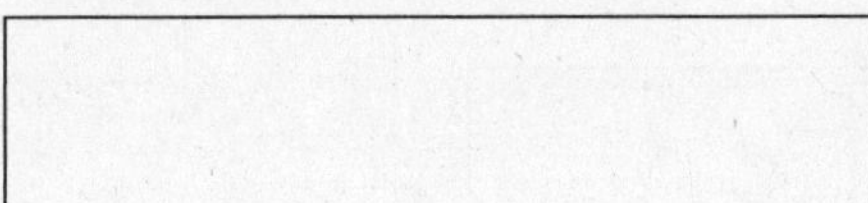

Name ____________________ Class ______________ Date ______________

Lesson 6-4

Solving Equations With Variables on Both Sides

Lesson Objective	**NAEP 2005 Strand:** Algebra
To write and solve equations with variables on both sides	**Topic:** Equations and Inequalities **Local Standards:** ____________________

Example

1 Variables on Both Sides Solve $9 + 2p = -3 - 4p$.

$9 + 2p = -3 - 4p$

$9 + 2p + \square = -3 - 4p + \square$ ← **Add $\square$ to each side.**

$9 + \square = -3$ ← **Combine like terms.**

$9 - \square + 6p = -3 - \square$ ← **Subtract $\square$ from each side.**

$6p = \square$ ← **Simplify.**

$\frac{6p}{\square} = \frac{\square}{\square}$ ← **Divide each side by $\square$.**

$p = \square$ ← **Simplify.**

Check $9 + 2p = -3 - 4p$

$9 + 2(\square) \stackrel{?}{=} -3 - 4(\square)$ ← **Substitute $\square$ for *p*.**

$\square = 5$ ✓ ← **The solution checks.**

Quick Check

1. Solve $7b - 2 = b + 10$. Check the solution.

Name ______________________ Class ______________ Date ____________

Example

❷ **Using the Distributive Property** The chess club decides to sell shirts and hats for fundraising. The total cost of a shirt and a hat is \$21. Paula purchased 4 hats for the same price as 3 shirts. What is the cost of one shirt?

Words [cost of 4 hats] is the same as [cost of 3 shirts].

Let x = cost of one shirt.

Equation $4 \cdot (21 - x) \quad = \quad 3x$

$4(21 - x) = 3x$

$\square - 4x = 3x$ ← $\square$ **Property**

$\square - 4x + \square = 3x + \square$ ← **Add** $\square$ **to each side.**

$\square = 7x$ ← **Simplify.**

$\frac{84}{7} = \frac{7x}{7}$ ← **Divide each side by** $\square$.

$\square = x$ ← **Simplify.**

The cost of one shirt is \$$\square$.

Quick Check

2. One cell phone plan costs \$29.94 per month plus \$.10 for each text message sent. Another plan costs \$32.99 per month plus \$.05 for each text message sent. For what number of text messages will the monthly bill for both plans be the same?

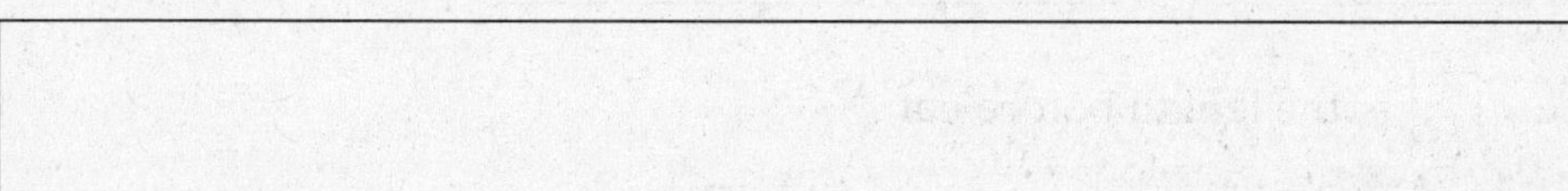

Name ______________________ Class ______________ Date ______________

Lesson 6-5

Solving Inequalities by Adding or Subtracting

Lesson Objective	**NAEP 2005 Strand:** Algebra
To write and solve inequalities using addition and subtraction	**Topic:** Equations and Inequalities
	Local Standards: ____________________

Vocabulary and Key Concepts

Addition and Subtraction Properties of Inequality

If you add or subtract the same number on each side of an inequality, the relationship between the two sides does not change.

Arithmetic	**Algebra**
$8 < 12$, so	If $a < b$, then
$8 + 3 < 12 + 3$ and $8 - 4$ ☐ $12 - 4$.	$a + c < b + c$ and $a - c$ ☐ $b - c$
$10 > 7$, so	If $a > b$, then
$10 + 5$ ☐ $7 + 5$ and $10 - 2$ ☐ $7 - 2$.	$a + c$ ☐ $b + c$ and $a - c$ ☐ $b - c$

An inequality is ____

Examples

1 Solving Inequalities by Adding After the hairdresser cut 3 in. from Rapunzel's hair, her hair was at least 15 in. long. How long was her hair before she had it cut?

Words → **Inequality**

length before cut − length cut | is at least | 15 in.

Let ☐ = the length before cut.

☐ − 3 ☐ 15

$\ell - 3 \geq 15$

$\ell - 3 +$ ☐ $\geq 15 +$ ☐ ← **Isolate the variable. Use the** ____________________.

$\ell \geq$ ☐ ← **Simplify.**

Rapunzel's hair was at least ☐ in. long before she had it cut.

Name ______________ Class ______________ Date ______________

❷ **Solving Inequalities by Subtracting** Solve $p + 3 < -5$. Graph the solutions.

$$p + 3 < -5$$

$p + 3 - \square < -5 - \square$ ← **Isolate the variable. Use the** ______________.

$p < \square$ ← **Simplify.**

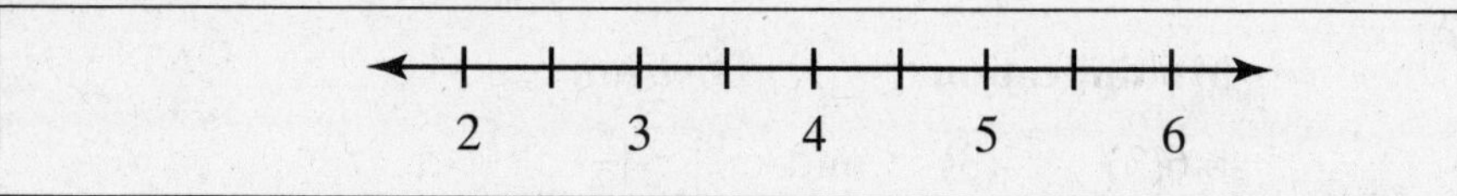

Quick Check

1. Solve $1 \leq u - 4$. Graph the solutions.

2 3 4 5 6

2. A school auditorium has 300 seats. If 89 people have tickets for the school play, how many more people can attend?

Name ______________________________ Class ________________ Date ______________

Lesson 6-6

Solving Inequalities by Multiplying or Dividing

Lesson Objective To write and solve inequalities using multiplication and division	**NAEP 2005 Strand:** Algebra **Topic:** Equations and Inequalities **Local Standards:** ____________________

Key Concepts

Multiplication and Division Properties of Inequality

Using Positive Numbers to Multiply or Divide When you multiply or divide each side of an inequality by a positive number, the relationship between the two sides does not change.

		Multiplication		Division
Arithmetic	$6 > 5$,	so $6(3) \square 5(3)$	and	$\frac{6}{2} \square \frac{5}{2}$
	$4 < 10$,	so $4(5) \square 10(5)$	and	$\frac{4}{2} \square \frac{10}{2}$
Algebra	If $a > b$ and $c > 0$,	then $ac \square bc$	and	$\frac{a}{c} \square \frac{b}{c}$
	If $a < b$ and $c > 0$,	then $ac \square bc$	and	$\frac{a}{c} \square \frac{b}{c}$

Note that these relationships are also true for $\leq$ and $\geq$.

Using Negative Numbers to Multiply or Divide When you multiply or divide each side of an inequality by a negative number, ________ the direction of the inequality sign.

		Multiplication		Division
Arithmetic	$6 > 5$,	so $6 \cdot (-3) \square 5 \cdot (-3)$	and	$\frac{6}{-2} \square \frac{5}{-2}$
	$4 < 10$,	so $4 \cdot (-5) \square 10 \cdot (-5)$	and	$\frac{4}{-2} \square \frac{10}{-2}$
Algebra	If $a > b$ and $c < 0$,	then $ac \square bc$	and	$\frac{a}{c} \square \frac{b}{c}$
	If $a < b$ and $c < 0$,	then $ac \square bc$	and	$\frac{a}{c} \square \frac{b}{c}$

Note that these relationships are also true for $\leq$ and $\geq$.

Name ______________________ Class ______________ Date ______________

Examples

1 Dividing by a Positive Number A small business sells each CD of its game software for \$12. How many CDs must they sell to meet the goal of at least \$84,000?

Words | number of CDs | times | \$12 | is at least | \$84,000 |

Let c = the number of CDs.

Inequality ☐ · 12 ☐ \$84,000

$12c \geq 84,000$

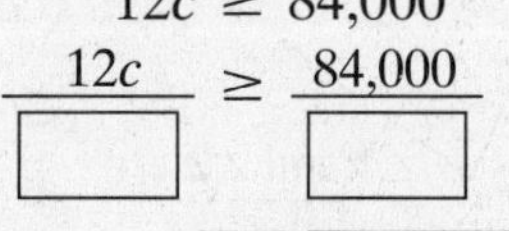

← **Isolate the variable. Use the** ______________________.

c ☐ ☐ ← **Simplify.**

The business must sell at least ______ CDs.

2 Multiplying by a Negative Number Solve $\frac{y}{-4} > 3$. Graph the solutions.

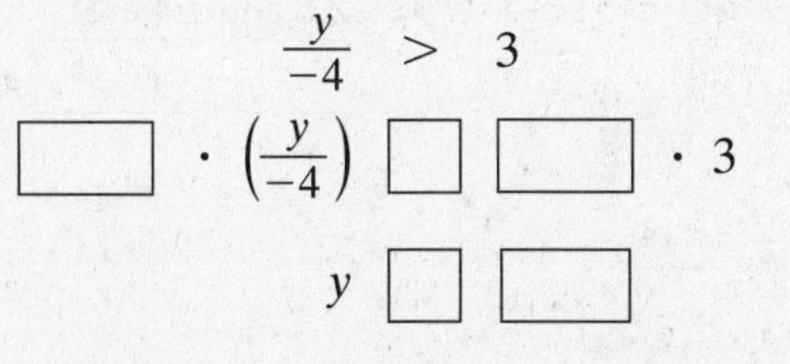

← **Multiply each side by** ______.

______ **the direction of the ine**

← **Simplify.**

← **Graph.**

−16 −14 −12 −10 −8

Quick Check

1. A hotel has an elevator with a limit of 2,000 lb. Suppose the average weight of a passenger is 160 lb. About how many passengers should the elevator safely hold?

2. Solve each inequality. Graph the solutions.

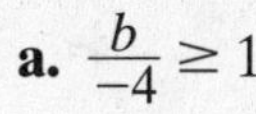

a. $\frac{b}{-4} \geq 1$ **b.** $-2p \geq 34$

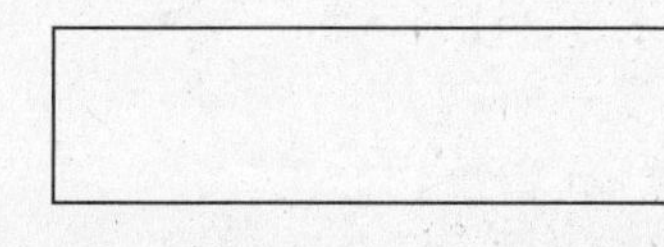

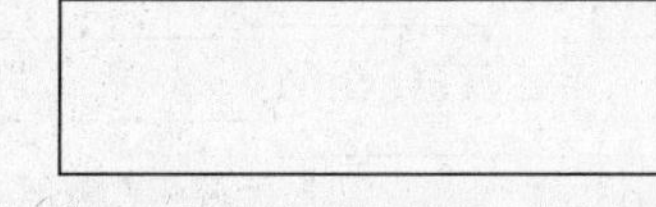

Name ______________________ Class ______________ Date ______________

Lesson 7-1

Pairs of Angles

Lesson Objective To identify types of angles and to find angle measures using the relationship between angles	**NAEP 2005 Strand:** Geometry **Topic:** Relationships Among Geometric Figures **Local Standards:** ____________________

Vocabulary

Adjacent angles have ______________________

____

Vertical angles are ______________________

____

1 2

side

same [ ]

∠1 and ∠2 are [ ] **angles.**

Two angles are supplementary if ______________________

____

Two angles are complementary if ______________________

____

6 5 3 4

∠5 and ∠3 are [ ] **angles.**

∠6 and ∠4 are [ ] **angles.**

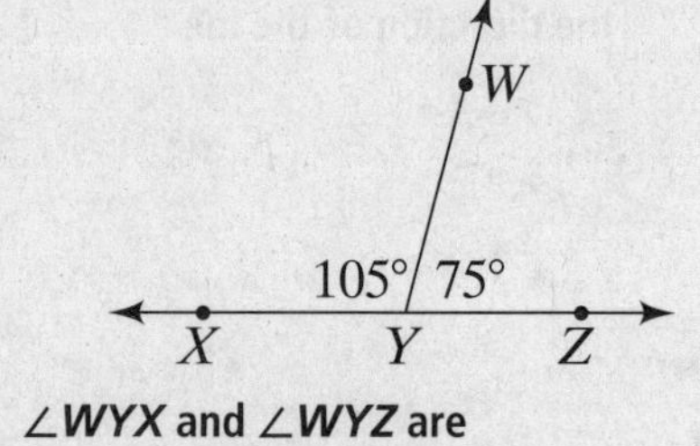

R V S T

∠WYX and ∠WYZ are [ ] **angles.**

∠VSR and ∠VST are [ ] **angles.**

Perpendicular lines are ______________________

____

Examples

1 Identifying Adjacent and Vertical Angles Name a pair of adjacent angles and a pair of vertical angles in the figure at the right.

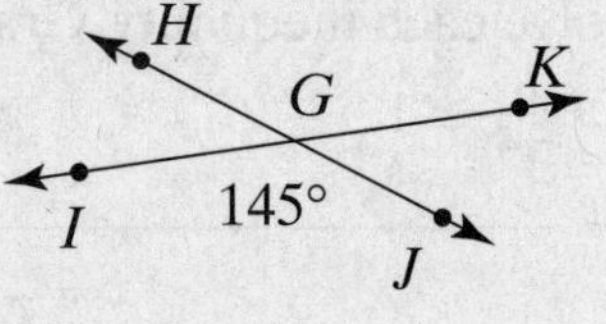

The adjacent angles are ∠*HGK* and [ ]; ∠*KGJ* and [ ]; ∠*JGI* and [ ]; ∠*IGH* and [ ].

The vertical angles are ∠*JGI* and [ ]; ∠*HGI* and [ ].

Since vertical angles are congruent, $m\angle HGK = m\angle JGI =$ [ ].

❷ Finding Supplementary Angles Suppose $m\angle DEF = 73°$. Find the measure of its supplement.

$x° + m\angle DEF = \square$ ← **The sum of the measures of supplementary angles is ☐.**

$x° + 73° = 180°$ ← **Substitute ☐ for $m\angle DEF$.**

$x° + 73° - \square = 180° - \square$ ← **Subtract ☐ from each side.**

$x° = \square$ ← **Simplify.**

The measure of the supplement of $\angle DEF$ is ☐.

❸ Finding Angle Measures A right angle is divided into two angles. If the measure of the larger angle is 67°, find the measure of the smaller angle.

$x° + 67° = \square$ ← **The angles are complementary.**

$x° + 67° - \square = 90° - \square$ ← **Subtract ☐ from each side.**

$x° = \square$ ← **Simplify.**

The measure of the complement of an angle whose measure is 67° is ☐.

Quick Check

1. $\angle DBJ$ and $\angle JBT$ are adjacent angles in the photo. $\angle DBY$ and $\angle JBT$ are vertical angles. Name another pair of vertical angles and another pair of adjacent angles.

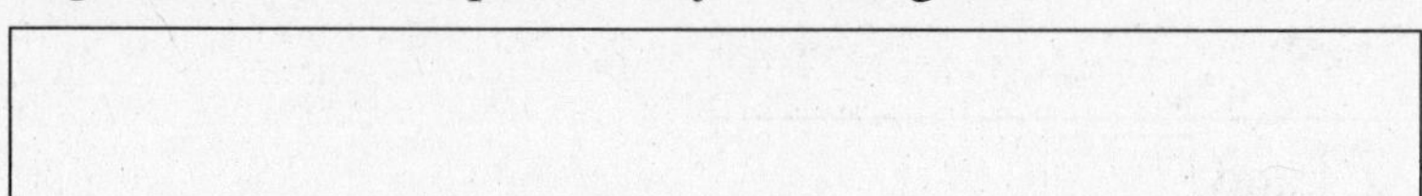

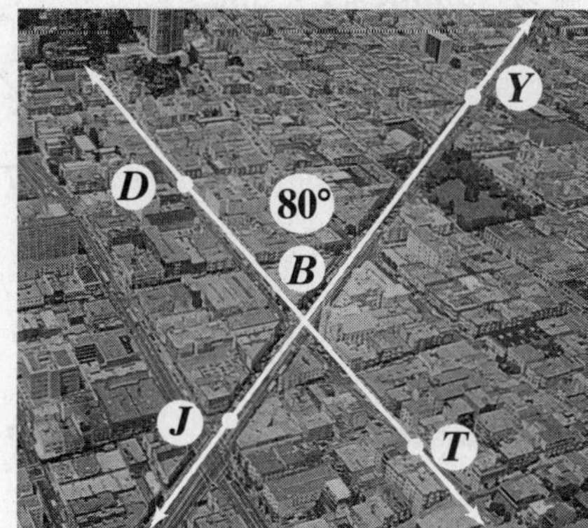

2. An angle has a measure of 47°. Find the measure of its supplement.

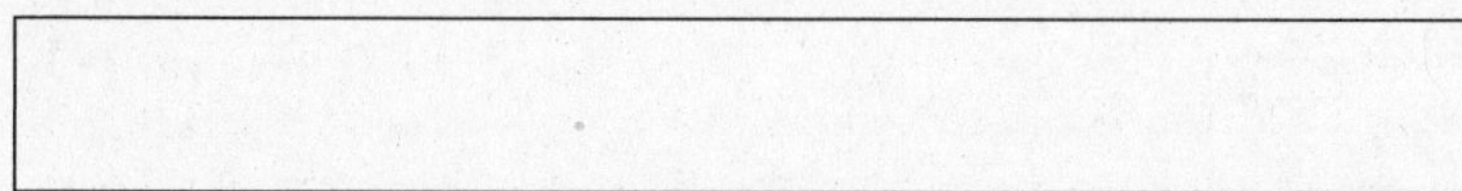

3. Find the measure of the complement of a 36° angle.

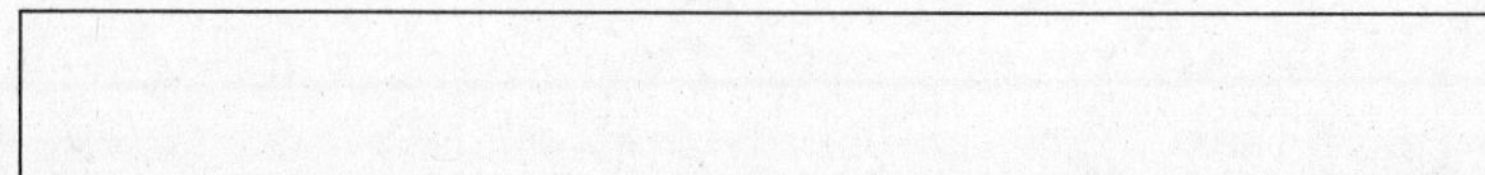

Name ______________________ Class ______________ Date ______________

Lesson 7-2

Angles and Parallel Lines

Lesson Objective To identify parallel lines and the angles formed by parallel lines	**NAEP 2005 Strand:** Geometry **Topic:** Relationships Among Geometric Figures **Local Standards:** ____________________

Vocabulary and Key Concepts

Transversals and Parallel Lines

When a transversal intersects two parallel lines,

- [ ] angles are congruent, and
- [ ] angles are congruent.

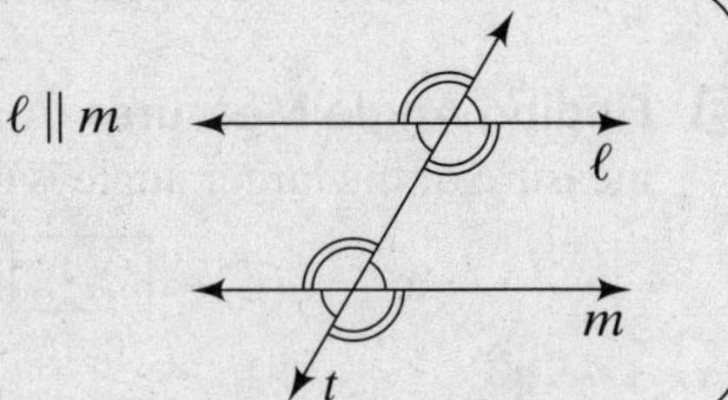

A transversal is ______________________________

____

Corresponding angles lie ______________________________

____

Examples: ∠1 and [ ] ∠2 and [ ]

∠3 and [ ] ∠4 and [ ]

Alternate interior angles lie ______________________________

____

Examples: ∠3 and [ ] ∠4 and [ ]

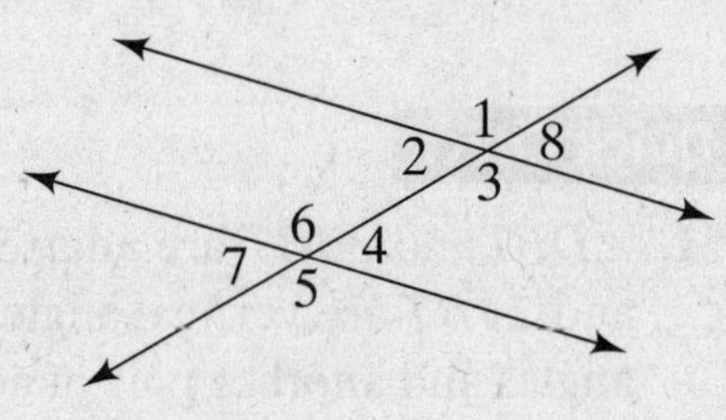

Examples

Use this diagram for Examples 1 and 2.

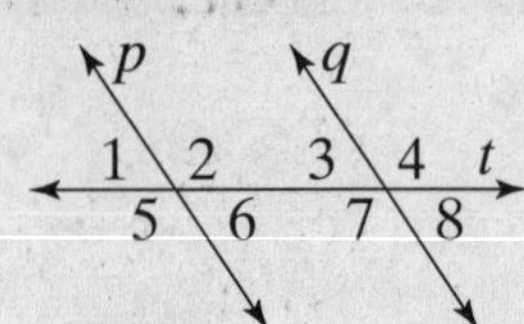

1 **Identifying Angles** Identify each pair of corresponding angles and each pair of alternate interior angles.

∠1 and [ ], ∠2 and [ ], ∠5 and [ ], ∠6 and [ ] are pairs of [ ] angles.

∠2 and [ ], ∠3 and [ ] are pairs of [ ] angles.

Name ______________________ Class ______________ Date ____________

❷ **Finding Angle Measures** If p is parallel to q, and $m\angle 3 = 56°$, find $m\angle 6$ and $m\angle 1$.

$m\angle 6 = m\angle 3 =$ ☐ ← ☐ **angles are congruent.**

$m\angle 1 = m\angle 3 =$ ☐ ← ☐ **angles are congruent.**

❸ **Identifying Parallel Lines** In the diagram below, $m\angle 5 = 80°$, $m\angle 6 = 80°$, and $m\angle 7 = 80°$. Explain why p and q are parallel and why s and t are parallel.

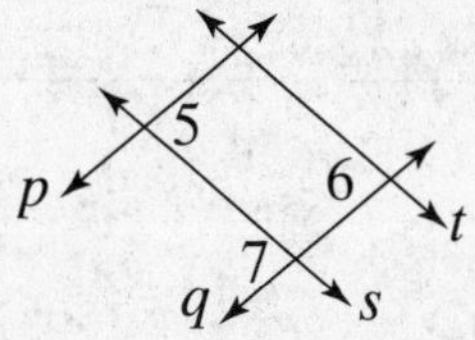

$p \parallel q$ because $\angle 5$ and $\angle 7$ are congruent ☐ angles.

$s \parallel t$ because $\angle 6$ and $\angle 7$ are congruent ☐ angles.

Quick Check

1. Use the diagram for Examples 1 and 2. Identify each pair of angles as *corresponding*, *alternate interior*, or *neither*.

a. $\angle 3, \angle 6$ **b.** $\angle 5, \angle 7$ **c.** $\angle 1, \angle 8$

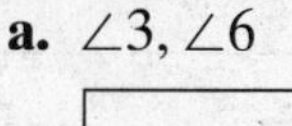

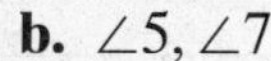

2. In the diagram for Examples 1 and 2, $m\angle 2 = 124°$. Find $m\angle 7$.

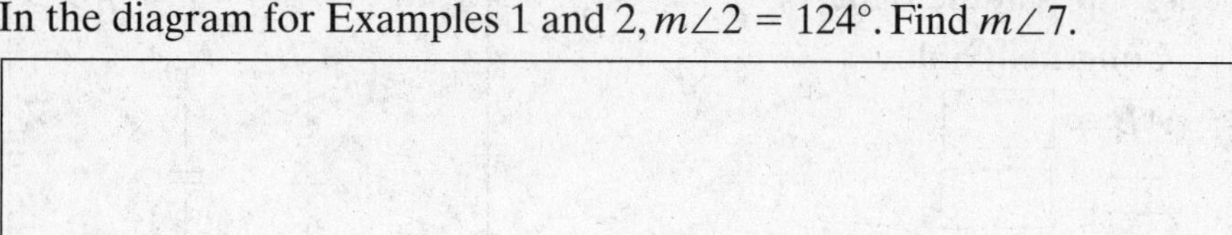

3. Transversal t is perpendicular to lines ℓ and m. Explain how you know $\ell \parallel m$.

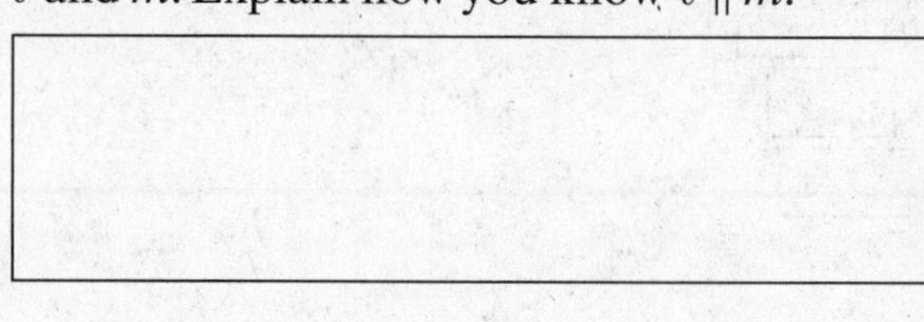

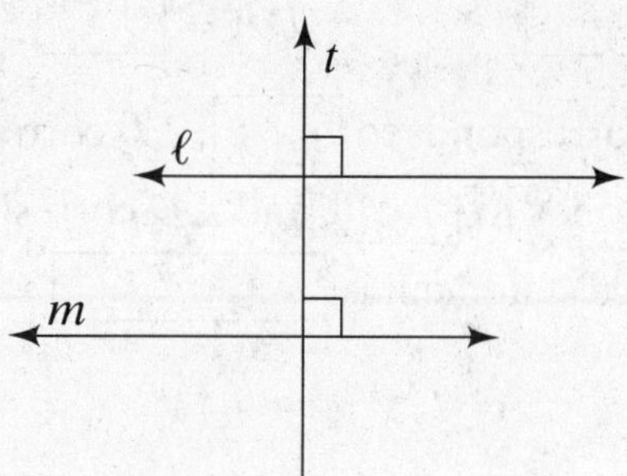

Name ________________ Class ________________ Date ________________

Lesson 7-3

Congruent Polygons

Lesson Objective To identify congruent figures and use them to solve problems	**NAEP 2005 Strand:** Geometry **Topic:** Transformation of Shapes and Preservation of Properties **Local Standards:** ____________

Vocabulary and Key Concepts

Showing Triangles Are Congruent

To demonstrate that two triangles are congruent, show that the following parts of one triangle are congruent to the corresponding parts of the other triangle.

[ ] (SSS)

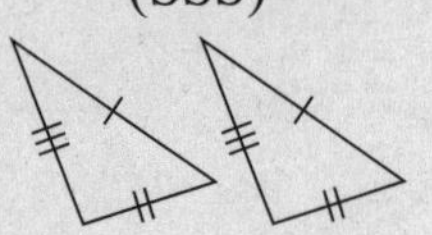

[ ] (SAS)

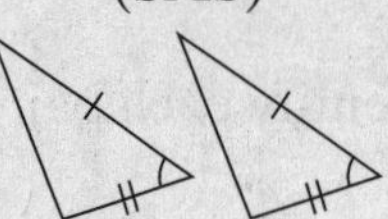

[ ] (ASA)

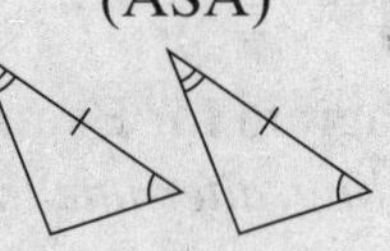

Congruent polygons are ________________________________

Example

1 Writing Congruence Statements Write a congruence statement for the congruent figures at the right.

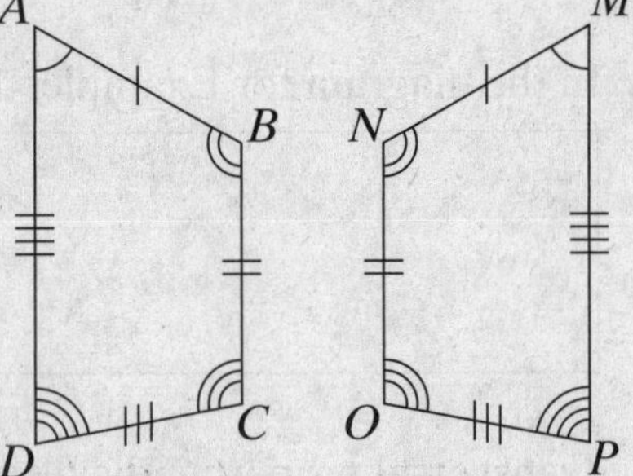

Congruent Angles	**Congruent Sides**
$\angle A \cong$ [ ]	$\overline{AB} \cong$ [ ]
$\angle B \cong$ [ ]	$\overline{BC} \cong$ [ ]
$\angle C \cong$ [ ]	$\overline{CD} \cong$ [ ]
$\angle D \cong$ [ ]	$\overline{DA} \cong$ [ ]

Since $\angle A$ corresponds to [ ], $\angle B$ corresponds to [ ], $\angle C$ corresponds to [ ], and $\angle D$ corresponds to [ ], a congruence statement is [ ] $\cong$ [ ].

Quick Check

1. Write a congruence statement for the congruent figures at the right.

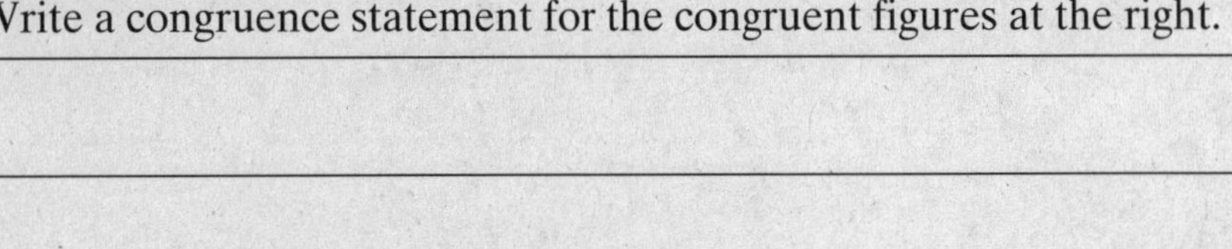

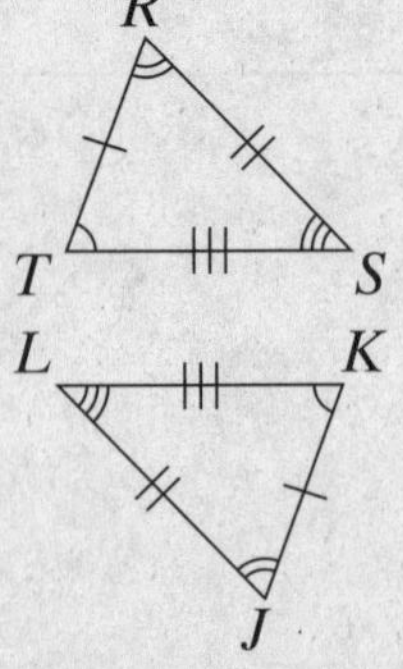

Name ______________________ Class ______________ Date ____________

Examples

❷ Congruent Triangles Show that the triangles are congruent.

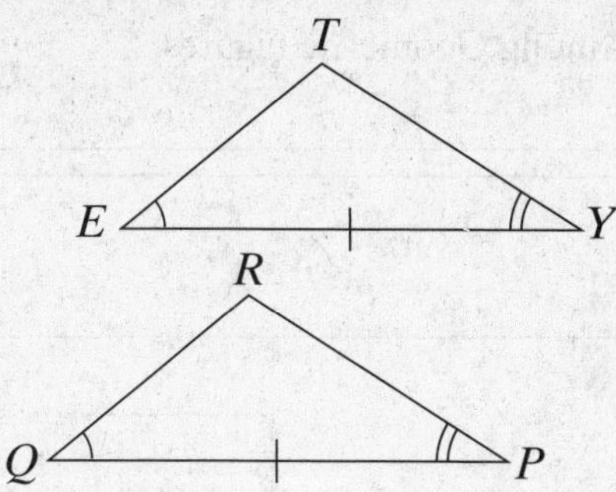

$\angle Q \cong \angle E$ [ ]

$\overline{QP} \cong \overline{EY}$ [ ]

$\angle P \cong \angle Y$ [ ]

$\triangle QPR \cong \triangle EYT$ [ ]

❸ Surveying A surveyor drew the diagram at the right to find the distance from J to I across the canyon. $\triangle GHI \cong \triangle KJI$. What is the distance $\overline{JI}$?

Corresponding parts of congruent triangles are [ ]. Since $\overline{JI}$ corresponds to $\overline{HI}$, $\overline{JI}$ = [ ] ft.

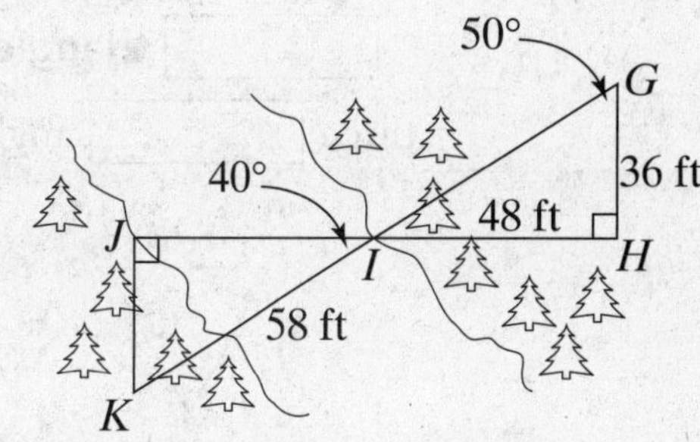

Quick Check

2. Show that each pair of triangles is congruent.

a.

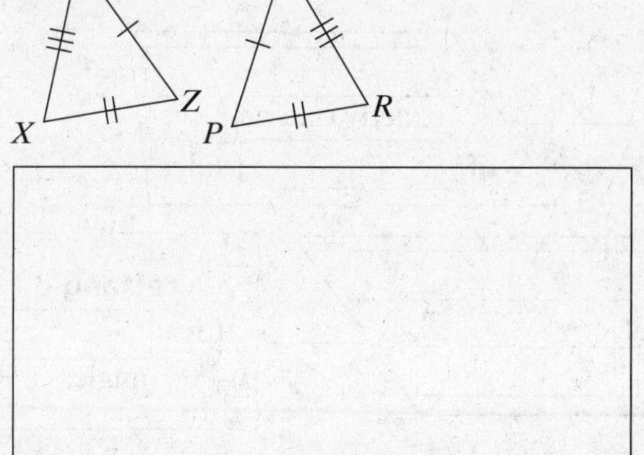

b.

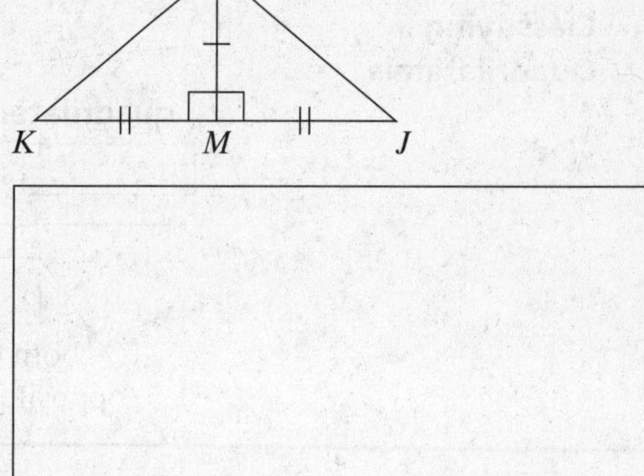

3. Use the diagram in Example 3 to find each measurement.

a. $\overline{JK}$ **b.** $m\angle K$ **c.** $m\angle GIH$

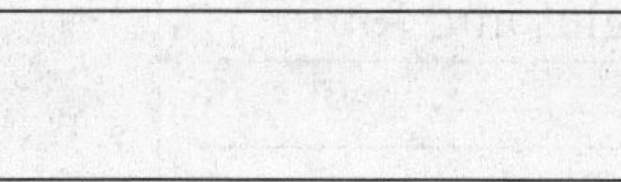

Name ______________________ Class ______________ Date ______________

Lesson 7-4

Classifying Triangles and Quadrilaterals

Lesson Objective	**NAEP 2005 Strand:** Geometry
To classify triangles and quadrilaterals	**Topic:** Relationships Among Geometric Figures
	Local Standards: ______________

Key Concepts

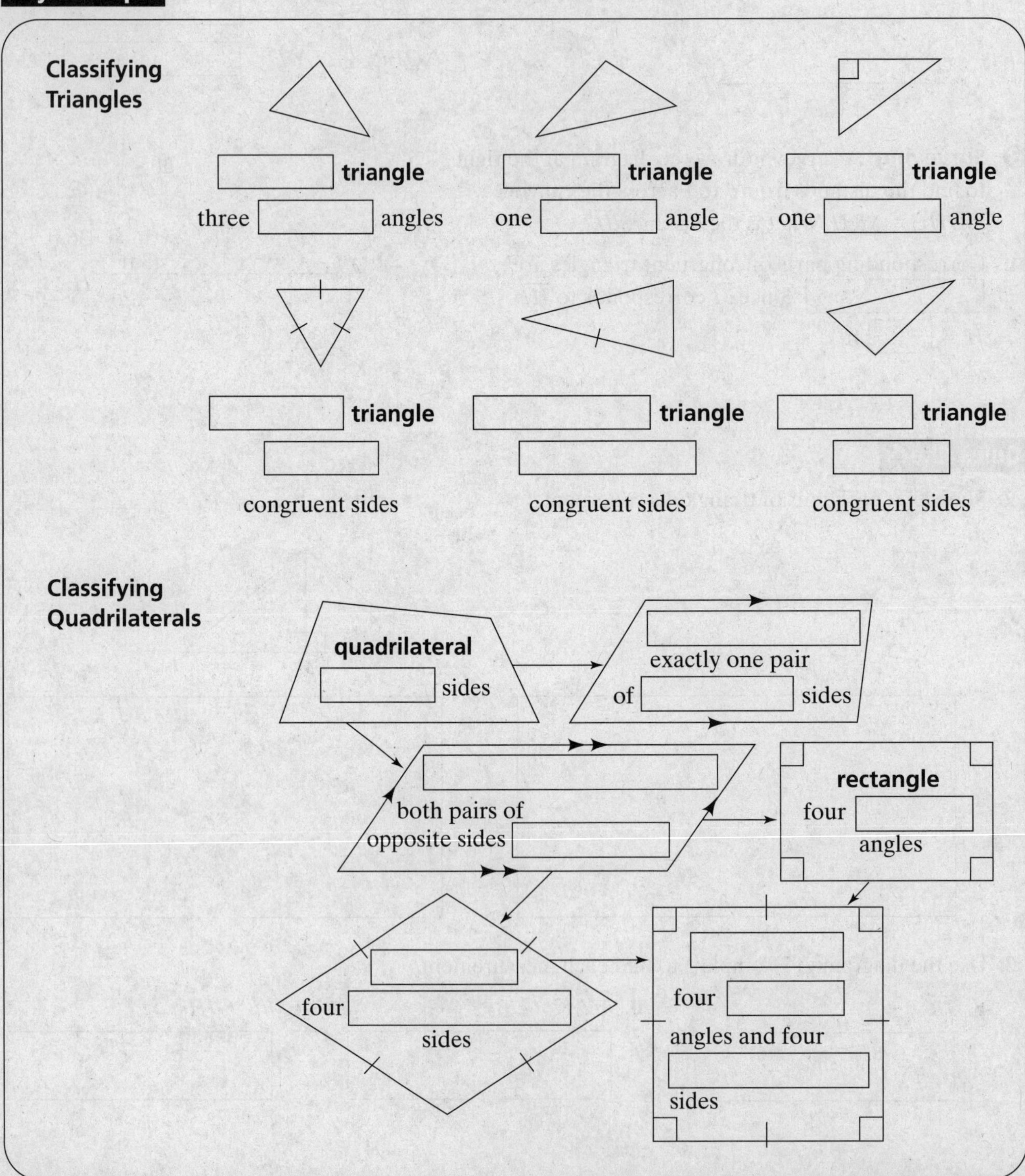

Name ____________________ Class ____________ Date ____________

Examples

1 Classifying Triangles Classify $\triangle LMN$ by its sides and angles.

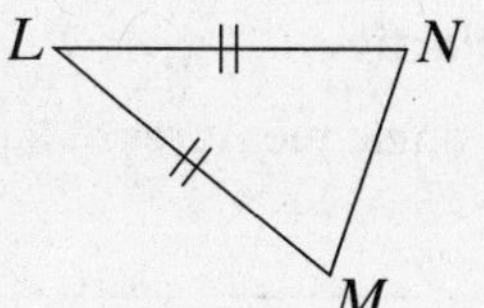

The triangle has [ ] sides that are congruent and three [ ] angles. It is an [ ] triangle.

2 Classifying Quadrilaterals Determine the best name for quadrilateral *WXYZ*. Explain your choice.

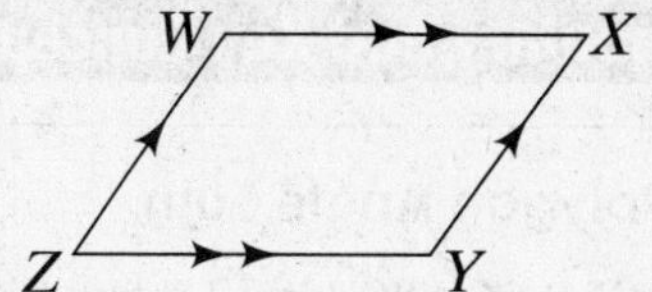

The opposite sides are [ ],
but the four sides are not [ ].
WXYZ is a [ ].

Quick Check

1. Classify each triangle by its sides and angles.

a.

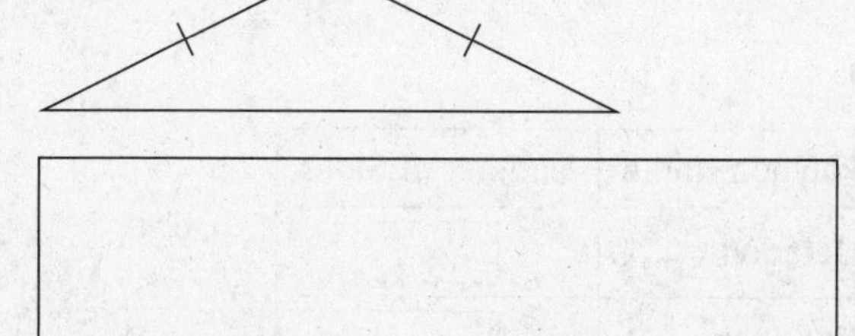

b.

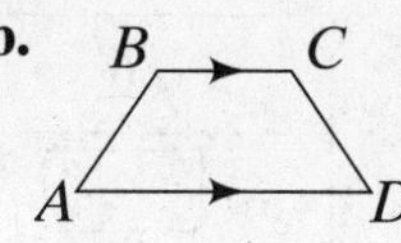

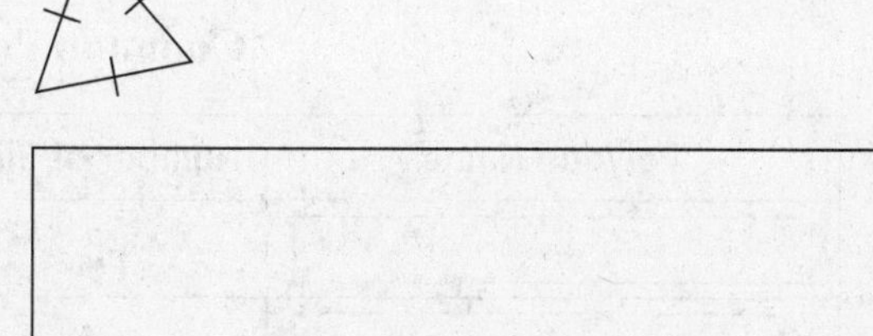

2. What is the best name for each quadrilateral? Explain.

a.

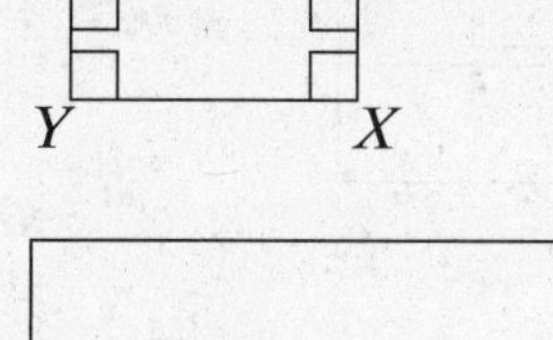

b.

Name ____________ Class ____________ Date ____________

Lesson 7-5

Angles and Polygons

Lesson Objective	**NAEP 2005 Strand:** Geometry
To find the angle measures of a polygon	**Topic:** Relationships Among Geometric Figures
	Local Standards: ____________

Vocabulary and Key Concepts

Polygon Angle Sum

For a polygon with n sides, the sum of the measures of the interior angles is ☐.

A regular polygon is ____________

____

Interior angles are ____________

____

Common Polygons

Polygon Name	Number of Sides	Polygon Name	Number of Sides
☐	3	Octagon	☐
☐	4	Nonagon	☐
☐	5	Decagon	☐
☐	6	Dodecagon	☐
Heptagon	☐		

Example

1 The Sum of Angle Measures of a Polygon Find the sum of the measures of the interior angles of an octagon.

An octagon has ☐ sides.

$(n - 2)180° = (\square - 2)180°$ ← **Substitute** ☐ **for** ***n*****.**

$= \square°$ ← **Simplify.**

Quick Check

1. What is the sum of the measures of the interior angles of a heptagon?

☐

Examples

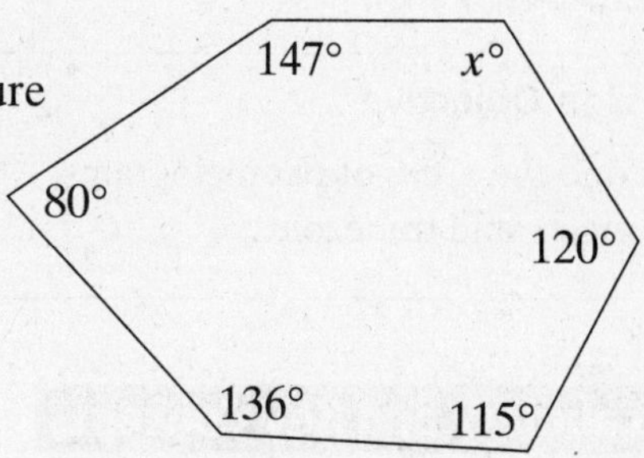

❷ Angle Measures of a Polygon Find the missing angle measure in the hexagon.

Step 1 Find the sum of the measures of the interior angles of a hexagon.

$(n - 2)180° = (\square - 2)180°$ ← **Substitute** ☐ **for *n*.**

$= \square$ ← **Simplify.**

Step 2 Write an equation.

Let x = the missing angle measure.

$\square = \square + \square + \square$
$+ \square + \square + x°$ ← **Write an equation.**

$720° = \square + x°$ ← **Add.**

$\square = x°$ ← **Subtract** ☐ **from each side.**

The missing angle measure is ☐.

❸ Angle Measures of a Regular Polygon A design on a tile is in the shape of a regular nonagon. Find the measure of each angle.

Find the sum of the measures of the interior angles of the nonagon.

$(n - 2)180° = (\square - 2)180°$ ← **Substitute** ☐ **for *n*.**

$= \square$ ← **Simplify.**

$1{,}260° \div \square = \square$ ← **Divide the sum by the number of angles.**

Each angle of a regular nonagon has a measure of ☐.

Quick Check

2. A hexagon has five angles with measures of 142°, 84°, 123°, 130°, and 90°. What is the measure of the sixth angle?

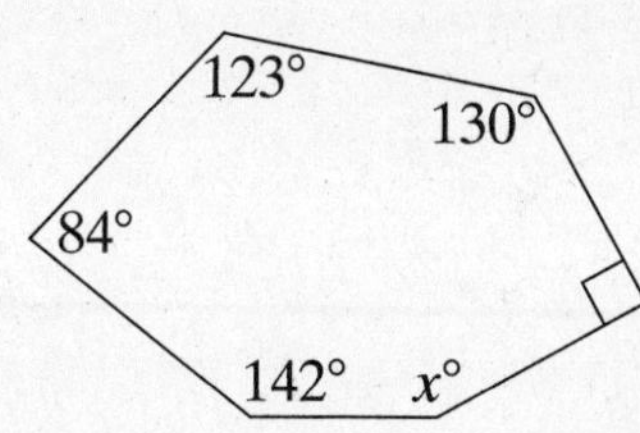

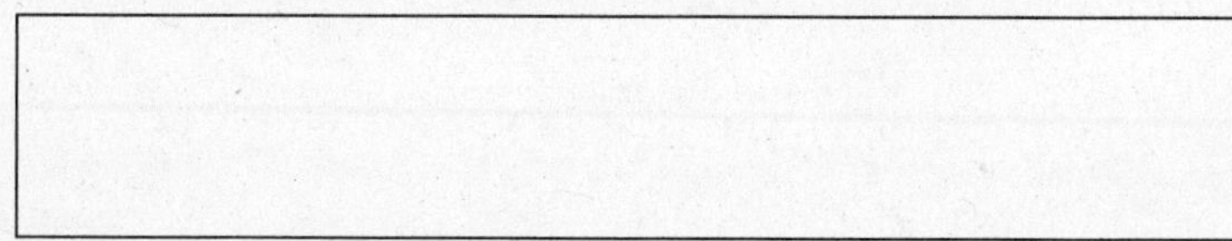

3. Find the measure of each angle of a regular polygon with 5 sides.

☐

Lesson 7-6

Areas of Polygons

Lesson Objective	**NAEP 2005 Strand:** Measurement
To find the areas of parallelograms, triangles, and trapezoids	**Topic:** Measuring Physical Attributes **Local Standards:** ____________________

Vocabulary and Key Concepts

Area of a Parallelogram

The area of a parallelogram equals the product of any base length b and the corresponding height h.

$A =$ ☐☐

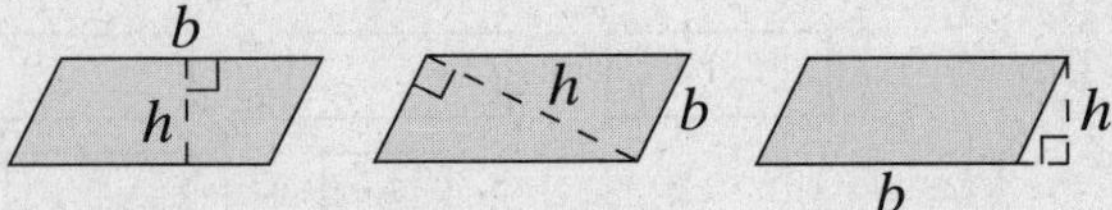

Area of a Triangle

The area of a triangle equals half the product of any base length b and the corresponding height h.

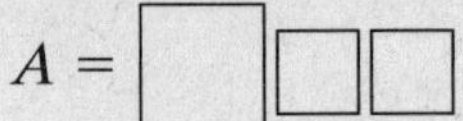

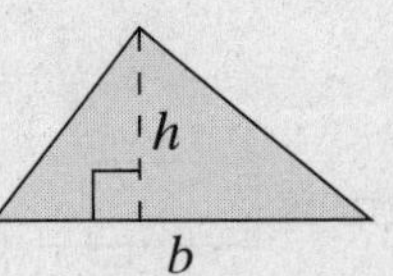

Area of a Trapezoid

The area of a trapezoid is one half the product of the height and the sum of the lengths of the bases.

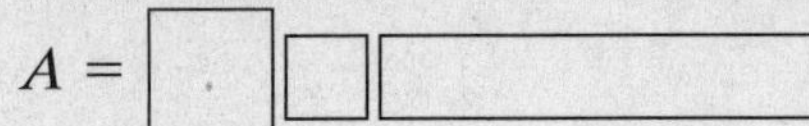

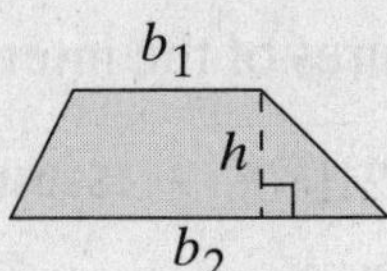

The area of a figure is ____

Name ______________________ Class ______________ Date ______________

Examples

1 Finding the Area of a Triangle Find the area of the triangular part of the doghouse.

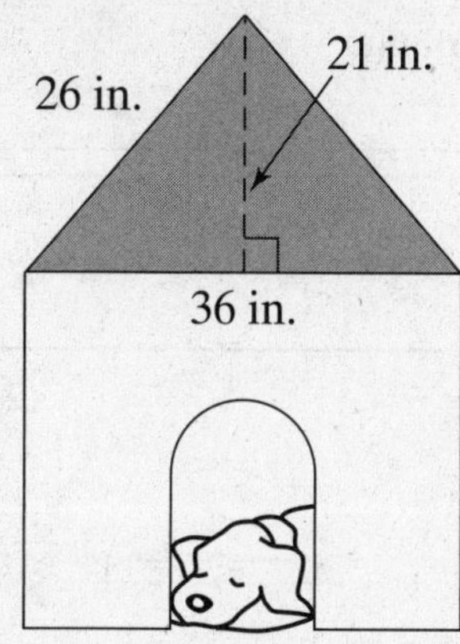

$A = \frac{\square}{\square}\,\square$ ← **Use the area of a triangle formula.**

$= \frac{1}{2} \cdot \square \cdot \square$ ← **Substitute $\square$ for *b* and $\square$ for *h*.**

$= \square$ ← **Simplify.**

The area of the triangular part of the doghouse is ______ in.².

2 Finding the Area of a Trapezoid Find the area of a trapezoid with height 4.4 in. and bases 6.7 in. and 9.3 in.

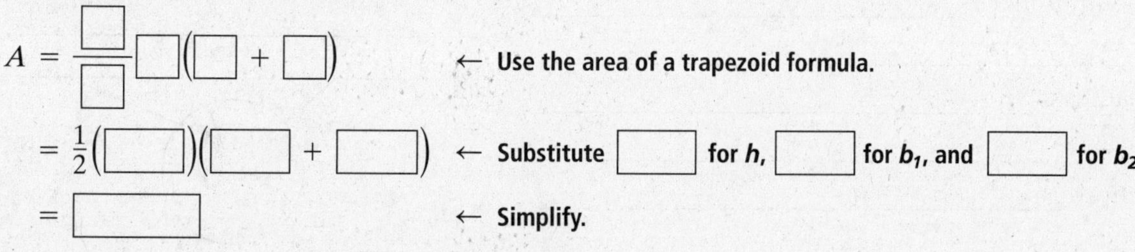

$A = \frac{\square}{\square}\,\square(\square + \square)$ ← **Use the area of a trapezoid formula.**

$= \frac{1}{2}(\square)(\square + \square)$ ← **Substitute $\square$ for *h*, $\square$ for b_1, and $\square$ for b_2.**

$= \square$ ← **Simplify.**

The area of the trapezoid is ______ in.².

Quick Check

1. Find the area of the triangle at the right.

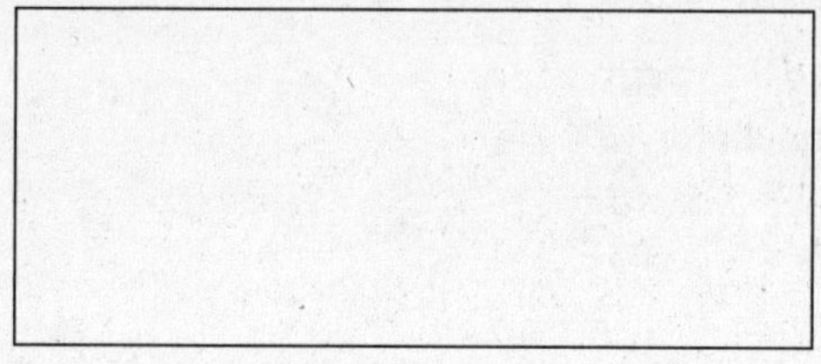

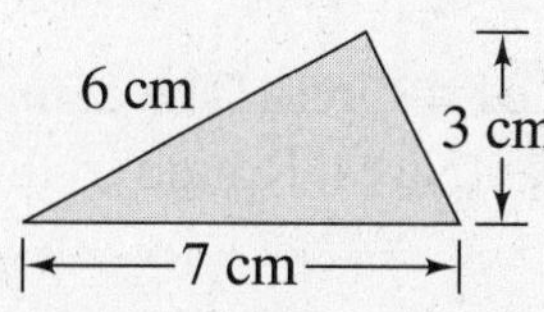

2. Find the area of the trapezoid at the right.

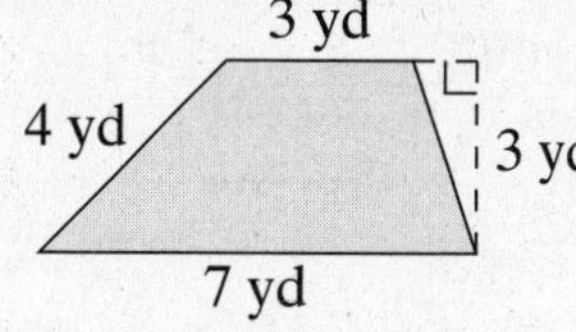

Name ______________________ Class ______________ Date ______________

Lesson 7-7

Circumference and Area of a Circle

Lesson Objective	**NAEP 2005 Strand:** Measurement
To find the circumference and area of a circle and the area of irregular figures	**Topic:** Measuring Physical Attributes **Local Standards:** ____________

Vocabulary and Key Concepts

Circumference of a Circle

The circumference of a circle is the product of π and the diameter d.

$C = \square\square$ or $\square\square\square$

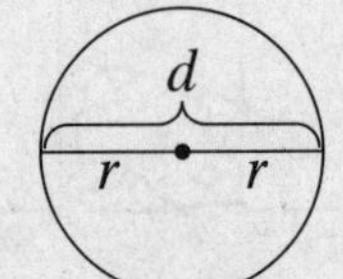

Area of a Circle

The area of a circle is the product of π and the square of the radius r.

$A = \square\square^{\square}$

Circumference is ______________________

____

A radius is ______________________

____

A chord is ______________________

____

A diameter is ______________________

____

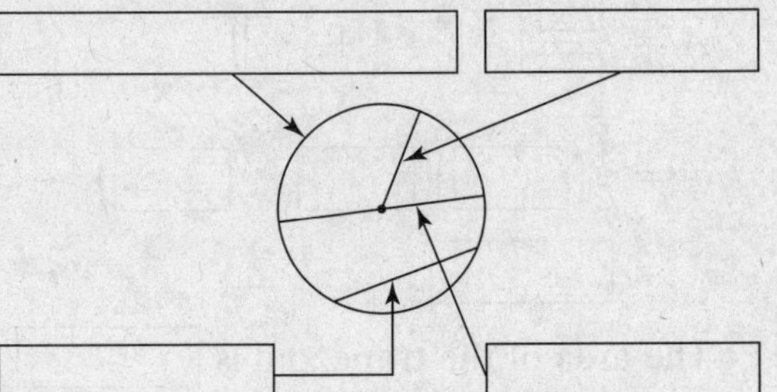

Examples

1 Finding the Measures of a Circle The diameter of a tractor tire is 125 cm. Find the circumference and area. Round to the nearest tenth.

$C = \square\square$ ← Use the formula for circumference.

$= \pi(\square)$ ← Substitute.

π × 125 = ______ ← Use a calculator.

The circumference is about ______ cm.

The radius of the tire is 125 ÷ ______, or ______ cm.

$A = \square\square^2$ ← Use the formula for the area of a circle.

$= \pi(\square)^2$ ← Substitute.

π × 62.5 x^2 = ______ ← Use a calculator.

The area of the tire is about ______ cm^2.

Name ______________________ Class ______________ Date ______________

❷ Finding the Area of an Irregular Figure Find the area of the unshaded region of the square tile with a circle inside of it, as shown at the right. Round to the nearest tenth.

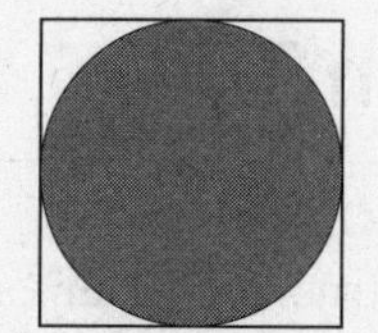

Separate the figure into a ☐ and a ☐.

Step 1 Find the area of the square. Area of square = ☐

$A = (\square)^2$ ← **Substitute ☐ for *s*.**

$= \square$ ← **Simplify.**

Step 2 Find the area of the circle. Area of circle = ☐

$A = \pi(\square)^2$ ← **Substitute ☐ for *r*.**

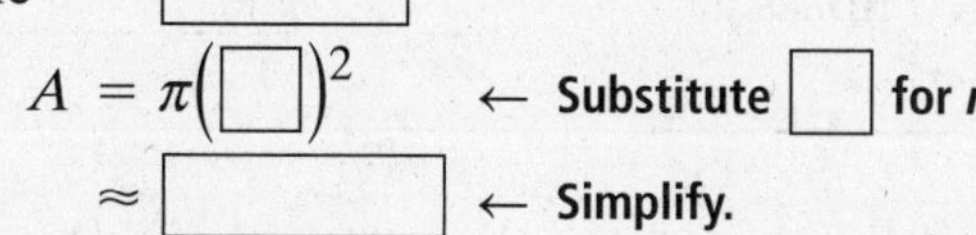

$\approx \square$ ← **Simplify.**

Step 3 Subtract the area of the ☐ from the area of the ☐.

The area of the unshaded region is about

☐ cm^2 − ☐ cm^2 = ☐ cm^2.

Quick Check

1. Find the circumference and area of the circle. Round to the nearest tenth.

2. Find the area of the shaded region. Round to the nearest tenth.

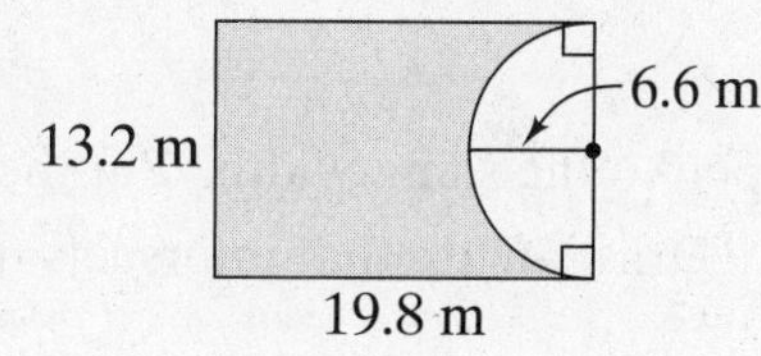

Name ______________________ Class ______________ Date ______________

Lesson 7-8

Constructions

Lesson Objective	**Local Standards:** ______________
To construct congruent angles and parallel lines	

Vocabulary

A compass is ____

____

Examples

1 Constructing Congruent Angles Construct ∠*D* congruent to ∠*A* shown at the right

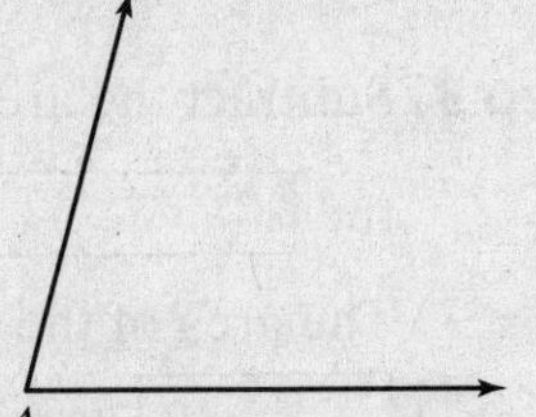

Step 1 Draw a ray with endpoint [ ].

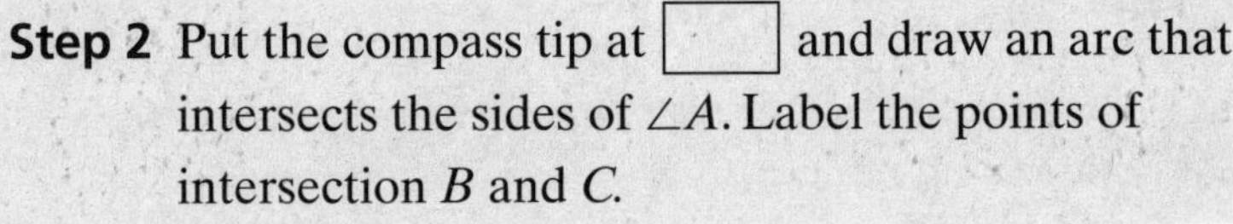

Step 2 Put the compass tip at [ ] and draw an arc that intersects the sides of ∠*A*. Label the points of intersection *B* and *C*.

Step 3 Keep the compass open to the same width. Put the compass tip as [ ]. Draw an arc that intersects the ray at point *E*.

Step 4 Adjust the compass so that the tip is at *B* and the pencil is at *C*. Using this compass opening, put the tip at [ ]. Draw an arc to determine point *F*. Draw $\overrightarrow{DF}$.

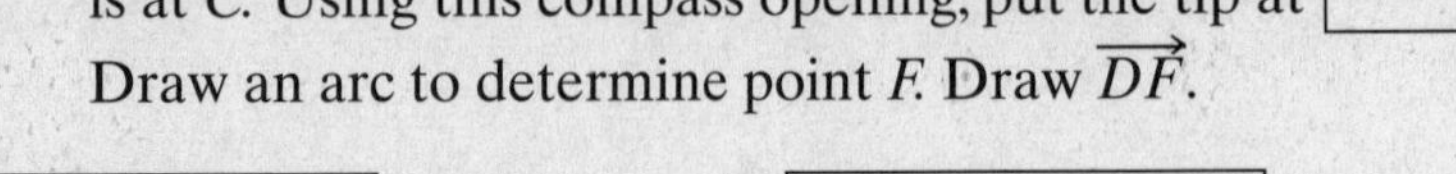

[ ] is congruent to [ ].

Name ______________________ Class ______________ Date ______________

❷ Constructing Parallel Lines Construct a line parallel to g.

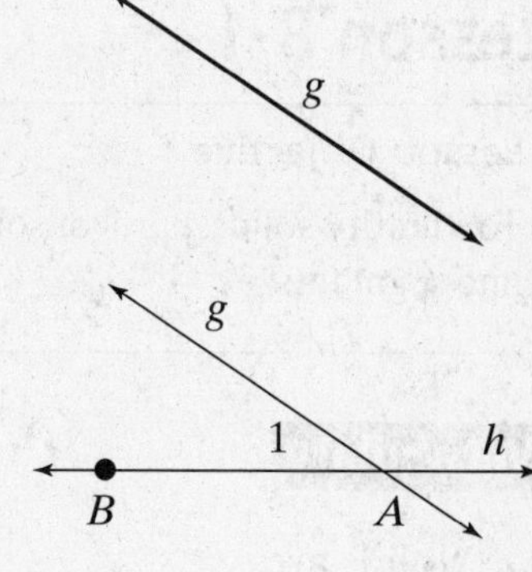

Step 1 Draw line h that intersects line g. Label the point of intersection A. Label the angle formed $\angle 1$. Then label point B on line h.

Step 2 Construct an angle at B that is congruent to $\angle 1$. Label point E on the line formed in the construction.

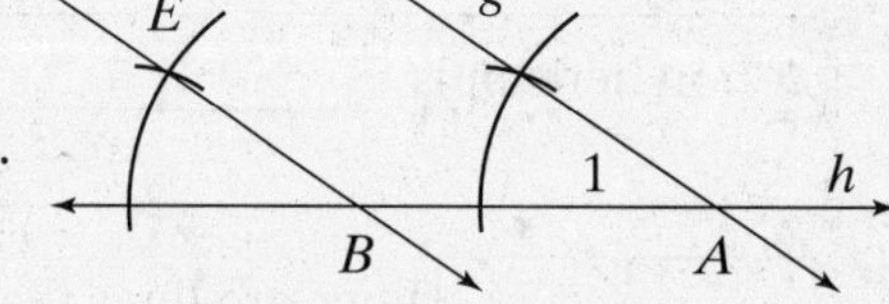

______________ is parallel to line g.

Quick Check

1. Draw an obtuse angle, $\angle F$. Construct $\angle N$ congruent to $\angle F$.

2. Draw a line d. Construct a line e parallel to line d.

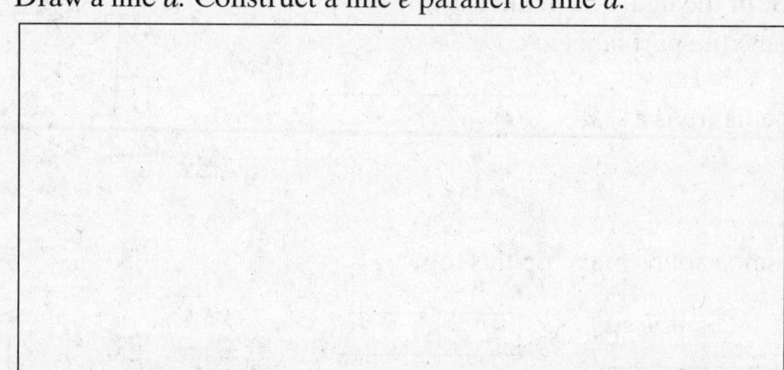

Name ____________________ Class ______________ Date ______________

Lesson 8-1

Solids

Lesson Objective	NAEP 2005 Strand: Geometry
To identify solids, parts of solids, and skew line segments	Topic: Dimension and Shape Local Standards: ____________

Vocabulary

Solids are ____

____

A polyhedron is ____

____

[ ] lines are lines that do not [ ] and are not [ ].

A [ ] is a solid that has two [ ] bases that are [ ] polygons.

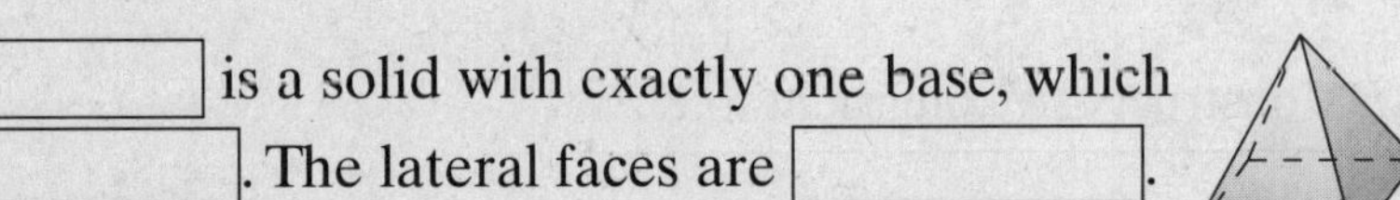

A [ ] is a solid with exactly one base, which is a [ ]. The lateral faces are [ ].

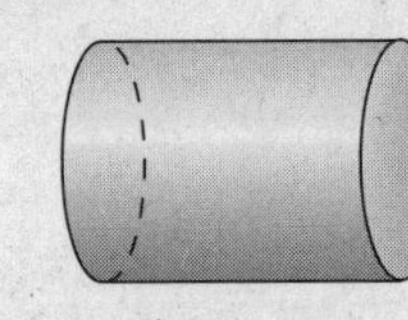

A [ ] is a solid with two bases that are parallel, congruent [ ].

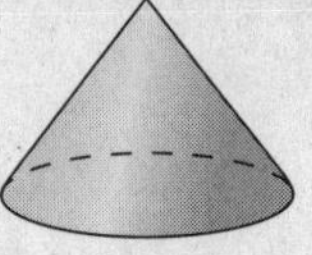

A [ ] is a solid with exactly one circular base and one [ ].

Examples

1 Naming Solids and Their Parts In the figure at right, describe the base, name the figure, and name the part labeled $\overline{CD}$.

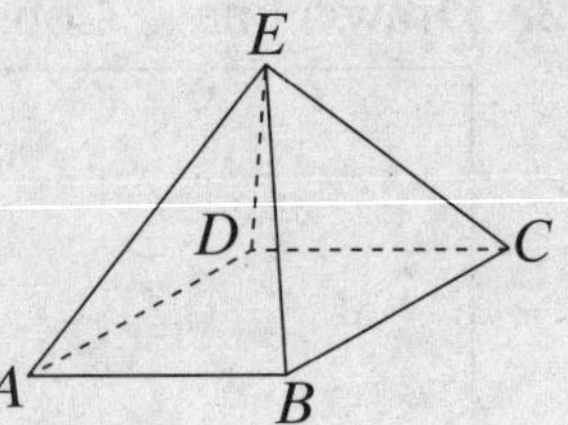

The base is a [ ]. The figure is a [ ].

$\overline{CD}$ is a [ ].

2 Recognizing Solids Which common solids make up this toy?

The box is a [ ]. The head is a [ ].

The hat is a [ ] with a [ ] on top.

Name ______________________ Class ______________ Date ______________

3 Identifying Skew Line Segments For each figure, name a pair of skew line segments, a pair of parallel line segments, and a pair of intersecting line segments.

a. A B D E C F

____ and ____ are skew. ____ and ____ are parallel.
____ and ____ intersect.

b.

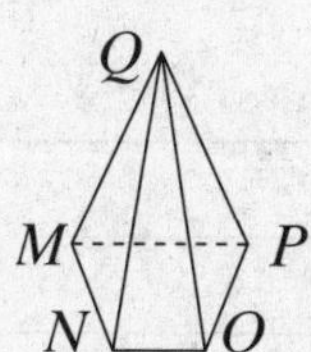

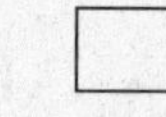

____ and ____ are skew. ____ and ____ are parallel.
____ and ____ intersect.

Quick Check

1. Refer to the figure at the right. Name the figure, $\overline{JK}$, and the points J and K.

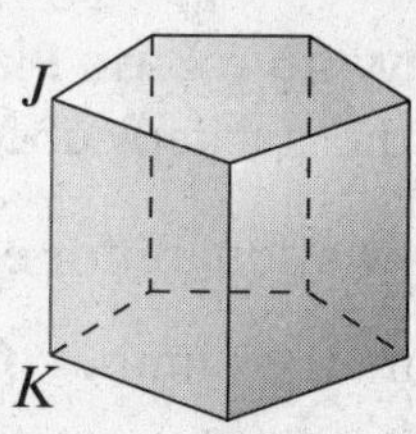

2. What common solids will a stage crew use to build the stage prop at right?

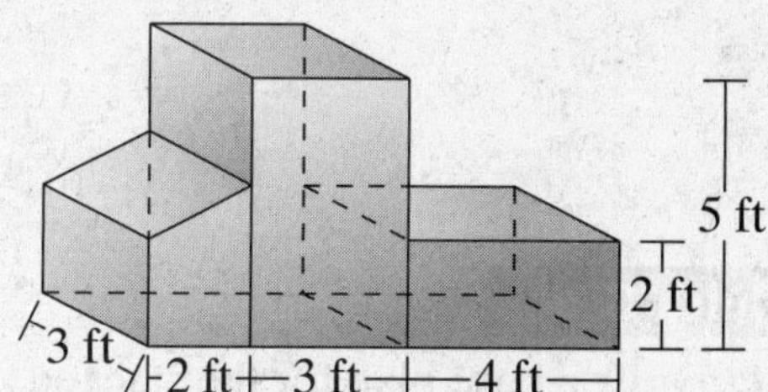

3. For the figure at the right, name a pair of intersecting line segments.

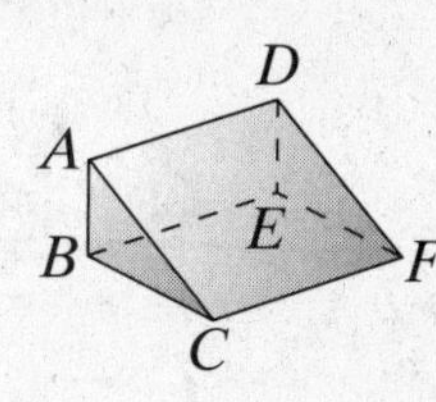

Lesson 8-2

Drawing Views of Three-Dimensional Figures

Lesson Objective	NAEP 2005 Strand: Geometry
To draw views of three-dimensional figures, including base plans and isometric views	**Topic:** Dimension and Shape **Local Standards:** ____________________

Vocabulary

A base plan shows ____

____

An isometric view is ____

____

Example

1 Drawing a Base Plan Draw the base plan for the stacked cubes.

Draw a square for each stack as seen from above.

Write the number of cubes in the stack inside each square.

Label the front and right sides.

Quick Check

1. Draw a base plan for the stacked cubes at the right.

Name ______________________ Class ______________ Date ______________

Examples

2 Drawing Top, Front, and Right Views Draw the top, front, and right view of the figure. Assume no blocks are hidden from view.

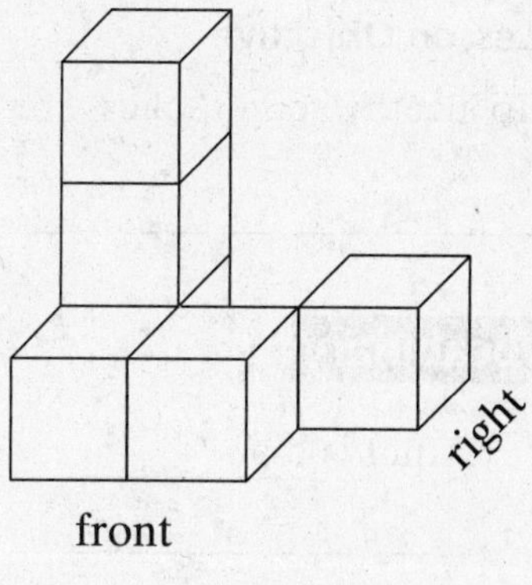

Treat each face like a two-dimensional figure.

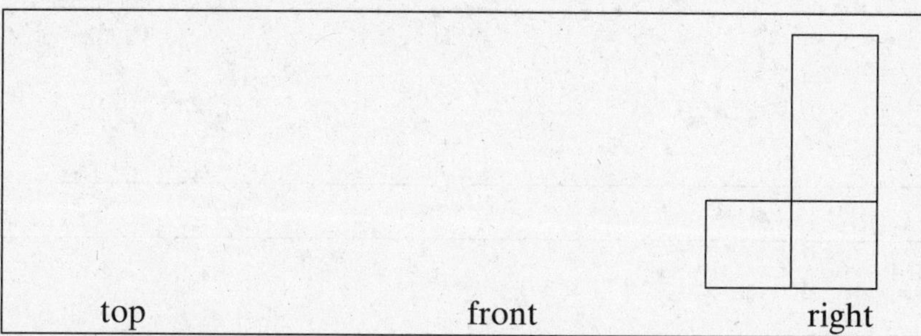

3 Performing The Rhythm Singers perform in three rows on steps 7 ft long and 1 ft deep. The first step is 1 ft high, and each row is 1 ft higher than the step in front of it. Draw a base plan for the steps where each square on graph paper is equal to one square foot.

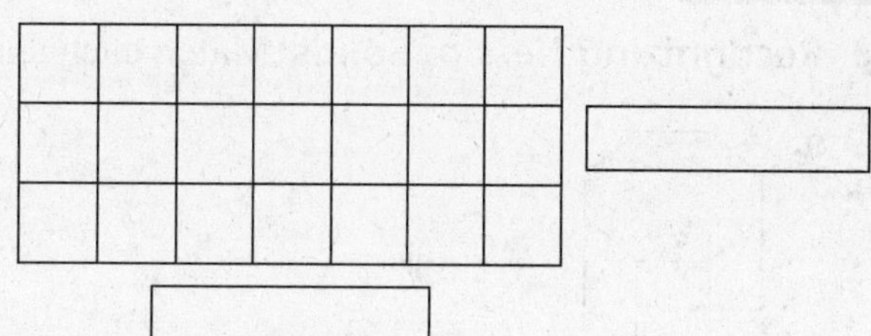

Draw one square for each square foot of the steps as seen from above.

Then write the height in feet of each square foot in the corresponding square.

Quick Check

2. Draw the top, front, and right views of the figure at the right. Assume no blocks are hidden from view.

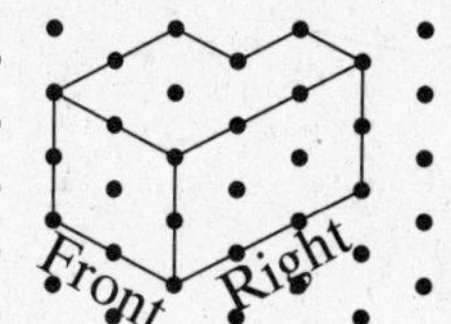

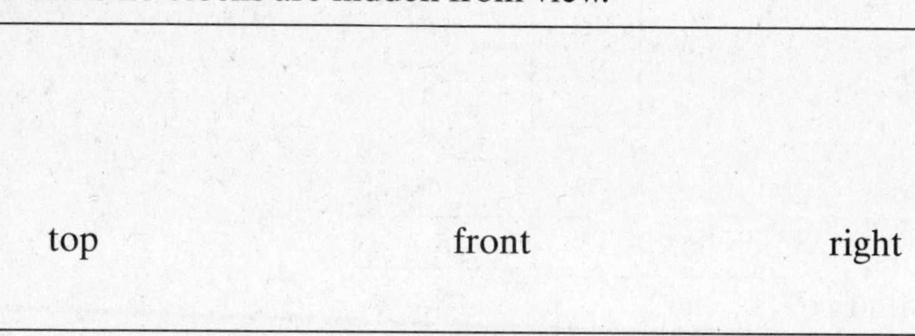

3. The Rhythm Singers need an additional step row. Draw a new base plan by continuing the pattern. How high off the ground is this extra step?

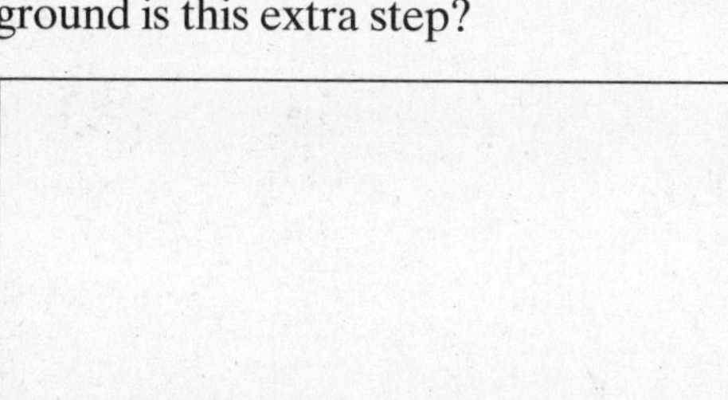

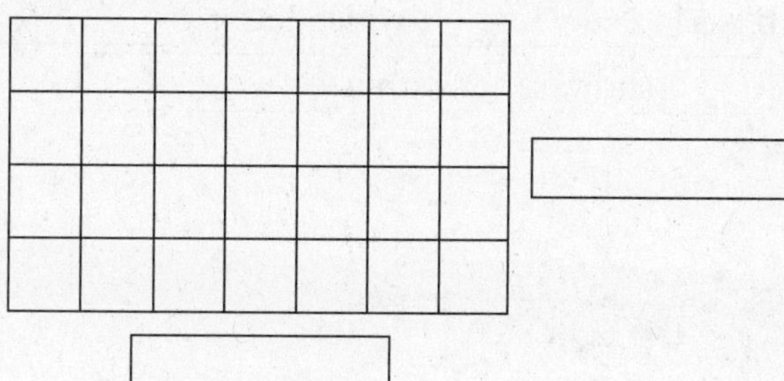

Name ______________________ Class ______________ Date ______________

Lesson 8-3

Nets and Three-Dimensional Figures

Lesson Objective	**NAEP 2005 Strand:** Geometry
To identify nets of solids	**Topic:** Dimension and Shape
	Local Standards: ____________

Vocabulary

A net is ____
____

Examples

1 Recognizing Nets of Solids Match each shape with its net.

a.

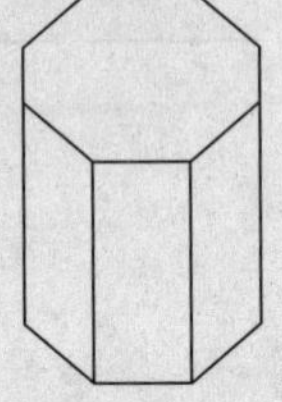

b.

I.

II.

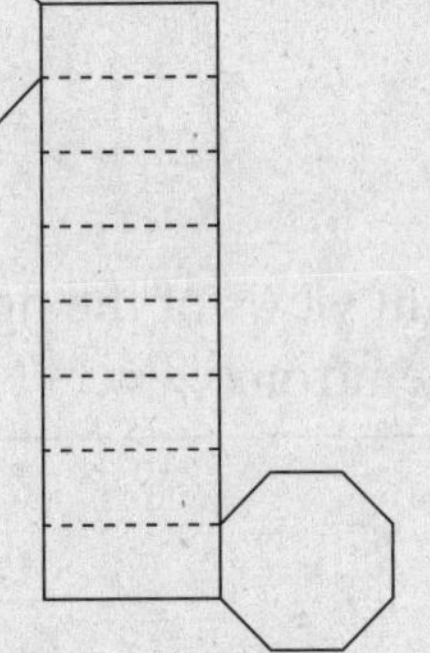

Shape **a** is an [ ], which has two [ ] bases. Figure [ ] shows a net with two [ ].

Shape **b** is a [ ], which has a [ ] base. Figure [ ] shows a net with a [ ].

Name ______________________ Class ______________ Date ______________

❷ **Identifying Solids From Nets** Identify the solid that this net forms.

The net shows one [ ] and six congruent [ ]. The one [ ] forms a base of a [ ] [ ].

Quick Check

1. Describe the net of a standard number cube.

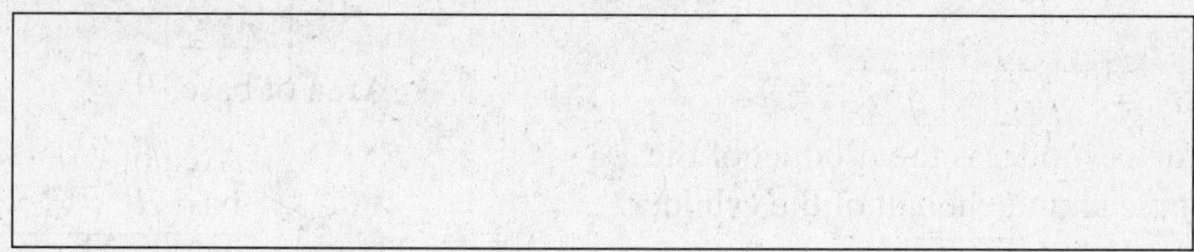

2. A net consists of one regular pentagon and five congruent triangles. What solid will it form?

Name ______________________ Class ______________ Date ______________

Lesson 8-4

Surface Areas of Prisms and Cylinders

Lesson Objective	NAEP 2005 Strand: Measurement
To find surface areas of prisms and cylinders using nets and formulas	**Topic:** Measuring Physical Attributes **Local Standards:** ______________

Vocabulary and Key Concepts

Lateral Area and Surface Area of Prisms and Cylinders

The lateral area L.A. of a prism is the product of the perimeter of the base and the height.

L.A. = ☐

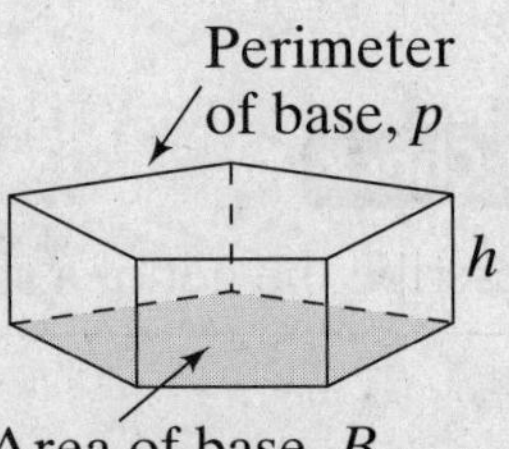

The surface area S.A. of a prism is the sum of the lateral area and the area of its two bases.

S.A. = ☐ + ☐

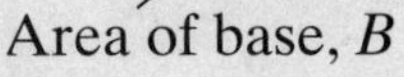

The lateral area L.A. of a cylinder is the product of the circumference of the base and the height of the cylinder.

L.A. = ☐

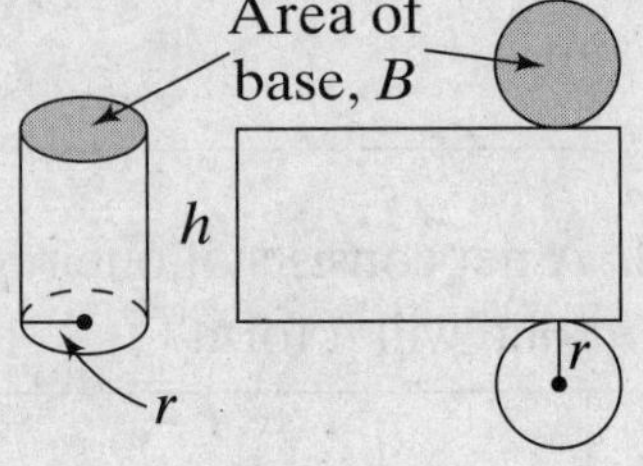

The surface area S.A. of a cylinder is the sum of the lateral area and the area of the bases.

S.A. = ☐ + ☐

Surface area is ______________________________

Lateral area is ______________________________

Examples

1 Using the Prism Surface Area Formula Use a formula to find the surface area of a prism with bases made of squares that are 2 in. on a side and with a height of 3 in.

S.A. = L.A. + $2B$ ← surface area formula

= $ph + 2s^2$ ← Use ph for L.A. and s^2 for B.

= (☐ · ☐)☐ + ☐(☐) ← The perimeter of the base is 4 · 2 in. The height of the prism is 3 in.

= ☐ + ☐ ← Use the order of operations.

= ☐ ← Add.

The surface area of the prism is ☐ in.^{2}.

❷ Finding Surface Area of a Cylinder Find the surface area needed to make a cylindrical can with a height of 7.2 cm and a diameter of 3.96 cm. Give the answer to the nearest whole unit.

$$\text{S.A.} = \square + \square \quad \leftarrow \textbf{cylinder surface area formula}$$

$$= \square + 2\square \quad \leftarrow \textbf{L.A.} = \square\textbf{; } B = \square$$

$$= 2\pi(\square)(\square) + 2\pi(\square^2) \quad \leftarrow \textbf{Substitute.}$$

$$= 36.3528\pi \approx \square \quad \leftarrow \textbf{Simplify.}$$

The surface area needed is approximately $\square$ cm^2.

Quick Check

1. The base of a decorative box for dolls is 8 in. by 5 in. Its height is 12 in. Estimate the surface area of the box.

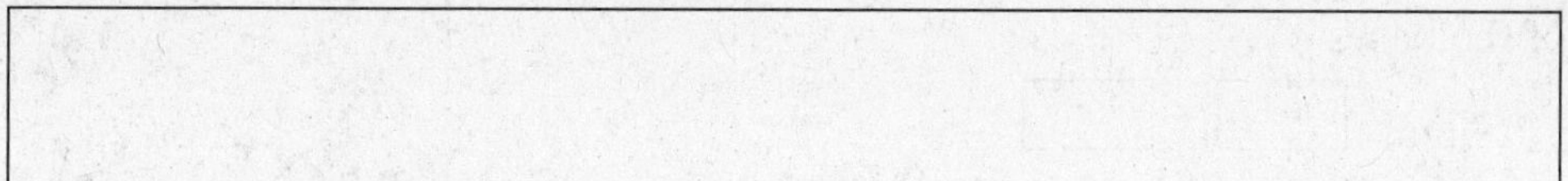

2. Find the surface area of the cylinder at the right to the nearest square meter.

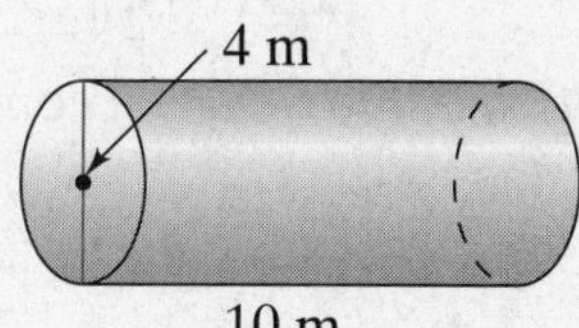

Name ____________ Class ____________ Date ____________

Lesson 8-5

Surface Areas of Pyramids and Cones

Lesson Objective	**NAEP 2005 Strand:** Measurement
To find surface areas of pyramids and cones using nets and formulas	**Topic:** Measuring Physical Attributes **Local Standards:** ____________

Vocabulary and Key Concepts

Lateral Area and Surface Area of Square Pyramids and Cones

The lateral area L.A. of a square pyramid is four times the area of one of the lateral faces.

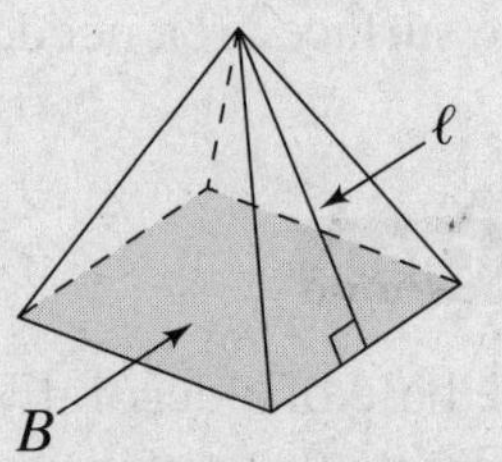

$$\text{L.A.} = 4 \cdot \left(\frac{\square}{\square}\square\right) = \square$$

The surface area S.A. of a square pyramid is the sum of the lateral area and the area of the base.

$$\text{S.A.} = \square + \square$$

The lateral area L.A. of a cone is one half the product of the circumference of the base and the slant height.

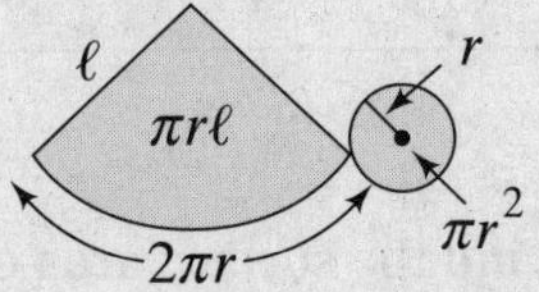

$$\text{L.A.} = \frac{1}{2}(\square)\square = \square$$

The surface area S.A. of a cone is the sum of the lateral area and the area of the base.

$$\text{S.A.} = \square + \square$$

Slant height is ____________

Examples

1 **Finding Surface Area** In order to buy paint to cover the inside of the roof and the floor of this playhouse, use the formula for S.A. of a square pyramid to find the area.

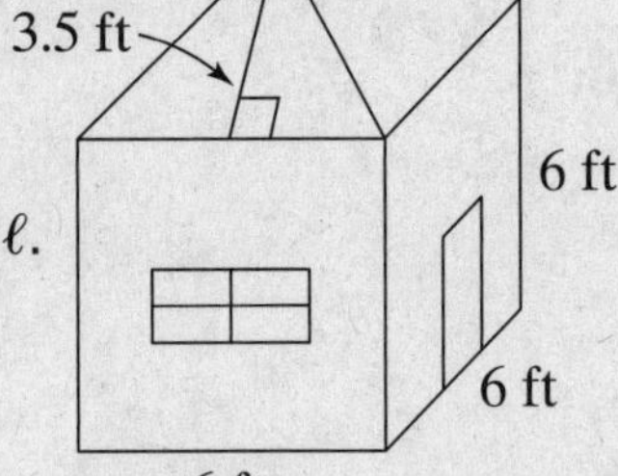

S.A. = L.A. + B ← **surface area formula**

$= 2b\ell + \square$ ← **Substitute $2b\ell$ for L.A. Substitute $\square$ for B.**

$= 2(\square)(\square) + \square$ ← **Substitute $\square$ for b and $\square$ for ℓ.**

$= \square + \square$ ← **Simplify.**

$= \square$ ← **Add.**

The surface area is $\square$ ft².

❷ Using the Cone Surface Area Formula Find the surface area of a cone with a radius of 9 ft and a slant height of 15 ft to the nearest square foot.

S.A. = L.A. + B ← **cone surface area formula**

$= \pi r \ell + \pi$ ☐ ← **Substitute $\pi r \ell$ for L.A. Substitute π ☐ for B.**

$= \pi(☐)(☐) + \pi(☐)^2$ ← **Substitute ☐ for r and ☐ for ℓ.**

= ☐ + ☐ ← **Use the order of operations.**

= ☐ ← **Simplify.**

≈ ☐ ← **Use a calculator.**

To the nearest square foot, the surface area of the cone is ☐ ft^2.

Quick Check

1. Find the surface area of the Great Pyramid of Khufu, shown at the right.

2. Find the surface area of the cone at right to the nearest square yard.

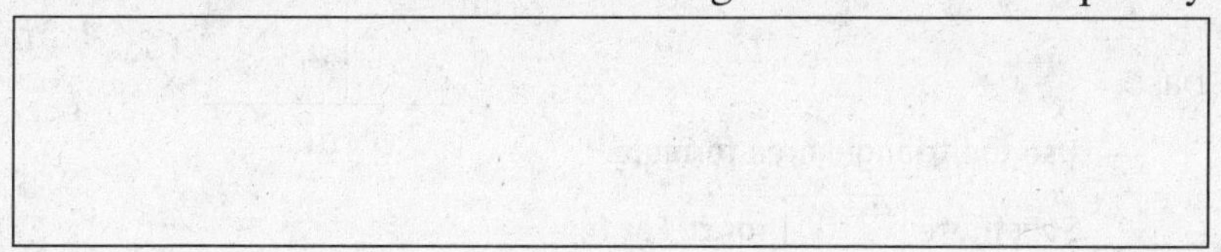

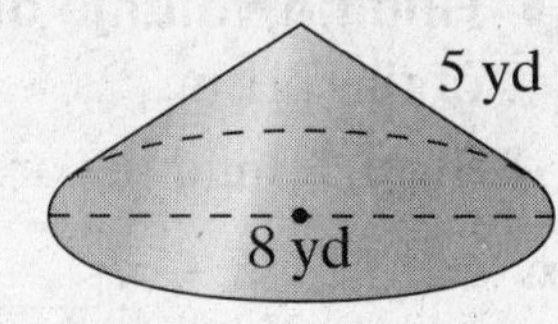

Name ______________________ Class ______________ Date ______________

Lesson 8-6

Volumes of Prisms and Cylinders

Lesson Objective	**NAEP 2005 Strand:** Measurement
To find the volumes of prisms and cylinders	**Topic:** Measuring Physical Attributes **Local Standards:** ____________________

Vocabulary and Key Concepts

Volume of Prisms and Cylinders

The volume V of a prism is the product of the base area B and the height h.

$$V = Bh$$

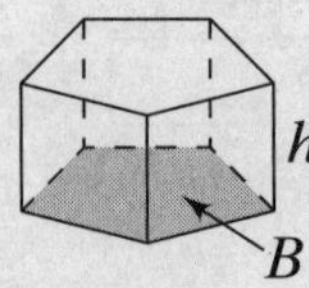

The volume V of a cylinder is the product of the base area B and the height h.

$$V = Bh$$

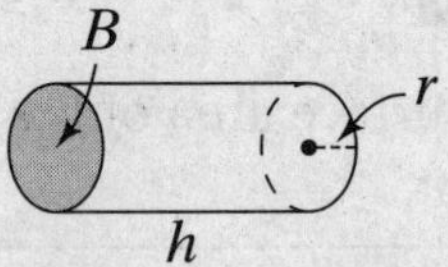

Volume is ____

____

Examples

1 Finding Volume of a Triangular Prism Find the volume of this prism.

2 cm
4 cm
3.5 cm

Step 1 Find the area B of the base.

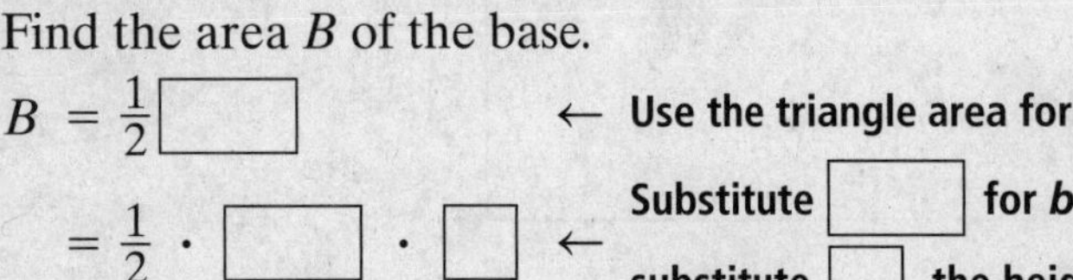

$B = \frac{1}{2}$ ☐ ← **Use the triangle area formula.**

$= \frac{1}{2} \cdot$ ☐ $\cdot$ ☐ ← **Substitute ☐ for *b*. For *h*, substitute ☐, the height of the triangle.**

$=$ ☐ ← **Multiply.**

The area of the base is ☐ cm^2.

Step 2 Use the base area to find the volume.

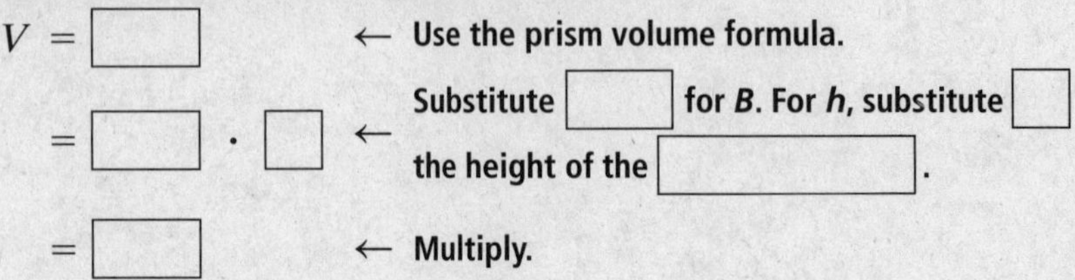

$V =$ ☐ ← **Use the prism volume formula.**

$=$ ☐ $\cdot$ ☐ ← **Substitute ☐ for *B*. For *h*, substitute ☐, the height of the ☐.**

$=$ ☐ ← **Multiply.**

The volume of the prism is ☐ cm^3.

❷ Finding Volume of a Cylinder Find the volume of a cylindrical cake that is 5 in. tall with a diameter of 15 in. Give your answer to the nearest cubic inch.

Estimate Use 3 for π. The area of the base is about 3×64 in.^{2}, or ______ in.^{2}. The volume is about 190×5 in.^{3}, or ______ in.^{3}.

Step 1 Find the area of the base.

$B = \pi$ ______

$= \pi($ ______ $)$ ← **Substitute.**

$\approx$ ______ ← **Simplify.**

The base area is about ______ in.^{2}.

Step 2 Use the base area to find the volume.

$V =$ ______

$\approx$ ______ $\cdot$ ______ **Substitute.** →

$=$ ______ **Simplify.** →

The volume of the cylindrical cake is about ______ in.^{3}.

Check for Reasonableness The answer ______ is close to the estimate of ______. The answer is reasonable.

Quick Check

1. Find the volume of the prism.

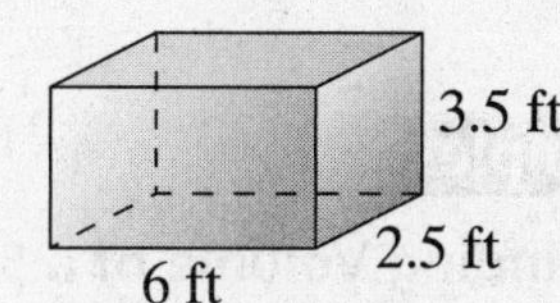

2. a. Estimation Estimate the volume of the cylinder at the right. Use 3 for π.

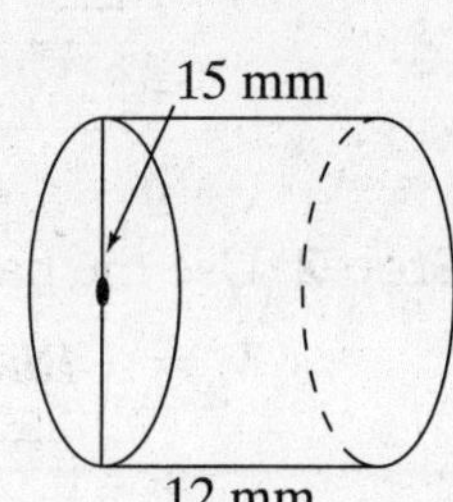

b. Find the volume of the cylinder to the nearest cubic millimeter.

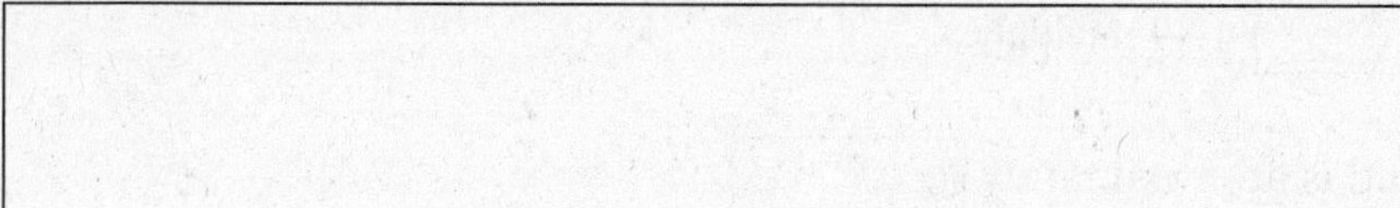

Name ______________________ Class ______________ Date ______________

Lesson 8-7

Volumes of Pyramids and Cones

Lesson Objective	NAEP 2005 Strand: Measurement
To find the volumes of pyramids and cones	Topic: Measuring Physical Attributes
	Local Standards: ____________

Key Concepts

Volume of a Pyramid

The volume V of a pyramid is one third the product of the base area B and the height h.

$$V = \frac{1}{3}Bh$$

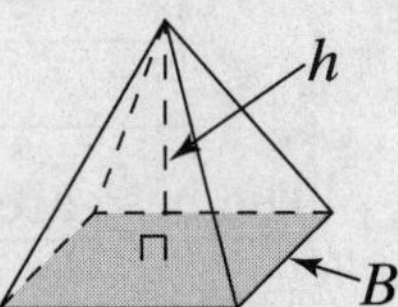

Volume of a Cone

The volume V of a cone is one third the product of the base area B and the height h.

$$V = \frac{1}{3}Bh$$

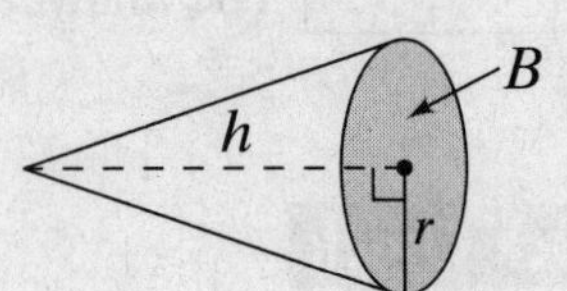

Examples

1 Finding Volume of a Square Pyramid Find the volume of this square pyramid to the nearest cubic foot.

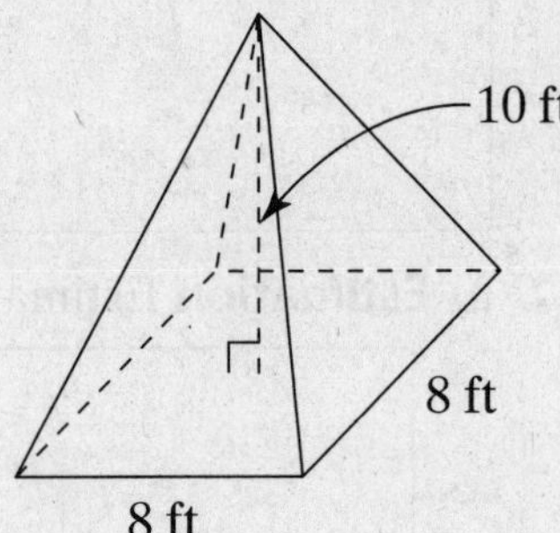

Step 1 Find the area of the base.

$B = \square$ ← **area of a square**

$= \square$ ← **Substitute $\square$ for *s*.**

$= \square$ ← **Simplify.**

Step 2 Use the base area to find the volume.

$V = \frac{1}{3}Bh$ ← **volume of a pyramid**

$= \frac{1}{3}(\square)(\square)$ ← **Substitute $\square$ for *B* and $\square$ for *h*.**

$\approx \square$ ← **Multiply.**

The volume of the pyramid is approximately $\square$ ft³.

❷ Finding Volume of a Cone Find the volume of this cone to the nearest cubic centimeter.

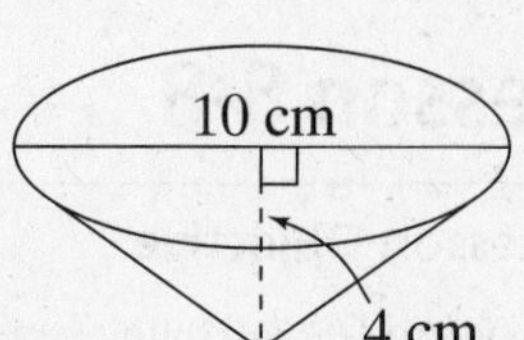

Step 1 Find the area of the base.

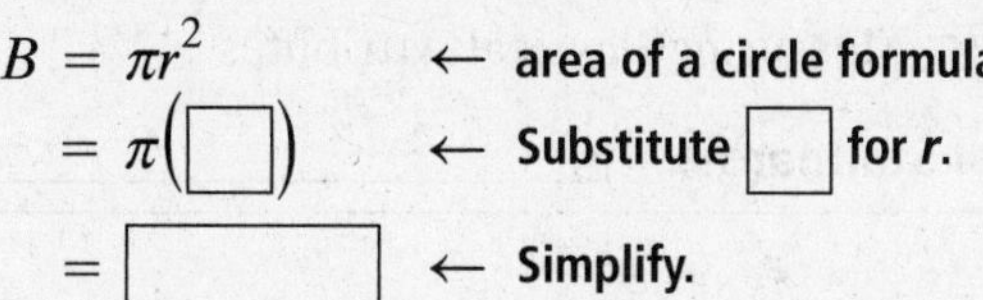

$B = \pi r^2$ ← **area of a circle formula**

$= \pi(\square)$ ← **Substitute $\square$ for *r*.**

$= \square$ ← **Simplify.**

Step 2 Use the base area to find the volume.

$V = \frac{1}{3}Bh$ ← **cone volume formula**

$= \frac{1}{3}(\square)\square$ ← **Substitute $\square$ for *B* and $\square$ for *h*.**

$= \square\frac{\square}{\square}\square$ ← **Multiply.**

≈ 105 ← **Simplify.**

To the nearest cubic centimeter, the volume of the cone is $\square$ cm^3.

Quick Check

1. Find the volume of the square pyramid at the right.

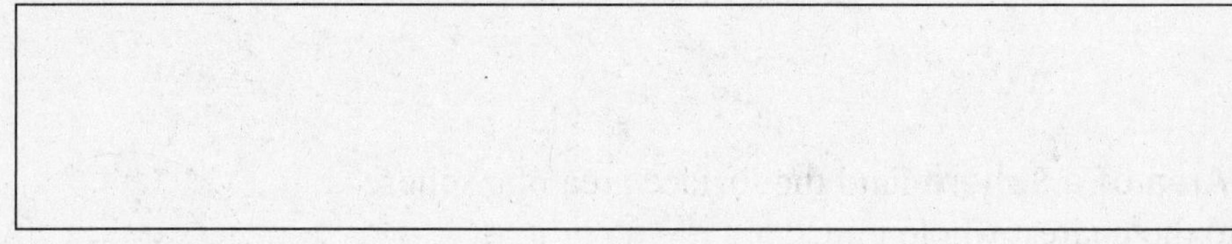

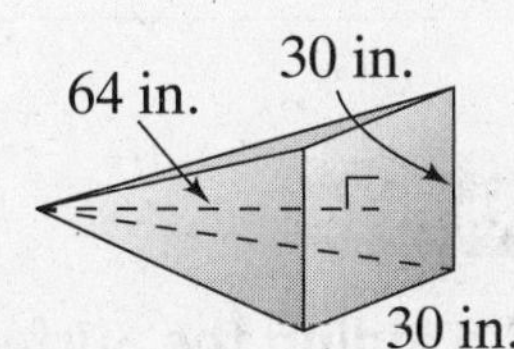

2. Find the volume of the cone at the right.
Round to the nearest cubic meter.

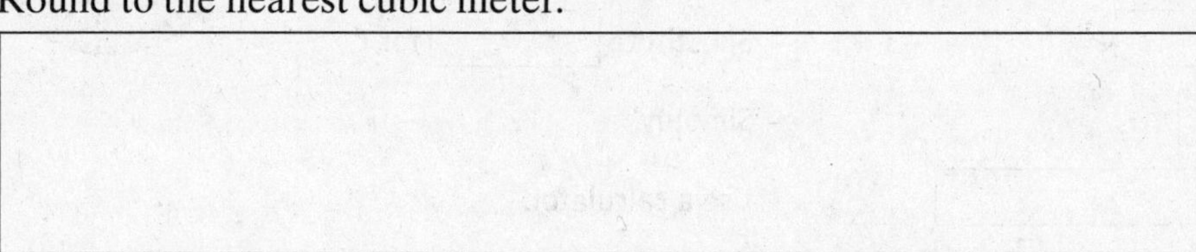

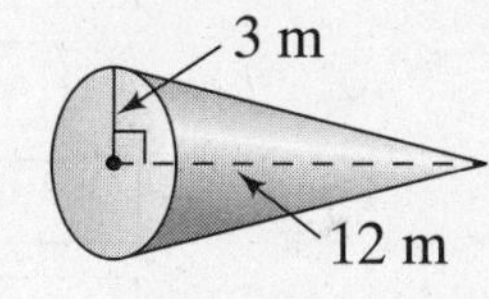

Name ______________________ Class ______________ Date ______________

Lesson 8-8

Spheres

Lesson Objective	**NAEP 2005 Strand:** Measurement
To find the surface area and volume of a sphere	**Topic:** Measuring Physical Attributes **Local Standards:** ______________

Vocabulary and Key Concepts

Surface Area and Volume of a Sphere

The surface area of a sphere is four times the product of π and the square of the radius r.

$$\text{S.A.} = 4\pi r^2$$

The volume of a sphere is four thirds of the product of π and the radius r cubed.

$$V = \frac{4}{3}\pi r^3$$

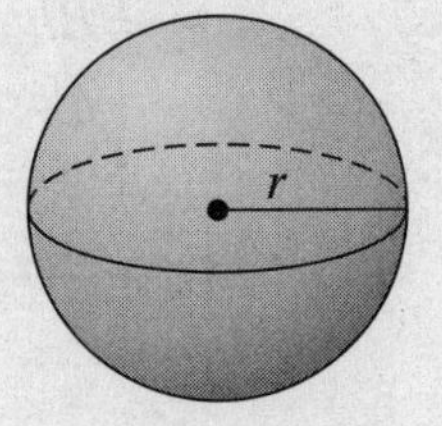

A sphere is ____

____

Example

1 Finding the Surface Area of a Sphere Find the surface area of a sphere with a radius of 12 m to the nearest whole unit.

S. A. = [ ] ← **surface area of a sphere**

$= 4\pi([\ \ ])^2$ ← **Substitute** [ ] **for** ***r*****.**

$= [\ \ ]\pi$ ← **Simplify.**

$\approx$ [ ] ← **Use a calculator.**

The surface area of the sphere is about [ ].

Quick Check

1. A sphere has a radius of 7 ft. Find its surface area to the nearest square foot.

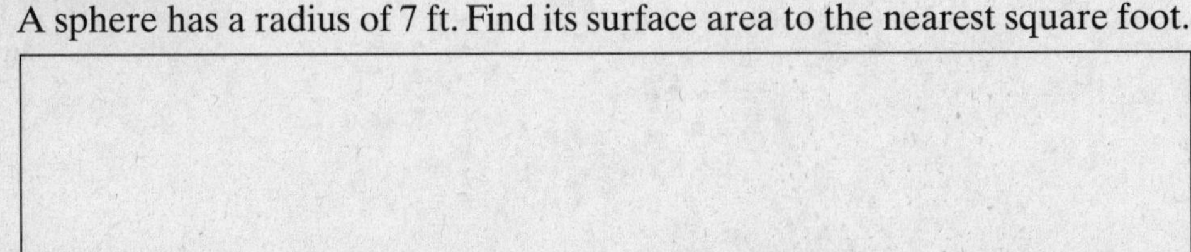

Name ____________ Class ____________ Date ____________

Example

❷ Finding the Volume of a Sphere A standard men's basketball has a diameter of 9.39 inches. What is the volume of a standard men's basketball to the nearest cubic inch?

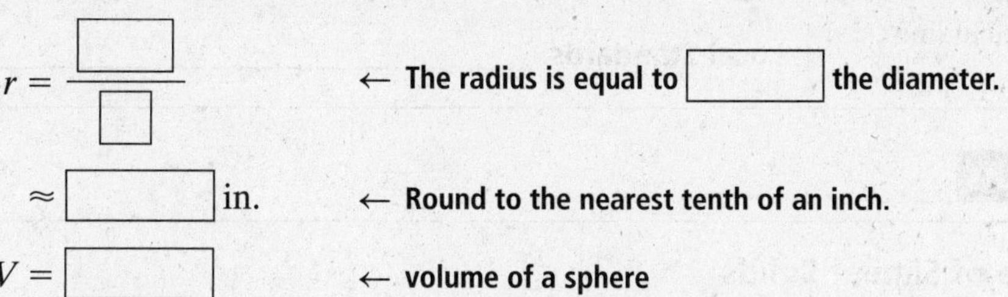

$r = \frac{\square}{\square}$ ← **The radius is equal to ☐ the diameter.**

$\approx \square$ in. ← **Round to the nearest tenth of an inch.**

$V = \square$ ← **volume of a sphere**

$\approx \frac{4}{3}\pi(\square)^3$ ← **Substitute ☐ for *r*.**

$\approx \square$ ← **Use a calculator.**

The volume of a standard men's basketball is about ☐.

Check for Reasonableness Use 3 for π and 5 for r. The volume is about $\frac{4}{3}(3)(5)^3$ in.^{3}, or ☐. The answer ☐ reasonable.

Quick Check

2. A globe in a brass stand has a diameter of 40 in. What is the volume of the globe to the nearest cubic inch?

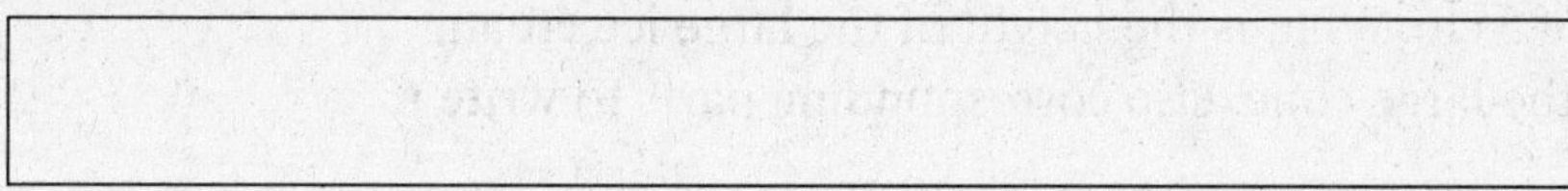

Name ______________________ Class ______________________ Date ______________________

Lesson 8-9

Exploring Similar Solids

Lesson Objective	**NAEP 2005 Strand:** Measurement
To use proportions to find missing measurements of similar solids, including surface area and volume	**Topic:** Systems of Measurement **Local Standards:** ____________

Vocabulary and Key Concepts

Surface Area and Volume of Similar Solids

If the ratio of the corresponding dimensions of similar solids is $\frac{a}{b}$, then

- the ratio of their surface areas is $\frac{a^2}{b^2}$ and
- the ratio of their volumes is $\frac{a^3}{b^3}$.

Similar solids ____

____

Example

1 Finding Dimensions of a Similar Solid At an ice cream shop, the small and large cones are similar. The small cone has a radius of 3 cm and a height of 12 cm. The large cone has a radius of 5 cm. What is the height of the large ice cream cone? Let h = the height of the large cone. Use corresponding parts to write a proportion.

$\frac{h}{\square} = \frac{\square}{\square}$ ← **dimensions of large cone** / ← **dimensions of small cone**

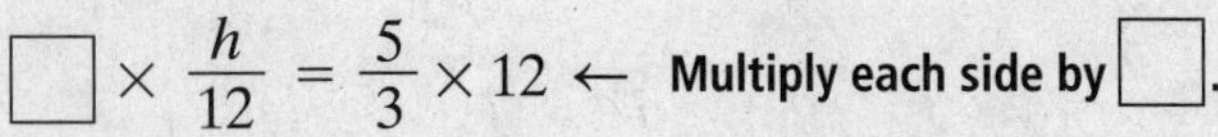

$\square \times \frac{h}{12} = \frac{5}{3} \times 12$ ← **Multiply each side by** $\square$.

$h = \frac{\square}{\square}$ ← **Simplify.**

$= \square$

The height of the large cone is $\square$.

Quick Check

1. Two cylinders are similar. The small cylinder has a diameter of 4 m and a height of h. The large cylinder has a diameter of 5 m and a height of 11 m. What is the value of h?

Name ______________________ Class ____________ Date ____________

Example

2 Surface Area and Volume of Similar Solids A square pyramid has a surface area of 39 cm^2 and a volume of 12 cm^3. The pyramid is similar to a larger pyramid, but its side length is $\frac{2}{3}$ that of the larger pyramid. Find the surface area and volume of the larger pyramid.

The ratio of the side lengths is $\frac{2}{3}$, so the ratio of the surface areas is $\frac{2^2}{3^2}$, or $\frac{\square}{\square}$.

$\frac{\text{surface area of the small pyramid}}{\text{surface area of the large pyramid}} = \frac{\square}{\square}$ ← **Write a proportion.**

$\frac{\square}{S} = \frac{\square}{\square}$ ← **Substitute the surface area of the small pyramid.**

$39 \cdot \square = S \cdot \square$ ← **Write the cross products.**

$S = \square$ ← **Simplify.**

The surface area of the large pyramid is ______.

If the ratio of the side lengths is $\frac{2}{3}$, the ratio of the volumes is $\frac{2^3}{3^3}$, or $\frac{\square}{\square}$.

$\frac{\text{volume of the small pyramid}}{\text{volume of the large pyramid}} = \frac{\square}{\square}$ ← **Write a proportion.**

$\frac{\square}{V} = \frac{\square}{\square}$ ← **Substitute the volume of the small pyramid.**

$12 \cdot \square = V \cdot \square$ ← **Write the cross products.**

$V = \square$ ← **Simplify.**

The volume of the large pyramid is ______.

Quick Check

2. A box has a surface area of about 54 $in.^2$ and a volume of about 27 $in.^3$. The edge lengths of the box are about $\frac{1}{3}$ of the edge lengths of a larger box. Find the surface area and volume of the larger box.

Name ________________ Class ________________ Date ________________

Lesson 9-1

Finding Mean, Median, and Mode

Lesson Objective To describe data using mean, median, mode, and range and to choose an appropriate measure of central tendency	**NAEP 2005 Strand:** Data Analysis and Probability **Topic:** Characteristics of Data Sets **Local Standards:** ________________

Vocabulary

A measure of central tendency is ________________

The mean is ________________

The median is ________________

____

The mode is ________________

Range is ________________

An outlier is ________________

____

Examples

1 Finding Mean, Median, and Mode Find the mean, the median, and the mode for the values in a set of coins with 4 pennies, 2 nickels, 3 dimes, and 1 quarter.

Mean

$$\frac{1 + 1 + 1 + 1 + 5 + 5 + 10 + 10 + 10 + 25}{\square} = \frac{\square}{\square} \quad \leftarrow \textbf{Add.}$$

$$= \square \quad \leftarrow \textbf{Divide.}$$

The mean is $\square$¢.

Median

1 1 1 1 5 5 10 10 10 25 ← **Order the data.**

$$\frac{\square + \square}{\square} = \square$$ ← **There are an even number of data items. Find the $\square$ of the middle two numbers.**

The median is $\square$¢.

Mode

1 1 1 1 5 5 10 10 10 25 ← **Use the data item(s) listed $\square$ often. $\square$ is the mode.**

The mode is $\square$¢.

Name ______________________ Class ______________ Date ______________

❷ **Finding Range** Find the range for the set of data:
5, −3.2, 1.5, 4.1, −7.3, 2.8, −5.6, 9.8, and 1.7

☐ − (☐) = ☐ ← **The greatest value is ☐. The least value is ☐. Subtract.**

The range is ☐.

❸ **Outliers** The prices of new books bought for the library are in dollars below. How does the outlier affect the mean?

7.95, 5, 12.05, 10, 6.25, 8, 56, 8.75, 9, 7

☐ is an outlier because it is ☐ than the other data items.

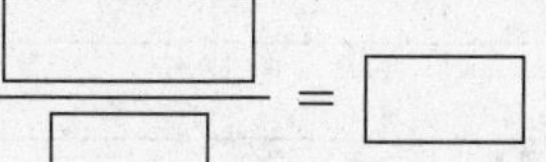

← **Find the mean with the outlier.**

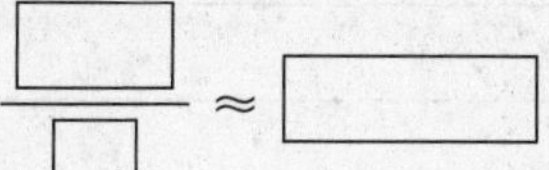

← **Find the mean without the outlier.**

The outlier raises the mean about $☐.

Quick Check

1. Find the mean, median, and mode of 11, 19, 11, 15, 16, 18, and 8.

2. Find the range of the data: −24.9, −26.5, −33.1, −24.2, −31.4, −32.1, −28.4, −30.

3. Find an outlier in each data set and tell how it affects the mean.
   a. 11, 14, 9, 1, 12, 15, 12, 13

   b. −5, −3, 0, 2, −1, −18, −6, 3, −2

Name ______________________ Class ______________ Date ______________

Lesson 9-2

Displaying Frequency

Lesson Objective	**NAEP 2005 Strand:** Data Analysis and Probability
To use line plots, frequency tables, and histograms to represent data	**Topic:** Data Representation **Local Standards:** ____________________

Vocabulary

Frequency is ______________________________

A line plot is ______________________________

____

A frequency table lists ______________________________

A histogram is ______________________________

____

Example

1 **Making a Line Plot** Make a line plot for the number of songs on a collection of CDs.

10 11 13 8 12 11 9 15 12 11 13 15 14

Songs on CDs

← **Each ✗ represents** [   ].

8 9 10 11 12 13 14 15 ← **The data are from** [   ] **to** [   ].

Number of Songs per CD

Quick Check

1. Make a line plot for these human body temperatures (°F):
98, 98, 99, 97, 98, 96, 99, 98, 97, 100, 99, 98, 99.

Examples

❷ Using a Line Plot Find the mean of the data in the line plot in Example 1.

Multiply each data value by its frequency.

$$\frac{(1 \cdot \square) + (1 \cdot \square) + (1 \cdot \square) + (\square \cdot 11) + (2 \cdot \square) + (\square \cdot 13) + (\square \cdot 14) + (\square \cdot 15)}{1 + 1 + 1 + 3 + 2 + 2 + 1 + 2}$$

Add the frequency of each item to find the total number of items.

$$= \frac{\square}{\square} \approx \square$$ ← **Simplify. Then round to the nearest tenth.**

❸ Making a Histogram The data set shows the number of goals a soccer team scored in each game of the season. Make a frequency table and histogram for the data.

0 3 0 0 7 2 1 0 4 1 0 3 6 0 1

The data range from ☐ to ☐.
Use equal-size intervals that begin with multiples of 2. →

Goals Scored

Goals	Tally	Frequency
0–1		
2–3		
4–5		
6–7		

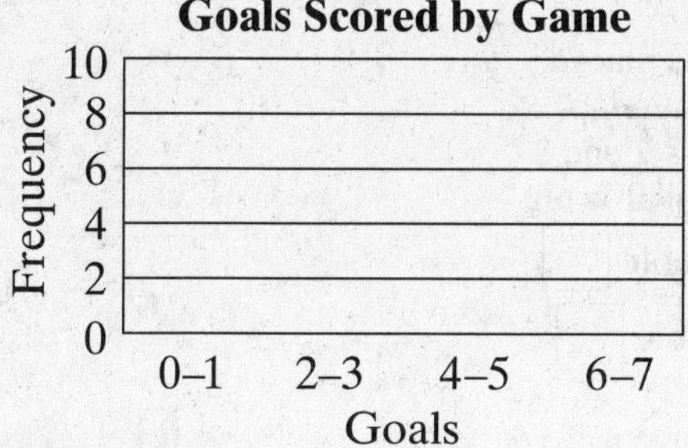

Quick Check

2. Use the line plot in Example 1. Find the median and mode.

3. Make a frequency table and histogram for the data. Cost of a movie: \$5.00, \$6.00, \$8.50, \$9.00, \$5.50, \$7.00, \$7.00, \$7.50, \$6.00, \$7.50, \$4.00, \$9.00, \$8.00, \$5.50

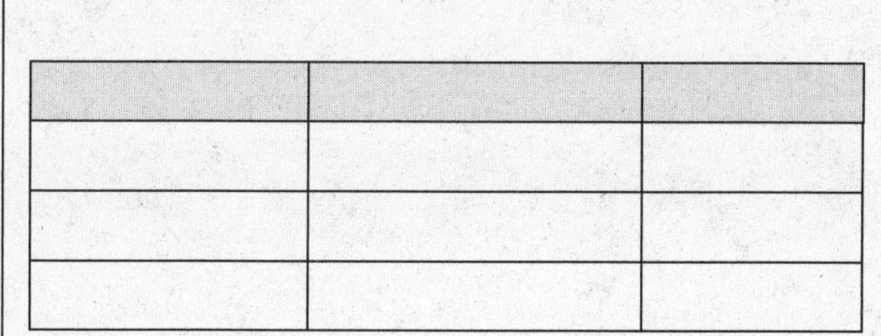

Name ______________________ Class ______________ Date ______________

Lesson 9-3

Venn Diagrams

Lesson Objective	Local Standards: ____________
To use Venn diagrams to represent relationships between data	

Example

1 **Use a Venn Diagram** Every table at the Country Café has white paper and crayons on it. The chart below shows colors of crayons at three tables. Use a Venn diagram to determine how many colors are available on all three tables. How many colors are available on just one table?

Crayon Colors at Each Table

Table 1	blue, brown, green, red, magenta, yellow, white
Table 2	black, brown, tan, maroon, orange, peach, yellow
Table 3	aqua, brown, gray, green, magenta, yellow, white

To draw a Venn diagram, draw a large rectangle. Inside it, draw three loops that overlap. Label the loops 1 (for Table 1), 2 (for Table 2), and 3 (for Table 3).

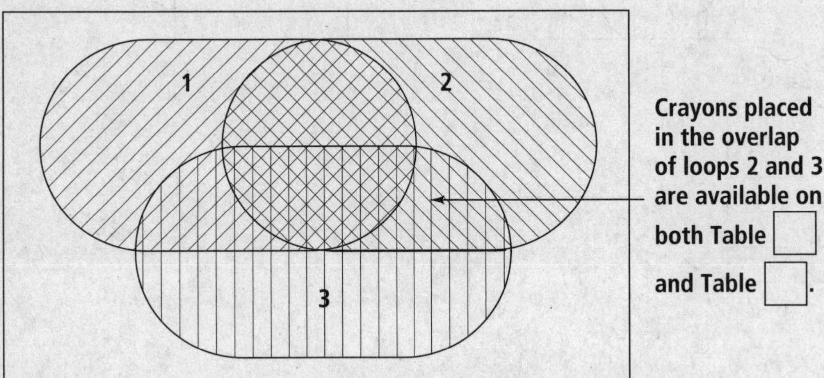

Use information from the table and logical reasoning to place each crayon color in the diagram.

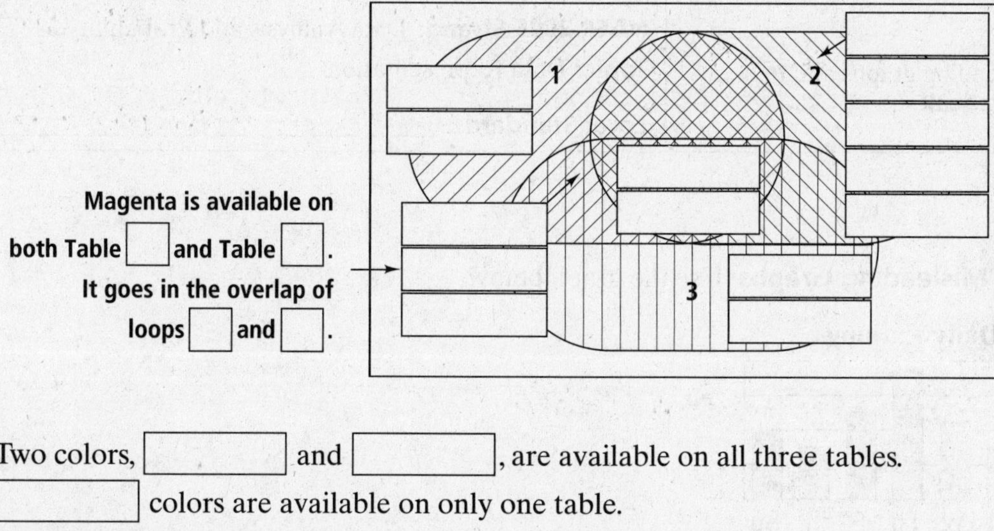

Two colors, ________ and ________, are available on all three tables.

________ colors are available on only one table.

Quick Check

1. A softball team has 18 players. Fourteen players bat right-handed. Two players can bat left- or right-handed. Four players bat left-handed. Draw a Venn diagram for this situation.

Name ______________________ Class ______________ Date ______________

Lesson 9-4

Reading Graphs Critically

Lesson Objective	**NAEP 2005 Strand:** Data Analysis and Probability
To recognize misleading graphs and to choose appropriate scales	**Topic:** Data Representation **Local Standards:** ____________________

Example

1 Recognizing Misleading Graphs Use the graph below.

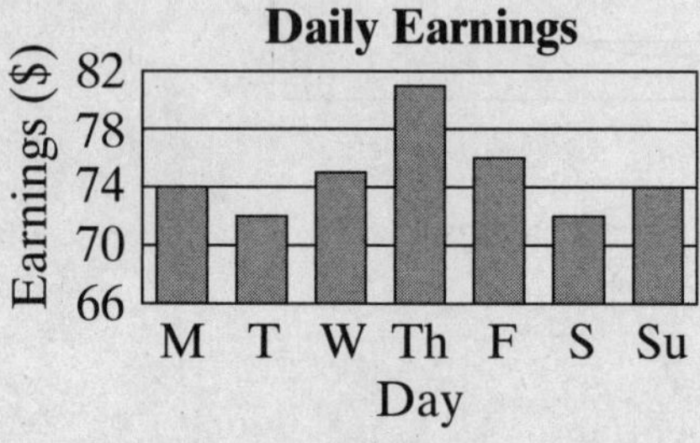

a. Which day appears to have almost twice the earnings of Monday?

[ ], because it extends up about [ ] units as compared with Monday's [ ] units.

b. Why might the graph appear misleading?

The vertical scale makes the differences between daily earnings appear greater than they are. For example, Thursday's earnings were about [ ], while Monday's earnings were [ ]. The graph, however, gives the impression that Thursday's earnings were [ ] as great as Monday's.

Quick Check

1. What scale on the vertical axis of the graph in Example 1 would show the data more clearly?

Example

❷ Selecting an Appropriate Scale Using different scales, make two bar graphs for the data. Use a break symbol in only one of the graphs.

Quarter Mile Records

Car	Time (s)
Dragster	5
Indy car	8
Sprint car	9
NASCAR stock car	10
Stock Pontiac Bonneville	17

The slowest time is ☐ seconds. Label the vertical axis with multiples of 5 from 0 to 20.

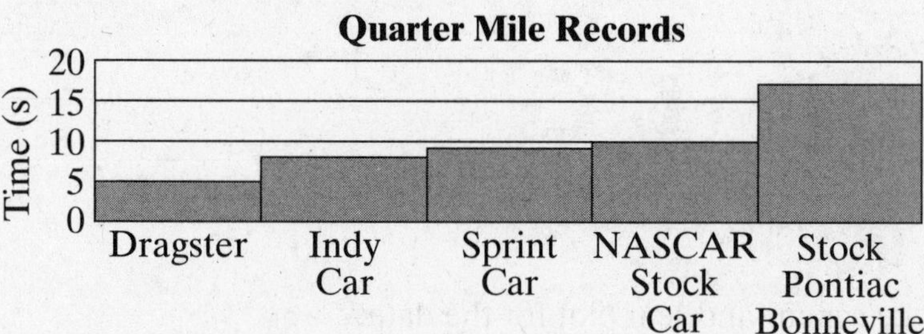

The data start at ☐. Label the vertical axis with multiples of 2.5, beginning with 5. Use a ☐ symbol.

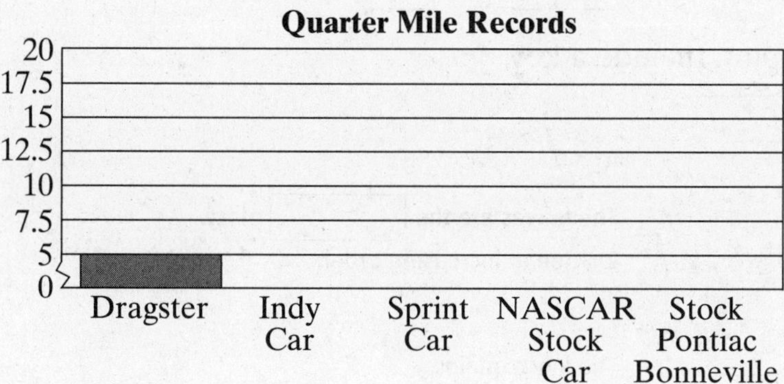

Quick Check

2. Which graph above shows the data more clearly? Explain.

Name ______________________ Class ______________ Date ______________

Lesson 9-5

Stem-and-Leaf Plots

Lesson Objective To represent and interpret data using stem-and-leaf plots	**NAEP 2005 Strand:** Data Analysis and Probability **Topic:** Data Representation **Local Standards:** ____________________

Vocabulary

A stem-and-leaf plot is ____

____

Example

1 Making Stem-and-Leaf Plots Make a stem-and-leaf plot for the data.

51, 56, 67, 44, 50, 63, 65, 58, 49, 51, 66, 59, 63, 47

Step 1 Choose the stems. The least value is ▢; the greatest value is ▢. Leaves are single digits, so use the first digits as the ▢. The stems in this case are ▢, ▢, and ▢.

Step 2 Draw the stem-and-leaf plot. Include a key.

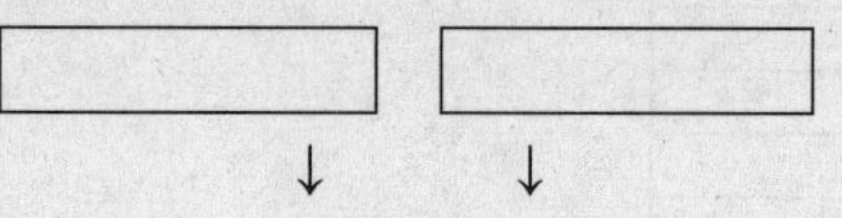

▢	4 7 9
▢	0 1 1 6 8 9
▢	3 3 5 6 7

← **The leaves are the ▢ place written in increasing order.**

Key: 4 | 4 means ▢. ← **The key explains what the stems and leaves represent.**

Quick Check

1. Below are the monthly high temperatures for Death Valley, California. Make a stem-and-leaf plot for the data.

87 91 101 111 120 125 134 126 120 113 97 86

Name ______________________ Class ______________ Date ______________

Example

❷ Using Back-to-Back Stem-and-Leaf Plots Compare the number of basketball and baseball cards using the mode of each data set.

Basketball and Baseball Cards

Basketball		Baseball
9 9 8	1	
4 2 1 0	2	8 9
	3	1 2 2 3 4

Key: means ☐ ← 4|2|9 → means ☐

The mode for basketball cards is ☐ cards, while the mode for baseball cards is ☐ cards. This measure of central tendency gives the impression that the number of baseball cards is ☐ than the number of basketball cards.

Quick Check

2. Compare the city mileage to the highway mileage using the mean and median.

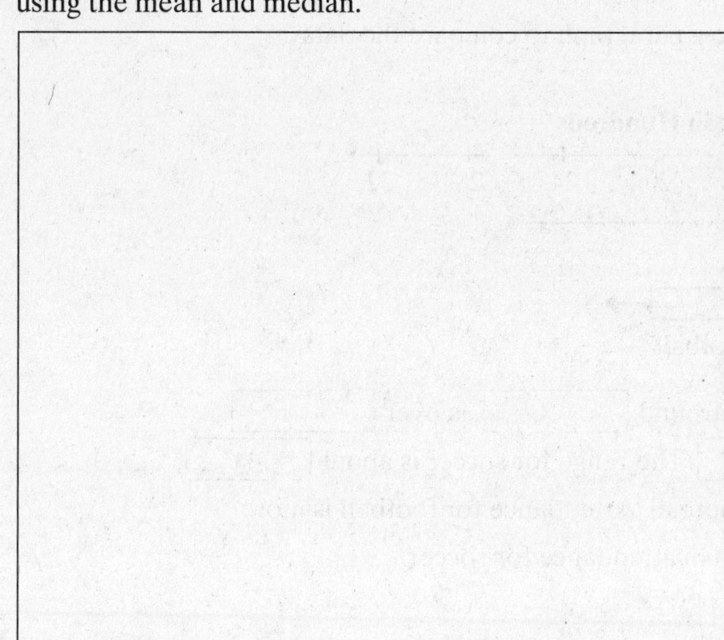

New Car Mileage (mi/gal)

City		Highway
9 8 8	1	
7 4 2	2	4 5 7 8
0	3	3 3
	4	0

Key: means 27 ← 7 | 2 | 8 → means 28

Name ____________ Class ____________ Date ____________

Lesson 9-6

Box-and-Whisker Plots

Lesson Objective	**Local Standards:** ____________
To represent and interpret data using box-and-whisker plots	

Vocabulary

A box-and-whisker plot is ____________

Quartiles divide ____________

Box-and-Whisker Plot

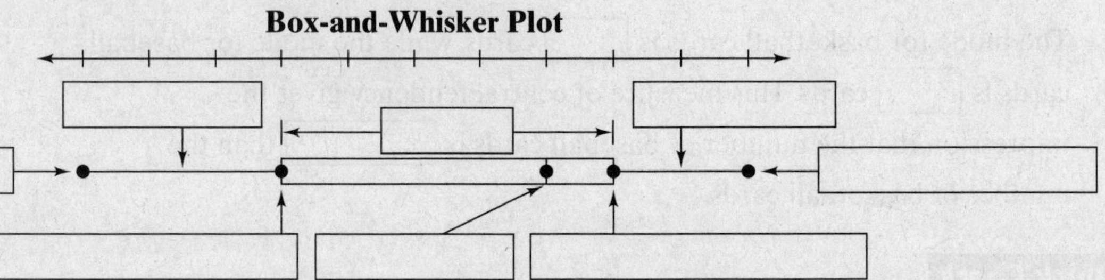

Example

❶ Comparing Two Sets of Data Write a paragraph to compare the data shown in this plot.

Game Attendance in Hundreds

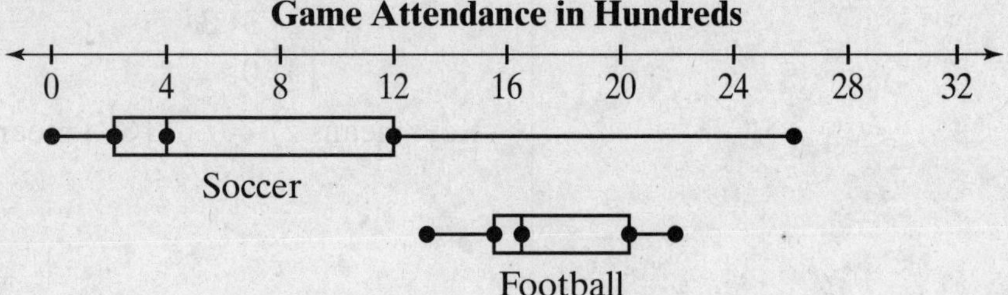

The median attendance for football, around ______, is over ______ times the median for soccer, ______. The range for soccer is about ______, which is greater than the range for football. Attendance for football is more tightly grouped around the median than attendance for soccer.

Quick Check

1. Write a paragraph comparing the data.

Students' Heights (in.)

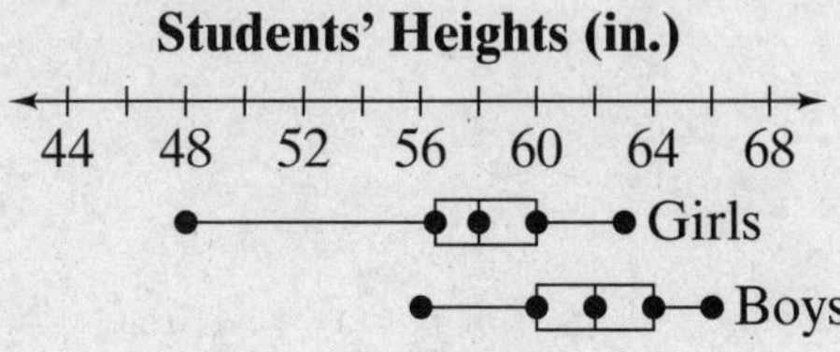

Name _______________ Class _______________ Date _______________

Example

2 Making Box-and-Whisker Plots Make a box-and-whisker plot for the data on study hours per week: 10, 13, 16, 17, 20, 22, 23, 24, 26, 30, 31.

Step 1 The data are in order from least to greatest. Find the median.

10 13 16 17 20 **22** 23 24 26 30 31

The median is the ______ number, ______.

Step 2 Find the lower quartile and the upper quartile. They are the ______ of the lower and upper halves.

10 13 **16** 17 20 22 23 24 **26** 30 31

The lower quartile is ______, and the upper quartile is ______.

Step 3 Draw a number line that spans all of the data values. Mark points below the number line at the least and greatest values, at the median, and at the lower and upper quartiles. Use the lower and upper quartiles to form a ______. Mark the median. Then draw the ______ from the box to the least and greatest values.

Study Hours Per Week

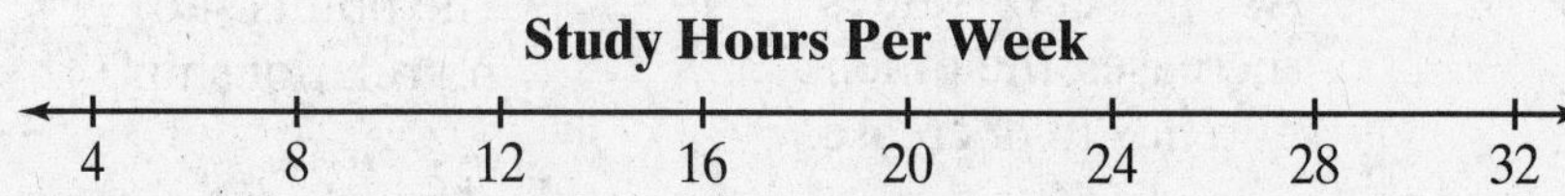

Quick Check

2. Make a box-and-whisker plot for the data below.

10 16 24 11 35 26 29 31 4 53 47 12 21 24 25 26

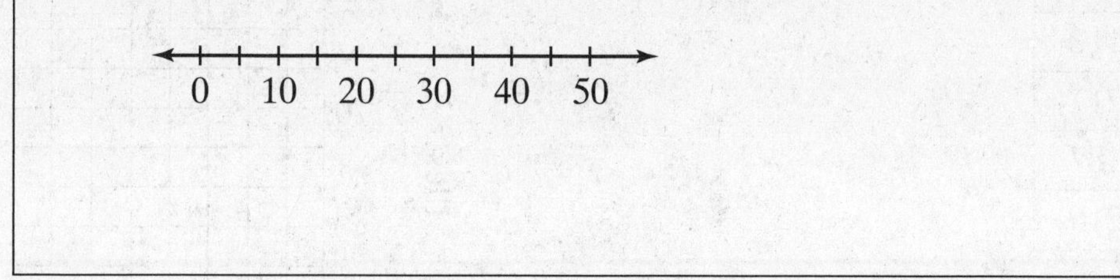

Name ______________________ Class ______________ Date ______________

Lesson 9-7

Making Predictions From Scatter Plots

Lesson Objective To make scatter plots and to use trends to make predictions	**NAEP 2005 Strand:** Data Analysis and Probability **Topics:** Data Representation; Characteristics of Data Sets **Local Standards:** ____________________

Vocabulary

A scatter plot is ____

A trend line is ____

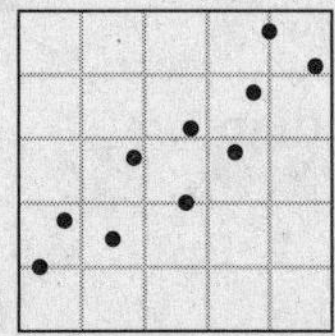

[ ] **trend**
As one set of values increases, the other set tends to increase.

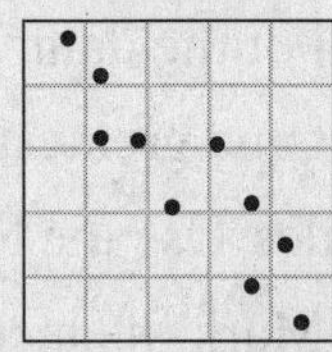

[ ] **trend**
As one set of values increases, the other set tends to decrease.

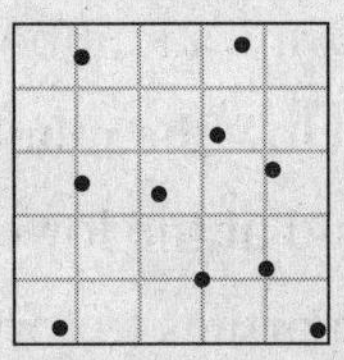

[ ] **trend**
The points show no relationship.

Examples

1 Making Scatter Plots Make a scatter plot for the data.

Miles Traveled and Gas Used

Gas (gal)	Miles
5	150
4	112
7	217
3	87
8	216
5	155

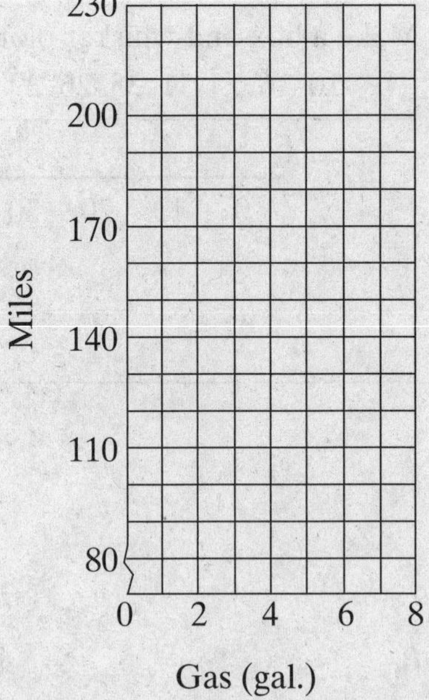

Step 1 Use the horizontal scale to show the [ ].

Use the vertical scale to represent the [ ].

Step 2 Plot each data pair. (5, 150) represents a data pair.

Name ________________ Class ________________ Date ________________

❷ **Drawing Trend Lines** Does the scatter plot in Example 1 show a positive trend, a negative trend, or no trend? Use a trend line to predict the amount of gas used to travel 170 miles.

Step 1 Determine the type of trend. The plotted points go [ ] from left to right. This scatter plot shows a [ ] trend.

Step 2 Draw a line with a [ ] slope. Make sure there are about as many points above the line as there are below it.

Step 3 Find 170 on the [ ] axis. Move right to the trend line. Then move down to the horizontal axis.

It takes about [ ] gallons of gas to travel 170 miles.

Quick Check

1. Make a scatter plot for the data below.

Age and Sleep Time

Age (yr)	1	15	6	19	12	3	5	13	20	6
Sleep Time (h)	15	8.5	9.5	7	9.25	12	11	9	7	9.75

2. Draw a trend line on the scatter plot from Quick Check 1.

Name ______________ Class ______________ Date ______________

Lesson 9-8

Circle Graphs

Lesson Objective To represent and interpret data using circle graphs	**NAEP 2005 Strand:** Data Analysis and Probability **Topic:** Data Representation **Local Standards:** ____________

Vocabulary

A circle graph is ______________

A central angle is ______________

Example

1 Reading Circle Graphs Use this circle graph for a school with a total enrollment of 1,308 students.

Step 1 What percent of the students are in the eighth grade?

Use the key. The enrollment for the eighth grade is graphed in ☐.

So ☐% of the students in Central Middle School are in the eighth grade. →

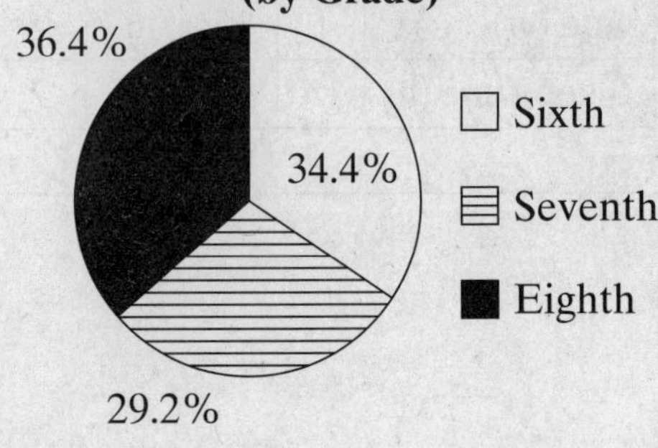

Step 2 How many students are in the eighth grade?

1,308 · ☐% = 1,308 ☒ ☐ ENTER ☐

There are about ☐ students enrolled in the eighth grade.

Quick Check

1. a. What percent of the students are in sixth grade?

b. How many students are in the sixth grade?

Name ______________________ Class ______________ Date ______________

Example

2 Making Circle Graphs Make a circle graph for the results of a survey of students' favorite season.

Favorite Season	Number
Spring	20
Summer	53
Fall	28
Winter	19

Step 1 Add each number of responses to find the total number of people in the survey.

☐ + ☐ + ☐ + ☐ = ☐

Step 2 Use proportions to find the measures of the central angles.

$\frac{20}{\square} = \frac{a}{\square}$ $\qquad$ $\frac{53}{\square} = \frac{b}{\square}$

$a = \square$ $\qquad$ $b = \square$

$\frac{28}{\square} = \frac{c}{\square}$ $\qquad$ $\frac{19}{\square} = \frac{d}{\square}$

$c = \square$ $\qquad$ $d = \square$

Step 3 Use a compass to draw a circle. Mark the center of the circle and draw a radius. Construct a central angle with a protractor.

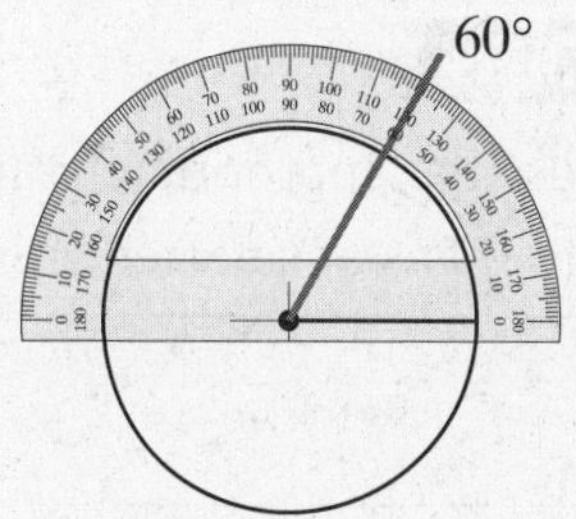

Step 4 Construct the other central angles using a protractor.

Step 5 Label each sector and title your graph. Set up a key to make the graph easier to read.

Favorite Season

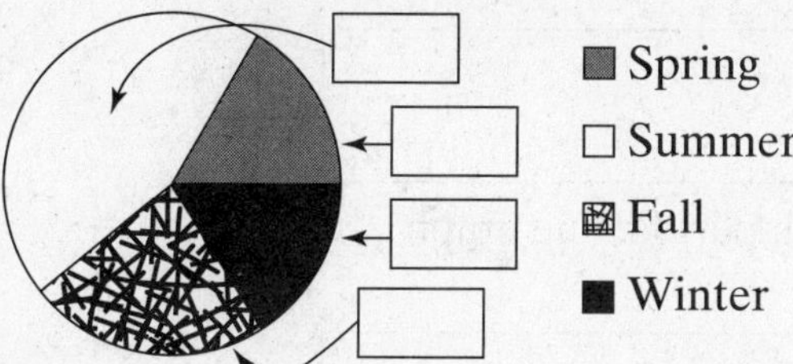

Quick Check

2. Make a circle graph for the data below.

Fuel Used by Types of Vehicles (billions of gallons)

Cars	Vans, Pickups, SUVs	Trucks	Other
75	55	37	1

SOURCE: U.S. Census Bureau. Go to **www.PHSchool.com** for a data update. Web Code: asg-9041

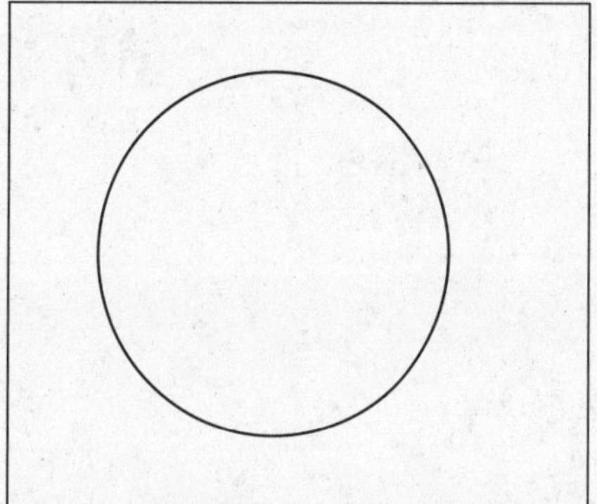

Name ______________________ Class ______________ Date ______________

Lesson 9-9

Choosing an Appropriate Graph

Lesson Objective	**NAEP 2005 Strand:** Data Analysis and Probability
To choose appropriate graphs to represent different data	**Topic:** Data Representation
	Local Standards: ____________________

Example

1 Choosing an Appropriate Graph Choose the appropriate graph—stem-and-leaf plot or circle graph—to display the data about a survey of students' favorite type of music. Explain your choice.

Use a ______________ to compare and find patterns in data that measure the same thing, which is not the case here. The limited number of categories and the percents in the survey adding up to 100% make the ______________ a good choice.

Quick Check

1. Choose the appropriate graph to display each set of data. Explain your choice.

   a. life spans of selected animals: bar graph or scatter plot?

   b. average household income and number of cars: histogram or scatter plot?

   c. price of a gallon of gas over a twelve-month period: line graph or circle graph?

Example

❷ **Club Membership** This table shows membership in the Computer Club over several years. Decide which type of graph would be most appropriate. Explain your choice and draw the graph.

Computer Club Members

Year	Number of Members
1999	13
2000	18
2001	23
2002	24
2003	28

Since the data show a change over time, a ________ graph is appropriate. Complete the graph.

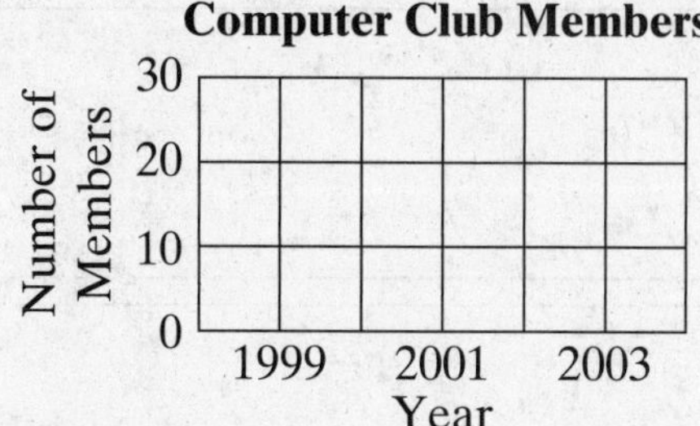

Quick Check

2. Decide which type of graph would be the most appropriate for the data in the table. Explain your choice. Then draw the graph.

Weekly Budget

Budget Item	Lunch	Recreation	Clothes	Savings
Amount	$27.00	$13.50	$31.50	$18.00

Name ______________________ Class ______________ Date ______________

Lesson 10-1

Theoretical and Experimental Probability

Lesson Objective	**NAEP 2005 Strand:** Data Analysis and Probability
To find theoretical probability, experimental probability, and odds	**Topic:** Probability **Local Standards:** ____________

Vocabulary and Key Concepts

Experimental Probability

$$P(\text{event}) = \frac{\text{number of times event occurs}}{\text{total number of trials}}$$

Odds

[ ] of an event is the ratio number of favorable outcomes : number of unfavorable outcomes.

[ ] an event is the ratio number of unfavorable outcomes : number of favorable outcomes.

Experimental probability is ______________________

Example

1 Finding Experimental Probability A gardener plants 250 sunflower seeds and 210 germinate. Find the experimental probability that a sunflower seed will germinate.

$P(\text{germinate}) = \frac{\text{number of seeds that germinate}}{[\ ]}$ ← **Write the probability ratio.**

$= \frac{[\ ]}{[\ ]}$ ← **Substitute.**

$= [\ ]$ ← **Divide.**

The probability that a sunflower seed will germinate is [ ]%.

Examples

❷ Identifying the Type of Probability The table shows the number of heads on 50 flips of a coin. Does 44% represent *experimental* or *theoretical* probability?

Number of Coin Flips	Number of Heads	Probability of Flipping Heads
50	22	44%

The table shows the actual number of heads that were flipped in 50 flips of a coin. 44% represents the ______ probability.

❸ Determining Odds Suppose you select a pen at random from a box containing three red pens and four blue pens. What are the odds in favor of selecting a red pen?

Three pens are red and four are blue. The odds in favor of selecting a red pen at random are ___ : ___.

Quick Check

1. Use the table at the right. Find the experimental probability of getting heads.

Heads	~~IIII~~ III
Tails	~~IIII~~ ~~IIII~~ II

2. A bag contains two red cubes and three white cubes. Does $P(\text{red}) = \frac{2}{5}$ represent *experimental* or *theoretical* probability?

3. In Example 3, what are the odds against selecting a red pen at random?

Name ______________________ Class ______________ Date ____________

Lesson 10-2

Making Predictions

Lesson Objective To make predictions based on theoretical and experimental probabilities	**NAEP 2005 Strand:** Data Analysis and Probability **Topic:** Probability **Local Standards:** ____________

Example

1 Using Probability A jar is filled with marbles, and the probability of choosing a yellow marble is $\frac{2}{5}$. If the jar has a total of 120 marbles, how many yellow marbles are in the jar?

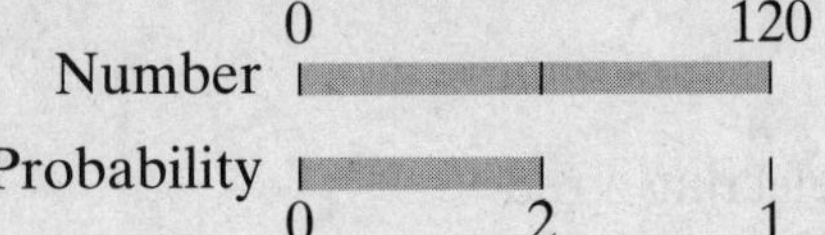

← **A diagram can help you understand the problem.**

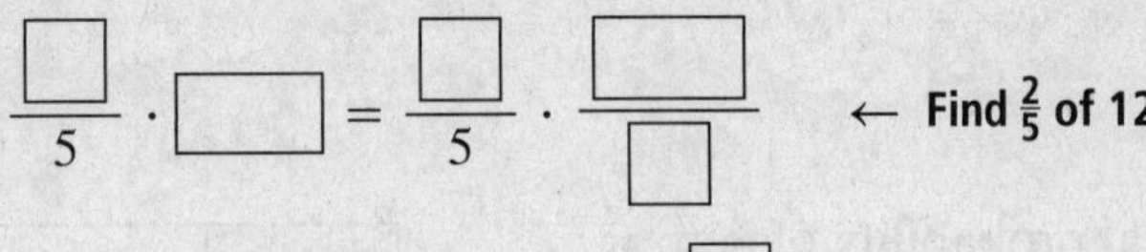

← **Find $\frac{2}{5}$ of 120.**

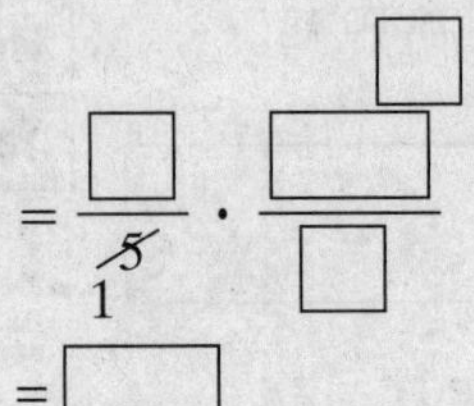

= ☐ ← **Simplify.**

There are ☐ yellow marbles in the jar.

Quick Check

1. According to game rules, the probability that a bottled-water cap can be redeemed for a prize is 1 out of 40. How many winning caps are likely among 500 bottles?

Name ______________________ Class ______________ Date ______________

Example

❷ Using Survey Results In a random survey of students, 42 out of 80 students plan to vote for Maria for student council president. If 400 people vote in the election, about how many votes will Maria receive?

Method 1 Write a proportion.

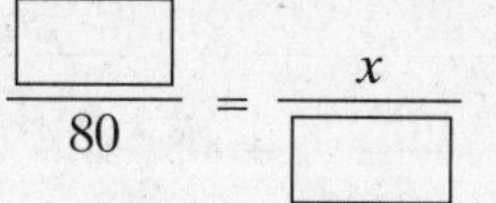

← **A diagram can help you understand the problem.**

$\frac{\square}{80} = \frac{x}{\square}$ ← **Set up a proportion.**

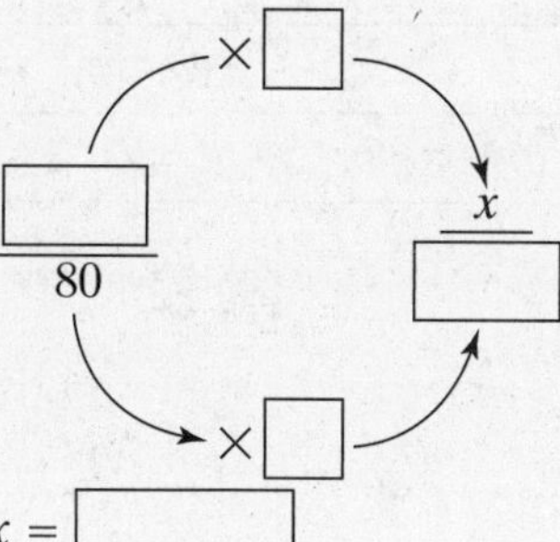

← **Use number sense to find a common multiplier.**

$x = \square$ ← **Simplify** $\square \times \square$.

Maria is likely to receive ☐ votes.

Method 2 From the survey, find the probability that a voter will vote for Maria. Apply this probability to all the voters.

$\frac{\square}{80} = \frac{\square}{40}$, or ☐% ← **The event "vote for Maria" occurred in 42 out of 80 trials.**

Find ☐% of 400.

☐% of 400 = ☐ × 400 ← **Find ☐% of 400.**

= ☐ ← **Simplify.**

Maria is likely to receive ☐ votes.

Quick Check

2. In a random survey of voters, 19 out of 60 people said they would vote for Mr. Chiu. If 1,200 people vote in the election, predict how many votes Mr. Chiu will receive.

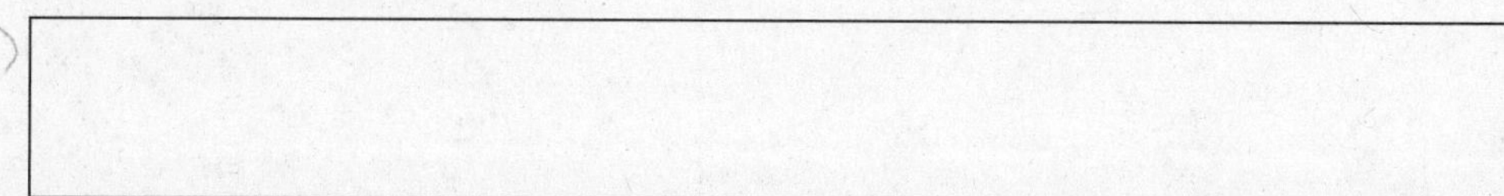

Name ______________ Class ______________ Date ______________

Lesson 10-3

Conducting a Survey

Lesson Objective To identify random samples and biased questions and to judge conclusions based on survey results	**NAEP 2005 Strand:** Data Analysis and Probability **Topic:** Experiments and Samples **Local Standards:** ______________

Vocabulary

A population is ______________

A sample is ______________

A random sample is ______________

____

Biased questions are ______________

Example

1 Determining Random Samples Determine whether each survey uses a random sample. Describe the population of the sample.

a. To find out how often students in your school go to movies, you select names at random from the school directory to interview.

This is ______________ sample. The population is ______________.

b. A country radio station asks listeners to call in and give their favorite song.

This is ______________ sample. The views of the people who listen to the radio station may not represent the views of all country music fans or all radio listeners. The population is country music fans who ______________.

Quick Check

1. To find out the type of music people in a city prefer, you survey people from 18 to 30 years old. Is the sample random? Explain.

____

Examples

❷ Identifying Bias in Questions Determine whether each question is biased.

a. Do you enjoy popular songs or old songs?

This question is [ ]. The terms "popular" and "old" are not neutral.

b. Do you watch more than one hour of television a week?

This question is [ ]. It does not influence the respondent.

❸ Judging Valid Conclusions To find the reading preferences in her town, Nadine conducted a survey of people entering the public library. From the results, she concluded that 20% of the people in her town preferred nonfiction books. Which of the following best describes the reason her conclusion may not be valid?

Romance	22
Science Fiction	18
Classics	28
Nonfiction	20
Other	12

A. The survey should have included fewer choices.
B. The survey should have included more choices.
C. The survey should have included a random sample from the people at the library.
D. The survey should have included a random sample from the people in town.

Nadine surveyed only people entering the public library. She did not get a random sample of [ ]. The answer is choice [ ].

Quick Check

2. What bias is there in the following question: "Which do you prefer, in-line skating or ice skating?" Revise the question to be unbiased.

3. In Example 3, suppose Nadine had surveyed only women. Would her conclusion be more valid? Explain why or why not.

Name ______________________ Class ______________ Date ______________

Lesson 10-4

Independent and Dependent Events

Lesson Objective	NAEP 2005 Strand: Data Analysis and Probability
To find the probabilities of independent and dependent events	Topic: Probability
	Local Standards: ____________

Vocabulary and Key Concepts

Independent Events

If A and B are independent events, then $P(A, \text{then } B) = P(A) \cdot P(B)$.

Dependent Events

If A and B are dependent events, then $P(A, \text{then } B) = P(A) \cdot P(B \text{ after } A)$.

Two events are ______________ if occurrence of one event does not affect the probability of the occurrence of the other.

Two events are ______________ if the outcome of one event affects the outcome of the other.

Example

1 Probability of Independent Events A box contains 3 red marbles and 7 blue ones. You draw a marble at random, replace it, and draw another. Find $P(\text{blue, then blue})$.

Because the first marble is replaced, these are ______________ events.

$P(\text{blue, then blue}) = P(\square) \cdot P(\square)$

$= \frac{\square}{\square} \cdot \frac{\square}{\square}$ ← **Substitute.**

$= \frac{\square}{\square}$ ← **Multiply.**

The probability of choosing a blue and then another blue is $\frac{\square}{\square}$.

Name ______________________ Class ______________ Date ______________

Example

❷ Probability of Dependent Events From a class of 12 girls and 14 boys, you select two students at random. What is the probability of selecting two boys?

A. $\frac{3}{13}$ **B.** $\frac{7}{25}$ **C.** $\frac{7}{26}$ **D.** $\frac{18}{25}$

First Student $P(\text{boy}) = \frac{\square}{26}$ ← $\square$ **of the students are boys.**

Second Student $P(\text{boy after boy}) = \frac{\square}{\square}$ ← $\square$ **boys are left of** $\square$ **students.**

$P(\text{boy then boy}) = P(\text{boy}) \cdot P(\text{boy after boy})$ ← **Use the formula for dependent events.**

$= \frac{\square}{26} \cdot \frac{\square}{\square}$ ← **Substitute.**

$= \frac{\square}{\square} = \frac{\square}{\square}$ ← **Multiply and simplify.**

The probability of selecting two boys is $\frac{\square}{\square}$. The correct answer is choice $\square$.

Quick Check

1. Use the information in Example 1 to find P(blue, then red).

2. In Example 2, find the probability that first a boy and then a girl are selected.

3. Are the events dependent or independent? Explain.

a. Flip a coin and then flip it again.

b. Pick a name from a hat. Without replacing it, pick another.

Name ______________________ Class ______________ Date ______________

Lesson 10-5

Permutations

Lesson Objective	**NAEP 2005 Strand:** Data Analysis and Probability
To find the number of permutations of a set of objects	**Topic:** Probability **Local Standards:** ____________

Vocabulary and Key Concepts

The Counting Principle

Suppose there are *m* ways of making one choice and *n* ways of making a second choice. Then there are ______ ways to make the first choice followed by the second choice.

Permutation Notation

The expression ${}_nP_r$ represents the number of permutations of *n* objects chosen *r* at a time.

$${}_{25}P_2 = 25 \cdot 24 = 600$$

25 objects **groups of 2 (two factors)**

A permutation is ____

____

A factorial is ____

____

Example

1 Permutations Using a Diagram In how many ways can three people form a line? Use the letters A, B, and C to represent each person.

A — B — ☐ ① (A, B, ☐)
A — ☐ — B ② (A, ☐, ☐)

B — ☐ — C ③ (B, ☐, ☐)
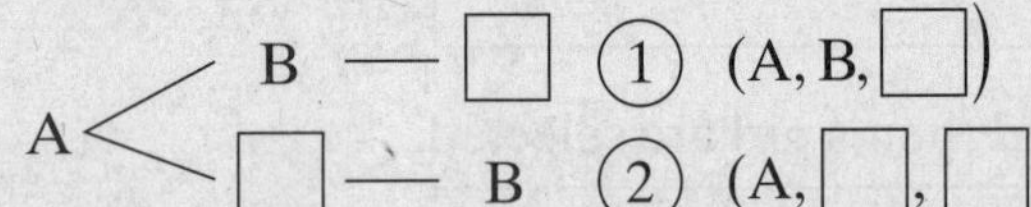
B — C — ☐ ④ (B, ☐, ☐)

☐ — A — ☐ ⑤ (☐, ☐, ☐)
☐ — ☐ — ☐ ⑥ (☐, ☐, ☐)

Three people can line up in ______ different ways. This means that there are ______ permutations.

Name ______________________ Class ______________ Date ______________

Example

2 Using the Counting Principle Suppose you choose four books to read out of six choices. In how many different sequences can you read them?

There are six books you can read first, five books you can read second, four books you can read third, and three books you can read fourth.

$\square \cdot \square \cdot \square \cdot \square = \square$ ← **Use the counting principle.**

There are $\square$ ways in which you can read the books.

3 Permutations Using Factorials Megan created a password using the numbers 1, 2, 3, 4, and 5. Find the number of possible passwords.

$5! = \square \cdot \square \cdot \square \cdot \square \cdot \square = \square$ ← **Simplify.**

There are $\square$ possible passwords.

Quick Check

1. Four geese fly in line. Use a tree diagram to find how many different orders they can fly.

2. A principal at a school presents awards to four out of seven students. How many different ways can the principal give out the awards?

3. Simplify each expression.

   a. 2!   b. 6!   c. 4!

Name ______________________ Class ______________ Date ______________

Lesson 10-6

Combinations

Lesson Objective	**NAEP 2005 Strand:** Data Analysis and Probability
To find the number of combinations of a set of objects using lists and combination notation	**Topic:** Probability **Local Standards:** ____________________

Vocabulary and Key Concepts

Combination Notation

The expression ${}_nC_r$ represents the number of combinations of n objects chosen r at a time.

$${}_nC_r = \frac{{}_nP_r}{r!}$$

Example ${}_7C_3 = \frac{{}_7P_3}{3!} = \frac{7 \cdot 6 \cdot 5}{3 \cdot 2 \cdot 1} = 35$

A combination is ____

____

Example

1 Finding Combinations How many groups of two can be formed from a committee of six members?

Use the letters A, B, C, D, E, and F to represent the six possible members.

Step 1 Make an organized list of all the possible combinations of members.

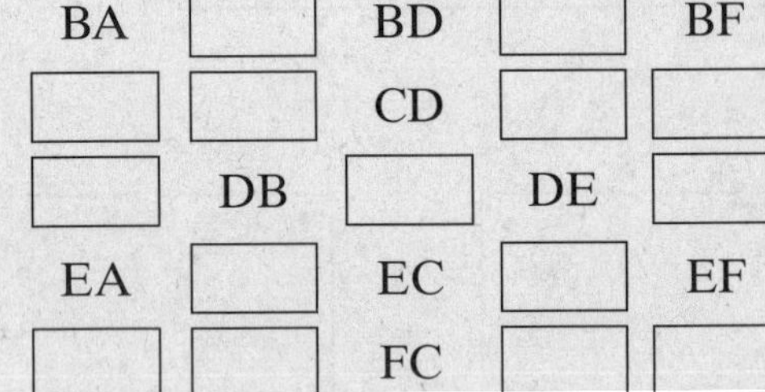

Step 2 Cross out any group that is a duplicate of another.

AB	AC	☐	AE	☐
~~BA~~	☐	BD	☐	BF
☐	☐	CD	☐	☐
☐	~~DB~~	☐	DE	☐
~~EA~~	☐	~~EC~~	☐	EF
☐	☐	~~FC~~	☐	☐

Step 3 Count the number of groups that remain.

There are ☐ different ways to form a group with two members.

Example

❷ Using Combination Notation Find the number of ways you can choose 3 pencils from a box of 8 colored pencils.

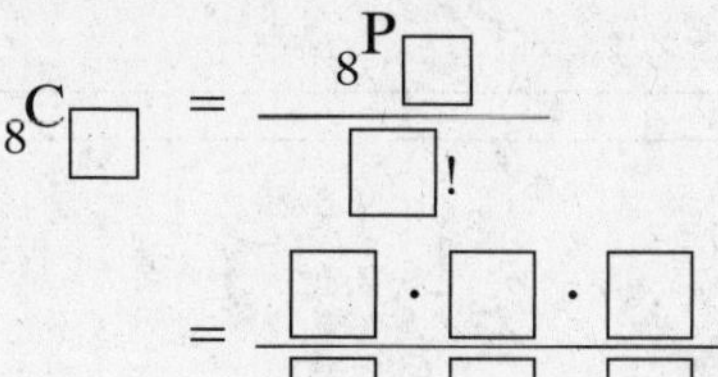

$${}_{8}C_{\square} = \frac{{}_{8}P_{\square}}{\square!}$$ ← **The numerator shows the number of ways to arrange 3 pencils out of 8.** ← **The denominator shows there are 3! arrangements of each group of 3 pencils.**

$$= \frac{\square \cdot \square \cdot \square}{\square \cdot \square \cdot \square}$$ ← **Simplify $_{\square}P_{\square}$ and $\square$!.**

$$= \square$$ ← **Simplify.**

There are $\square$ different combinations of colored pencils.

Quick Check

1. Make an organized list to find the number of different groups of three tutors your teacher can choose from four students.

2. Simplify each expression.

a. $_{7}C_{5}$

b. $_{8}C_{4}$

c. $_{5}C_{3}$

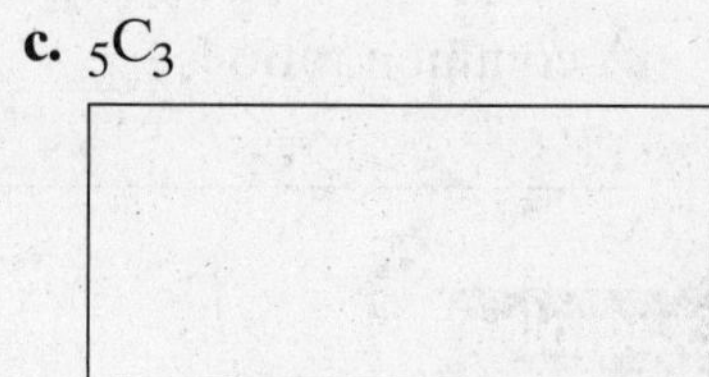

Name ______________________ Class ______________ Date ____________

Lesson 11-1

Sequences

Lesson Objective To write rules for sequences and to use the rules to find terms in a sequence	**NAEP 2005 Strand:** Algebra **Topic:** Patterns, Relations, and Functions **Local Standards:** ____________

Vocabulary

A sequence is ______________________

A term is ______________________

You are using inductive reasoning when ______________________

An arithmetic sequence is ______________________

A common difference is ______________________

A geometric sequence is ______________________

A common ratio is ______________________

Examples

1 Finding Terms of a Sequence Find the next three terms in the sequence 12.4, 11.2, 10, 8.8, . . .

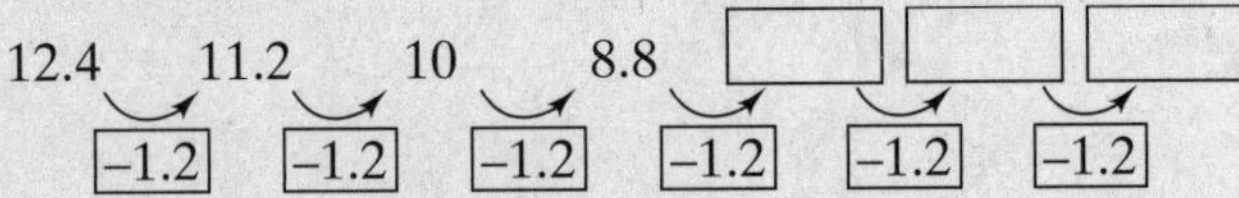

You find each term by adding ☐ to the previous term. The next three terms are ☐, ☐, and ☐.

2 Evaluating Algebraic Expressions Find the first four terms of the sequence represented by the expression $1 + 2(n - 1)$.

A. 0, 2, 4, 6 **B.** 1, 3, 5, 7 **C.** 2, 4, 6, 8 **D.** 3, 5, 6, 9

Position, (*n*)	1	2	3	4
1 + 2(*n* − 1)	☐ + 2(☐ − 1)	☐ + 2(☐ − 1)	☐ + 2(☐ − 1)	☐ + 2(☐ − 1)
Term	☐	☐	☐	☐

The correct answer is choice ☐.

Name ________________ Class ________________ Date ________________

❸ **Writing an Algebraic Expression** Write an algebraic expression for the sequence $\frac{1}{2}, 1, \frac{3}{2}, 2, \ldots$ Then find the 20th term in the sequence.

Make a table that pairs each term's position with its value.

Position, (*n*)	1	2	3	4	...	20
	$\square \cdot \frac{1}{2}$	$\square \cdot \frac{1}{2}$	$\square \cdot \frac{1}{2}$	$\square \cdot \frac{1}{2}$	$n \cdot \frac{1}{2}$	$\square \cdot \frac{1}{2}$
Term	$\square$	$\square$	$\square$	$\square$	$\square$	$\blacksquare$

You find a term in the sequence by multiplying the term's position number by ______. The algebraic expression ______ represents the sequence.

______ = ______(20) ← **Substitute 20 for *n* to find the 20th term.**

= ______ ← **Simplify.**

The 20th term in the sequence is ______.

❹ **Describing a Geometric Sequence**

A scientist isolates 10 cells in a dish. The next day there are 40 cells in the dish. The day after, there are 160 cells. Describe the geometric sequence and find the next three terms.

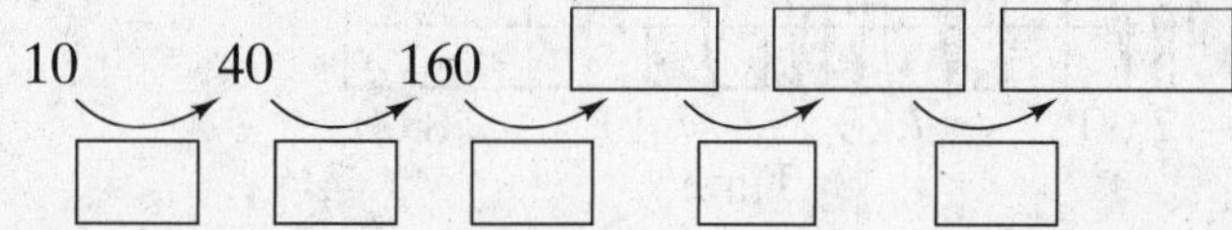

The common ratio is ______. You can describe the sequence as

Start with ______ *and multiply by* ______ *repeatedly.*

The next three terms are ______, ______, and ______.

Quick Check

1. Find the next three terms in each sequence.

   a. 5, 12, 19, 26, . . .

   b. 4, 9, 14, 19, . . .

   c. 2, 12, 22, 32, . . .

2. Find the first four terms of the sequence represented by $3(n - 1)$.

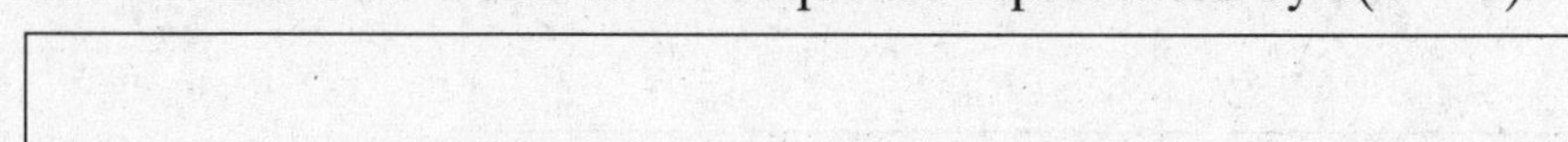

3. Write an algebraic expression for the sequence −2, −4, −6, −8, . . . Then find the 20th term.

4. Find the common ratio in the sequence 0.1, 1, 10, 100, . . . Describe the sequence and find the next three terms.

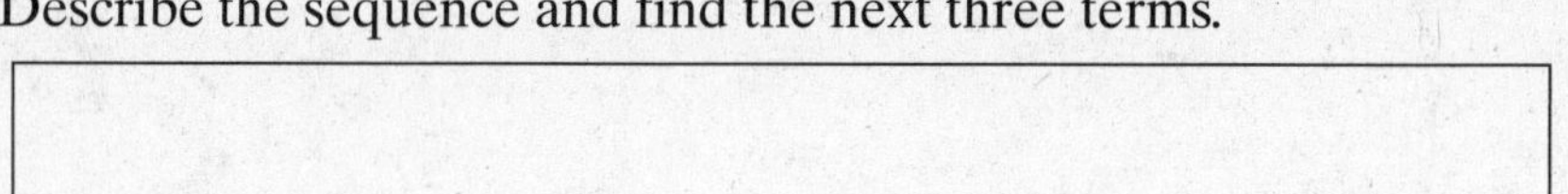

Name ______________________ Class ______________ Date ______________

Lesson 11-2

Relating Graphs to Events

Lesson Objective	**Local Standards:** ______________
To interpret and sketch graphs that represent real-world situations	

Example

1 Interpreting a Graph The line graph below shows the speed of a car traveling across town.

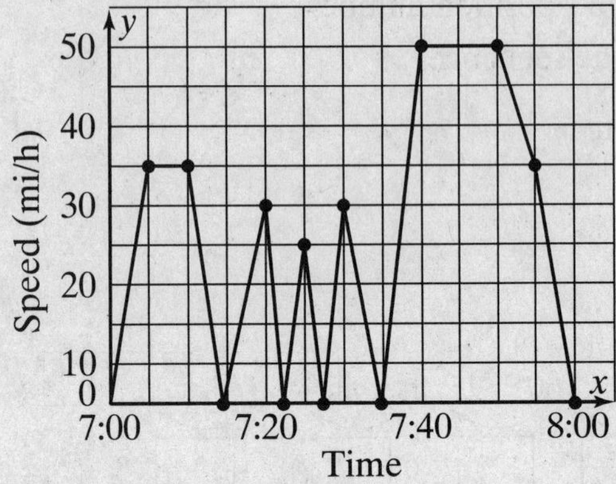

a. How long did the trip take?

Time is shown on the ☐-axis. The trip lasted ☐ hour, from ☐ to ☐.

b. What was the fastest speed?

The fastest speed was ☐ mi/h. This speed was maintained between ☐ and ☐.

Quick Check

1. Use the graph in Example 1. Between which two times did the car's speed increase the most?

☐

Name ______________________ Class ______________ Date ______________

Example

② Sketching a Graph An athlete jogs for 30 min, sprints for 5 min, and walks for 10 min. Sketch and label a graph showing his speed.

As the athlete starts jogging, the speed increases and then becomes constant for about 30 minutes. Then the speed increases again for the sprint and becomes constant for about 5 minutes. Then the speed decreases when the athlete slows to a walk for 10 minutes.

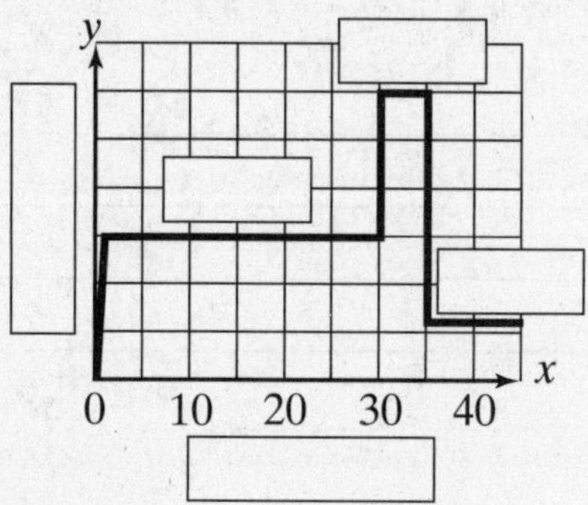

Quick Check

2. You walk to your friend's house. For the first 10 min, you walk from home to a park. For the next 5 min, you watch a ball game in the park. For the last 5 min, you run to your friend's house. Sketch and label a graph showing your distance from home during your trip.

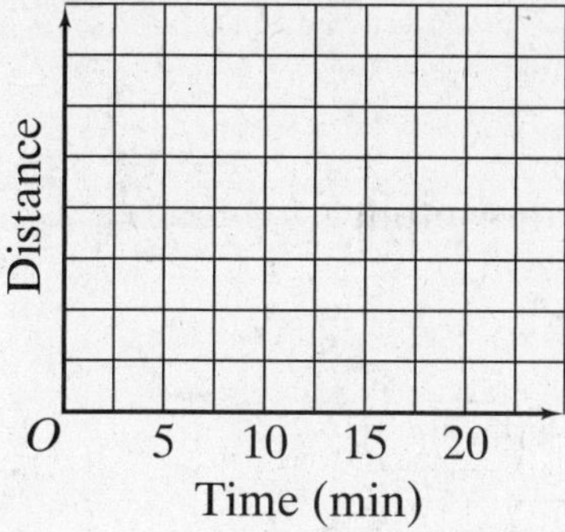

Name ____________________ Class ____________________ Date ____________________

Lesson 11-3

Functions

Lesson Objective	**NAEP 2005 Strand:** Algebra
To represent functions with equations, tables, and function notation	**Topics:** Patterns, Relations, and Functions; Algebraic Representations **Local Standards:** ____________________

Vocabulary

A function is ____________________

____

A function rule is ____________________

____

Examples

1 Representing Functions Complete the table for $p = 4s$.

Input s	$p = 4s$	Output p
3	$4 \times \square = \square$	
5	$4 \times \square = \square$	
7	$4 \times \square = \square$	
9	$4 \times \square = \square$	

2 Evaluating a Function Rule Use the rule $f(x) = 3x - 1$. Find the output values $f(2)$, $f(-1)$, and $f(5)$.

$f(x) = 3x - 1$ ← **Write the function rule.** → $f(x) = 3x - 1$

$f(2) = 3 \cdot \square - 1$ ← **Substitute the input value for *x*.** → $f(-1) = 3 \cdot (\square) - 1$

$= \square - 1$ ← **Simplify.** → $= \square - 1$

$= \square$ $\qquad$ $= \square$

$f(x) = 3x - 1$ ← **Write the function rule.**

$f(5) = 3 \cdot \square - 1$ ← **Substitute the input value for *x*.**

$= \square - 1$ ← **Simplify.**

$= \square$

Example

3 Using Function Notation Use function notation to show the relationship between the total number of cars and the number of tires. Identify your variables.

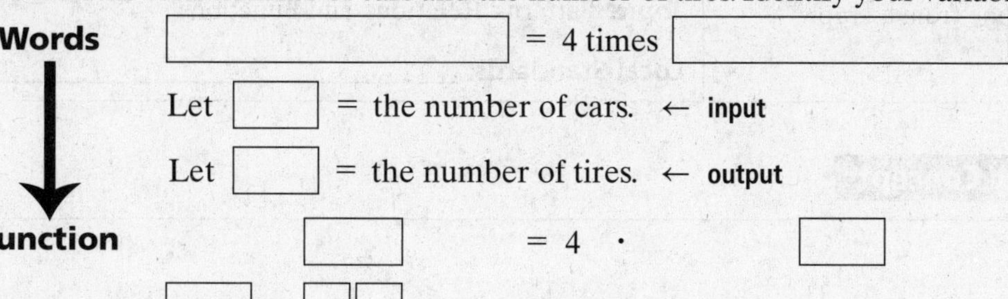

Quick Check

1. The deposit on a drink container is \$.10 in the state of Michigan. Use the function rule $d = 0.1c$. Make a table of input-output pairs to show the total deposits on 5, 10, and 15 containers.

Input c	$d = 0.1c$	Output d	Total Deposit (\$)

2. Use the function rule $f(x) = -4x + 12$. Find $f(-7)$ and $f(3)$.

3. Use the function in Example 3. Find $f(6)$. What does $f(6)$ represent?

Name ________________ Class ________________ Date ________________

Lesson 11-4

Understanding Slope

Lesson Objective To find the slope of a line from a graph or table	**NAEP 2005 Strand:** Algebra **Topic:** Patterns, Relations, and Functions **Local Standards:** ________________

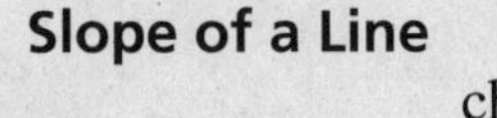

Vocabulary and Key Concepts

Slope of a Line

slope of a line = $\dfrac{\text{change in } \square\text{-coordinates}}{\text{change in } \square\text{-coordinates}}$ ← rise / ← run

Slope is ________________

Examples

1 Finding the Slope of a Line Using coordinates, find the slope of the line between $P\,(-2, 3)$ and $Q\,(-1, -1)$.

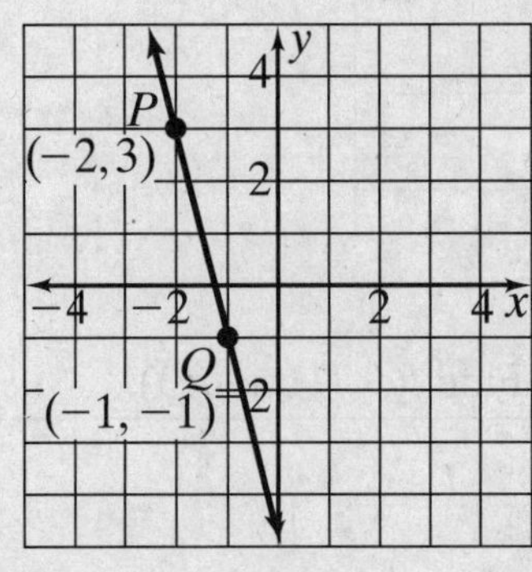

slope $= \dfrac{\text{change in } \square\text{-coordinates}}{\text{change in } \square\text{-coordinates}}$

$= \dfrac{\square - (\square)}{\square - (\square)}$ ← **Subtract coordinates of Q from coordinates of P.**

$= \dfrac{\square}{\square}$ or $\square$ ← **Simplify.**

2 Slopes of Horizontal and Vertical Lines Find the slope of each line. State whether the slope is zero or undefined.

a. line k

slope $= \dfrac{1 - (\square)}{\square - 2} = \dfrac{\square}{\square}$

Division by zero is $\square$.

The slope of a vertical line is $\square$.

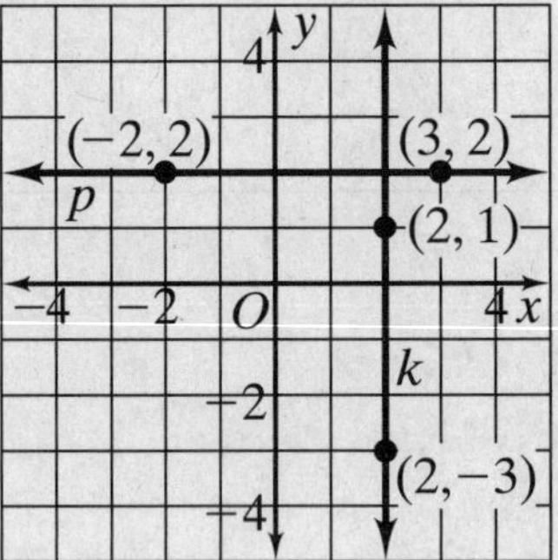

b. line p

slope $= \dfrac{2 - \square}{\square - 3} = \dfrac{\square}{\square} = \square$

The slope of a horizontal line is $\square$.

Name ______________________ Class ______________ Date ______________

Example

3 Finding Slope From a Table Graph the data in the table. Connect the points with a line. Then find the rate of change.

Distance (mi)	Cost ($)
100	25
200	50
300	75
400	100

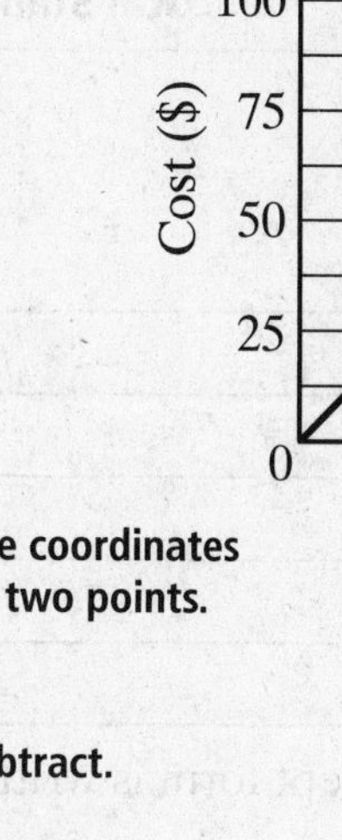

$$\text{rate of change} = \text{slope} = \frac{\text{change in } \square}{\text{change in } \square}$$

$$= \frac{75 - \square}{\square - 100} \quad \leftarrow \textbf{Use coordinates of two points.}$$

$$= \frac{\square}{\square} \quad \leftarrow \textbf{Subtract.}$$

$$= \frac{\square}{\square} \quad \leftarrow \textbf{Simplify.}$$

The cost increases by $\$\square$ for every $\square$ miles traveled.

Quick Check

1. Find the slope of each line.

a.

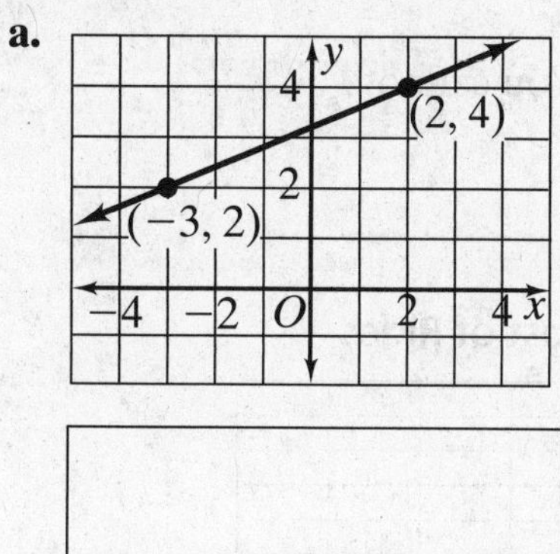

b.

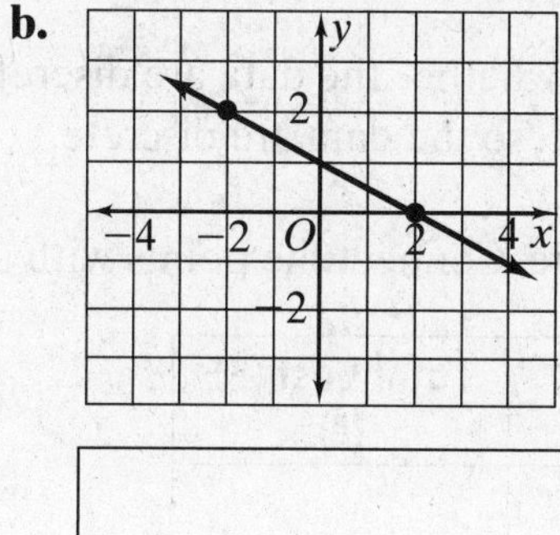

2. Find the slope of a line through the points (3, 1) and (3, −2). State whether the slope is zero or undefined.

3. Graph the data in the table and connect the points with a line. Then find the slope.

x	−1	0	1	2
y	2	0	−2	−4

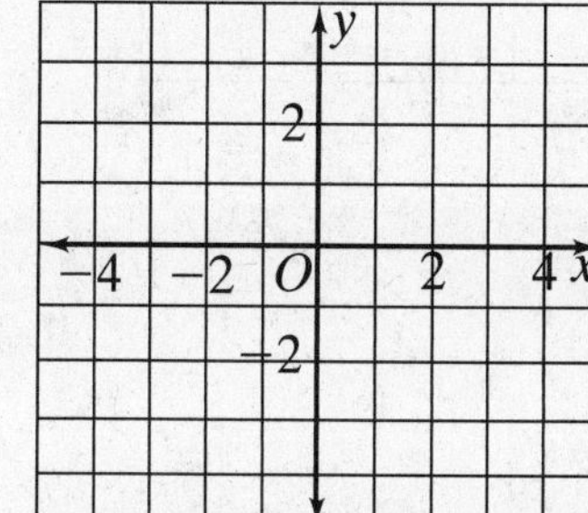

Slope = $\square$

Name ______________________ Class ______________ Date ______________

Lesson 11-5

Graphing Linear Functions

Lesson Objective	NAEP 2005 Strand: Algebra
To use tables and equations to graph linear functions	Topic: Algebraic Representations Local Standards: ____________

Vocabulary

Discrete data are ______________________

Continuous data are ______________________

The *y*-intercept is ______________________

An equation written in slope-intercept form is written in the form ______________________

A linear function is ______________________

Example

1 Graphing Discrete Data The function $c = 4r$ represents the cost (in dollars) of riding r rides at an amusement park. Make a table and graph the function.

Step 1 Determine whether the data are discrete or continuous. You cannot ride part of the ride, so the data are discrete.

Step 2 Make a table. Connect the points with a dashed line.

Number of Rides (r)	Total Cost ($) (c)

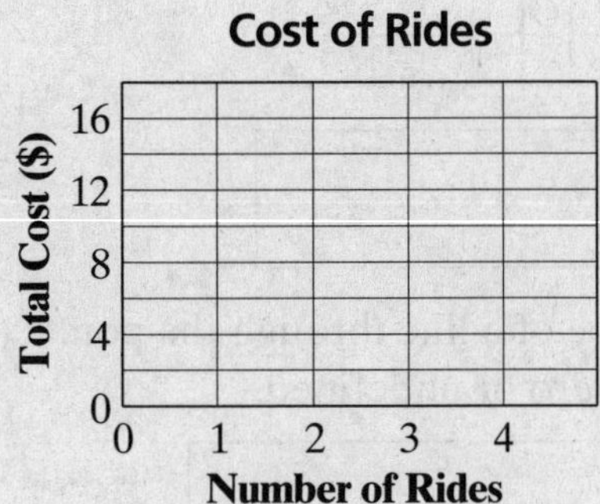

Name ______________________ Class ______________ Date ____________

❷ **Graphing Continuous Data** Amber earns \$7 per hour. Make a table to describe Amber's earnings (output) as a function of the number of hours she works (input). Graph the function.

Amber can work for part of an hour so the data are continuous. Plot the data and connect the data points with a solid line.

Input (h)	0	1	2	3	4	5
Output (\$)	0					

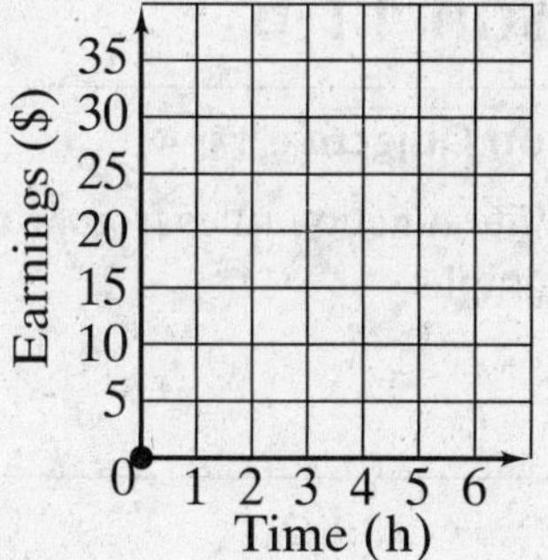

Quick Check

1. **Tickets** The function $c = 15t$ represents the cost (in dollars) of t adult tickets to a museum. Make a table and graph the function.

t				
c				

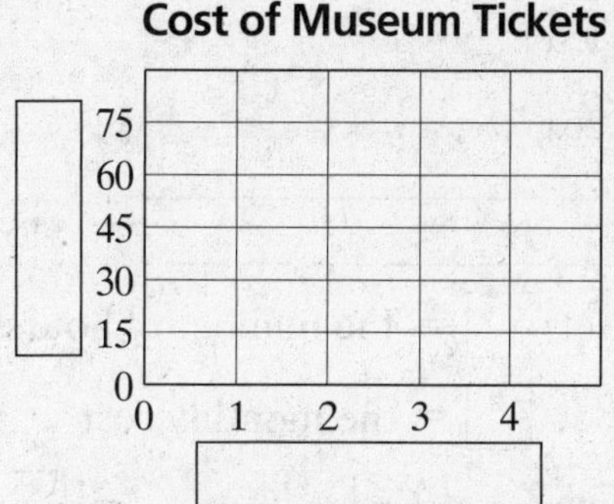

2. The function $h = 4{,}000 - 600m$ gives the height h of a skydiver in feet after she has been falling for m minutes. Make a table and graph the function.

m	*h*

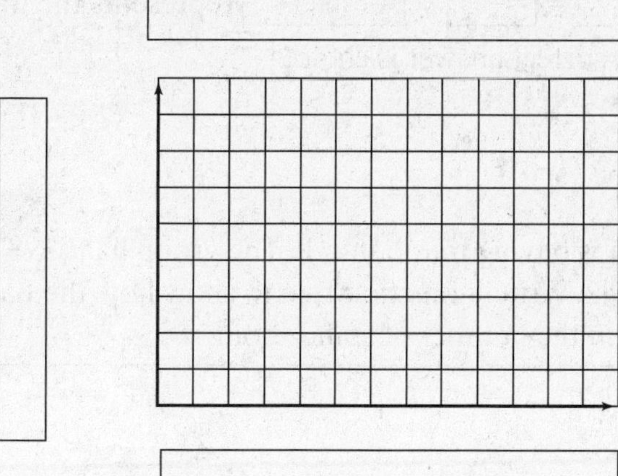

Lesson 11-6

Writing Rules for Linear Functions

Lesson Objective	**NAEP 2005 Strand:** Algebra
To write function rules from words, tables, and graphs	**Topic:** Patterns, Relations, and Functions; Algebraic Representations; Variables, Expressions, and Operations
	Local Standards: ____________________

Example

1 Writing a Function Rule From Words A rate for Internet access is \$15 per month plus \$.25 per hour of use. Write a function rule to show how the monthly bill depends on the number of hours used.

A. $y = 0.25 + 15x$

B. $y = 15 + 0.25x$

C. $y = 15 - 0.25x$

D. $y = 0.25x - 15$

Words 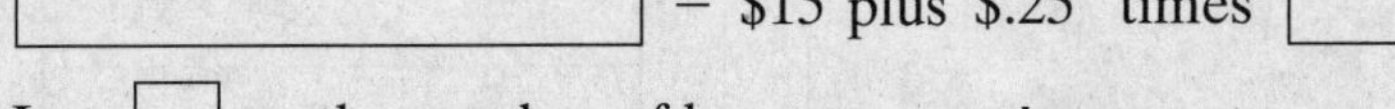

= \$15 plus \$.25 times

Let ☐ = the number of hours. ← **input**

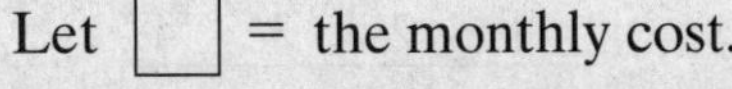

Let ☐ = the monthly cost. ← **output**

Function ☐ = ☐ + ☐ · ☐

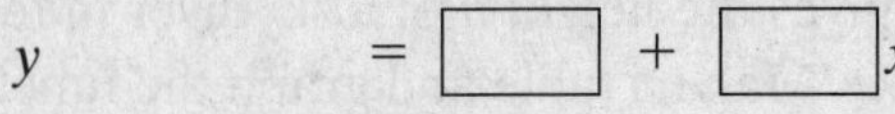

y = ☐ + ☐ x

The function rule ☐ = ☐ + ☐ represents the monthly cost for x hours of use. The correct answer is choice ☐.

Quick Check

1. A school orchestra is buying music stands. The group has \$298 in its treasury. Each stand costs \$42. Write a function rule to show how the balance in the treasury depends on the number of stands bought.

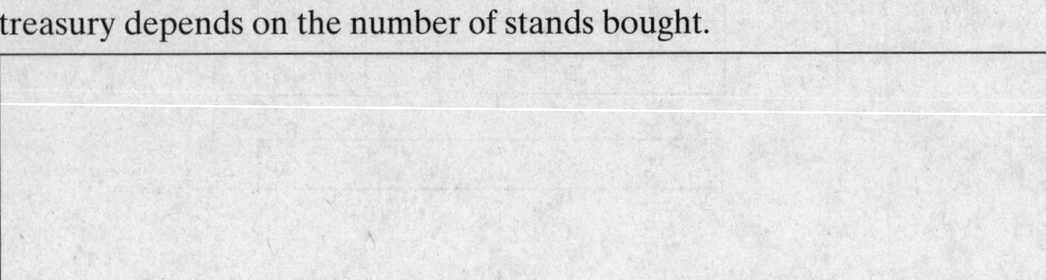

Name ____________________ Class ____________ Date ____________

Examples

❷ Writing a Rule From a Table Do the values in the table below represent a linear function? If so, write a function rule.

+1 +1 +1 ← **Find the changes in inputs.**

x	0	1	2	3
y	5	2	–1	–4

–3 –3 –3 ← **Find the changes in outputs.**

$$\frac{\text{change in } y}{\text{change in } x} = \frac{-3}{1} = \frac{-3}{1} = \frac{-3}{1}$$ ← **Compare the changes as ratios.**

Since each ratio is the same, the function ☐ linear. The slope is ☐. The point (0, ☐) lies on the graph of the function. So the *y*-intercept is ☐. Use the slope-intercept form to write a function rule.

$y =$ ☐ $x +$ ☐ ← **Substitute ☐ for *m* and ☐ for *b*.**

❸ Writing an Equation From a Graph Find the equation of the line in the graph.

Step 1 Find the slope.
Use the points $(-4, 0)$ and $(1, 8)$.

slope = 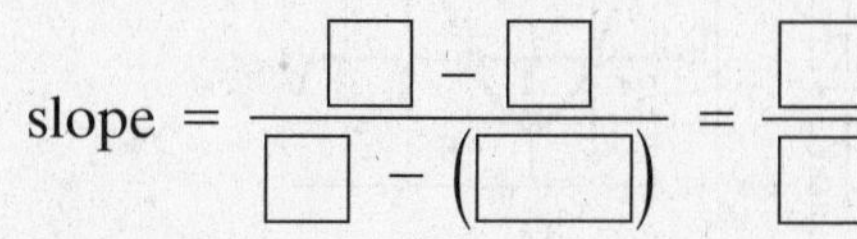

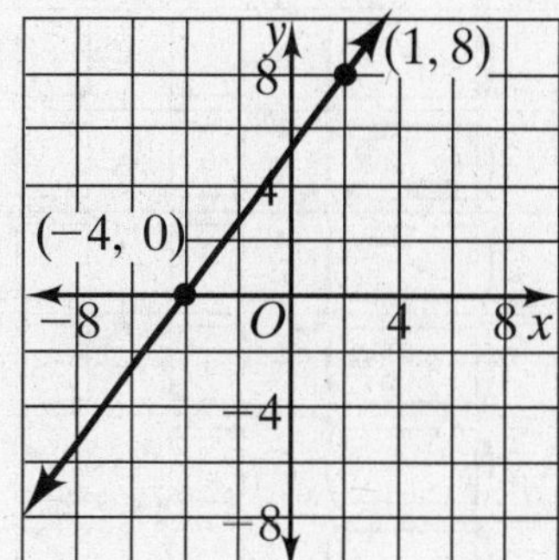

Step 2 Use the slope and one point to write an equation.

$y - y_1 = m(x - x_1)$

$y - 8 =$ ☐ $(x -$ ☐ $)$ ← **Use the point (1, ☐) for (x_1, y_1)**

$y - 8 =$ ☐ $(x -$ ☐ $)$

Using the point (1, ☐), the equation of the line is $y - 8 =$ ☐ $(x -$ ☐ $)$.

Quick Check

2. Do the values in the table represent a linear function? If so, write a function rule.

x	0	1	2	3
y	2	4	7	8

3. Use the point $(-2, 1)$ to write an equation for the line in Example 3.

Name ______________________ Class ______________ Date ______________

Lesson 11-7

Quadratic and Other Nonlinear Functions

Lesson Objective To graph and write quadratic functions and other nonlinear functions	**NAEP 2005 Strand:** Algebra **Topic:** Algebraic Representations **Local Standards:** ____________

Vocabulary

A quadratic function is ____

____

The graph of a quadratic function is a U-shaped curve called a [ ].

Example

1 Graphing a Quadratic Function Make a table and graph the quadratic function $f(x) = x^2 - 2x$.

x	$x^2 - 2x$	$= f(x)$
–2	$(\square)^2 - 2(\square) = \square + \square$	$= \square$
–1	$(\square)^2 - 2(\square) = \square + \square$	$= \square$
0	$(\square)^2 - 2(\square) = \square + \square$	$= \square$
1	$(\square)^2 - 2(\square) = \square - \square$	$= \square$
2	$(\square)^2 - 2(\square) = \square - \square$	$= \square$
3	$(\square)^2 - 2(\square) = \square - \square$	$= \square$

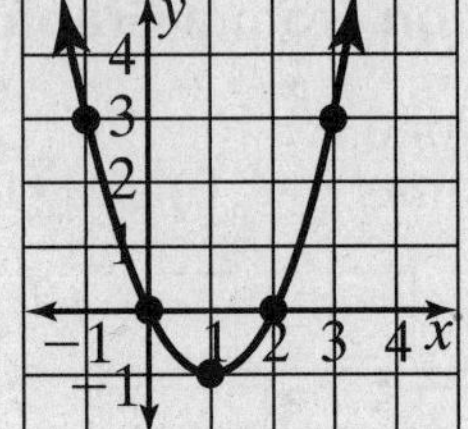

Quick Check

1. Make a table and a graph for the function $y = 2x^2 - 5$.

x					
y					

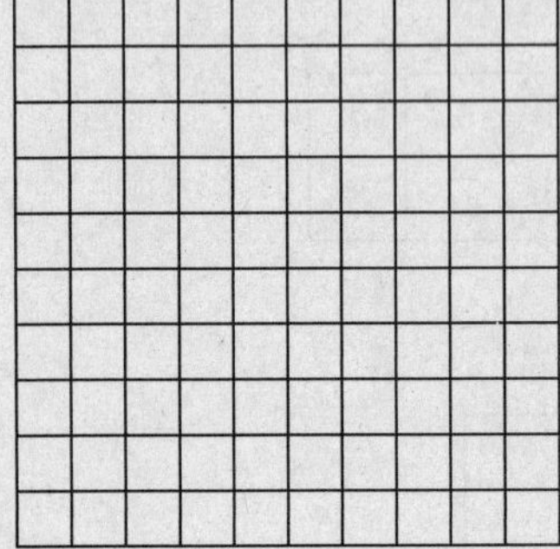

Name ______________________ Class ______________ Date ______________

Examples

❷ Graphing Other Nonlinear Functions The function $y = \frac{50}{s}$ relates the time (in hours) for a 50-mile bicycle ride to the speed traveled s (in miles per hour). Make a table and then graph the function.

Speed	Time
5	50 ÷ 5 = ☐
10	50 ÷ 10 = ☐
15	50 ÷ 15 = ☐
20	50 ÷ 20 = ☐

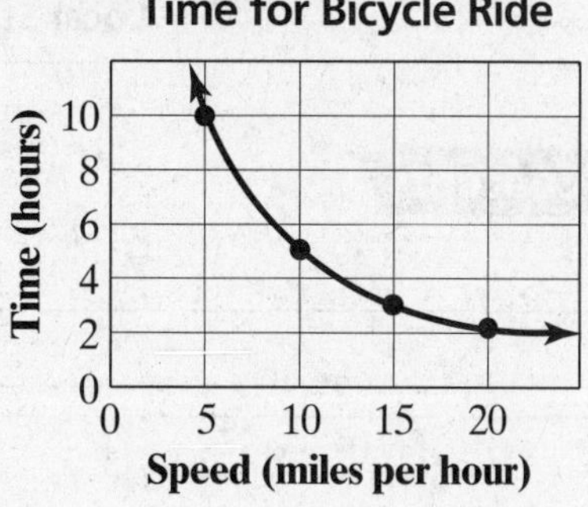

The data are continuous, so the curve is solid.

❸ Writing a Quadratic Function Rule Write a quadratic function rule for the data in the table below.

x	y
−2	1
−1	−2
0	−3
1	−2
2	1

Input x	(Input)^2 x^2	Output y
−2	☐	1
−1	☐	−2
0	☐	−3
1	☐	−2
2	☐	1

← Compare each output to (input)^2.
Each output is less than (input)^2 by ☐.

The function rule is ______.

Quick Check

2. The function $y = \frac{200}{s}$ relates the time y (in hours) for a 200-mile trip to the speed traveled s (in miles per hour). Make a table showing speed and number of hours traveled. Then graph the data.

Speed	Time
20	200 ÷ 20 = ☐
40	200 ÷ 40 = ☐
50	200 ÷ 50 = ☐
60	200 ÷ 60 = ☐

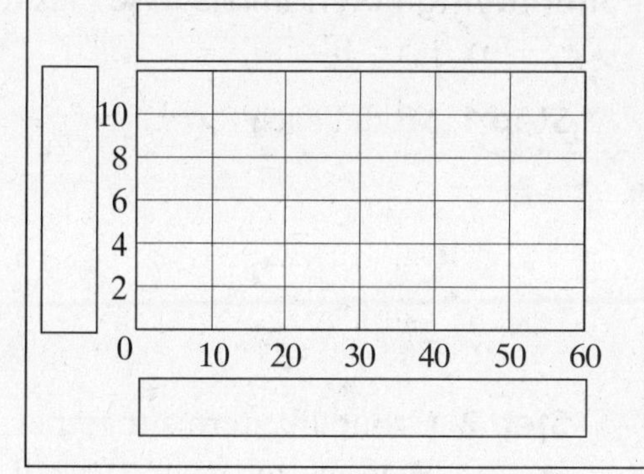

3. Write a quadratic function rule for the data in the table.

x	−3	−1	0	2	4
y	7	−1	−2	2	14

Name ______________________ Class ______________ Date ______________

Lesson 12-1

Exploring Polynomials

Lesson Objective	**NAEP 2005 Strand:** Algebra
To write variable expressions and to simplify polynomials	**Topic:** Variables, Expressions, and Operations **Local Standards:** ____________________

Vocabulary and Key Concepts

A polynomial is ____

A constant is ____

Using Algebra Tiles

□ represents 1.  represents x. represents x^2.

■ represents -1. represents $-x$. represents $-x^2$.

Examples

1 Writing Algebraic Expressions Write an algebraic expression for the model below.

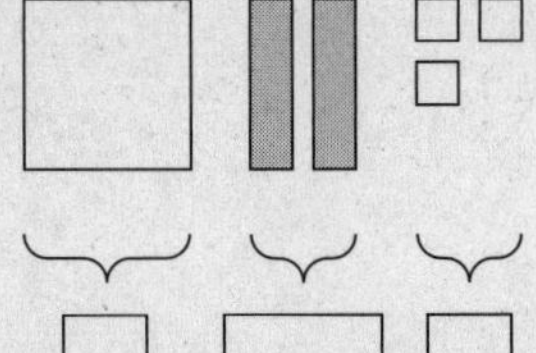

The model shows the expression ______.

2 Simplifying Polynomials Use tiles to simplify the polynomial $-x^2 + 3x + x^2 + x^2 + 3 - x - 4$.

Step 1 Model each term.

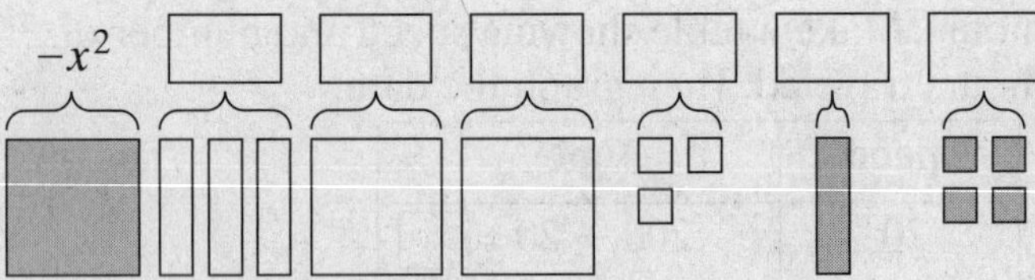

Step 2 Group like terms together. Remove zero pairs. Recall that a zero pair is a pair of algebra tiles whose sum is zero.

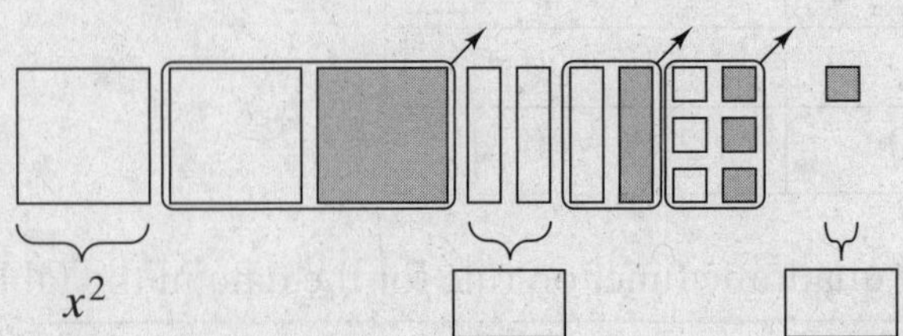

The simplified polynomial is ______ + ______ − ______.

Name ______________________ Class ______________ Date ______________

❸ Using Properties to Simplify Polynomials Use properties of numbers to simplify the polynomial $2b^2 - 2b - 3b^2 + 4 + b - 4$.

$2b^2 - 2b - 3b^2 + 4 + b - 4$

$= 2b^2 - 3b^2 - 2b + b + 4 - 4$ ← ______ **Property.**

$= (2b^2 - 3b^2) + (-2b + b) + (4 - 4)$ ← ______ **Property.**

$= (2 - 3)b^2 + (-2 + 1)b + (4 - 4)$ ← ______ **Property.**

$=$ ______ ← **Simplify.**

Quick Check

1. Write an algebraic expression for each model.

a.

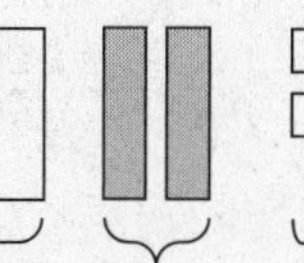

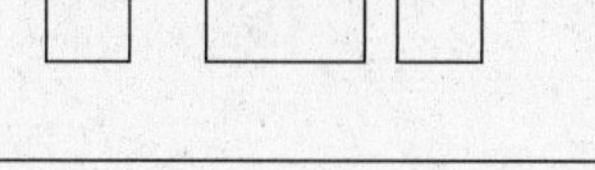

b.

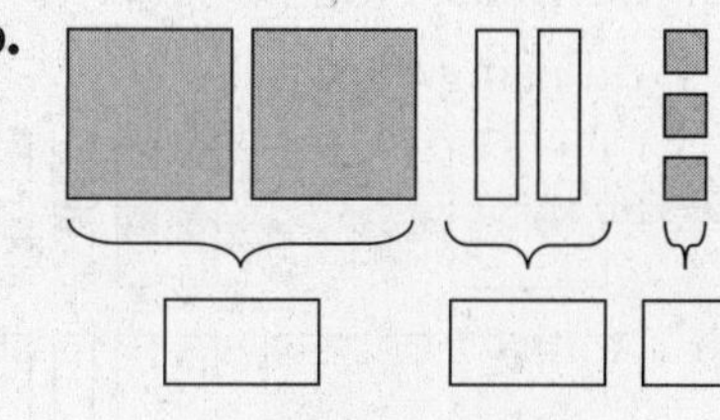

2. Draw or use tiles to simplify each polynomial.

a. $5x^2 - 4x + 3x - 7x^2 + 6$

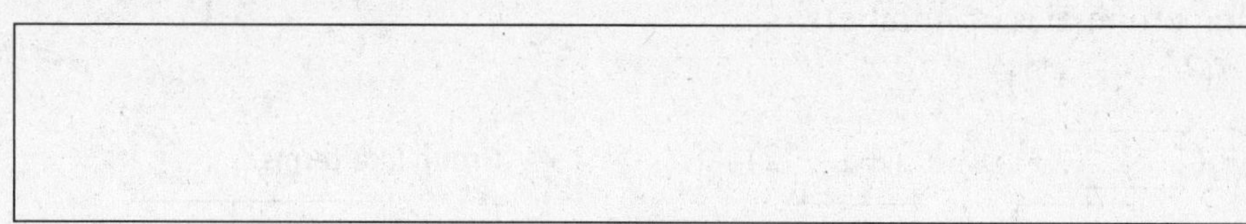

b. $8x^2 + 7 - 3x - 2x^2 - 5$

3. The polynomials below represent the areas of two neighborhoods. Use properties of numbers to simplify each polynomial.

a. $4g^2 - 5g - 2g^2 + 7g$

b. $3y - 5y^2 - y + 7$

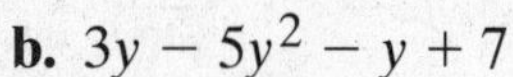

Name ______________________ Class ______________ Date ______________

Lesson 12-2

Adding and Subtracting Polynomials

Lesson Objective	**NAEP 2005 Strand:** Algebra
To add and subtract polynomials	**Topic:** Variables, Expressions, and Operations
	Local Standards: ______________________

Vocabulary

A coefficient is ____

Examples

1 Adding Polynomials Add $(x^2 - 4x - 1) + (-2x^2 + 5x - 2)$.

Method 1 Add using tiles.

$x^2 - 4x - 1$

$-2x^2 + 5x - 2$

$-x^2$ $\quad x \quad -3$

The sum is ☐ + ☐ − ☐.

Method 2 Add using properties of numbers.

$(x^2 - 4x - 1) + (-2x^2 + 5x - 2)$

$= (x^2 -$ ☐ $) + ($ ☐ $+ 5x) + (-1 - 2)$ ← **Group like terms.**

$= (1 -$ ☐ $)\, x^2 + ($ ☐ $+ 5)$ ☐ $+ (-1 - 2)$ ← **Use the** ☐ **Property.**

$=$ ☐ + ☐ − ☐ ← **Simplify.**

2 Gardening A garden has sides of length $3x + 5$, $4x - 2$, $5x + 2$, and $7x - 6$. Write a polynomial to express the length of edging that is needed to go around the garden.

To find the perimeter of the garden, find the ☐ of the lengths of the four sides.

$P = (3x + 5) + (4x - 2) + (5x + 2) + (7x - 6)$

$=$ (☐ $x +$ ☐ $x +$ ☐ $x +$ ☐ x) + (☐ − ☐ + ☐ − ☐) ← **Group like terms.**

$=$ ☐ $x - 1$ ← **Add the coefficients.**

The perimeter of the garden is ☐. The edging must be ☐ units long to go around the garden.

Name ______________________ Class ______________ Date ____________

❸ Subtracting Polynomials Subtract $(3q^2 - 2q + 4) - (2q^2 - 2q + 3)$.

$(3q^2 - 2q + 4) - (2q^2 - 2q + 3)$

$= 3q^2 - 2q + 4 - \square q^2 + \square q - \square$ ← **Add the opposite of each term in the second polynomial.**

$= (\square q^2 - \square q^2) + (\square q + \square q) + (\square - \square)$ ← **Group like terms.**

$= (3 - 2)\square + (-2 + 2)\square + (4 - 3)$ ← **Use the ______ Property.**

$= \square + \square$ ← **Simplify.**

Quick Check

1. Find each sum.
2. Write the perimeter of each figure as a polynomial. Simplify.

a. $(c^2 + 3c - 5) + (4c^2 - c + 7)$

b. $(x^2 + 3x - 1) + (2x^2 - 6)$

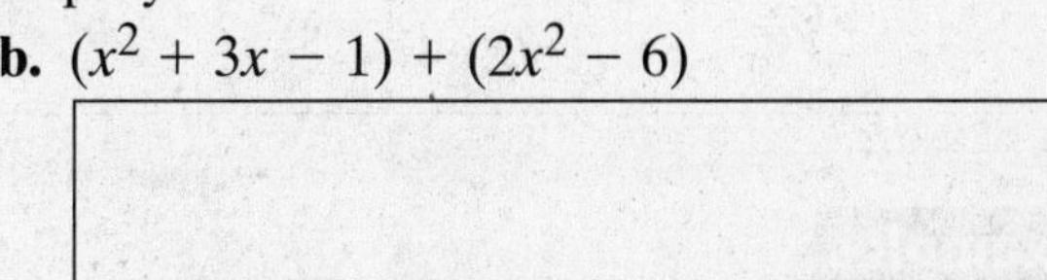

a.

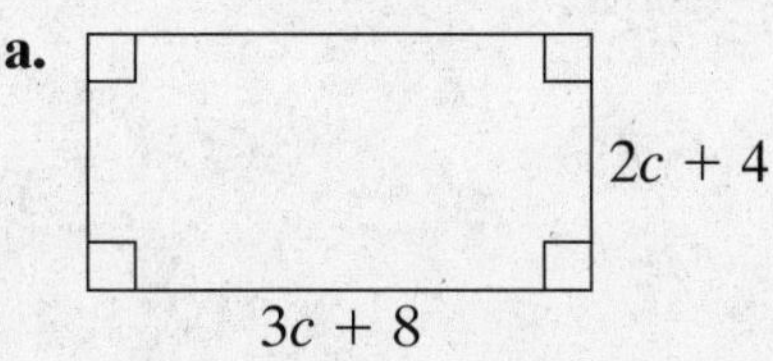

b.

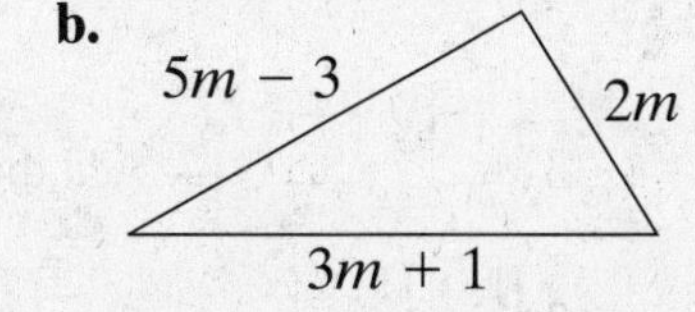

3. Subtract $(4y^2 - 3y + 1) - (6y^2 - 3y + 3)$. Check the solution.

Name ______________________ Class ______________ Date ______________

Lesson 12-3

Exponents and Multiplication

Lesson Objective	**NAEP 2005 Strand:** Algebra
To multiply powers with the same base and to multiply numbers in scientific notation	**Topic:** Variables, Expressions, and Operations
	Local Standards: ____________________

Key Concepts

Multiplying Powers With the Same Base

To multiply numbers or variables with the same base, ☐ the exponents.

Arithmetic	**Algebra**
$3^2 \cdot 3^7 = 3^{(2+7)} = 3^9$	$a^m \cdot a^n = a^{(m+n)}$

Examples

1 Multiplying Powers Write the expression $(-3)^2 \cdot (-3)^4$ using a single exponent.

$(-3)^2 \cdot (-3)^4 = (-3)^{(\square + \square)}$ ← **Add the exponents.**

$= (-3)^{(\square)}$ ← **Simplify the exponent.**

2 Multiplying With Scientific Notation Multiply $(3 \times 10^3)(7 \times 10^5)$. Write the product in scientific notation.

$(3 \times 10^3)(7 \times 10^5) = (\square \times \square) \times (10^{\square} \times 10^{\square})$ ← **Use the ☐ and ☐ properties.**

$= \square \times (10^{\square} \times 10^{\square})$ ← **Multiply ☐ and ☐.**

$= \square \times 10^{\square}$ ← **Add the exponents for the powers of 10.**

$= \square \times 10^{\square} \times 10^{\square}$ ← **Write ☐ in scientific notation.**

$= \square \times 10^{\square}$ ← **Add the exponents.**

Name ______________________ Class ______________ Date ______________

3 **Science** A light-year is about 5.9×10^{12} miles. A mile is about 1.609×10^3 meters. How many meters are in a light-year? Write your answer in scientific notation.

A. 9.5×10^{15} **B.** 9.5×10^{16} **C.** 9.5×10^{36} **D.** 95×10^{16}

$(5.9 \times 10^{12})(1.609 \times 10^3)$ ← **Multiply by conversion factor.**

$= (\square \times \square) \times (10^{\square} \times 10^{\square})$ ← **Use the** ______ **and** ______ **properties.**

$\approx \square \times (10^{\square} \times 10^{\square})$ ← **Multiply** ______ **and** ______. **Round to the nearest tenth.**

$= \square \times 10^{\square}$ ← **Add the exponents.**

There are about ______ meters in a light-year. The correct answer is choice ______.

Quick Check

1. Write each expression using a single exponent.

a. $6^2 \cdot 6^3$ **b.** $(-4) \cdot (-4)^7$ **c.** $m^1 \cdot m^{11}$

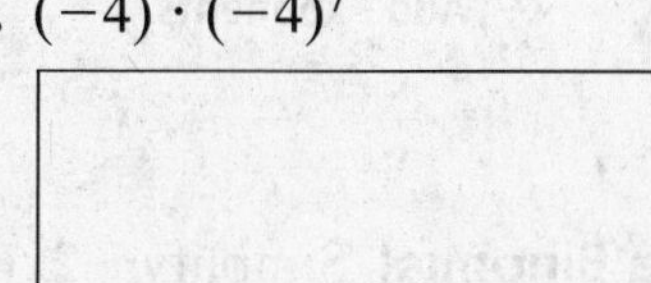
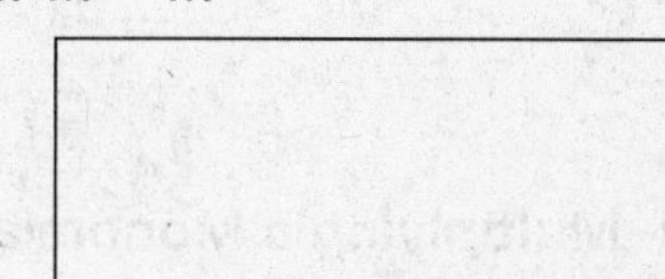

2. Multiply. Write each product in scientific notation.

a. $(2 \times 10^6)(4 \times 10^3)$ **b.** $(3 \times 10^5)(2 \times 10^8)$ **c.** $12(8 \times 10^{20})$

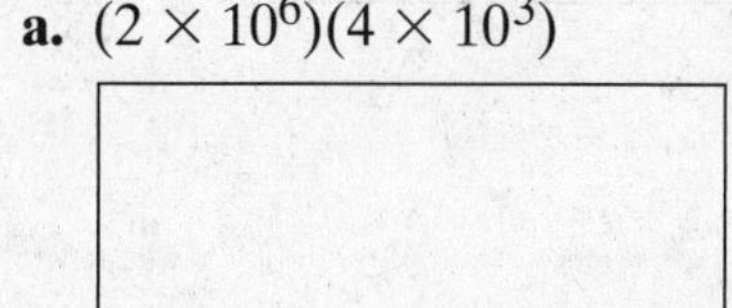

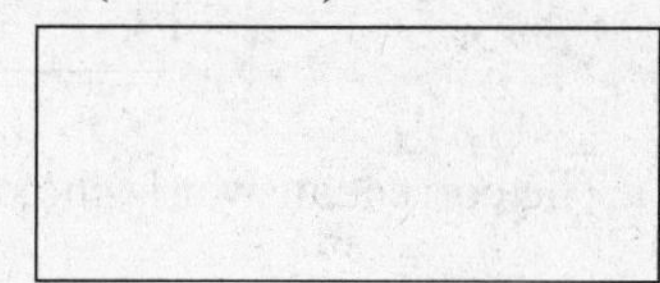

3. **Astronomy** The speed of light is about 3.00×10^5 kilometers/second. Use the formula $d = r \cdot t$ to find the distance light travels in an hour, which is 3.6×10^3 seconds.

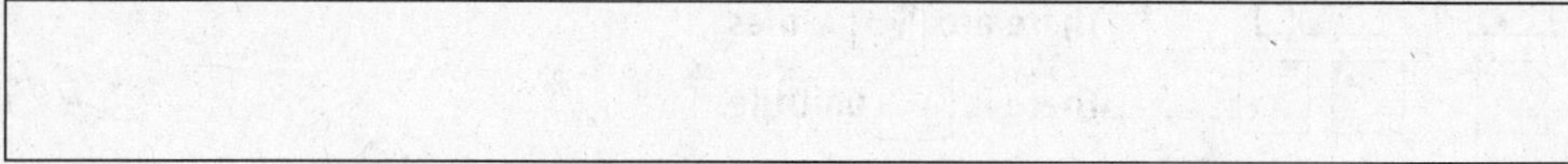

Name ______________________ Class ______________ Date ______________

Lesson 12-4

Multiplying Polynomials

Lesson Objective	**NAEP 2005 Strand:** Algebra
To multiply monomials and binomials	**Topic:** Variables, Expressions, and Operations
	Local Standards: ______________

Vocabulary

A monomial is ____

____

A binomial is ____

____

Examples

1 Multiplying Monomials Simplify $(3x^2)(-4x^3)$.

$(3x^2)(-4x^3) = (3)(-4) \cdot x^2 \cdot x^3$ ← **Use the ______ Property of Multiplication to rearrange the factors.**

$= \square \cdot x^2 \cdot x^3$ ← **Multiply coefficients.**

$= \square \cdot \square$ ← **Add exponents.**

2 Multiplying a Monomial and a Binomial Simplify $-2x(4x^3 + 6)$.

A. $-8x^4 - 12x$ **B.** $-6x^4 - 8x$ **C.** $8x^4 - 12x$ **D.** $2x^4 + 4x$

$-2x(4x^3 + 6) = -2x \cdot \square + (-2x) \cdot \square$ ← **Use the ______ Property.**

$= \square - \square$ ← **Simplify.**

The correct answer is choice $\square$.

3 Using Area Models to Multiply Binomials Simplify $(x + 1)(3x + 1)$.

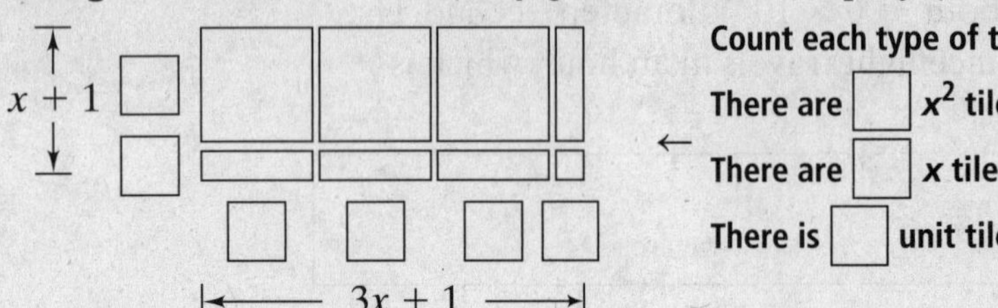

Count each type of tile.

There are $\square$ **x^2 tiles.**

There are $\square$ **x tiles.**

There is $\square$ **unit tile.**

So $(x + 1)(3x + 1) = \square$.

Name ______________________ Class ______________ Date ______________

Quick Check

1. Simplify $(2y^3)(4y)$.

2. Your neighbor is building an addition to her house. The expression $3r(5r + 5)$ represents the planned area of the house after it is remodeled. Simplify the polynomial to find the total area of the house, including the addition.

3. Draw an area model or use algebra tiles to simplify each expression.

   a. $(x + 2)(2x + 3)$

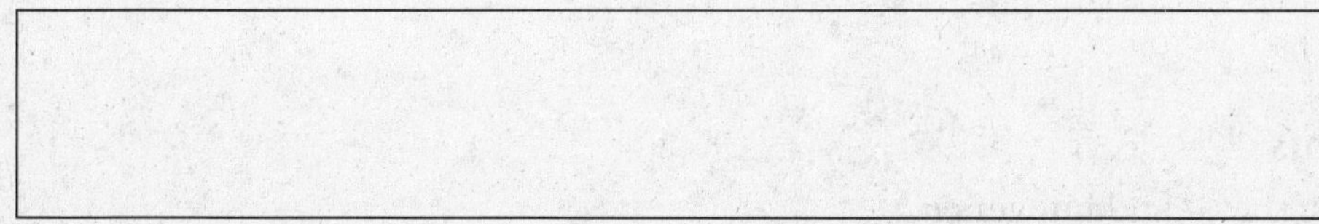

   b. $(3x + 4)(2x + 1)$

   c. $(x + 1)(2x + 5)$

Name ______________________ Class ______________ Date ______________

Lesson 12-5

Exponents and Division

Lesson Objective	NAEP 2005 Strand: Algebra
To divide powers with the same base and to simplify expressions with negative exponents	**Topic:** Variables, Expressions, and Operations **Local Standards:** ____________________

Key Concepts

Dividing Powers With the Same Base

To divide nonzero numbers or variables with the same nonzero base, ☐ the exponents.

Arithmetic	Algebra
$\frac{8^5}{8^3} = 8^{(5 \square 3)} = 8^{\square}$	$\frac{a^m}{a^n} = a^{(m \square n)}$, where $a \neq 0$.

Zero as an Exponent

For any nonzero number a, $a^0 = \square$.

Example $9^0 = \square$

Negative Exponents

For any nonzero number a and integers n,
$a^{-n} = \frac{1}{a^n}$.

Example $8^{-5} = \frac{1}{8^5}$.

Examples

❶ **Dividing Powers** Write $\frac{x^{14}}{x^9}$ using a single exponent.

$\frac{x^{14}}{x^9} = x^{(14 \square 9)}$ ← ☐ **exponents with the same base.**

$= x^{\square}$ ← **Simplify.**

❷ **Dividing Numbers in Scientific Notation** Simplify $(3.5 \times 10^6) \div (2.45 \times 10^2)$.
Write your answer in standard form and round to the nearest tenth.

$\frac{3.5 \times 10^6}{2.45 \times 10^2} = \frac{3.5}{2.45} \times \frac{10^6}{10^2}$ ← **Write as a product of quotients.**

$= \frac{3.5}{2.45} \times \square$ ← **Subtract exponents.**

$\approx \square = \square$ ← **Divide.**

❸ Expressions With a Zero Exponent Simplify each expression.

a. $(-5)^0$

$(-5)^0 = \square$ ← **Simplify.**

b. $2y^0, y \neq 0$

$2y^0 = \square$ ← **Simplify.**

❹ Expressions With Negative Exponents Simplify each expression.

a. 2^{-3}

b. $(p)^{-8}$

$2^{-3} = \frac{\square}{2^{\square}}$ ← **Use a** 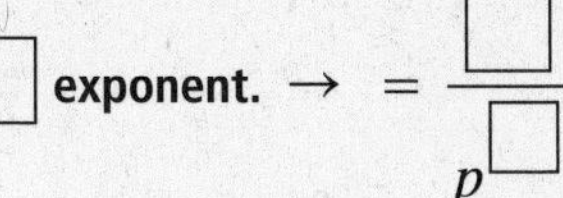 **exponent.** → $= \frac{\square}{p^{\square}}$

$= \frac{\square}{\square}$ ← **Simplify.**

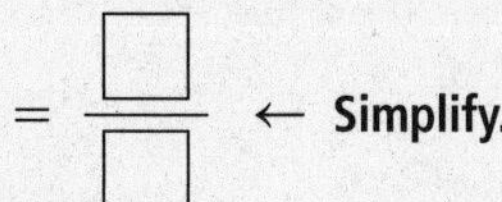

Quick Check

1. Write $\frac{w^8}{w^5}$ using a single exponent.

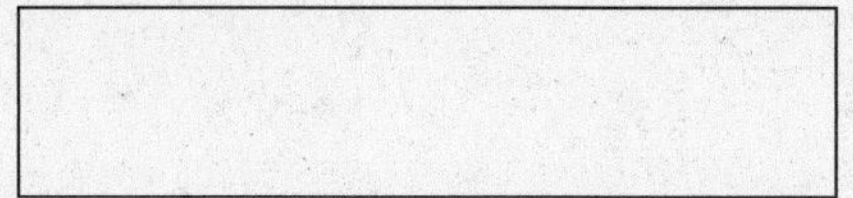

2. The distance between the sun and Earth is about 9.3×10^7 miles. Light travels about 1.1×10^7 miles per minute. Use the formula time $= \frac{\text{distance}}{\text{speed}}$ to estimate how long sunlight takes to reach Earth. Write your answer in standard form and round to the nearest tenth.

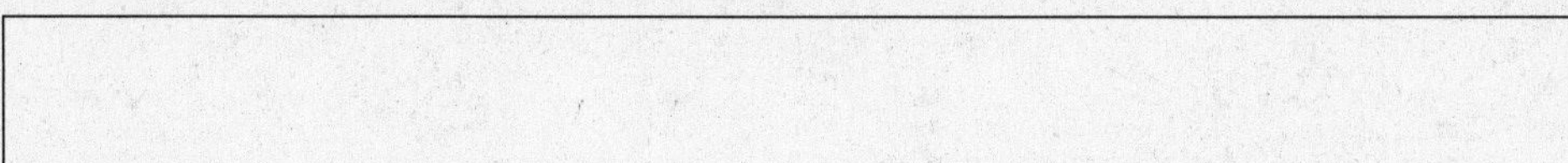

3. Simplify each expression.

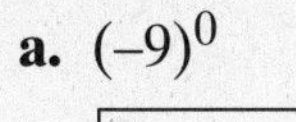

a. $(-9)^0$

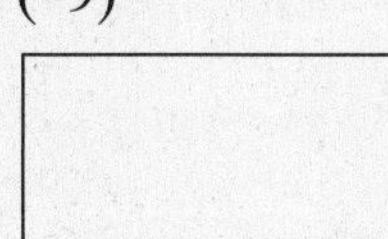

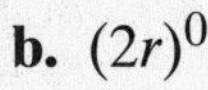

b. $(2r)^0$

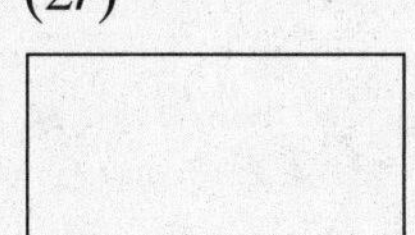

c. $2r^0$

4. Simplify each expression.

a. 3^{-1}

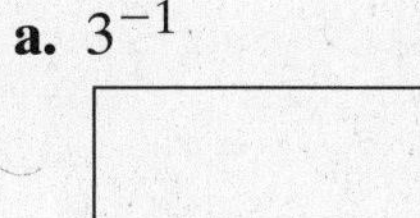

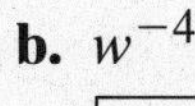

b. w^{-4}

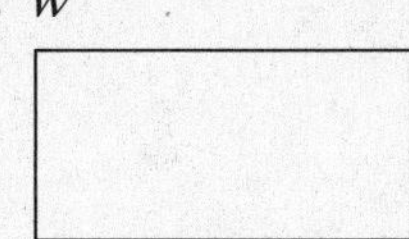

c. $(-2)^{-3}$

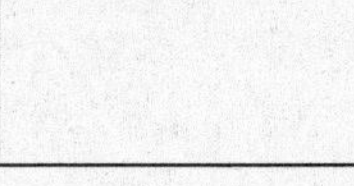

A Note to the Student:

This section of your workbook contains a series of pages that support your mathematics understandings for each chapter and lesson presented in your student edition.

- Practice pages provide additional practice for every lesson.
- Guided Problem Solving pages lead you through a step-by-step solution to an application problem in each lesson.
- Vocabulary pages contain a variety of activities to increase your reading and math understanding, ranging from graphic organizers to vocabulary review puzzles.

Name ______________________ Class ______________ Date ______________

Practice 1-1

Algebraic Expressions and the Order of Operations

Write an algebraic expression for each word phrase.

1. 5 less than a number n ______
2. 15 more than the absolute value of a number ______
3. the number of minutes in n hours ______
4. 5 more than a number, divided by 9 ______
5. 3 more than the product of 8 and a number ______
6. 3 less than the absolute value of a number, times 4 ______

Write an algebraic expression for each situation. Explain what the variable represents.

7. the amount of money Waldo has if he has $10 more than Jon
8. the amount of money that Mika has if she has some quarters
9. how much weight Kirk can lift if he lifts 30 lb more than his brother
10. how fast Rya runs if she runs 5 mi/h slower than Danae

Write a word phrase that can be represented by each variable expression.

11. $n \div (4)$
12. $n + 4$
13. $3n$
14. $n - 8$

Evaluate each expression for $n = 5.6$, $x = 2.4$, and $y = 4$.

15. $6(n + 8)$ ______
16. $29y - 15$ ______
17. $(x + n) \div y$ ______
18. $(24 \div x) + 18$ ______
19. $(6 \cdot 8 + y) \cdot n$ ______
20. $xn + y$ ______
21. $6 \cdot 8 + y \cdot n$ ______
22. $6(8 + y) \cdot n$ ______
23. $12 \div x + xy$ ______
24. $4n + x(y + 1)$ ______

Name ______________________ Class ______________ Date ______________

1-1 • Guided Problem Solving

GPS Student Page 7, Exercise 17:

a. **Amusement Park** An amusement park charges $5 for admission and $2 for each ride. Write an expression for the total cost of admission and *r* rides.

b. **Number Sense** How many rides can you go on if you have $16?

Understand

1. What information is given in the problem?

____

____

2. What are you being asked to do?

____

____

3. What does it cost to enter the park? ______________

4. What does a ride cost? ______________________

Plan and Carry Out

5. Write an expression for riding *r* rides costing $2 each, after paying the cost for the admission.

____

6. Using your expression, how many rides can you go on with $16?

____

Check

7. Is your expression reasonable? Does the expression check?

____

____

Solve Another Problem

8. A car-rental agency charges $35 per day and $.25 per mile. Write an expression for the cost of renting a car for one day and driving *m* miles. How many miles could you drive if you have only $50?

____

Practice 1-2

Integers and Absolute Value

Write an integer to represent each situation.

1. The top of the world's lowest known active volcano is 160 ft below sea level.

   ____

2. The football team gained three yards on a play.

   ____

3. Jenni owes her friend $20.

   ____

4. The temperature yesterday was five degrees above zero.

   ____

Use the information in the graph at the right for questions 5–8.

5. The highest outdoor temperature ever recorded in Nevada, 122°F, was recorded on June 23, 1954. Was it ever that hot in Idaho? Explain.

   ____

   ____

6. The lowest temperature ever recorded in Maine, −48°F, was recorded on January 17, 1925. Was it ever that cold in Minnesota? Explain.

7. Which state on the graph had a recorded low temperature of 60°F below zero?

   ____

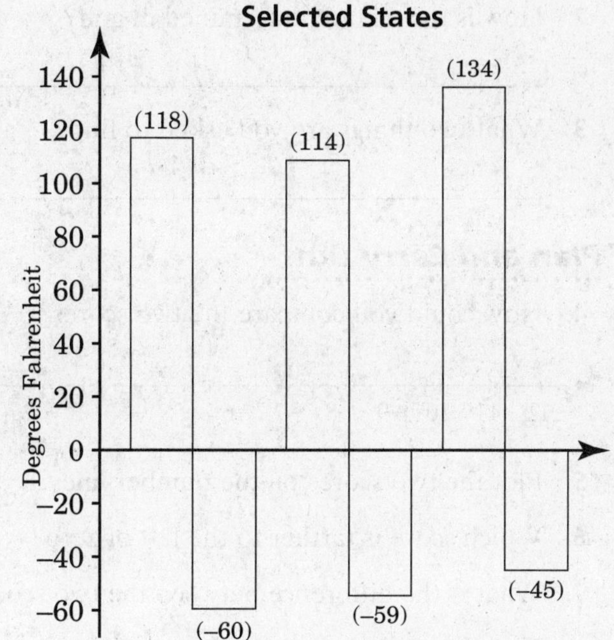

Compare. Write >, <, or =.

8. -12 ☐ 10
9. $|26|$ ☐ $|-26|$
10. $|42|$ ☐ $|-93|$
11. 53 ☐ -21
12. $|6|$ ☐ 0
13. $|9|$ ☐ $|-13|$

Order the integers in each set from least to greatest.

14. 0, −5, 5, −15, 15, 25, −25

    ____

15. 27, −10, −6, −18, 3, 9, −8

    ____

Name ______________________ Class ______________ Date ______________

1-2 • Guided Problem Solving

Student Page 12, Exercise 20:

Golf In golf, the lowest score wins. One golfer finishes a course at −9. A second golfer finishes at −12.

a. Which golfer wins?

b. By how much does the winner beat the other golfer?

Understand

1. What information in the problem do you need?

____

2. How is the winner determined in golf?

____

3. What two things are you asked to find?

____

Plan and Carry Out

4. How could you compare the two scores?

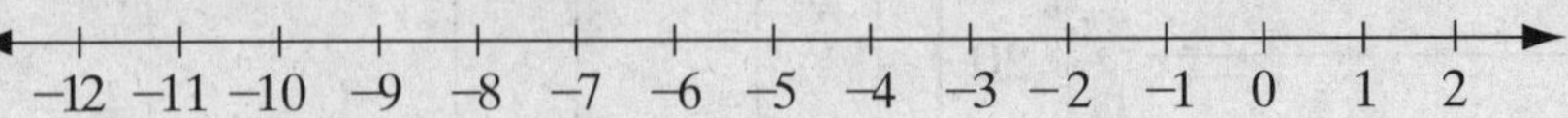

5. Plot the two scores on the number line.

6. Which score is farther to the left of zero? ______________

7. What is the difference between the two scores? ______________

8. By how much does the golfer win? ______________

Check

9. Is your answer reasonable? Is there another method you could use to check the problem?

____

____

Solve Another Problem

10. A diver located 250 feet below sea level spots a whale at 135 feet below sea level. Who is deeper and by how much?

____

Name ______________________ Class ______________ Date ______________

Practice 1-3

Adding and Subtracting Integers

Write the addition expression that is suggested by each model.

1. 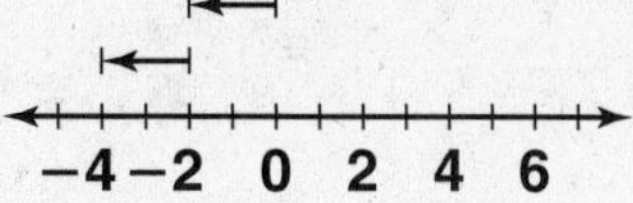

2. 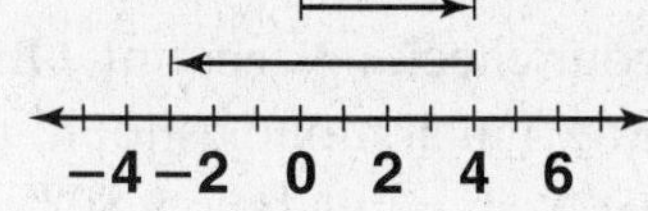

3. 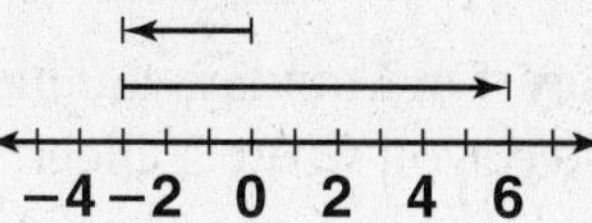

Write an algebraic expression to find the sum for each situation.

4. The varsity football team gained 7 yd on one play and then lost 4 yd. ______

5. The airplane descended 140 ft and then rose 112 ft. ______

6. The squirrel climbed 18 in. up a tree, slipped back 4 in., and then climbed up 12 in. more. ______

7. The temperature was 72°F at noon. At midnight a cold front moved in, dropping the temperature 12°F. ______

Simplify each expression.

8. $8 + (7)$ ______
9. $9 + (-4)$ ______
10. $-6 + (-8)$ ______
11. $9 + (-17)$ ______
12. $-15 + (-11)$ ______
13. $-23 + 18$ ______
14. $27 + 34$ ______
15. $-8 + (-17)$ ______
16. $19 + (-8)$ ______
17. $-14 - 33$ ______
18. $-32 - (-18)$ ______
19. $-15 - (-26)$ ______
20. $-19 - (-12)$ ______
21. $-16 - (-21)$ ______
22. $27 - 19$ ______

Evaluate each expression for $x = 5$, $y = -6$, and $z = -7$.

23. $x + y$ ______
24. $15 - z$ ______
25. $y - z$ ______
26. $y - 15 + x$ ______
27. $32 - z + x$ ______
28. $|x| - |y|$ ______

29. Jill and Joe are playing a game. The chart at the right shows the points gained or lost on each round.

   a. Who has the most points after the fifth round?

   ______

   b. To win, a player must have 20 points. How many points does each player need to win?

   ______

Round	Jill	Joe
1	10	12
2	−2	3
3	6	−8
4	4	0
5	−2	7

1-3 • Guided Problem Solving

GPS Student Page 18, Exercise 29:

Money On Monday, you had $151 in your checking account. On Tuesday, you wrote a check for $248. How much money should you deposit to prevent your account balance from going below $0?

Understand

1. What was your checking account balance on Monday? ______

2. How much did you write the check for on Tuesday? ______

3. What are you being asked to find?

____

____

Plan and Carry Out

4. When writing a check, do you add or subtract it from your checking account balance? ______

5. To subtract an integer, what do you add?

____

6. Subtract the amount of the check from the balance on Monday.

____

7. How much would you have to deposit to make your checking account balance zero?

____

Check

8. Does writing a check for more than the amount in your checking account give you a positive or a negative checking account balance?

____

Solve Another Problem

9. On a winter day in Colorado, the afternoon high temperature was recorded at 3°F. By midnight the temperature had dropped 8°F. What was the midnight temperature?

____

Name ____________ Class ____________ Date ____________

Practice 1-4

Multiplying and Dividing Integers

Simplify each expression.

1. $-4 \cdot 8$
2. $-7 \cdot (-9)$
3. $-5 \cdot (-11)$
4. $2(-3)(-3)$
5. $(-4)(-4)(-4)$
6. $(5)(2)(-20)$
7. $-63 \div 7$
8. $81 \div (-9)$
9. $\frac{96}{-12}$
10. $\frac{-54}{-6}$
11. $-1000 \div (-100)$
12. $\frac{-120}{10}$
13. The value of Jim's telephone calling card decreases 12 cents for every minute he uses it. Yesterday he used the card to make a 6-minute call. What was the change in the value of the card?
14. One day the temperature in Lone Grove, Oklahoma, fell 15 degrees in 5 hours. What was the average temperature change per hour?

Evaluate each expression for $x = -4$ and $y = 6$.

15. $2x + xy$
16. $(y - x) + 7x$
17. $4 + 2y \div x$
18. $\frac{x - y - 11}{-7}$

Name ______________________ Class ______________ Date ______________

1-4 • Guided Problem Solving

GPS Student Page 23, Exercise 41:

Geology Scientists drill 40,230 ft into Earth's crust.

a. Write an integer to represent this depth.

b. Estimation Estimate the depth drilled, to the nearest mile.

Understand

1. How far did the scientists drill? ______________________
2. In part *b,* what unit of measure do you need to convert feet to?

   ____

Plan and Carry Out

3. Will the depth the scientists have drilled into Earth be represented as a positive or a negative number?

   ____
4. Write the depth the scientists drilled as an integer.

   ____
5. To convert feet to miles what operation do you need to perform?

   ____
6. About how many feet, to the nearest thousand, does one mile equal? ______________________
7. Find the estimated depth in miles by rounding the depth to 40,000 feet. ______________________

Check

8. Find the exact depth and compare your estimation to see if it is reasonable.

   ____

   ____

Solve Another Problem

9. A roller coaster plunges down a hill with a vertical drop of 52.3 feet.

   a. Write an integer to represent this change in height. __________

   b. Estimate the vertical change, to the nearest yard. __________

Name ______________________ Class ______________ Date ______________

Practice 1-5

Properties of Numbers

Determine whether each equation is true or false.

1. $9 \cdot 8 + 6 = 9 \cdot 6 + 8$ ______________
2. $-7(11 - 4) = 7(15)$ ______________
3. $12 \cdot 7 = 10 \cdot 7 + 2 \cdot 7$ ______________
4. $15 + (-17) = -17 + 15$ ______________
5. $93 \cdot (-8) = -93 \cdot 8$ ______________
6. $53 + (-19) = -53 + 19$ ______________

Use mental math to simplify each expression.

7. $8 + (-2) + 7 + (-5)$ ______________
8. $65 + 23 + 35$ ______________
9 $17 + (-9) + 18 + (-11)$ ______________
10. $220 + 343 + 80$ ______________
11. $21 - 74$ ______________
12. $36 - 63$ ______________
13. $(-5)(38)(-20)$ ______________
14. $2 \cdot 83 \cdot (-5)$ ______________
15. $4 \cdot (25 \cdot 27)$ ______________

Find each product.

16. $25(-99)$ ______________
17. $19(-6)$ ______________
18. $6 \cdot \$2.99$ ______________
19. $102 \cdot \$21$ ______________
20. $19 \cdot 21$ ______________
21. $26 \cdot 97$ ______________
22. $21 \cdot (-11)$ ______________
23. $9 \cdot \$4.98$ ______________
24. $103 \cdot \$32$ ______________

The table to the right shows daily changes in temperature over a 5-day period.

25. Which two-day period had the greatest change in temperature?

____

26. On Sunday the temperature was 20°F. What was the temperature at the end of the day on Friday?

____

Day	Change in Temperature
Mon	−12°F
Tues	+6°F
Wed	−4°F
Thurs	−9°F
Fri	+8°F

Name ______________________ Class ______________ Date ______________

1-5 • Guided Problem Solving

GPS Student Page 29, Exercise 33:

Shopping Find the total cost of buying 4 pairs of candles for $2.97 per pair, 3 cards for $1.99 each, and 5 colored markers for $.99 each.

Understand

1. Are the prices given for each item or as the total for the type of item? ______________________

2. What are you being asked to find?

____

3. Draw a circle around each price.

Plan and Carry Out

4. What is the total cost of the candles?

____

5. What is the total cost of the cards?

____

6. What is the total cost of the markers?

____

7. Find the total cost of buying all the items.

____

Check

8. Check your answer by adding each item separately. Do your totals match?

____

____

____

Solve Another Problem

9. At the fabric store, Jane buys 3 yards of material at $4.79 per yard, 4 spools of thread at $0.89 each, and 6 yards of lace at $1.29 per yard. What is the total cost of materials?

____

Name ______________________ Class ______________ Date ______________

Practice 1-6

Solving Equations by Adding and Subtracting

Solve each equation. Check the solution.

1. $x - 6 = -18$ ______

2. $-14 = 8 + j$ ______

3. $4.19 + w = 19.72$ ______

4. $b + \frac{1}{6} = \frac{7}{8}$ ______

5. $9 + k = 27$ ______

6. $14 + t = -17$ ______

7. $v - 2.59 = 26$ ______

8. $r + 9 = 15$ ______

9. $n - 19 = 26$ ______

10. $14 = -3 + s$ ______

11. $9 = d - 4.3$ ______

12. $g - \frac{1}{4} = \frac{5}{8}$ ______

Write and solve an equation for each situation.

13. Yesterday Josh sold some boxes of greeting cards. Today he sold seven boxes. If he sold 25 boxes in all, how many did he sell yesterday?

______

14. After Simon donated four books to the school library, he had 28 books left. How many books did Simon have to start with?

______

15. Jana baked some muffins. After she served 13 of them to her friends for brunch, she had 17 left. How many muffins did she bake?

______

16. A scuba diver descended to a depth of –22 meters (or 22 meters below sea level). The ocean floor is at a depth of –71 meters. How much farther would she need to descend to reach the ocean floor?

______

______

Choose from –4, –3, –2, –1, 0, 1, 2, 3, 4. Find *all* the numbers that are solutions of each equation.

17. $|x| = 2$ ______

18. $5 + |x| = 9$ ______

19. $|x - 1| = 3$ ______

1-6 • Guided Problem Solving

GPS Student Page 36, Exercise 34:

A collector sold a baseball card for \$9.30. This was \$3.75 more than the price he paid. How much did the collector pay for the card?

Understand

1. At what price did the card collector sell his baseball card?

   ____

2. What are you being asked to find?

   ____

3. Did the collector pay more or less than \$9.30 for the baseball card?

   ____

Plan and Carry Out

4. Write an equation for the situation. Let y equal the amount that the collector paid for the baseball card.

   ____

5. How will you solve for the variable y?

   ____

6. What is the value of y? ______________________________

Check

7. Add \$3.75 to your solution. Is the sum \$9.30? ______________

Solve Another Problem

8. A real estate investor bought a house for \$125,000. After spending \$23,000 renovating the house, she sold it for \$196,000. How much profit did the investor make when she sold the house?

   ____

Name ______________________ Class ______________ Date ______________

Practice 1-7

Solving Equations by Multiplying and Dividing

Solve each equation. Check the solution.

1. $\frac{a}{-6} = 2$ ______
2. $18 = \frac{v}{-1.8}$ ______
3. $46 = 2.3m$ ______
4. $-114 = -6k$ ______
5. $0 = \frac{b}{19}$ ______
6. $136 = 8y$ ______
7. $0.6j = -1.44$ ______
8. $\frac{q}{7.4} = 8.3$ ______
9. $28b = -131.6$ ______
10. $\frac{n}{-9} = -107$ ______
11. $37c = -777$ ______
12. $\frac{n}{-1.28} = 4.96$ ______

Write and solve an equation for each situation.

13. Skylar spent \$90.65 on books that cost \$12.95 each. How many books did Skylar buy?

______

14. Eugenio has five payments left to make on his computer. If each payment is \$157.90, how much does he still owe?

______

15. Judy spent \$83.86 to buy T-shirts for the 14 members of the Chess Club. How much did each T-shirt cost?

______

16. Alison uses a total of 94.5 cups of dog food each week to feed her three dogs. Each dog eats the same amount. How much does each dog eat in one day?

______

Choose from –4, –3, –2, –1, 0, 1, 2, 3, 4. Find *all* the numbers that are solutions of each equation.

17. $|x| = 4$ ______
18. $5 + |x| = 6$ ______
19. $|x - 2| = 2$ ______

Name ______________________ Class ______________ Date ______________

1-7 • Guided Problem Solving

GPS Student Page 40, Exercise 30:

Surveys In a survey, 124 students reported they do community service. This is four times as many as those who reported they are in the band. How many of the students surveyed are in the band?

Understand

1. How many students reported that they do community service?

____

2. Is this four times more or less than the number of students who said they are in the band?

____

3. What are you being asked to find?

____

____

Plan and Carry Out

4. Write an equation for the situation. Let x equal the number of students in the band.

____

5. How will you solve for the variable x?

____

6. What is the value of x?

____

Check

7. Multiply your solution by 4. Is the product 124?

____

Solve Another Problem

8. There are 288 animal crackers in a package. If each child in the after-school program gets a dozen crackers, how many students are in the after-school program?

____

Name ______________________ Class ______________ Date ____________

1A: Graphic Organizer

For use before Lesson 1-1

Study Skill When you begin a new chapter in any textbook, take a few minutes to look through the lessons. Get an idea of how the lessons in the chapter are related. When you have completed the chapter, use the notes you have taken to review the material.

Write your answers.

1. What is the chapter title? ______________________
2. How many lessons are there in this chapter? ______________________
3. What is the topic of the Test-Taking Strategies page? ______________________
4. Complete the graphic organizer below as you work through the chapter.
   - In the center, write the title of the chapter.
   - When you begin a lesson, write the lesson name in a rectangle.
   - When you complete a lesson, write a skill or key concept in a circle linked to that lesson block.
   - When you complete the chapter, use this graphic organizer to help you review.

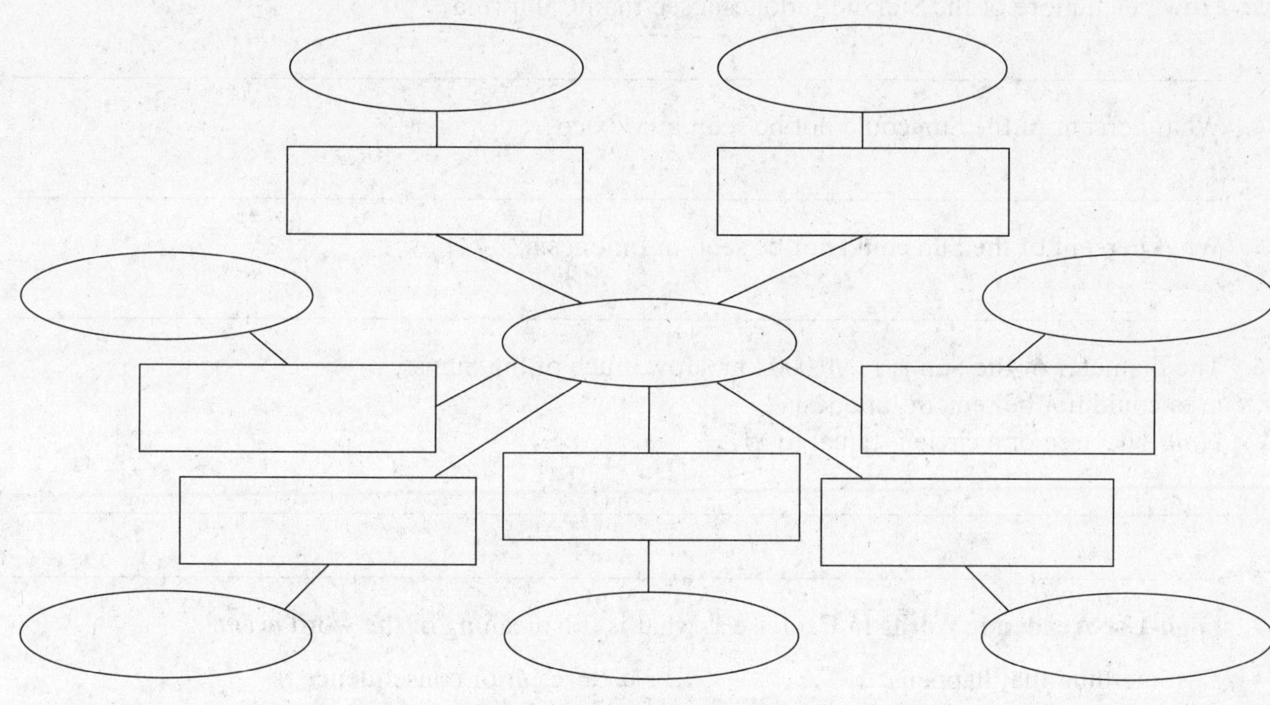

Name ______________________ Class ______________ Date ______________

1B: Reading Comprehension

For use after Lesson 1-4

Study Skill Highlight important information in your notes and on handouts from class.

Read the paragraph below and answer the questions.

A solar eclipse occurs when the moon passes between Earth and the Sun, partially blocking the view of the Sun. On June 11, 2002, a solar eclipse began at sunrise in Indonesia. The coastal town of Toli was the first to see the eclipse. Views of the eclipse lasted about $\frac{1}{4}$ of an hour with approximately $\frac{1}{5}$ of the Sun covered by the moon. In Mexico, residents witnessed about 97 percent of the Sun disappearing behind the moon, while in California about one-quarter of the Sun could be seen.

1. What event is described in the paragraph?

____

2. In Indonesia, how many minutes did the eclipse last?

____

3. How much more of the Sun did Indonesia see than California?

____

4. What percent of the Sun could not be seen in Mexico?

____

5. What percent of the Sun could not be seen in Indonesia?

____

6. The diameter of the Sun is 1,390,000 km. How much of the Sun's area could not be seen in Indonesia?
Hint: The area of a circle is equal to πr^2.

____

____

7. **High-Use Academic Words** In Exercise 1, what is the meaning of the word *event*?

a. something that happens

b. a result or consequence

1C: Reading/Writing Math Symbols

For use after Lesson 1-2

Study Skill To be successful in mathematics, you need to be able to read and understand mathematical symbols. These symbols will help you to determine relationships between figures and diagrams.

Write each of the following expressions or statements in words.

1. $|5|$ ______________________
2. -6 ______________________
3. $-|8|$ ______________________
4. $-2 < -1$ ______________________
5. $3 \neq 5$ ______________________
6. $|-2| = |2|$ ______________________

____

7. 803 cm ≈ 8 m ______________________

____

8. $\frac{9}{2} = 4.5$ ______________________

Write each of the following expressions using appropriate symbols.

9. the absolute value of negative four

____

10. four times a number increased by five

____

11. the quotient of a number and twelve

____

12. the opposite of negative seven

____

13. The opposite of three is less than zero. ______________________
14. Four less than a number is six. ______________________
15. One degree Celsius is approximately 32 degrees Fahrenheit.

____

Name ______________________ Class ______________ Date ______________

1D: Visual Vocabulary Practice

For use after Lesson 1-7

Study Skill The Glossary contains the key vocabulary for this course.

Concept List

Commutative Property of Addition	Distributive Property
Identity Property of Multiplication	integers
Associate Property of Multiplication	order of operations
Addition Property of Equality	evaluate
Division Property of Equality	

Write the concept that best describes each exercise. Choose from the concept list above.

1. $-(a^3 - 8) = -a^3 + 8$ ______	**2.** $1 \times 3z = 3z$ ______	**3.** $(8n \times \frac{3}{4})4 = 8n(\frac{3}{4} \times 4)$ ______
4. PEMDAS ______	**5.** $24 + (4 + c) = (4 + c) + 24$ ______	**6.** $-4, 0, 1$, and 5 are examples. ______
7. $3b = 2$ $\frac{3b}{3} = \frac{2}{3}$ $b = \frac{2}{3}$ ______	**8.** When $a = -2$, $5a - 4 = 5(-2) - 4$ $= -10 - 4$ $= -14$ ______	**9.** If $x = 3y$, then $x + 5 = 3y + 5$. ______

1E: Vocabulary Check

For use after Lesson 1-5

Study Skill Strengthen your vocabulary. Use these pages and add cues and summaries by applying the Cornell Notetaking style.

Write the definition for each word or term at the right. To check your work, fold the paper back along the dotted line to see the correct answers.

Definition	Term
______________________________	Commutative Property of Multiplication
______________________________	Identity Property of Addition
______________________________	Associative Property of Multiplication
______________________________	integers
______________________________	additive inverse

Name ______________________ Class ______________ Date ______________

1E: Vocabulary Check (continued)

For use after Lesson 1-5

Write the vocabulary word or term for each definition. To check your work, fold the paper forward along the dotted line to see the correct answers.

Changing the order of the factors does not change the product. ______________________

The sum of 0 and a is a. ______________________

Changing the grouping of factors does not change the product. ______________________

the set of whole numbers, their opposites, and zero ______________________

two numbers whose sum is zero ______________________

Name ____________________ Class ____________ Date ____________

1F: Vocabulary Review Puzzle

For use with the Chapter Review

Study Skill Vocabulary is an important part of every subject you learn. Review new words and their definitions using flashcards.

Complete the crossword puzzle using the words below. For help, use the Glossary in your textbook.

absolute value	additive inverses	equation	evaluate	integers
isolate	opposites	simplify	solution	variable

ACROSS

1. symbol that stands for one or more numbers
5. to replace each variable with a number and then simplify an algebraic expression
6. to get the variable alone on one side of an equation
8. to replace an expression with its simplest name
9. two numbers whose sum is zero
10. a mathematical sentence with an equal sign

DOWN

2. the distance a number is from zero
3. set of whole numbers and their opposites
4. any value that makes an equation true
7. numbers that are the same distance from zero on a number line, but in opposite directions

Name ____________ Class ____________ Date ____________

Practice 2-1

Factors

List all the factors of each number.

1. 36 ____________
2. 42 ____________
3. 50 ____________
4. 41 ____________

Tell whether the first number is a factor of the second.

5. 2; 71 ________
6. 1; 18 ________
7. 3; 81 ________
8. 4; 74 ________
9. 9; 522 ________
10. 8; 508 ________
11. 13; 179 ________
12. 17; 3,587 ________

Identify each number as *prime* or *composite.* If the number is *composite,* use a factor tree to find its prime factorization.

13. 74 ____________
14. 83 ____________
15. 23 ____________
16. 73 ____________
17. 91 ____________
18. 109 ____________

Write the prime factorization of each number.

19. 70 ____________
20. 92 ____________
21. 120 ____________
22. 200 ____________
23. 180 ____________
24. 360 ____________
25. 187 ____________
26. 364 ____________
27. 1,287 ____________

Find the GCF by finding the prime factorization.

28. 24, 40 ____________
29. 20, 42 ____________
30. 56, 63 ____________
31. 18, 24, 36 ____________
32. 20, 45, 75 ____________
33. 120, 150, 180 ____________

34. Mr. Turner distributed some supplies in his office. He distributed 120 pencils, 300 paper clips, and 16 pens. What is the greatest number of people there can be in the office if each person received the same number of items? ____________

35. The baseball league bought new equipment for the teams. The managers bought 288 baseballs, 40 bats, and 24 equipment bags. What is the greatest number of teams there can be if all the new equipment is distributed equally among the teams? ____________

Name ______________________ Class ______________ Date ______________

2-1 • Guided Problem Solving

GPS Student Page 56, Exercise 48:

Art The art teacher hands out her entire inventory of art supplies, listed at the right. Each class gets the same number of each item.

paintbrushes 120
boxes of markers 78
packs of paper 24
sets of watercolors 54

a. How many classes receive supplies?

b. How many of each item does each class get?

Understand

1. What are you being asked to do?

____

____

Plan and Carry Out

2. Write the prime factorization of 120. ______________

3. Write the prime factorization of 78. ______________

4. Write the prime factorization of 24. ______________

5. Write the prime factorization of 54. ______________

6. What is the product of the common prime factors of each number?

____

7. What is the greatest number of classes that can receive supplies?

____

8. How many of each item will each class receive?

____

____

Check

9. Is your answer reasonable? ______________

____

Solve Another Problem

10. You have three pieces of string with lengths of 42 inches, 63 inches, and 77 inches. You need to cut pieces of equal length from these three pieces of string. How long should each piece be, and how many pieces can you get from each length of string?

____

____

____

Name ____________ Class ____________ Date ____________

Practice 2-2

Equivalent Forms of Rational Numbers

Write each number as a fraction or mixed number in simplest form.

1. -5 ____________
2. 0.63 ____________
3. -3.9 ____________
4. $4\frac{5}{6}$ ____________
5. $\frac{77}{99}$ ____________
6. $\frac{21}{-56}$ ____________
7. $-\frac{28}{52}$ ____________
8. $\frac{195}{105}$ ____________
9. A baseball player averaged 0.375 last season. Express the batting average as a fraction. ____________

Write each fraction or mixed number as a decimal rounded to three places.

10. $\frac{7}{21}$ ____________
11. $-\frac{9}{21}$ ____________
12. $-\frac{2}{3}$ ____________
13. $3\frac{1}{6}$ ____________
14. $-4\frac{7}{8}$ ____________
15. $3\frac{11}{12}$ ____________
16. $-4\frac{7}{11}$ ____________
17. $3\frac{1}{18}$ ____________
18. $-1\frac{7}{18}$ ____________
19. $-2\frac{7}{9}$ ____________
20. $5\frac{7}{15}$ ____________
21. $-4\frac{14}{15}$ ____________

Write each decimal as a mixed number or fraction in simplest form.

22. 0.006 ____________
23. -4.8 ____________
24. 0.97 ____________
25. 0.4 ____________
26. 9.05 ____________
27. -0.28 ____________
28. 3.082 ____________
29. -1.41 ____________
30. 4.23 ____________
31. 8.05 ____________
32. -3.02 ____________
33. 7.13 ____________

Solve.

34. The eighth grade held a magazine sale to raise money for their spring trip. They wanted each student to sell subscriptions. After the first day of the sale, 25 out of 125 students turned in subscription orders. Write a rational number in simplest form to express the student response on the first day.

____

35. Pete wanted to win the prize for selling the most subscriptions. Of 240 subscriptions sold, Pete sold 30. Write a rational number in simplest form to express Pete's part of the total sales.

____

Name ______________________ Class ______________ Date ______________

2-2 • Guided Problem Solving

GPS Student Page 59, Exercise 33:

Population In 2003, 0.219 of the people in the United States were younger than 15 years old. Write the decimal as a fraction.

Understand

1. What are you being asked to do?

____

Plan and Carry Out

2. Write the fraction with a denominator of one.

____

3. How many digits are there to the right of the decimal point?

____

4. Multiply the numerator and denominator by 1,000.

____

5. Can the fraction be simplified? Why or why not?

____

____

Check

6. Is your answer reasonable? Write the decimal in word form.

____

____

____

Solve Another Problem

7. A group of teenagers is surveyed about their preference for music performers. Of the teenagers surveyed, 0.275 preferred individual artists. Express the decimal as a fraction.

____

Name ________________________ Class ______________ Date ______________

Practice 2-3

Comparing and Ordering Rational Numbers

Determine which rational number is greater by rewriting each pair of fractions using their LCD.

1. $\frac{2}{9}, \frac{3}{6}$ ______
2. $-\frac{2}{4}, -\frac{4}{5}$ ______
3. $\frac{2}{12}, \frac{1}{4}$ ______
4. $\frac{5}{12}, \frac{9}{15}$ ______
5. $-\frac{6}{16}, -\frac{4}{9}$ ______
6. $\frac{5}{10}, \frac{8}{12}$ ______
7. $\frac{4}{6}, \frac{1}{3}$ ______
8. $-\frac{3}{8}, -\frac{8}{9}$ ______
9. $\frac{3}{6}, \frac{1}{3}$ ______
10. $\frac{2}{6}, \frac{4}{5}$ ______
11. $\frac{5}{20}, \frac{1}{2}$ ______
12. $\frac{1}{7}, \frac{1}{10}$ ______

13. During the 1992 Summer Olympic Games, the top three women's long jumpers were Inessa Kravets ($23\frac{3}{8}$ ft), Jackie Joyner-Kersee ($23\frac{5}{24}$ ft), and Heike Drechsler ($23\frac{7}{16}$ ft). Write these women's names in order from the shortest jump to the longest.

____

Compare. Write >, <, or =.

14. $-\frac{4}{9}$ ☐ $-\frac{5}{8}$
15. $\frac{1}{3}$ ☐ $\frac{6}{18}$
16. $\frac{5}{7}$ ☐ 0.63
17. -0.76 ☐ $-\frac{3}{4}$
18. $-1\frac{9}{12}$ ☐ $-1\frac{15}{20}$
19. $\frac{6}{11}$ ☐ $\frac{5}{9}$
20. $\frac{7}{12}$ ☐ 0.59
21. $\frac{6}{13}$ ☐ 0.45

Order each set of numbers from greatest to least.

22. $0.74, \frac{3}{4}, \frac{6}{7}, 0.64$ ______
23. $\frac{16}{32}, 0.45, \frac{2}{5}, \frac{9}{25}$ ______
24. $\frac{7}{8}, -\frac{5}{8}, \frac{15}{30}, -\frac{8}{11}$ ______
25. $\frac{14}{15}, 0.743, -0.65, \frac{14}{31}$ ______
26. $0.8, 0.5, \frac{5}{8}, \frac{3}{8}$ ______
27. $-\frac{9}{10}, -\frac{4}{5}, -\frac{1}{2}, -\frac{17}{18}$ ______

Name ______________ Class ______________ Date ______________

2-3 • Guided Problem Solving

GPS Student Page 65, Exercise 33:

Erika worked from 4:55 P.M. to 5:30 P.M. Maria worked $\frac{2}{3}$ of an hour. Who worked longer?

Understand

1. What information is given in the problem?

____

2. Underline the question.

Plan and Carry Out

3. How many minutes are in one hour? ______________
4. How many minutes did Erika work? ______________
5. Write an expression to represent the part of an hour that Erika worked.

____

6. What fraction of an hour did Erika work? ______________
7. Compare the fraction of an hour Erika worked to the $\frac{2}{3}$ of an hour Maria worked.

____

8. Who worked longer, Erika or Maria? ______________

Check

9. Is your answer reasonable? Determine how many minutes Maria worked.

____

____

Solve Another Problem

10. Anita swam from 3:25 P.M. to 4:05 P.M. Martin swam for $\frac{2}{5}$ of an hour. Who swam the greater part of an hour?

____

____

Name ______________________ Class ______________ Date ____________

Practice 2-4

Adding and Subtracting Rational Numbers

Find each sum or difference. Write each answer as a mixed number or fraction in simplest form.

1. $\frac{3}{4} + \frac{7}{8}$ ____________
2. $-1\frac{1}{6} + 2\frac{2}{3}$ ____________
3. $-3\frac{5}{6} - \left(-4\frac{1}{12}\right)$ ____________
4. $\frac{5}{18} + \frac{7}{12}$ ____________
5. $5\frac{8}{21} - \left(-3\frac{1}{7}\right)$ ____________
6. $1\frac{19}{24} + 2\frac{23}{20}$ ____________
7. $5\frac{1}{14} + 2\frac{3}{7} + 1\frac{4}{21}$ ____________
8. $\frac{11}{12} - \frac{5}{16} + \frac{11}{18}$ ____________
9. $\frac{5}{6} + \frac{7}{8} - \frac{11}{12}$ ____________
10. $-19\frac{5}{6} + 10\frac{9}{10}$ ____________
11. $4\frac{7}{18} - 3\frac{7}{12}$ ____________
12. $-1\frac{4}{5} - \left(-4\frac{1}{12}\right)$ ____________
13. $14.6 + \left(-3\frac{1}{5}\right)$ ____________
14. $-7\frac{3}{4} - 4.125$ ____________
15. $5.75 + \left(-2\frac{1}{8}\right)$ ____________
16. $1\frac{3}{4} - 2.75 - 4\frac{5}{8}$ ____________
17. $3\frac{1}{2} - 6\frac{7}{10} + 4\frac{1}{5}$ ____________
18. $\frac{3}{16} + \frac{1}{8} - \frac{1}{4}$ ____________

Solve each equation. Write each answer as a mixed number or as a fraction in simplest form.

19. $x + \frac{3}{8} = -\frac{1}{4}$ ____________
20. $y - \frac{1}{5} = -\frac{4}{5}$ ____________
21. $z + \left(-\frac{2}{3}\right) = -\frac{1}{6}$ ____________
22. $m - \frac{9}{10} = \frac{1}{5}$ ____________
23. $n - 1\frac{1}{3} = -3$ ____________
24. $p + \frac{7}{12} = -\frac{1}{4}$ ____________
25. $c - 7.2 = -3.7$ ____________
26. $d - 0.16 = 2.3$ ____________
27. $\frac{1}{8} + a = -2\frac{1}{4}$ ____________
28. Stanley is helping in the library by mending torn pages. He has cut strips of tape with lengths of $5\frac{1}{2}$ in., $6\frac{7}{8}$ in., $3\frac{3}{4}$ in., and $4\frac{3}{16}$ in. What is the total length of tape he has used?

____

Name ______________________ Class ______________ Date ______________

2-4 • Guided Problem Solving

GPS Student Page 68, Exercise 30:

Carpentry The piece of wood that a carpenter calls a "2-by-4" is actually $1\frac{1}{2}$ in. thick by $3\frac{1}{2}$ in. wide. If two 2-by-4 pieces are joined with their $3\frac{1}{2}$-in. surfaces touching, what is the thickness of the new piece?

Understand

1. Circle the information you need.
2. What are you asked to find?

____

____

Plan and Carry Out

3. What operation needs to be performed with the fractions?

____

4. Write an expression to show the operation that is to be performed.

____

5. Do the fractions have a common denominator? ____________
6. Add the whole numbers and add the fractions.

____

7. Simplify and change the improper fraction to a mixed number.

____

Check

8. Does your answer make sense? Could you do the problem another way?

____

Solve Another Problem

9. It rained $5\frac{1}{2}$ inches in June and $4\frac{1}{4}$ inches in July. What was the total rainfall for the months of June and July?

____

Name ____________________ Class ____________ Date ____________

Practice 2-5

Multiplying and Dividing Rational Numbers

Find each product or quotient. Write each answer as a fraction or mixed number in simplest form.

1. $-\frac{1}{6} \cdot 2\frac{3}{4}$ ______
2. $\frac{3}{16} \div \left(-\frac{1}{8}\right)$ ______
3. $-5\frac{7}{12} \div 12$ ______
4. $-8 \div \frac{1}{4}$ ______
5. $8\frac{3}{4} \cdot 3\frac{7}{8}$ ______
6. $-\frac{11}{12} \div \frac{5}{6}$ ______
7. $-1\frac{1}{15} \div 15$ ______
8. $-3 \div \frac{3}{4}$ ______
9. $-2\frac{7}{8} \div 3\frac{3}{4}$ ______
10. $-\frac{23}{24} \cdot (-8)$ ______
11. $\frac{7}{8} \cdot \left(-\frac{2}{7}\right)$ ______
12. $-7 \div \frac{1}{9}$ ______
13. $-6\frac{5}{6} \div \frac{1}{6}$ ______
14. $-8 \cdot 3\frac{3}{4}$ ______
15. $\frac{7}{10} \cdot \left(-3\frac{1}{4}\right)$ ______
16. $5 \cdot \left(-3\frac{5}{6}\right)$ ______
17. $-\frac{8}{9} \div \left(-3\frac{2}{3}\right)$ ______
18. $2\frac{1}{3} \div \frac{2}{3}$ ______

Solve each equation.

19. $\frac{1}{3}a = \frac{3}{10}$ ______
20. $-\frac{3}{4}b = 9$ ______
21. $-\frac{7}{8}c = 4\frac{2}{3}$ ______
22. $\frac{5}{6}n = -3\frac{3}{4}$ ______
23. $-\frac{3}{5}x = 12$ ______
24. $-2\frac{2}{3}y = 3\frac{1}{3}$ ______
25. $\frac{7}{12}y = -2\frac{4}{5}$ ______
26. $2\frac{1}{4}z = -\frac{1}{9}$ ______
27. $2\frac{1}{5}d = -\frac{1}{2}$ ______

28. One pound of flour contains about four cups. A recipe calls for $2\frac{1}{4}$ c of flour. How many full recipes can you make from a two-pound bag of flour?

______

29. Kim needs $2\frac{1}{2}$ ft of wrapping paper to wrap each package. She has five packages to wrap. How many packages can she wrap with a 12-ft roll of wrapping paper?

______

30. Gina and Paul are making pizza for the cast and crew of the school play. They estimate that the boys in the cast and crew will eat $\frac{1}{2}$ pizza each. They estimate that the girls will each eat $\frac{1}{3}$ of a pizza. There are 7 boys and 10 girls working on the play. How many pizzas do they need to make?

______

Name ______________________ Class ______________ Date ______________

2-5 • Guided Problem Solving

GPS Student Page 75, Exercise 33:

Recycling A family uses $14\frac{1}{2}$ pounds of paper in a week and recycles about $\frac{3}{4}$ of its waste. How many pounds of paper does the family recycle?

Understand

1. Circle the information you will need to solve the problem.
2. What are you being asked to do?

____

____

Plan and Carry Out

3. What operation should be performed on the fractions?

____

4. Write the expression using the values in the problem.

____

5. Convert the mixed number to an improper fraction.

____

6. Perform the multiplication and simplify.

____

Check

7. Is your answer reasonable?

____

____

____

Solve Another Problem

8. You have a candy bar that is $4\frac{1}{2}$ inches long. You are going to split the candy bar evenly among three people. How much candy does each person get?

____

____

Name ______________________ Class ____________ Date ____________

Practice 2-6

Formulas

Find the area and the perimeter of each figure.

1. 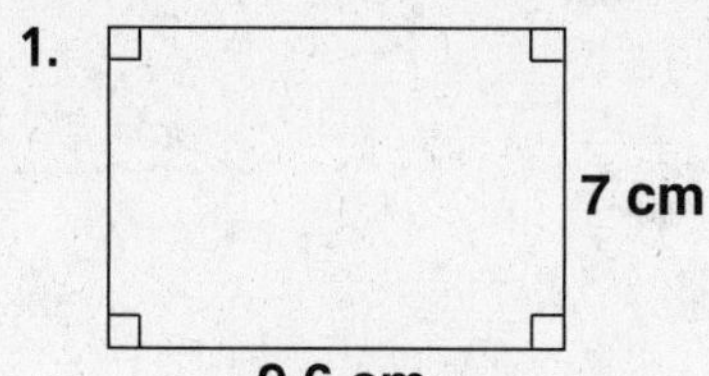

2. 20 m
17 m
21 m
32 m

____

____

____

Write an equation to find the solution for each problem. Use the formula $d = rt$. Solve the equation. Then give the solution for the problem.

3. Kent left college at 7:00 A.M. and drove to his parents' house 400 mi away. He arrived at 3:00 P.M. What was his average speed?

____

4. An airplane flew for 4 h 30 min at an average speed of 515 mi/h. How far did it fly?

____

5. Marcia rowed her boat 18 mi downstream at a rate of 12 mi/h. How long did the trip take?

____

In Exercises 6–9, use the formula $F = \frac{9}{5}C + 32$ or $C = \frac{5}{9}(F - 32)$ to find a temperature in either degrees Fahrenheit, °F, or degrees Celsius, °C.

6. What is the temperature in degrees Fahrenheit when it is 0°C?

____

7. What is the temperature in degrees Fahrenheit when it is 100°C?

____

8. What is the temperature in degrees Celsius when it is −4°F?

____

9. What is the temperature in degrees Celsius when it is 77°F?

____

Name ____________ Class ____________ Date ____________

2-6 • Guided Problem Solving

GPS Student Page 84, Exercise 23:

Algebra Find the height h of a cone with a radius of 3 ft and a volume of 27 ft^3. Use the formula $V = \frac{1}{3}\pi r^2 h$.

Understand

1. What formula are you given?

2. What are you being asked to do?

Plan and Carry Out

3. What do you do first?

4. What is the next step?

Check

5. How can you check to see if your answer is correct?

Solve Another Problem

6. For adults, a blood pressure reading around $\frac{120}{80}$ is considered normal. The upper number measures the force of the blood pushing against the walls of the arteries and is called the systolic pressure. An estimate of a person's systolic pressure, P, can be found with the formula $P = 100 + \frac{a}{2}$, where a is age. Solve the formula for a.

Name ______________________ Class ______________ Date ______________

Practice 2-7

Powers and Exponents

Write using exponents.

1. $8 \cdot 8 \cdot 8 \cdot 8 \cdot 8$
2. $(-2)(-2)(-2)(-2)$
3. $x \cdot x \cdot x \cdot x \cdot x \cdot x$
4. $(-3m)(-3m)(-3m)$
5. $4 \cdot t \cdot t \cdot t$
6. $(5v)(5v)(5v)(5v)(5v)$

Simplify each expression.

7. 19^3
8. -6^2
9. $(-5)^4$
10. 4^3
11. $-(10)^2$
12. 20^1
13. $(-4)^2 + 10 \cdot 2$
14. $-4^2 + 10 \cdot 2$
15. $(5 \cdot 3)^2 + 8$
16. $5 \cdot 3^2 + 8$
17. $9 + (7 - 4)^2$
18. $(-6)^2 + 3^3 - 7$
19. $-6^2 + 3^3 - 7$
20. $(2^3 + 8) - 5 \cdot 4 - 5^2$
21. $2^3 \cdot 3 - 5 \cdot 5^2 + 8$

Evaluate each expression for the given value.

22. $4x^2$ for $x = 3$
23. $(5b)^2$ for $b = 2$
24. $-6x^2$ for $x = 3$
25. $(-3g)^2$ for $g = 2$
26. $7 + 3q; q = 6$
27. $j^2 + 6; j = 4$
28. $2m^2 - 3m; m = 16$
29. $y^2 - 19y + 16; y = 25$
30. $x^2 + 7x - 19; x = 21$
31. $v^2 + v; v = 9$

32. Suppose you own a card shop. You buy one line of cards at a rate of 4 cards for $5. You plan to sell the cards at a rate of 3 cards for $5. How many cards must you sell in order to make a profit of $100?

Name ______________________ Class ______________ Date ______________

2-7 • Guided Problem Solving

GPS Student Page 89, Exercise 38:

Model Rockets You can use the formula $h = 160t - 16t^2$ to estimate the number of feet a model rocket rises in t seconds. How high is a rocket 2 seconds after takeoff?

Understand

1. Write the formula given in this problem. ______________
2. What does the h stand for and what is its unit of measure?
____
3. What does the t stand for and what is its unit of measure?
____
4. What are you being asked to estimate?
____
____

Plan and Carry Out

5. What does 2 seconds represent in the formula? ______________
6. What are you solving for in the formula? ______________
7. Write the formula, substituting the values that you know.
____
8. What operation do you do first? ______________
9. Solve the equation. How high does the rocket rise? ______________

Check

10. Is your expression reasonable? Does the expression check?
____

Solve Another Problem

11. A farmer puts out a salt cube for deer. The salt cube has an edge that measures 15 inches. The formula $S = 6e^2$ allows you to find the surface area of a cube, where S is the surface area and e is the length of an edge. What is the surface area of the salt cube?
____

Name ______________________ Class ______________ Date ______________

Practice 2-8

Scientific Notation

Write each number in scientific notation.

1. 45
2. 250
3. 90
4. 670
5. 4,100
6. 500
7. 43,200
8. 97,100
9. 38,050
10. 480,000
11. 960,000
12. 8,750,000

Write each number in standard form.

13. 3.1×10^1
14. 8.07×10^2
15. 4.501×10^4
16. 9.7×10^6
17. 2.86×10^5
18. 3.58×10^6
19. 8.1×10^1
20. 9.071×10^2
21. 4.83×10^9
22. 2.73×10^8
23. 2.57×10^5
24. 8.09×10^4

Order each set of numbers from least to greatest.

25. $8.9 \times 10^2, 6.3 \times 10^3, 2.1 \times 10^4, 7.8 \times 10^5$
26. $2.1 \times 10^4, 2.12 \times 10^3, 3.46 \times 10^5, 2.112 \times 10^2$
27. A mulberry silkworm can spin a single thread that measures up to 3,900 ft in length. Write the number in scientific notation.

Write each number in scientific notation.

28. 0.025
29. 0.00003
30. 0.00197
31. 0.000407

Write each number in standard form.

32. 8.1×10^{-3}
33. 3.42×10^{-5}
34. 9.071×10^{-6}
35. 2.57×10^{-4}

Name ______________________ Class ______________ Date ______________

2-8 • Guided Problem Solving

GPS Student Page 95, Exercise 33:

Astronomy When the sun emits a solar flare, the blast wave can travel through space at 3×10^6 km/h. Use the formula $d = rt$ to find how far the wave will travel in 30 min.

Understand

1. What does each of the variables stand for in the formula?

____

2. What is it that you are being asked to find?

____

Plan and Carry Out

3. Which variable are you solving for in the formula? ______________

4. To write the rate in standard form, which way and how many places will you move the decimal point? What is the rate in standard form?

____

5. Convert 30 minutes to hours. ______________

6. Substitute what you know into the formula and solve.

____

7. Write the distance back into scientific notation. Which way will you move the decimal point and how many places?

____

Check

8. How can you check to see if your answer is reasonable?

____

____

Solve Another Problem

9. A state animal shelter had 4.2×10^4 unwanted animals dropped off last year. If the goal of the shelter is to decrease the number by one-sixth this year, how many fewer animals will enter the shelter? Write your answer in scientific notation.

____

Name ______________________ Class ______________ Date ____________

2A: Graphic Organizer

For use before Lesson 2-1

Study Skill Take notes when your teacher presents new material in class and when you read the lesson yourself. Organize your notes, reviewing them as you go.

Write your answers.

1. What is the chapter title? ______________________

2. How many lessons are there in this chapter? ______________________

3. What is the topic of the Test-Taking Strategies page?

____

4. Complete the graphic organizer below as you work through the chapter.
   - In the center, write the title of the chapter.
   - When you begin a lesson, write the lesson name in a rectangle.
   - When you complete a lesson, write a skill or key concept in a circle linked to that lesson block.
   - When you complete the chapter, use this graphic organizer to help you review.

Name ______________________ Class ______________ Date ______________

2B: Reading Comprehension

For use after Lesson 2-5

Study Skill Make a realistic study schedule. Try to balance your study time with before- or after-school free time, meals, and other activities.

Use the recipe below to answer the questions.

Saffron Rice Salad

2 tablespoons white wine vinegar
1 teaspoon olive oil
2 to 3 drops hot pepper sauce, optional
1 clove garlic, minced
$\frac{1}{4}$ teaspoon ground white pepper
$2\frac{1}{2}$ cups cooked rice (cooked in chicken broth and $\frac{1}{8}$ teaspoon saffron or ground turmeric), cooled to room temperature
$\frac{1}{2}$ cup diced red bell pepper
$\frac{1}{2}$ cup diced green bell pepper
$\frac{1}{2}$ cup sliced green onions
$\frac{1}{4}$ cup sliced black olives

Combine vinegar, oil, pepper sauce (if desired), garlic, and white pepper in large bowl; mix well. Add rice, peppers, onions, and olives; toss lightly. Serve on lettuce leaves. Serves four.

1. What can you make by combining the ingredients above?

____

2. How many ingredients are used in the recipe? ______________

3. What is the smallest quantity used in the recipe? ______________

4. How many servings can you make using this recipe? ______________

5. How many ingredients require an amount that is a rational number but not an integer? ______________

6. Which ingredient(s) require an amount that is a mixed number?

____

7. Calculate the total quantity of bell peppers used in the recipe.

____

8. For a picnic, you need to make the saffron rice salad to serve 6 people.

   a. How many cups of sliced black olives will you need? ______________

   b. How many cups of sliced green onions will you need? ______________

9. **High-Use Academic Words** In Exercise 7, what does it mean to *calculate*?

   a. to determine using mathematical processes

   b. to place in order

Name ______________________ Class ______________ Date ______________

2C: Reading/Writing Math Symbols

For use after Lesson 2-3

Study Skill Create a list of mathematical symbols and their meanings. Keep the list in your math notebook for reference.

Explain the meaning of the bar (−) in the following examples.

1. $4 - 7$ ______________________

2. $\frac{3}{5}$ ______________________

____

3. $3 + (-5)$ ______________________

4. $3.\overline{6}$ ______________________

Explain the meaning of the dot (·) in the following examples.

5. 14.2222 . . .

____

6. 2.7

____

7. $3 \cdot 9$

____

8. Sarah is 6 years old.

____

9. 1, 3, 5, 7, . . .

____

Write the following expressions using the appropriate math symbols. Use a bar or a dot.

10. the sum of four and negative three ______________________

11. the difference between two and five tenths and three point three repeating

____

Name ______________________ Class ______________ Date ______________

2D: Visual Vocabulary Practice

For use after Lesson 2-6

Study Skill When a math exercise is difficult, try to determine what makes it difficult. Is it a word that you don't understand? Are the numbers difficult to use?

Concept List

composite numbers	factors	formula
prime numbers	greatest common factor	least common denominator
least common multiple	reciprocals	relatively prime

Write the concept that best describes each exercise. Choose from the concept list above.

1. $C = \frac{5}{9}(F - 32)$ ____________	**2.** The number 336 represents this for the numbers 28 and 48. ____________	**3.** 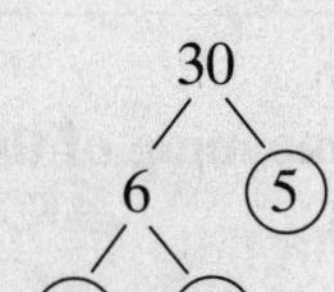 ____________
4. The number 2 represents this for the numbers 24 and 70. ____________	**5.** 2, 13, 23, and 37 are examples of these. ____________	**6.** $\frac{a}{b}$ and $\frac{b}{a}$ ____________
7. 15 and 22 ____________	**8.** 4, 14, 22, and 36 are examples of these. ____________	**9.** The number 105 represents this for the fractions $\frac{5}{7}$ and $\frac{14}{15}$. ____________

Name ______________________ Class ______________ Date ______________

2E: Vocabulary Check

For use after Lesson 2-7

Study Skill Strengthen your vocabulary. Use these pages and add cues and summaries by applying the Cornell Notetaking style.

Write the definition for each word or term at the right. To check your work, fold the paper back along the dotted line to see the correct answers.

______________________	base
______________________	prime number
______________________	least common multiple
______________________	repeating decimal
______________________	multiplicative inverse

2E: Vocabulary Check (continued)

For use after Lesson 2-7

Write the vocabulary word or term for each definition. To check your work, fold the paper forward along the dotted line to see the correct answers.

the number that is used as a factor when a number is written in exponential form ______________________

a whole number with exactly two factors, 1 and the number itself ______________________

For any two or more numbers, it is the smallest number that is a multiple of all of the numbers. ______________________

a decimal that repeats the same digits without end ______________________

the reciprocal of a number ______________________

Name ______________________ Class ______________ Date ______________

2F: Vocabulary Review Puzzle

For use with the Chapter Review

Study Skill Review vocabulary words often to keep them fresh in your mind.

Complete the crossword puzzle using the words below. For help, use the Glossary in your textbook.

scientific notation	reciprocals	power	exponent	formula
greatest common factor	divisible	base	rational	

ACROSS

2. two numbers whose product is 1
5. a way to abbreviate very large or very small numbers
8. an expression using a base and an exponent
9. A number is __________ by a second whole number if it can be divided by the second number with a remainder of 0.

DOWN

1. the greatest number that is a factor of two or more numbers
3. the number used as a factor in exponential expressions
4. This term applies to numbers that can be written in the form $\frac{a}{b}$, where a is an integer and b is any nonzero integer.
6. a small raised number indicating how many times a base is used as a factor
7. a rule using variables and showing a relationship between two or more quantities

Name ______________________ Class ______________ Date ______________

Practice 3-1

Exploring Square Roots and Irrational Numbers

Find the two square roots of each number.

1. 81

2. $\frac{9}{49}$

3. $\frac{1}{121}$

4. 289

Find each square root. Round to the nearest tenth if necessary.

5. $\sqrt{130}$

6. $\sqrt{8}$

7. $\sqrt{144}$

8. $\sqrt{160}$

9. $\sqrt{182}$

10. $\sqrt{256}$

11. $\sqrt{301}$

12. $\sqrt{350}$

Identify each number as *rational* or *irrational*.

13. $\sqrt{16}$

14. $\sqrt{11}$

15. $\sqrt{196}$

16. $\frac{4}{5}$

17. $0.\overline{712}$

18. -8

19. $\sqrt{3}$

20. 5.2

21. 0.1010010001 . . .

22. $-\sqrt{25}$

23. $\sqrt{306}$

24. 2.7064

Use $s = 20\sqrt{273 + T}$ to estimate the speed of sound s in meters per second for each Celsius temperature T. Round to the nearest integer.

25. 37°C

26. −1°C

27. 15°C

28. −18°C

Find the value of each expression.

29. $\sqrt{(49)^2}$

30. $\left(\sqrt{169}\right)^2$

31. $\sqrt{(2.7)^2}$

32. $-\sqrt{(4)^2}$

Estimate the value of each expression to the nearest integer.

33. $\sqrt{5}$

34. $-\sqrt{4}$

35. $\sqrt{3}$

36. $-\sqrt{245}$

37. $-\sqrt{21}$

38. $\sqrt{50}$

Name ______________________ Class ______________ Date ____________

3-1 • Guided Problem Solving

GPS Student Page 110, Exercise 47:

Ferris Wheels The formula $d = 1.23\sqrt{h}$ represents the distance in miles d you can see from h feet above ground. On the London Eye Ferris Wheel, you are 450 ft above ground. To the nearest tenth of a mile, how far can you see?

Understand

1. What are you being asked to find?

____

____

____

Plan and Carry Out

2. What is the formula? ____________________

3. What is the height? ____________________

4. Substitute known values into the formula.

____

5. Simplify using a calculator. Round to the nearest tenth.

____

Check

6. Use estimation to check your answer.

____

____

____

____

Solve Another Problem

7. The formula $d = 1.23\sqrt{h}$ represents the distance in miles d you can see from h feet above ground. At the top of the Ferris wheel at Cedar Point, you are 140 ft above ground. To the nearest tenth of a mile, how far can you see?

____

Name ______________________ Class ______________ Date ______________

Practice 3-2

The Pythagorean Theorem

Find the length of the hypotenuse of each triangle. If necessary, round to the nearest tenth.

1. 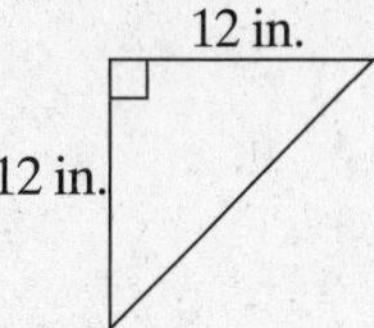

____

2. 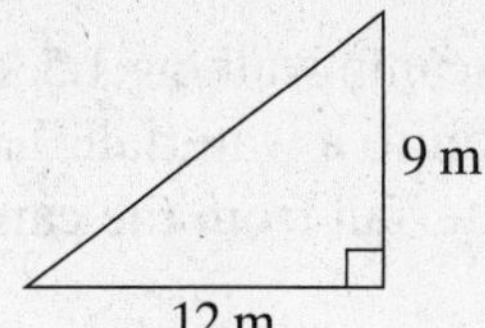

____

3. 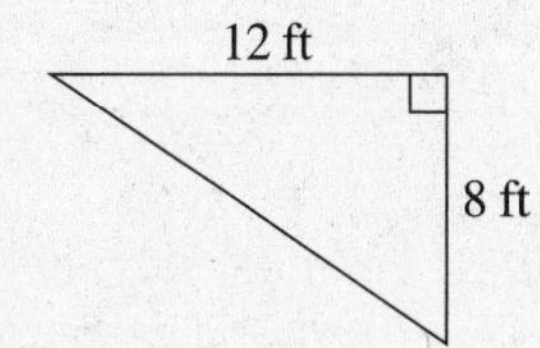

____

4. 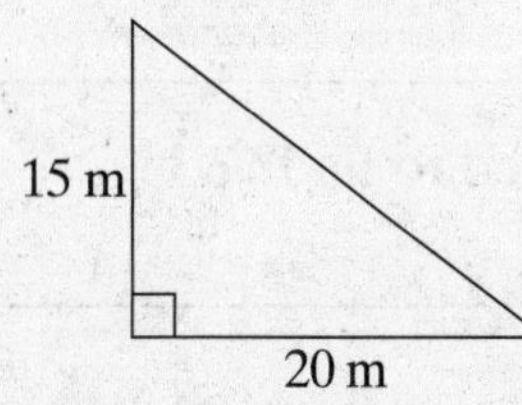

____

Let *a* and *b* represent the lengths of the legs of a right triangle. Find the length of the hypotenuse. If necessary, round to the nearest tenth.

5. $a = 14, b = 18$ _______________

6. $a = 7, b = 23$ _______________

7. $a = 15, b = 8$ _______________

Solve.

8. A circus performer walks on a tightrope 25 feet above the ground. The tightrope is supported by two beams and two support cables. If the distance between each beam and the base of its suppport cable is 15 feet, what is the length of the support cable? Round to the nearest foot.

____

You are given three circles, as shown. Points *A, B, C, D, E, F,* and *G* lie on the same line. Find each length to the nearest tenth.

9. *HD* _______________

10. *IE* _______________

11. *JD* _______________

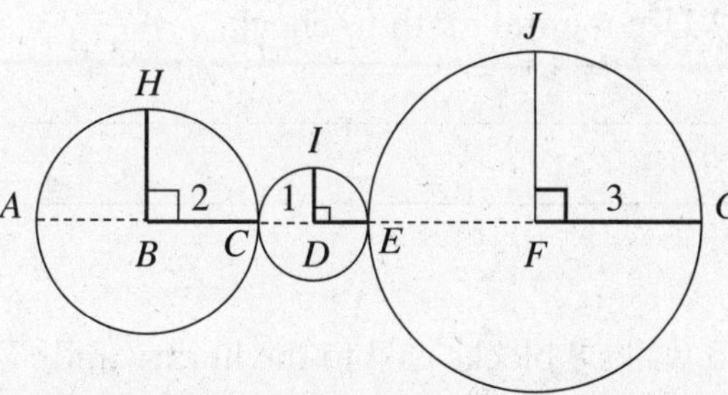

Name ______________________ Class ______________ Date ______________

3-2 • Guided Problem Solving

GPS Student Page 115, Exercise 20:

Two hikers start a trip from a camp walking 1.5 km due east. They turn due north and walk 1.7 km to a waterfall. To the nearest tenth of a kilometer, how far is the waterfall from the camp?

Understand

1. Distances are given for walking in which two directions?

   ____

2. What are you being asked to find?

   ____

Plan and Carry Out

3. Draw a picture.
4. Write the formula for the Pythagorean Theorem. ______________
5. What part of the triangle has a missing length? ______________
6. Substitute known values into the Pythagorean Theorem.

   ____

7. Simplify. ______________________
8. Add. ______________________
9. Find the positive square root of the hypotenuse, the missing length.

   ____

10. Estimate, or simplify, using a calculator. ______________
11. How far is the waterfall from the camp? ______________

Check

12. Is your answer reasonable? Use mental math to check.

    ____

    ____

Solve Another Problem

13. Leah starts at her house and walks 8 blocks east to the library and then 12 blocks south to school. How far is she from her house?

    ____

    ____

Name ______________________ Class ______________ Date ______________

Practice 3-3

Using The Pythagorean Theorem

Find the missing leg length. If necessary, round the answer to the nearest tenth.

1.

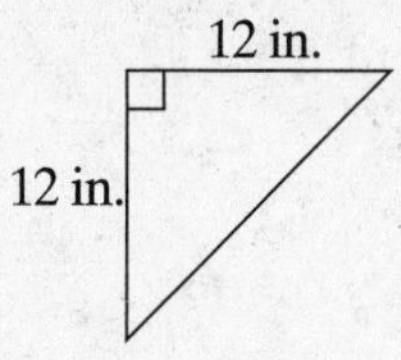

____

2.

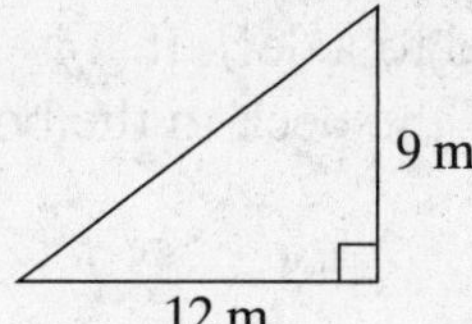

____

3.

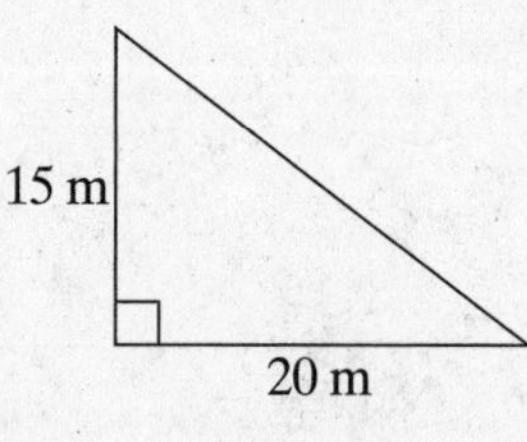

____

4.

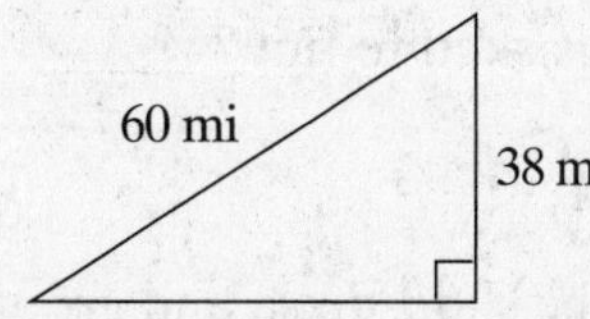

____

For Exercises 5–14, *a* and *b* represent leg lengths and *c* represents the length of the hypotenuse. Find the missing leg length. If necessary, round to the nearest tenth.

5. $a = 8$ cm, $c = 12$ cm ______________

6. $b = 9$ in., $c = 15$ in. ______________

7. $b = 5$ m, $c = 25$ m ______________

8. $a = 36$ in., $c = 39$ in. ______________

9. $a = 10$ m, $c = 20$ m ______________

10. $b = 24$ mm, $c = 25$ mm ______________

11. $a = 9$ yd, $c = 41$ yd ______________

12. $b = 10$ cm, $c = 26$ cm ______________

13. $b = 27$ yd, $c = 130$ yd ______________

14. $a = 11$ mi, $c = 61$ mi ______________

15. One leg of a right triangle is 4 ft long and the hypotenuse is 5 ft long. Ritchie uses $\sqrt{4^2 + 5^2}$ to find the length of the other leg. Is Ritchie correct in his approach? Why or why not?

____

____

____

Name ______________________________ Class ____________________ Date ________________

3-3 • Guided Problem Solving

GPS Student Page 120, Exercise 13:

A 10-ft-long slide is attached to a deck that is 5 ft high. Find the distance from the bottom of the deck to the bottom of the slide to the nearest tenth.

Understand

1. What two lengths are given in the problem? ____________________
2. What are you being asked to find? ____________________

Plan and Carry Out

3. Draw a picture of the slide, deck, and ground.
4. What kind of a triangle is formed by the picture? ____________
5. Is the unknown length a leg or hypotenuse of the triangle?

   ____
6. Write down the formula for the Pythagorean Theorem.

   ____
7. Substitute values from your picture into the Pythagorean Theorem. ________________________________
8. Simplify. ________________________________
9. Use a calculator to find the square root. Round to the nearest tenth. ____________________________
10. What is the distance from the bottom of the deck to the bottom of the slide? ____________________________

Check

11. Use the Pythagorean Theorem to check the length of the slide based on your answer, and the height of the deck. Is your answer the same as the given slide length? Why or why not?

    ____

    ____

Solve Another Problem

12. Mason is on the southwest corner of a 90° intersection. One street in the intersection is 23 ft wide. If Mason crosses diagonally to the northeast corner, he will walk 34 ft. Find the width of the other street. If necessary, round your answer to the nearest tenth. ____________________________

Name ______________________ Class ______________ Date ______________

Practice 3-4

Graphing in the Coordinate Plane

Name the coordinates of each point in the graph.

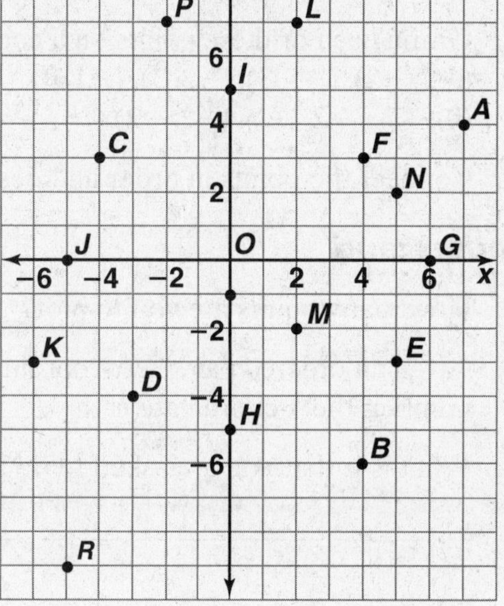

1. *J* ______

2. *R* ______

3. *K* ______

4. *M* ______

5. *I* ______

6. *P* ______

7. *N* ______

8. *L* ______

In which quadrant or on which axis is each point located?

9. $(-3, -2)$ ______

10. $(7, 0)$ ______

11. $(4, 0)$ ______

12. $(-3, -9)$ ______

13. $(4, -7)$ ______

14. $(7, -5)$ ______

15. $(2, 9)$ ______

16. $(-3, 2)$ ______

17. Arnie plotted points on the graph below. He placed his pencil point at *A*. He can move either right or down any whole number of units until he reaches point *B*. In how many ways can he do this?

______

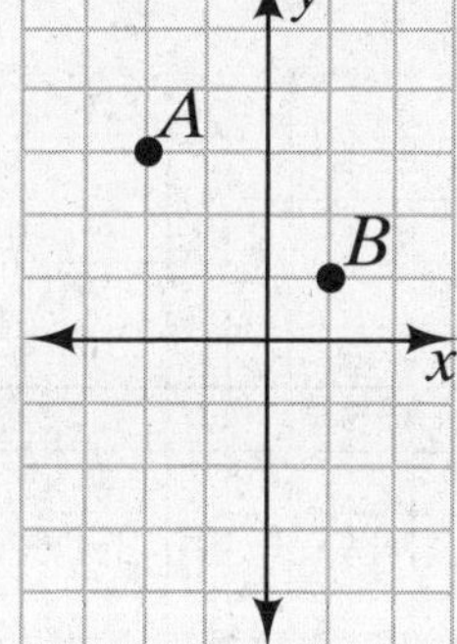

18. Marika had to draw $\triangle ABC$ that fit several requirements.
    a. It must fit in the box shown.
    b. The endpoints of $\overline{AB}$ have coordinates $A(-2, 0)$ and $B(2, 0)$.
    c. Point *C* must be on the *y*-axis and its *y*-coordinate is an integer.

    Name all the points that could be point *C*.

______

______

Name ______________________ Class ______________ Date ______________

3-4 • Guided Problem Solving

GPS Student Page 126, Exercise 25:

a. Graph each of these points on a coordinate plane: $(-2, -2), (-5, 3), (-3, 3), (-1, 0), (1, 3), (3, 3), (0, -2), (0, -7), (-2, -7), (-2, -2)$.

b. Connect the points in order and describe the figure formed.

Understand

1. How many points are you to plot? ______________________

2. Given an ordered pair, the x-coordinate is the ______________ number; the y-coordinate is the ______________ number.

3. What is it that you are asked to do after plotting the points?

____

____

Plan and Carry Out

4. What does the x-coordinate indicate?

____

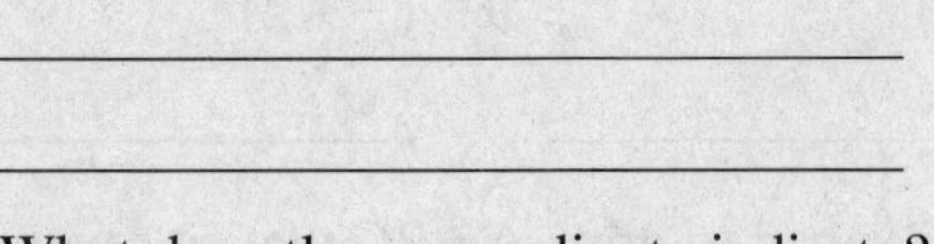

____

5. What does the y-coordinate indicate?

____

____

6. Plot the points on the graph.

7. Which quadrant is the first point in? ______________________

8. Connect the points in order.

9. What shape is formed? ______________________

Check

10. Is every point plotted correctly to create the figure?

____

Solve Another Problem

11. Plot the following points on the grid at the right. Connect the points in order, connecting the last point to the first. What shape is formed?
$(-3, -2), (0, 4), (3, -2), (-3, 2), (3, 2)$

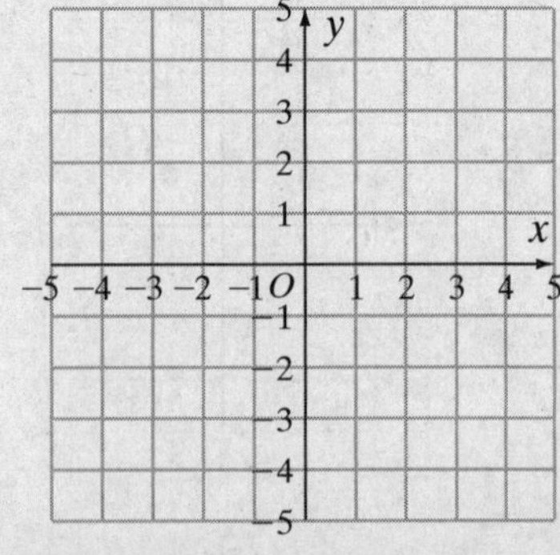

____

Name ______________________ Class ______________________ Date ______________

Practice 3-5

Equations, Tables, and Graphs

Use the equation $y = -2x + 1$. Complete each solution.

1. $(0, \underline{?})$ ______________

2. $(-5, \underline{?})$ ______________

3. $(20, \underline{?})$ ______________

4. $(-68, \underline{?})$ ______________

5. Determine whether each ordered pair is a solution of $y = 3x - 8$.

a. $(0, -8)$ ________ **b.** $(6, -10)$ ________ **c.** $(-2, -2)$ ________ **d.** $(4, 4)$ ________

6. Determine whether each ordered pair is a solution of $y = -5x + 19$.

a. $(-3, 4)$ ________ **b.** $(0, 19)$ ________ **c.** $(2, 9)$ ________ **d.** $(-4, 39)$ ________

Graph each linear equation.

7. $y = -4x + 6$

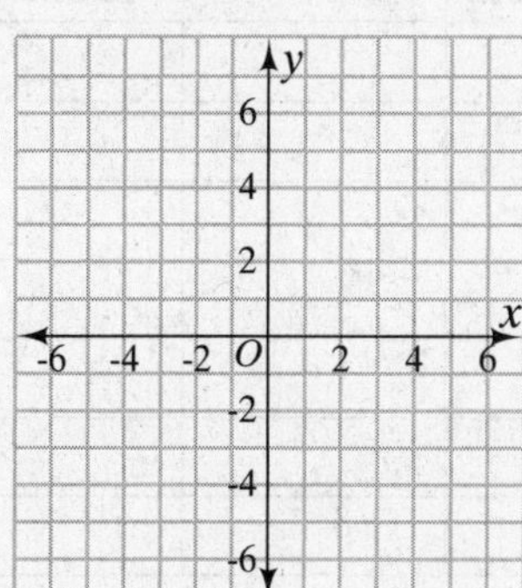

8. $y = \frac{5}{2}x - 5$

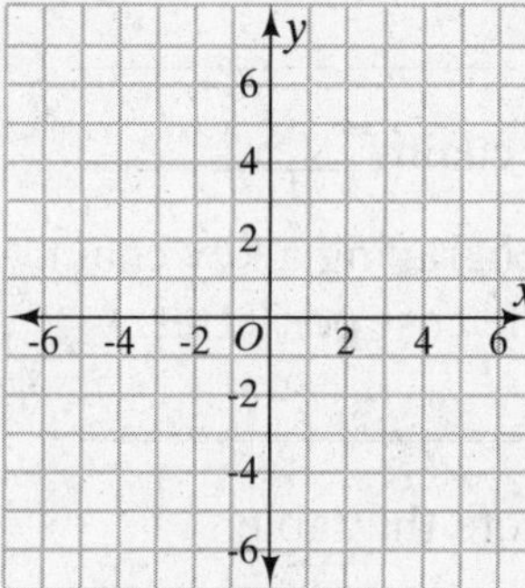

9. $y = -\frac{1}{2}x + 3$

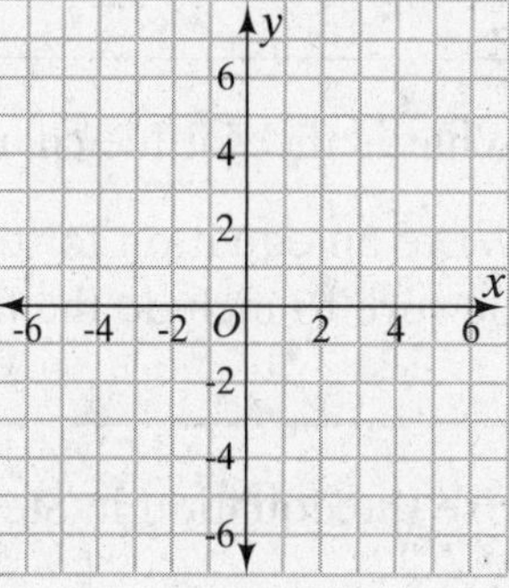

10. $y = \frac{1}{2}x - \frac{1}{2}$

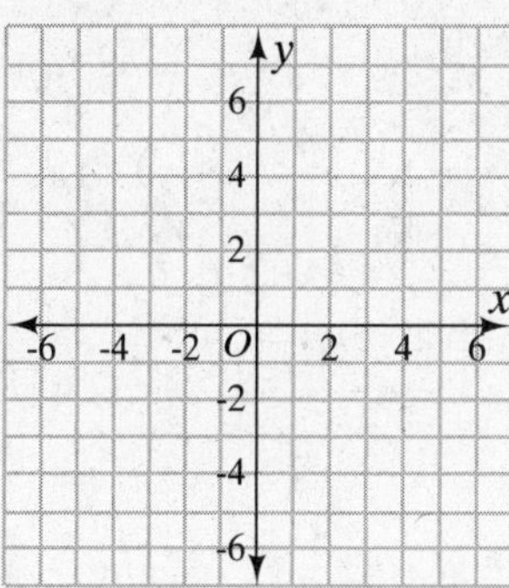

11. $y = -2x + 7$

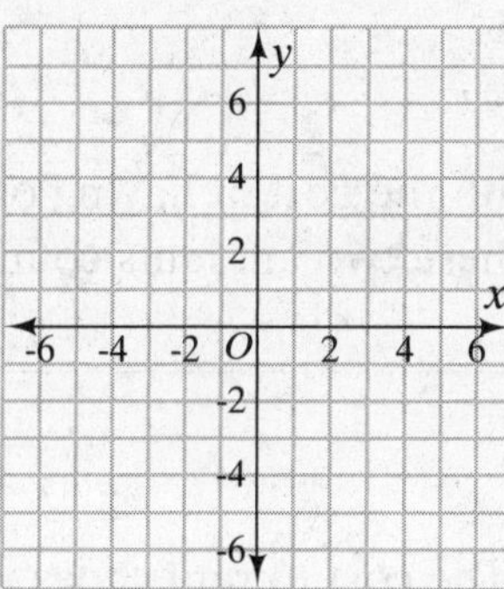

12. $y = -3x - 1$

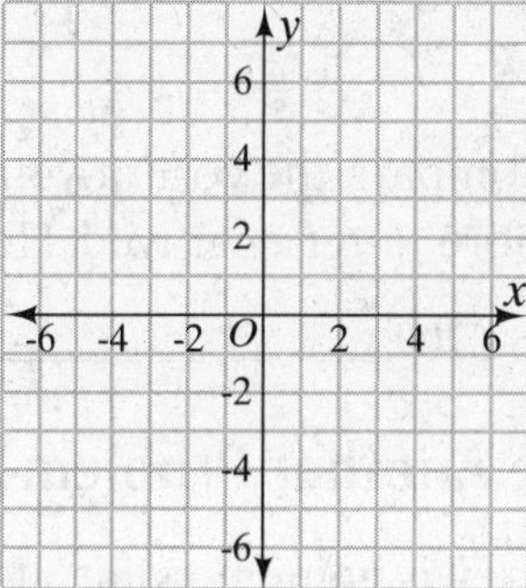

13. Jan wants to buy maps for her trip. The maps cost \$2 each and she has \$25. Make a table and write an equation to represent the amount she will have left if she buys m maps.

____

Name ______________________ Class ______________ Date ____________

3-5 • Guided Problem Solving

GPS Student Page 133, Exercise 15:

Engraving a key chain costs $10 plus $1.50 for each engraved letter. You can only spend $20. What is the maximum number of letters you can engrave? Solve by making a table and writing an equation.

Understand

1. What are you being asked to do?

____

____

Plan and Carry Out

2. Write an expression for the cost of l engraved letters.

____

3. What is the flat fee charged per key chain? ____________

4. Write an equation for the cost c of engraving a key chain. Be sure to include the flat fee and the cost per letter.

____

5. Use the equation in Step 4 to complete the table.

Number of Letters	Expression	Total Cost (dollars)
1		
2		
3		
4		
5		
6		
7		

6. What is the maximum number of letters you can engrave for $20 or less? ____

Check

7. Compare the cost of your answer with the cost of having one more letter engraved. How should these two amounts compare to $20? ____

Solve Another Problem

8. Suzy is going bowling at EZ Lanes. The cost to rent shoes is $4, and each bowling game costs $3.50. If Suzy needs to rent shoes and has $16, how many games can she play? Solve by drawing a table and writing an equation.

____

____

Name ______________________ Class ______________ Date ______________

Practice 3-6

Translations

Use arrow notation to write a rule that describes the translation shown on each graph.

1. 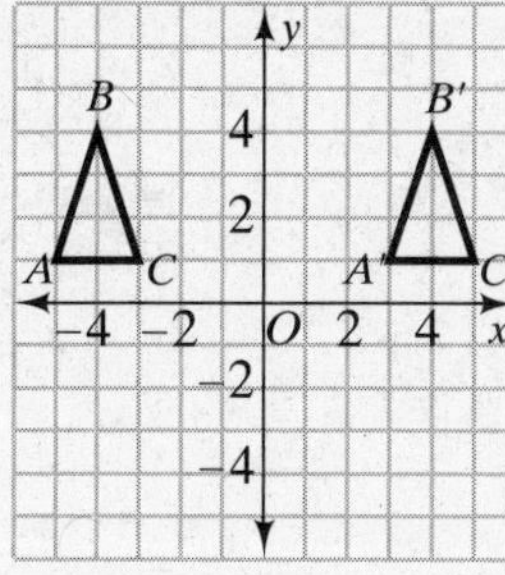

2. 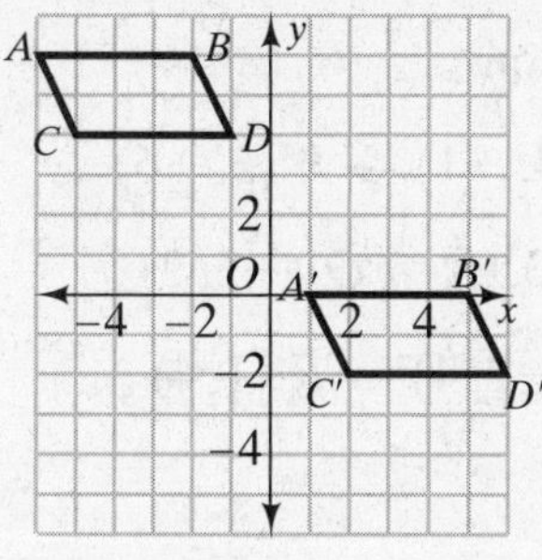

3. 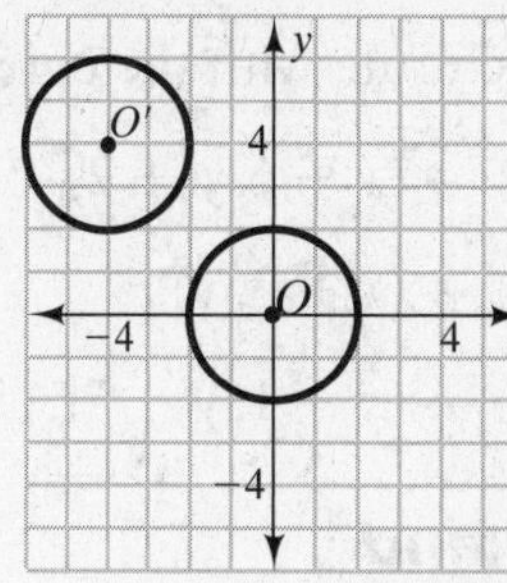

______________________ ______________________ ______________________

Copy $\triangle MNP$. Then graph the image after each translation. List the coordinates of each image's vertices.

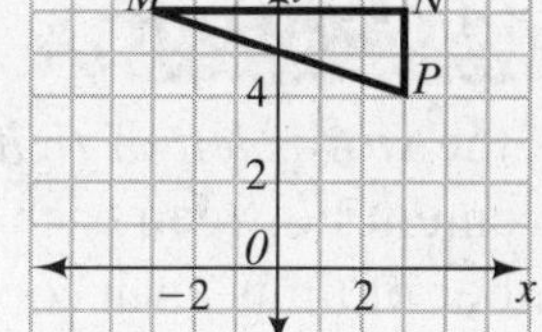

4. left 2 units, down 2 units

____

5. right 2 units, down 1 unit

____

6. left 2 units, up 3 units

____

Copy $\square RSTU$. Then graph the image after each translation. List the coordinates of each image's vertices.

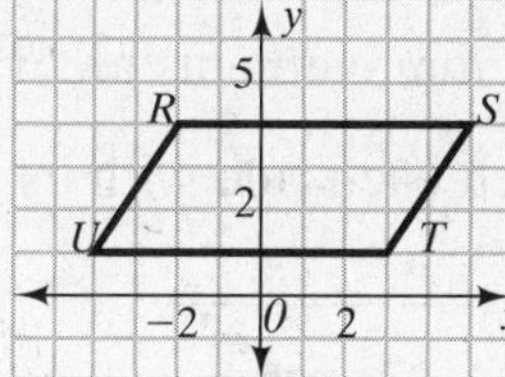

7. right 1 unit, down 2 units

____

8. left 3 units, up 0 units

____

9. right 2 units, up 4 units

____

10. A rectangle has its vertices at $M(1, 1)$, $N(6, 1)$, $O(6, 5)$, and $P(1, 5)$. The rectangle is translated to the left 4 units and down 3 units. What are the coordinates of M', N', O', and P'? Graph the rectangles $MNOP$ and $M'N'O'P'$.

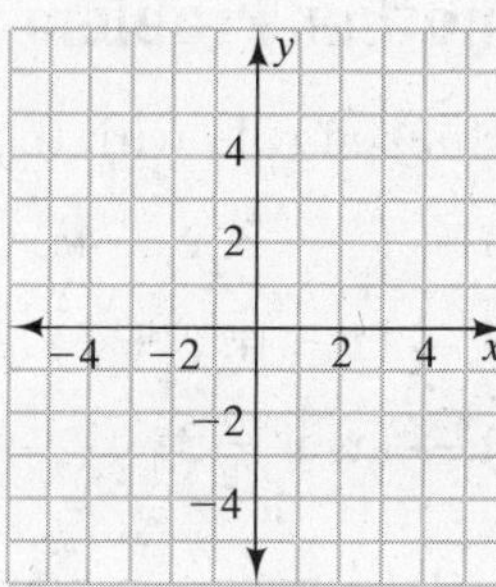

____

11. Use arrow notation to write a rule that describes the translation of $M'N'O'P'$ to $MNOP$.

____

Name ______________________ Class ______________ Date ____________

3-6 • Guided Problem Solving

GPS Student Page 139, Exercises 16-18:

Match each rule with the correct translation.

A. $(x, y) \to (x - 6, y + 2)$ **I.** $P(4, -1) \to P'(3, -6)$

B. $(x, y) \to (x + 3, y)$ **II.** $Q(3, 0) \to Q'(-3, 2)$

C. $(x, y) \to (x - 1, y - 5)$ **III.** $R(-2, 4) \to R'(1, 4)$

Understand

1. What are you asked to do?

____

Plan and Carry Out

2. Use the words *left* or *right* and *up* or *down* to describe the movement between each point and its image. Be sure to give the number of units each coordinate is translated.

   Point $P(4, -1)$ to $P'(3, -6)$ ______________________

   Point $Q(3, 0)$ to $Q'(-3, 2)$ ______________________

   Point $R(-2, 4)$ to $R'(1, 4)$ ______________________

3. Which movements are written as addition? ______________

4. Which movements are written as subtraction? ______________

5. Match each rule with its translation.

   A = __________ B = __________ C = __________

Check

6. How could you check your answers?

____

____

Solve Another Problem

7. Match each rule with the correct translation.

A. $(x, y) \to (x - 3, y - 4)$ **I.** $P(5, -2) \to P'(5, -5)$

B. $(x, y) \to (x + 4, y + 2)$ **II.** $Q(1, 6) \to Q'(5, 8)$

C. $(x, y) \to (x, y - 3)$ **III.** $R(-4, 2) \to R'(-7, -2)$

____

Name ______________________ Class ______________ Date ______________

Practice 3-7

How many lines of symmetry can you find for each letter?

1. W ________ **2.** X ________ **3.** H ________ **4.** T ________

Graph the given point and its image after each reflection. Name the coordinates of the reflected point.

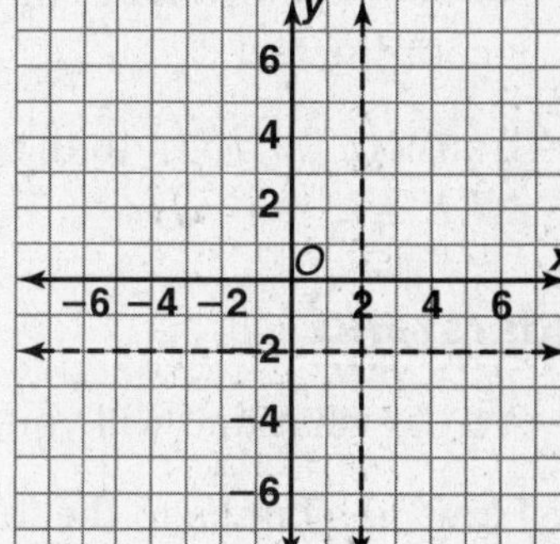

5. $A(5, -4)$ over the vertical dashed line

____

6. $B(-3, 2)$ over the horizontal dashed line

____

7. $C(-5, 0)$ over the y-axis

____

8. $D(3, 4)$ over the x-axis

____

$\triangle ABC$ has vertices $A(2, 1)$, $B(3, -5)$, and $C(-2, 4)$. Graph $\triangle ABC$ and its image, $\triangle A'B'C'$, after a reflection over each line. Name the coordinates of A', B', and C'.

9. the x-axis

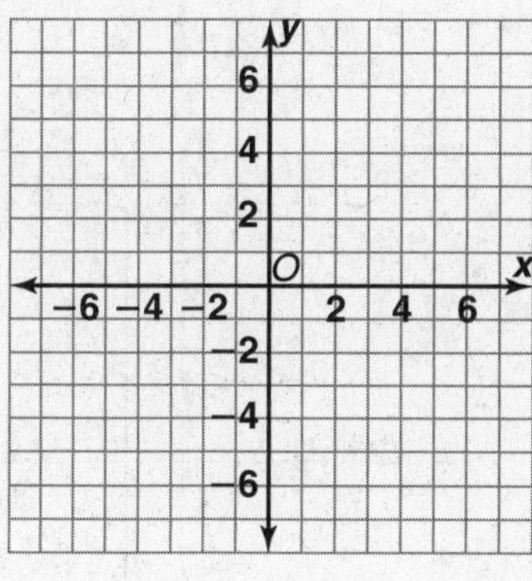

____

____

10. the line through $(-1, 2)$ and $(1, 2)$

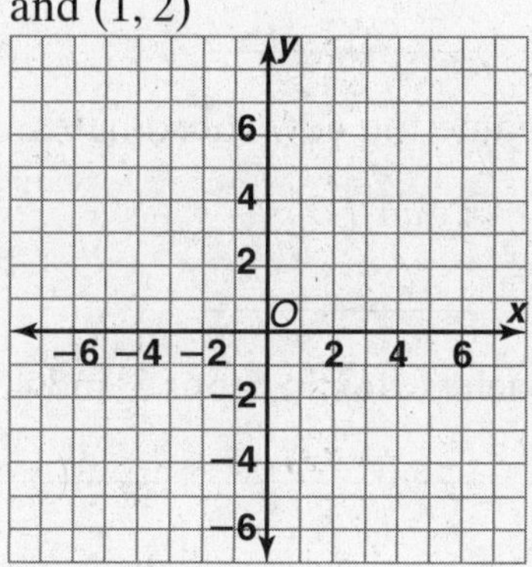

____

____

11. the y-axis

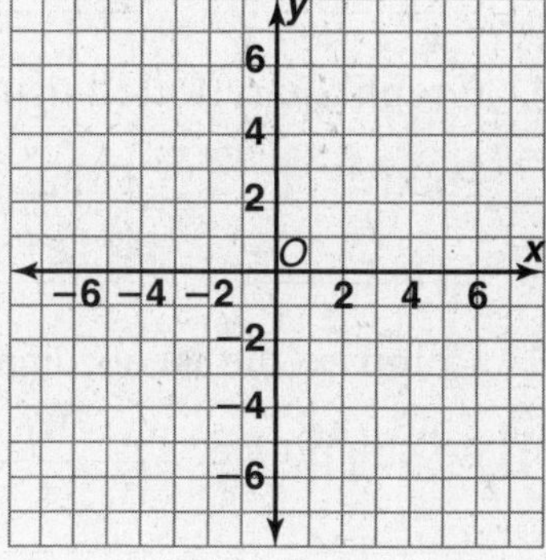

____

____

Fold your paper over each dashed line. Are the figures reflections of each other over the given line?

12.

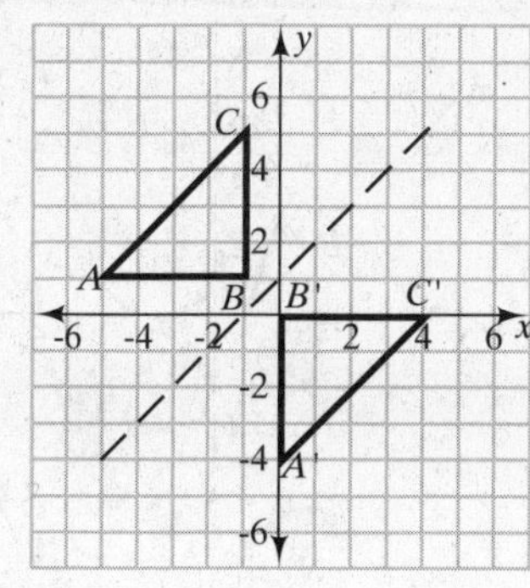

____

13.

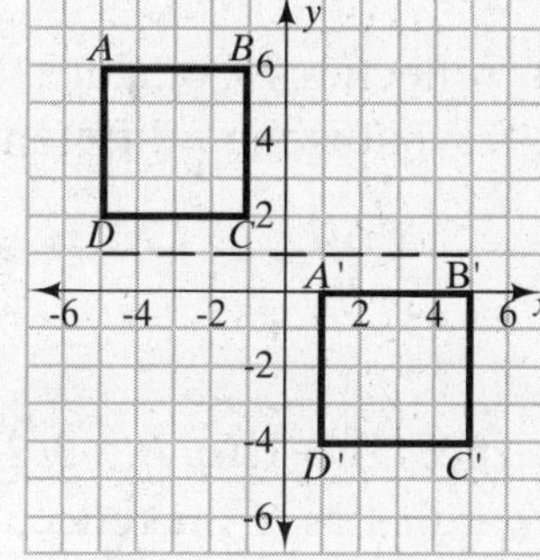

____

14.

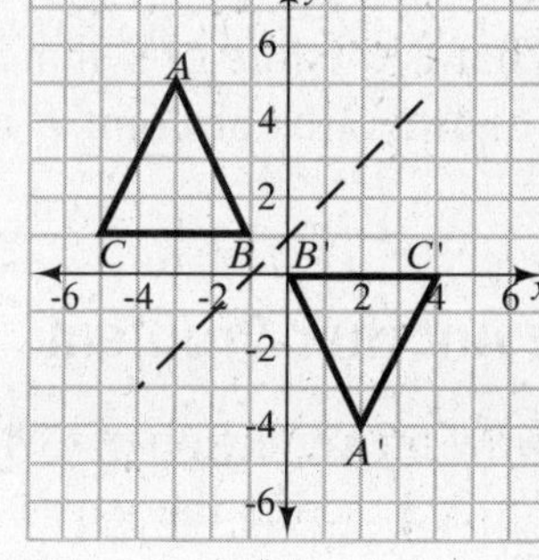

____

Name ______________________ Class ______________ Date ______________

3-7 • Guided Problem Solving

GPS Student Page 144, Exercise 22:

a. Graph the image of $\triangle JKL$ after it is reflected over the line m. Name the coordinates of $\triangle J'K'L'$. What do you notice about the y-coordinates?

b. Translate $\triangle J'K'L'$ to the left 3 units. Name the coordinates of $\triangle J''K''L''$.

Understand

1. Across what line will you reflect $\triangle JKL$? ______________
2. How many units to the left will you translate $\triangle JKL$? ________

Plan and Carry Out

3. Write the coordinates for each vertex of $\triangle JKL$.

   Point J ________ Point K ________ Point L ________

4. Graph the reflected figure and name the new coordinates.

   Point J' ________ Point K' ________ Point L' ________

5. Compare the y-coordinates of each vertex in Steps 3 and 4. What do you notice? ______________________________

   ____

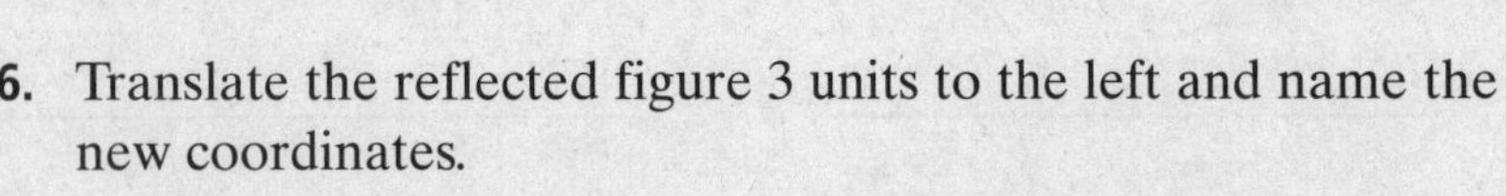

6. Translate the reflected figure 3 units to the left and name the new coordinates.

   Point J'' ________ Point K'' ________ Point L'' ________

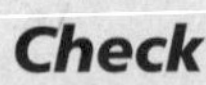

Check

7. What is the line of symmetry in your reflection? Compare the x-coordinates of Point J' and Point J''. What is their difference?

   ____

Solve Another Problem

8. Draw the reflection of $\triangle ABC$ with vertices $A(-1, 0)$, $B(-3, 2)$, and $C(-2, 3)$ across the y-axis. Give the coordinates of the reflection's vertices.

   ____

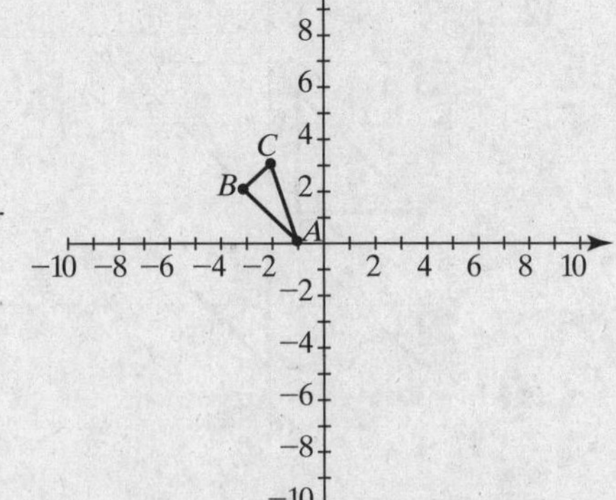

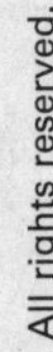

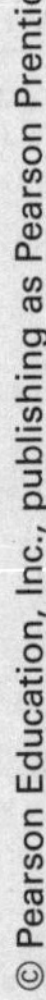

Name ______________________ Class ______________ Date ______________

Practice 3-8

Rotations

Graph each point. Then rotate it the given number of degrees about the origin. Give the coordinates of the image.

1. $V(2, -3)$; 90° ______________
2. $M(-4, 5)$; 270° ______________
3. $V(0, 5)$; 180° ______________
4. $V(3, 4)$; 360° ______________
5. Graph $\triangle RST$ with vertices $R(-1, 3)$, $S(4, -2)$, and $T(2, -5)$. Graph the image formed by rotating the triangle about the origin by each angle.

a. 90°

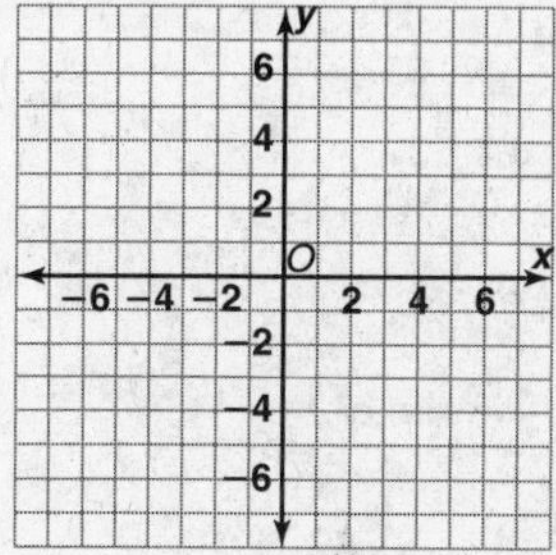

b. 180°

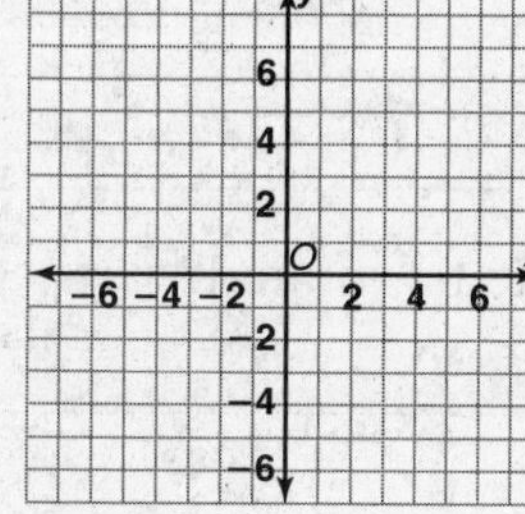

c. 270°

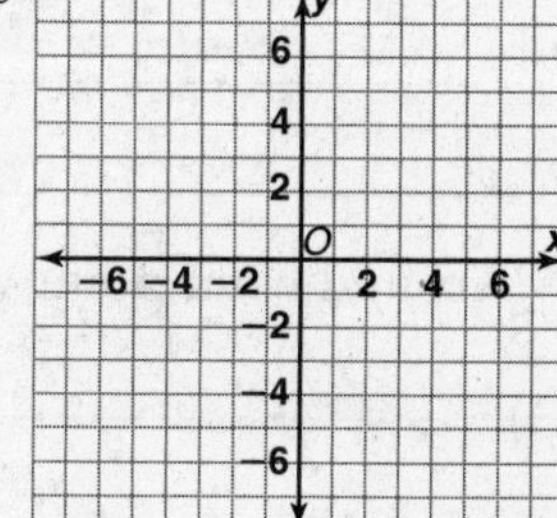

Determine if each figure could be a rotation of the figure at the right. For each figure that could be a rotation, tell what the angle of rotation appears to be.

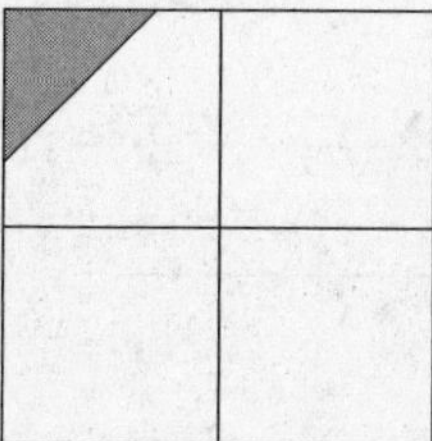

6.

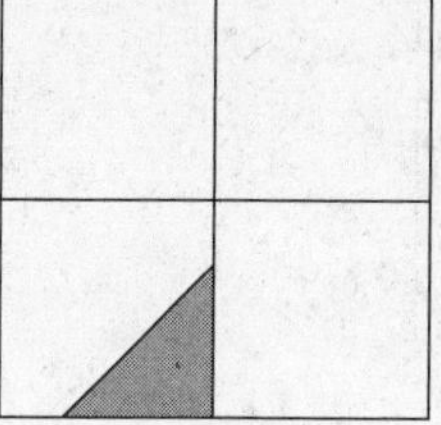

____

7.

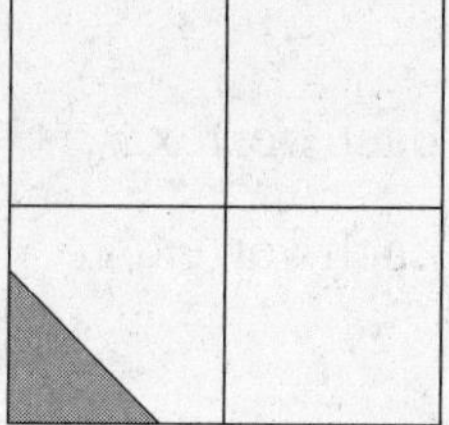

____

8.

____

9.

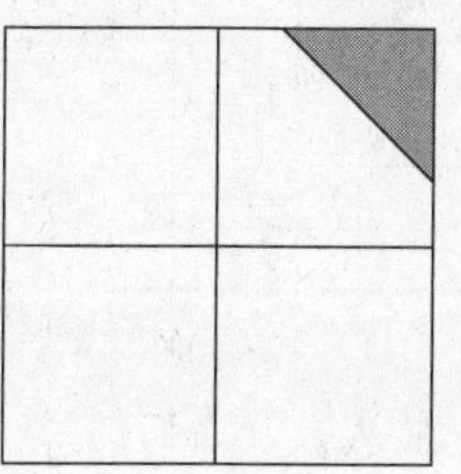

____

10.

____

11.

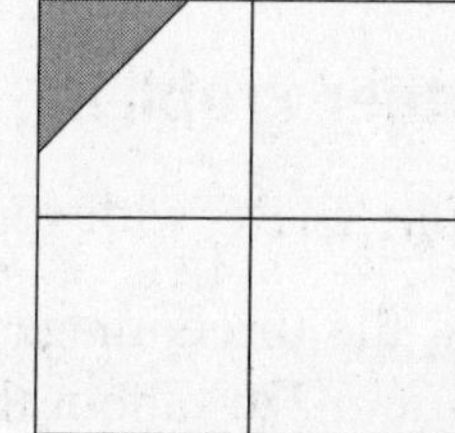

____

Name ______________________ Class ______________ Date ______________

3-8 • Guided Problem Solving

GPS Student Page 148, Exercise 12:

Graph $\triangle JKL$ with vertices $J(1, -3)$, $K(6, -2)$, and $L(6, -4)$. Graph the three images formed by rotating the triangle 90°, 180°, and 270° about the origin.

Understand

1. What are you asked to do?

____

____

2. Around what point will the triangle be rotated?

____

Plan and Carry Out

3. Graph the triangle.

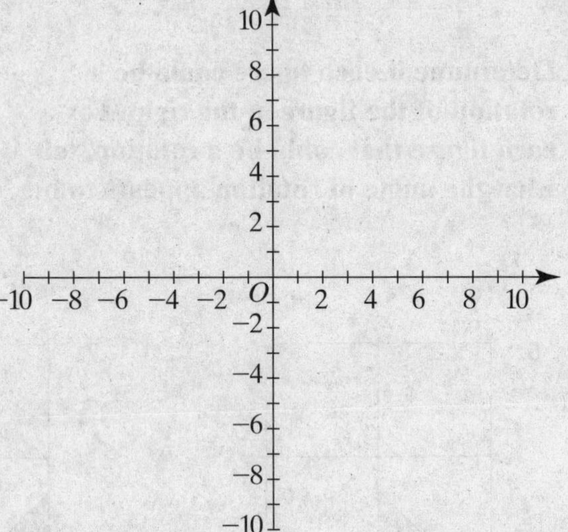

4. What is a rotation?

____

5. What direction does the figure rotate?

____

6. Rotate the figure 90° and mark each vertex.
7. Rotate the original figure 180° and mark each vertex.
8. Rotate the original figure 270° and mark each vertex.

Check

9. How can you check that your figures are rotated correctly?

____

____

____

Solve Another Problem

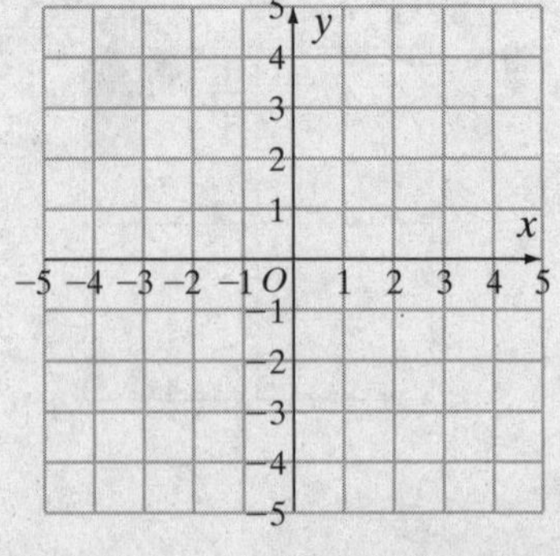

10. a. Graph $\triangle ABC$ with vertices $A(2, 2)$, $B(1, 1)$, and $C(1, 3)$.

    b. Draw the three images formed by rotating the triangle 90°, 180°, and 270° about the origin.

Name ______________________ Class ______________ Date ______________

3A: Graphic Organizer

For use before Lesson 3-1

Study Skill Many skills build on each other. Before you begin a new lesson, do a quick review of the material covered in earlier lessons. Ask for help if there are any concepts you did not understand.

Write your answers.

1. What is the chapter title? ______________________
2. How many lessons are there in this chapter? ______________________
3. What is the topic of the Test-Taking Strategies page? ______________________
4. Complete the graphic organizer below as you work through the chapter.
   - In the center, write the title of the chapter.
   - When you begin a lesson, write the lesson name in a rectangle.
   - When you complete a lesson, write a skill or key concept in a circle linked to that lesson block.
   - When you complete the chapter, use this graphic organizer to help you review.

Name ______________________ Class ______________ Date ______________

3B: Reading Comprehension

For use after Lesson 3-3

Study Skill Finish one assignment before starting another. It may help if you begin with the most difficult assignment first.

The map below is a coordinate map of New York City. The horizontal scale uses letters and the vertical scale uses numbers to identify various locations. Use the map to answer the questions below. The letters are typically written first, followed by the numbers.

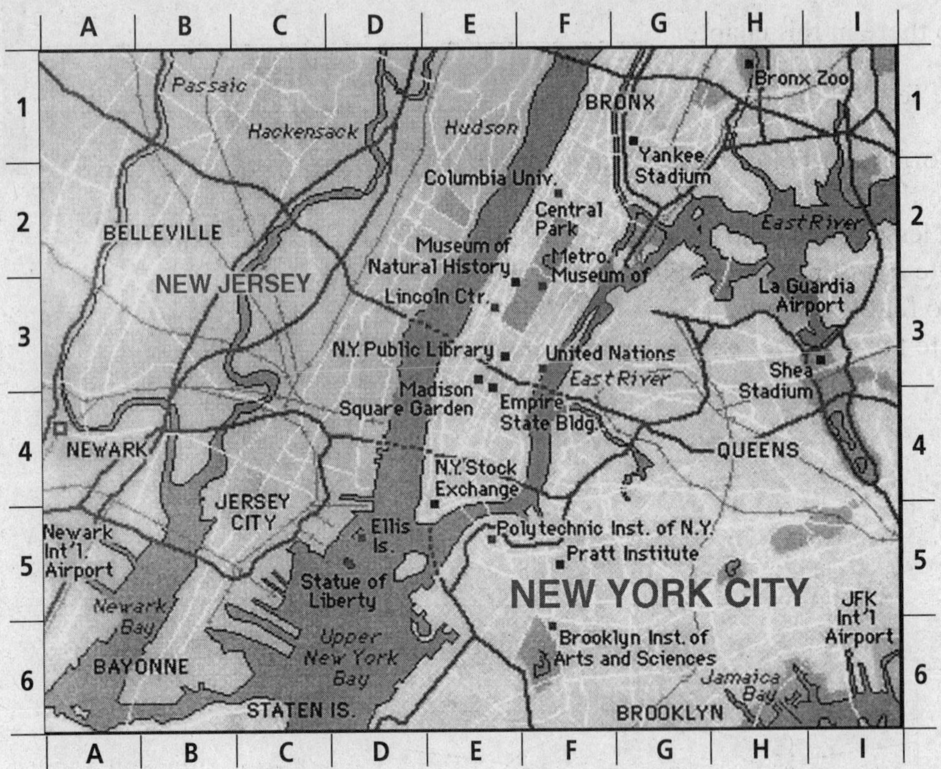

1. What are the coordinates of Columbia University? ______________________

2. What are the coordinates of JFK International Airport? ______________________

3. What landmark is located close to H4? ______________________

4. Identify the location of the New York Stock Exchange.

____

5. The Bronx Zoo is how many horizontal and vertical coordinates from the Statue of Liberty?

____

6. **High-Use Academic Words** In Exercise 4, what does the word *identify* mean?

a. to show that you recognize something b. to have power over

Name ______________________ Class ______________ Date ______________

3C: Reading/Writing Math Symbols

For use after Lesson 3-4

Study Skill Learning is when you figure out how to get past an obstacle.

Match each number in Column A with its word form in Column B.

Column A	Column B
1. 16^2	A. three raised to the seventh power
2. 0.416	B. two and seven tenths
3. $\sqrt{16}$	C. four hundred sixteen thousandths
4. 2.7	D. sixteen squared
5. 3^7	E. the square root of sixteen

Match each term in Column A with an appropriate example from Column B.

Column A	Column B
6. repeating decimal	F. 39.125
7. ordered pair	G. $\sqrt{n}$
8. scientific notation	H. 1.4142135...
9. terminating decimal	I. 0.0333333...
10. square root	J. 5.67×10^4
11. irrational number	K. $(0, -3)$

Write out the following mathematical statements in word form.

12. $2^5 = 32$

____

13. $\sqrt{25} = 5$

____

14. $6^2 > 3^3$

____

Name ______________________ Class ______________ Date ____________

3D: Visual Vocabulary Practice

For use after Lesson 3-6

High-Use Academic Words

Study Skill If a word is not in the glossary, use a dictionary to find its meaning.

Concept List

sum	table	estimate
evaluate	solve	define
order	equivalent	compare

Write the concept that best describes each exercise. Choose from the concept list above.

1.

$\frac{z}{8} = 7 - 2$

$\frac{z}{8} \times 8 = (7 - 2) \times 8$

$z = 5 \times 8$

$z = 40$

____

2.

The World's Longest Rivers

Name	Country	Length
Nile	Egypt	4,160 mi
Amazon	Brazil	4,000 mi
Yangtze	China	3,964 mi

____

3.

$7\frac{1}{6}$ and $7.1\overline{6}$

____

4.

$|-28| > 27$

____

5.

$3a + 6 + (-4.25) + (-a) + 7$

$= 2a + 8.75$

____

6.

$4n - (9 \div m)$ for $n = -3$

and $m = 7$

____

7.

$x + 29\frac{5}{8} = 42\frac{1}{9}$

$x + 30 \approx 42$

$x \approx 12$

____

8.

A *transformation* is a change in the position, shape, or size of a figure.

____

9.

$-10.1, 6.7, -10\frac{2}{3}, -4, 7.8$

$-10\frac{2}{3}, -10.1, -4, 6.7, 7.8$

____

Name ______________________ Class ______________ Date ____________

3E: Vocabulary Check

For use after Lesson 3-7

Study Skill Strengthen your vocabulary. Use these pages and add cues and summaries by applying the Cornell Notetaking style.

Write the definition for each word or term at the right. To check your work, fold the paper back along the dotted line to see the correct answers.

______________________	perfect square
______________________	real numbers
______________________	transformation
______________________	legs
______________________	irrational number

Vocabulary and Study Skills

3E: Vocabulary Check (continued)

For use after Lesson 3-7

Write the vocabulary word or term for each definition. To check your work, fold the paper back along the dotted line to see the correct answers.

a number that is the square of an integer ______________________

the set of rational and irrational numbers ______________________

a change in position, shape, or size of a figure ______________________

the two shorter sides of a right triangle ______________________

a number that cannot be written as the ratio of two integers ______________________

3F: Vocabulary Review

For use with the Chapter Review

Study Skill Taking short breaks can help you stay focused. Every 30 minutes, take a 5-minute break, then return to studying.

I. Match the term in Column A with its definition in Column B.

Column A

1. quadrant
2. origin
3. hypotenuse
4. real numbers
5. Pythagorean Theorem
6. translation
7. rotation

Column B

A. a transformation that turns a figure about a fixed point

B. the longest side in a right triangle, which is opposite the right angle

C. any one of the four sections into which the coordinate plane is divided

D. the point where the x-axis and the y-axis intersect, indicated by the ordered pair (0, 0)

E. a transformation that moves each point of a figure the same distance and in the same direction

F. a formula that describes the relationship of length between the legs and the hypotenuse, in a right triangle

G. the set of numbers that includes rational and irrational numbers

II. Match the term in Column A with its definition in Column B.

Column A

1. perfect square
2. coordinate plane
3. ordered pair
4. linear equation
5. reflection
6. line of symmetry
7. irrational numbers

Column B

A. numbers that cannot be written in the form $\frac{a}{b}$, where a is any integer and b is any nonzero integer

B. an equation whose solutions all lie on a line

C. a transformation that flips a figure over a line

D. a number that is the square of a whole number

E. a line that divides a figure into mirror images

F. gives the coordinates of the location of a point

G. a grid formed by the intersection of two number lines

Name ______________ Class ______________ Date ______________

Practice 4-1

Ratios and Rates

Write three ratios that each diagram can represent.

1. 

2. 

3. 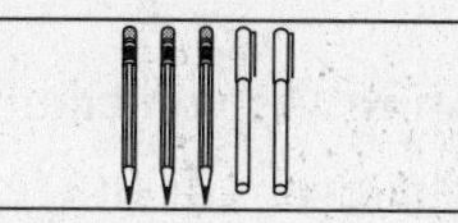

Write each ratio in simplest form.

4. 9 cm : 12 cm

5. 20 in. out of 25 in.

6. $\frac{18\text{ km}}{30\text{ km}}$

7. 6 in. to 2 ft

8. 10 min to 3 h

9. 20 s to 5 min

Find each unit rate.

10. $67.92 for 4 gal

11. $21.00 for 6 h

12. 250 mi in 4 h

13. 141 words in 3 min

14. $5.94 for 6 carnations

15. 36 min for 12 songs

The table at the right shows the results of a survey. Write each of the ratios in simplest form and as a decimal to the nearest hundredth.

Which Meal Do You Want for the Party?

Tacos	Pizza
𝍸 |||| 𝍸	𝍸 𝍸 𝍸 |

16. *Tacos* to *Pizza* ______

17. *Pizza* to *Tacos* ______

18. *Tacos* to the total ______

19. *Pizza* to the total ______

20. Which is the better buy: a 16-oz box of cereal for $3.89 or a 6-oz box of cereal for $1.55?

21. A bag contains 8 yellow marbles and 6 blue marbles. What number of yellow marbles can you add to the bag so that the ratio of yellow to blue marbles is 2 : 1?

Name ______________________ Class ______________ Date ______________

4-1 • Guided Problem Solving

GPS Student Page 162, Exercise 23:

Temperature As you climb a mountain, the temperature of the air around you drops. If the temperature decreases at a rate of $\frac{-6.5°F}{1000 \text{ m}}$, what is the unit rate of decrease? Round to the nearest thousandth.

Understand

1. Place a circle around the rate at which the temperature drops.
2. What are you being asked to find? ______________

Plan and Carry Out

3. What is the unit of the rate for the decrease in temperature and the distance traveled?

____

4. What operation will be used to find the unit rate? ______________
5. Calculate the unit rate. Round to the nearest thousandth.

____

Check

6. Another way to divide a decimal by 1,000 is to move the decimal point three places to the left. Check to see that your answer has the correct number of zeros. Then round to the nearest thousandth.

____

Solve Another Problem

7. An automobile uses 15 gallons of gas to travel 429 miles on a highway. A truck uses 18 gallons of gas to travel 477 miles on the highway. Find the unit rate of each vehicle to determine which one gets better gas mileage.

____

____

Name ______________________ Class ______________ Date ______________

Practice 4-2

Converting Units

Convert each measure. Round answers to the nearest tenth where necessary.

1. 56 in. = _?_ ft
2. 240 days = _?_ h
3. 4 gal = _?_ pt
4. 0.75 day = _?_ h
5. 2.25 t = _?_ lb
6. 84 ft = _?_ yd
7. 0.25 day = _?_ min
8. 18 days = _?_ h
9. 0.01 t = _?_ oz

Use the table to convert the following measures. Round answers to the nearest hundredth where necessary.

Customary Units	Metric Units
1 in.	2.54 cm
1 mi	1.61 km
1 ft	0.30 m
1.06 qt	1 L

10. 5 mi ≈ __________ km
11. 10 cm ≈ __________ in.
12. 12 qt ≈ __________ L
13. 9 cm ≈ __________ ft
14. 11 yd ≈ __________ m

Solve.

15. At one time, trains were not permitted to go faster than 12 mi/h. How many yards per minute is this?
16. A mosquito can fly at 0.6 mi/h. How many inches per second is this?
17. An Arctic tern flew 11,000 miles in 115 days. How many feet per minute did the bird average?
18. A sneeze can travel up to 100 mi/h. How many feet per second is this?

Use compatible numbers to find a reasonable estimate.

19. 118 in. is about _?_ ft.
20. 3,540 seconds is about _?_ hours.

4-2 • Guided Problem Solving

GPS Student Page 170, Exercise 38:

Population In 2004, about 129,405,000 babies were born in the world.

a. Find the approximate number of births per day for a 365-day year.

b. Find the number of births per hour.

Understand

1. What are you being asked to find?

____

____

2. Do you need to find an exact answer or an approximate answer?

____

Plan and Carry Out

3. How many days were in the year 2004? ______________

4. Multiply the number of births per year by the *conversion factor* of days in a year so that the time unit cancels out.

____

5. Simplify to the nearest whole number. Remember to add the units. ______________

6. How many hours are in a day? ______________

7. Multiply the number of births per day that you found in Step 5 by the conversion factor of hours in a day. Round the answer to the nearest whole number.

____

Check

8. Multiply the number of births per day by 365. Is this close to the given number of births per year?

____

Solve Another Problem

9. A shower head dispenses 2.5 gallons of water per minute. How many pints/second is this to the nearest hundredth of a unit?

____

Name ____________________ Class ____________ Date ____________

Practice 4-3

Solving Proportions

Solve each proportion.

1. $\frac{3}{8} = \frac{m}{16}$ ______
2. $\frac{9}{4} = \frac{27}{x}$ ______
3. $\frac{18}{6} = \frac{j}{1}$ ______
4. $\frac{12}{q} = \frac{3}{4}$ ______
5. $\frac{3}{2} = \frac{15}{r}$ ______
6. $\frac{5}{x} = \frac{25}{15}$ ______

Estimate the solution of each proportion.

7. $\frac{m}{25} = \frac{16}{98}$ ______
8. $\frac{7}{3} = \frac{52}{n}$ ______
9. $\frac{30}{5.9} = \frac{k}{10}$ ______
10. $\frac{y}{12} = \frac{2.89}{4.23}$ ______
11. $\frac{5}{8} = \frac{b}{63}$ ______
12. $\frac{9}{4} = \frac{35}{d}$ ______

Solve each proportion.

13. $\frac{4}{5} = \frac{b}{40}$ ______
14. $\frac{11}{7} = \frac{88}{c}$ ______
15. $\frac{x}{1.4} = \frac{28}{5.6}$ ______
16. $\frac{42.5}{20} = \frac{x}{8}$ ______
17. $\frac{15}{25} = \frac{7.5}{y}$ ______
18. $\frac{16}{b} = \frac{56}{38.5}$ ______
19. $\frac{8}{12} = \frac{e}{3}$ ______
20. $\frac{v}{35} = \frac{15}{14}$ ______
21. $\frac{60}{n} = \frac{12}{5}$ ______
22. $\frac{4}{7} = \frac{r}{35}$ ______
23. $\frac{18}{16} = \frac{27}{t}$ ______
24. $\frac{n}{12} = \frac{12.5}{15}$ ______
25. 5 is to 8 as 15 is to *w* ______
26. *y* is to 8 as 22.5 is to 10 ______
27. 14 is to *b* as 28 is to 18 ______
28. 10 is to 7 as *m* is to 10.5 ______
29. 30 is to 16 as *j* is to 8 ______
30. *r* is to 17 as 81 is to 51 ______

Write a proportion for each situation. Then solve.

31. Jaime paid $1.29 for three ponytail holders. At that rate, what would eight ponytail holders cost her?

______

32. According to a label, there are 25 calories per serving of turkey lunchmeat. How many calories are there in 2.5 servings?

______

33. Arturo paid $8 in tax on a purchase of $200. At that rate, what would the tax be on a purchase of $150?

______

34. Chris drove 200 mi in 4 h. At that rate, how long would it take Chris to drive 340 mi?

______

Name ______________________ Class ______________ Date ____________

4-3 • Guided Problem Solving

GPS Student Page 178, Exercise 35:

Money Before a trip to Quebec, you want to exchange 1,500 U.S. dollars to Canadian dollars. The exchange rate for U.S. dollars to Canadian dollars is 0.7975 U.S. dollar = 1 Canadian dollar from one bank and 0.8352 U.S. dollar = 1 Canadian dollar from another bank. How many more Canadian dollars will you get from the first bank than from the second bank?

Understand

1. How much money do you want to exchange? ______________
2. What are the 2 exchange rates from the banks?

   ____

   ____
3. Underline what you are being asked to determine.

Plan and Carry Out

4. Let C represent the number of Canadian dollars. Write and solve a proportion of American dollars to Canadian dollars equal to the rate of the first bank.

   ____
5. Let C represent the number of Canadian dollars. Write and solve a proportion of American dollars to Canadian dollars equal to the rate of the second bank.

   ____
6. How do you find how much more money you received?

   ____

Check

7. Multiply the exchange rate at the first bank by your answer to Step 4. The product should equal the amount of U.S. dollars you started with.

   ____

Solve Another Problem

8. Two friends are running in a marathon. One runner averages 6.12 minutes per mile. The other runner averages 6.39 minutes per mile. What will be the difference in their finish times (rounded to the nearest hundredth of a minute) for the 26.2-mile race?

   ____

Name ________________________ Class ____________ Date ____________

Practice 4-4

Similar Figures and Proportions

Tell whether each pair of polygons is similar. Explain why or why not.

1.

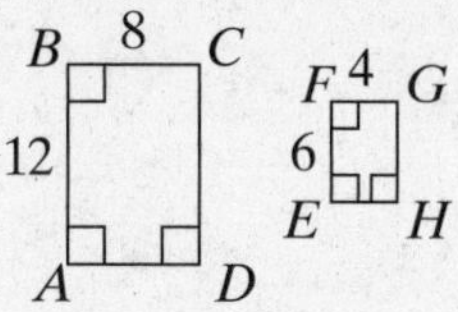

____

2.

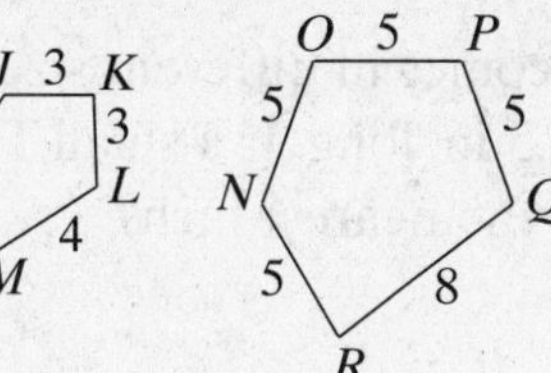

____

3.

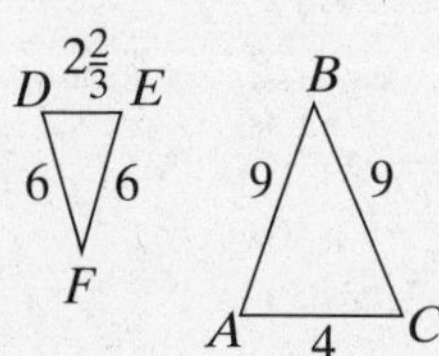

____

4.

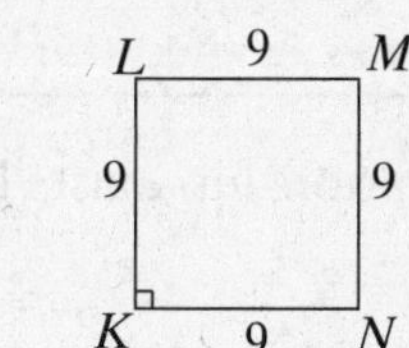

____

Exercises 5–12 show pairs of similar polygons. Find the unknown lengths.

5.

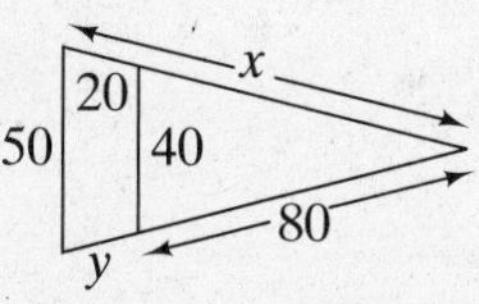

____

6.

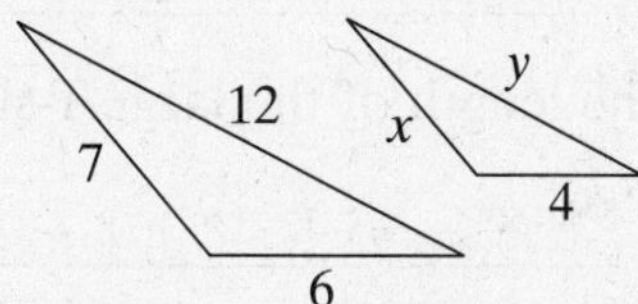

____

7.

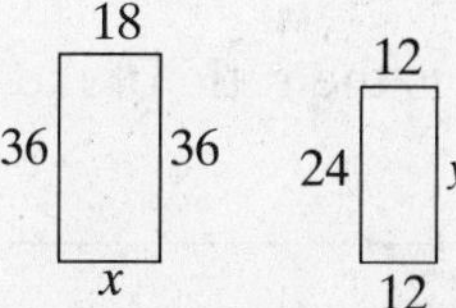

____

8.

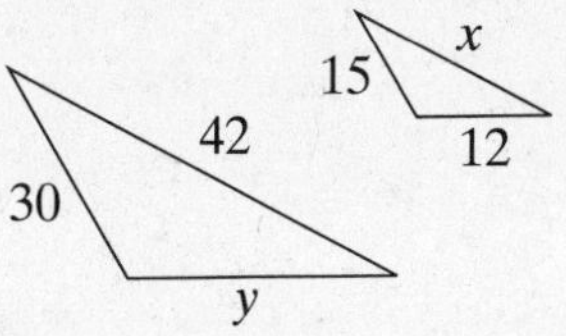

____

9.

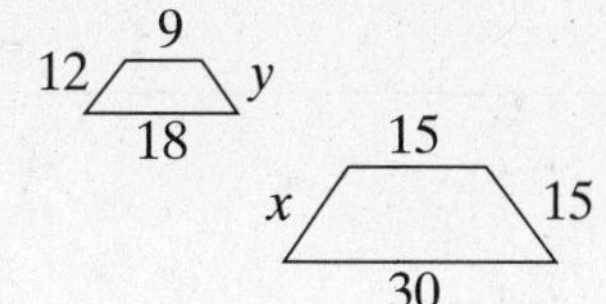

____

10.

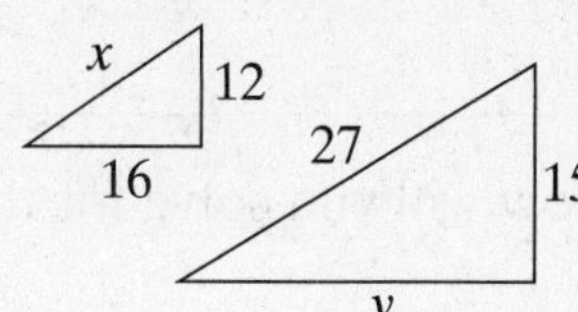

____

11.

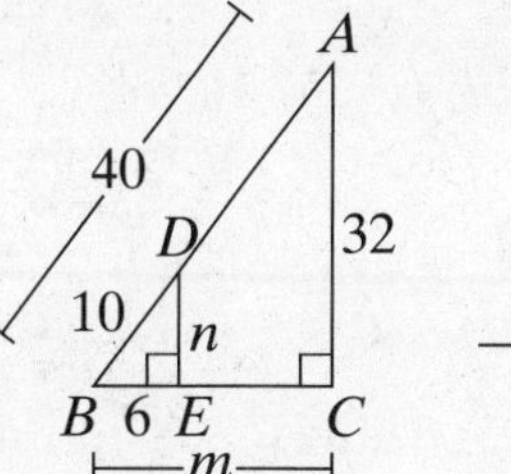

____

12.

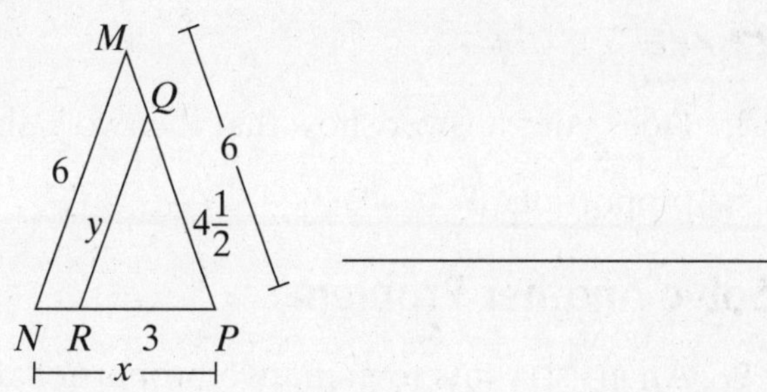

____

Solve.

13. A rock show is being televised. The lead singer, who is 75 inches tall, is 15 inches tall on a TV monitor. The image of the bass player is 13 inches tall on the monitor. How tall is the bass player?

____

14. A 42-inch-long guitar is 10.5 feet long on a stadium screen. A drum is 21 inches wide. How wide is the image on the stadium screen?

____

Name ______________________ Class ______________ Date ______________

4-4 • Guided Problem Solving

GPS Student Page 184, Exercise 15:

Clothing A T-shirt comes in different sizes. A large T-shirt is 21.5 in. wide and 26.5 in. long. If a small T-shirt is 15.5 in. wide, what is its length to the nearest inch?

Understand

1. What are you being asked to find? ______________________

   ____

2. What type of relationship exists between the two shirts?

   ____

Plan and Carry Out

3. What are the dimensions of the large T-shirt? ______________________

   ____

4. What is the ratio of the width to the length of the large T-shirt?

   ____

5. Set up a proportion for the situation. Let y equal the length of the small T-shirt.

   ____

6. How will you solve for the variable y?

   ____

7. What is the value of y? ______________________

Check

8. Does your answer show that the two T-shirt sizes are

   proportional? ______________________

Solve Another Problem

9. An artist wants to paint two proportional rectangular paintings on canvas. One painting is larger than the other. The large painting is 20 in. wide and 8 in. long. The smaller painting is 16 in. wide and 6 in. long. Are the two paintings proportional in size?

   ____

   ____

Name ______________________ Class ______________ Date ______________

Practice 4-5

Similarity Transformations

Graph the coordinates of the quadrilateral *ABCD*. Find the coordinates of its image *A′B′C′D′* after a dilation with the given scale factor.

1. $A(2, -2), B(3, 2), C(-3, 2), D(-2, -2)$; scale factor 2

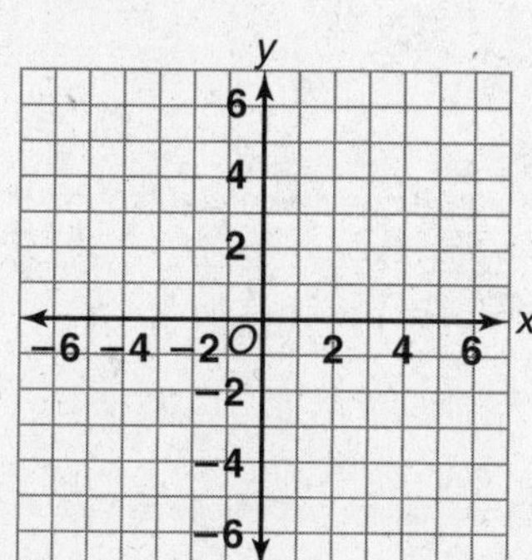

2. $A(6, 3), B(0, 6), C(-6, 2), D(-6, -5)$; scale factor $\frac{1}{2}$

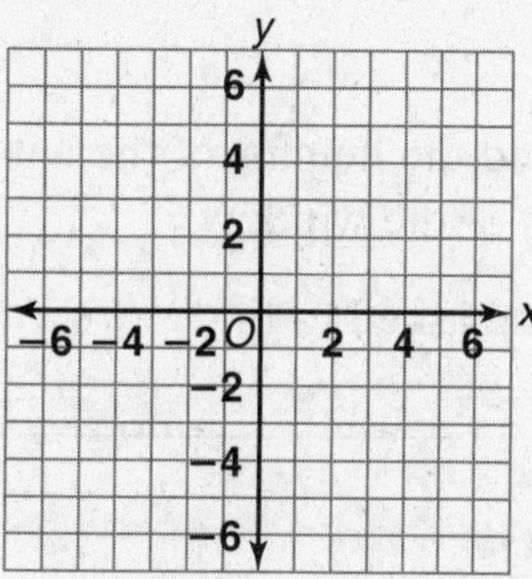

Quadrilateral *A′B′C′D′* is a dilation of quadrilateral *ABCD*. Find the scale factor. Classify each dilation as an enlargement or a reduction.

3.

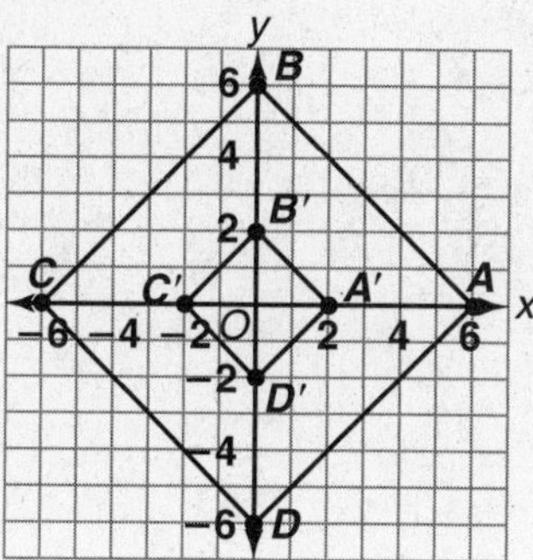

____

4.

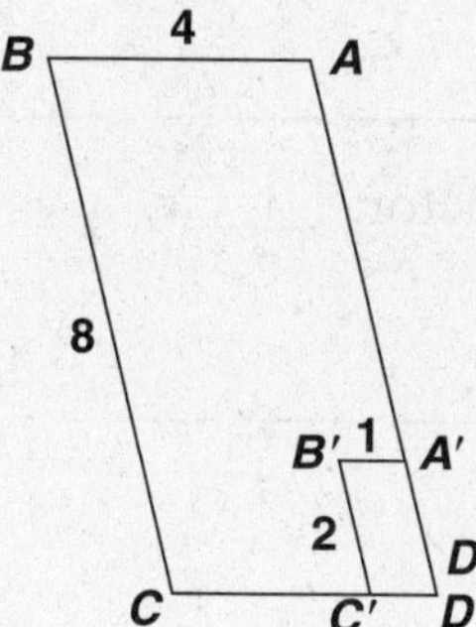

____

5.

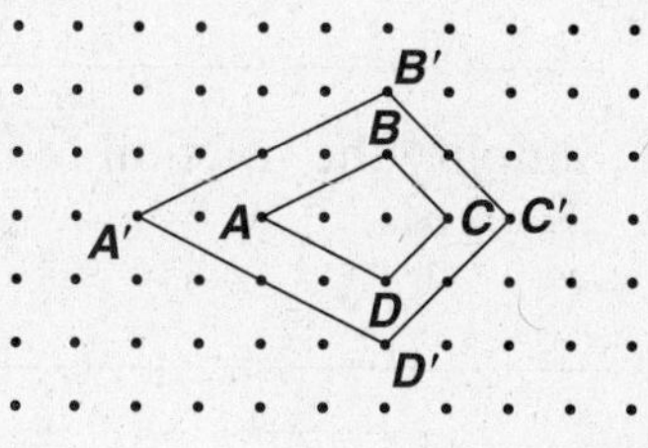

____

6. A triangle has coordinates $A(-2, -2)$, $B(4, -2)$, and $C(1, 1)$. Graph its image $A'B'C'$ after a dilation with scale factor $\frac{3}{2}$. Give the coordinates of $A'B'C'$, and the ratio of the areas of the figures $A'B'C'$ and ABC.

____

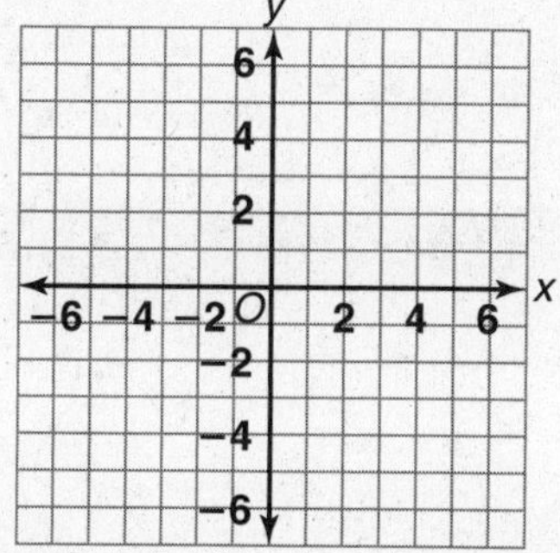

Name ______________________ Class ______________ Date ______________

4-5 • Guided Problem Solving

GPS Student Page 190, Exercise 15:

Computers A window on a computer screen is $1\frac{1}{2}$ in. high and 2 in. wide. After you click the "size reduction" button, the window is reduced to $1\frac{1}{8}$ in. high and $1\frac{1}{2}$ in. wide. What is the scale factor?

Understand

1. Place circles around the heights of the window and squares around the widths of the window.

2. What are you being asked to find?

____

Plan and Carry Out

3. Use the width dimension to find the scale factor by placing the values in the formula $\frac{\text{image}}{\text{original}}$.

____

4. Simplify the fraction to find the scale factor.

____

Check

5. Use the height dimension to find the scale factor. Does the value match your answer to Step 4?

____

Solve Another Problem

6. A picture frame has an opening that is 12 in. by 15 in. If a matting is placed inside the frame to create an opening that is $7\frac{1}{2}$ in. by $9\frac{3}{8}$ in., what is the scale factor of the reduction?

____

Name _______________ Class _______________ Date _______________

Practice 4-6

Scale Models and Maps

The scale of a map is 1 in. : 40 mi. How many actual miles does each measurement on the map represent?

1. 3 in. **2.** 1.5 in. **3.** $7\frac{3}{4}$ in.

Suppose you want to make a map with scale 1 in. : 12 mi. How many inches does each distance occupy on the map?

4. 60 mi **5.** 9 mi **6.** 40 mi

Solve.

7. Two cities on a map were $2\frac{1}{4}$ in. apart. The cities are actually 56.25 mi apart. What scale was used to draw the map?

8. Four ounces of a certain perfume cost $20.96. How much would six ounces of perfume cost?

9. The human brain weighs about 1 lb for each 100 lb of body weight. What is the approximate weight to the nearest ounce of the brain of a person weighing 85 lb?

10. Two towns are 540 km apart. If the scale on the map is 2 cm to 50 km, how far apart are the towns on the map?

11. Cans of tuna cost $1.59 for $6\frac{1}{2}$ oz. At that rate, how much would 25 oz of tuna cost?

12. Students are building a model of a volcano. The volcano is about 8,000 ft tall. The students want the model to be 18 in. tall. What scale should they use?

13. A certain shade of paint requires 3 parts of blue to 2 parts of yellow to 1 part of red. If 18 gal of that shade of paint are needed, how many gal of blue are needed?

Name ____________________ Class ____________ Date ____________

4-6 • Guided Problem Solving

GPS Student Page 195, Exercise 26:

Geometry You draw a 6 in.-by-8 in. rectangle on a piece of paper to represent the roof of a 300 ft-by-400 ft rectangular building. What is the scale of your drawing?

Read and Understand

1. What are the dimensions of the drawing of the roof?

   ____

2. What are the actual dimensions of the roof? ____________

3. What are you asked to find? ____________

Plan and Solve

4. Which ratio best represents the scale of the model? ________

   a. $\frac{8 \text{ in.}}{300 \text{ ft}}$ b. $\frac{6 \text{ in.}}{400 \text{ ft}}$ c. $\frac{6 \text{ in.}}{300 \text{ ft}}$

5. How can you rewrite the ratio so that the first number in the ratio is 1 inch?

   ____

6. Write a sentence to express the scale in inches per foot.

   ____

   ____

Look Back and Check

7. Could you have solved the problem another way? Explain.

   ____

   ____

Solve Another Problem

8. The window of a house is 3 ft × 5 ft. On the blueprint it is shown as $\frac{3}{4}$ in. × $1\frac{1}{4}$ in. What is the scale of the blueprint?

   ____

Name ______________________ Class ______________ Date ______________

Practice 4-7

Similarity and Indirect Measurement

In each figure, find *x*.

1.
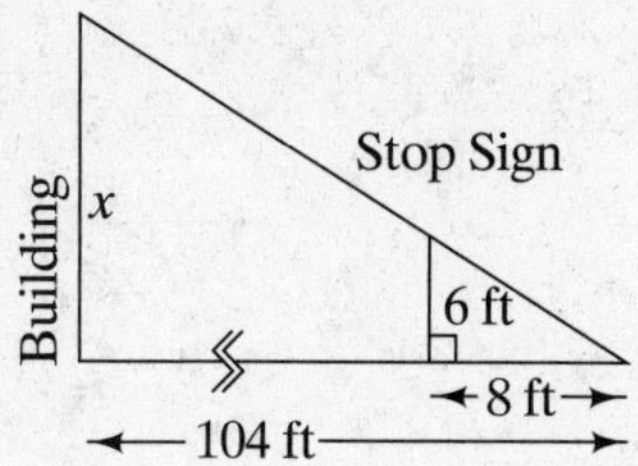

____

2.
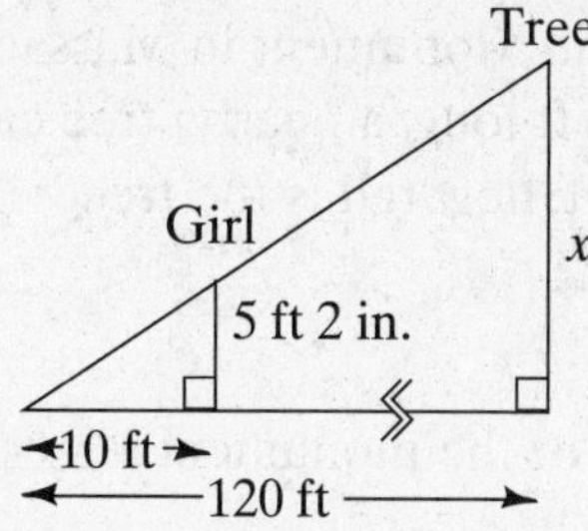

____

3.
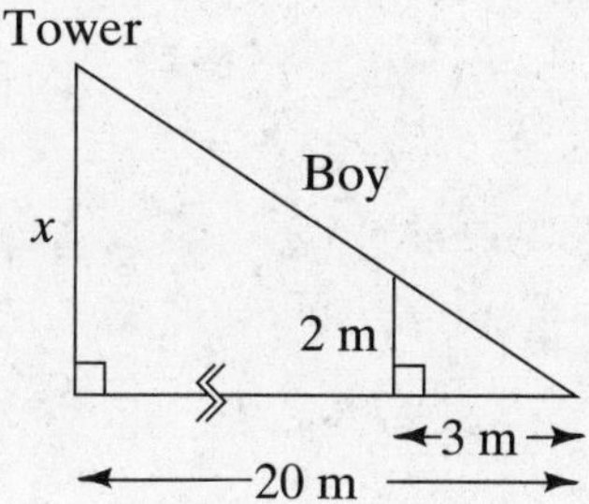

____

4.
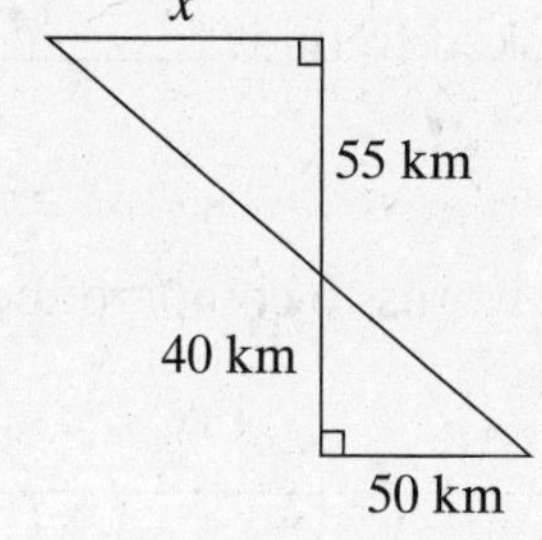

____

5.
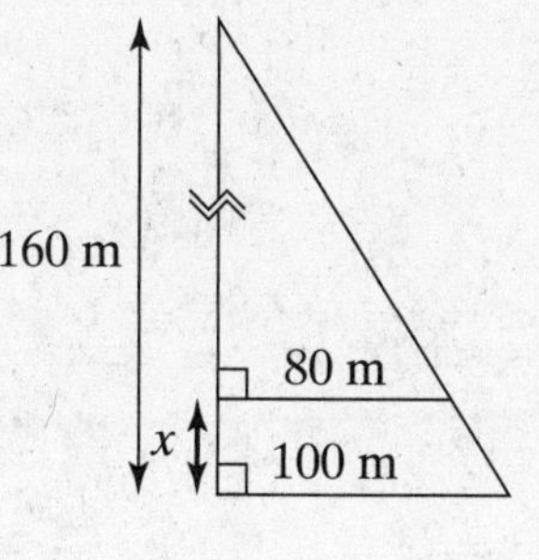

____

6.
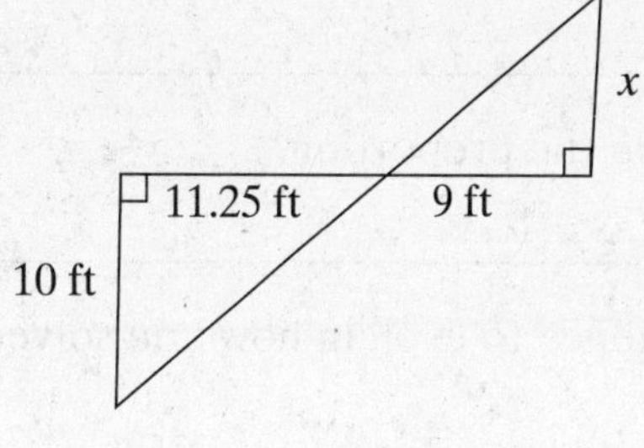

____

Solve.

7. An office building 55 ft tall casts a shadow 30 ft long. How tall is a person standing nearby who casts a shadow 3 ft long?

____

8. A 20-ft pole casts a shadow 12 ft long. How tall is a nearby building that casts a shadow 20 ft long?

____

9. A fire tower casts a shadow 30 ft long. A nearby tree casts a shadow 8 ft long. How tall is the fire tower if the tree is 20 ft tall?

____

10. A house casts a shadow 12 m long. A tree in the yard casts a shadow 8 m long. How tall is the tree if the house is 20 m tall?

____

Name ____________________ Class ____________ Date ____________

4-7 • Guided Problem Solving

GPS Student Page 200, Exercise 17:

History The Bunker Hill Monument in Massachusetts is 221 ft tall. When its shadow is 189 ft long, a nearby tree casts a shadow 29 ft long. To the nearest foot, how tall is the tree?

Understand

1. What is the height of the monument? ____________

2. How long is the shadow of the monument? ____________

3. How long is the shadow of the tree? ____________

4. What are you being asked to find? ____________

Plan and Carry Out

5. Write a proportion in words to compare the measurements.

   ____

6. Place the values of what you know in the proportion. Let h represent the tree's height.

   ____

7. Solve for h in the proportion.

   ____

8. Write a sentence to explain how you solved the problem.

   ____

   ____

Check

9. Divide the monument's height by its shadow. Next, divide the tree's height by its shadow. Are these quotients the same? Should they be?

   ____

   ____

Solve Another Problem

10. A flagpole casts a shadow that is 35.75 ft long. At the same time a 4-ft child casts a shadow that is 6.5 ft long. How tall is the flagpole?

    ____

4A: Graphic Organizer

For use before Lesson 4-1

Study Skill As you learn new math skills, practice them as much as possible. Make a list of any problems that you had trouble with and get extra help.

Write your answers.

1. What is the chapter title? ______________________
2. How many lessons are there in this chapter? ______________________
3. What is the topic of the Test-Taking Strategies page? ______________________
4. Complete the graphic organizer below as you work through the chapter.
   - In the center, write the title of the chapter.
   - When you begin a lesson, write the lesson name in a rectangle.
   - When you complete a lesson, write a skill or key concept in a circle linked to that lesson block.
   - When you complete the chapter, use this graphic organizer to help you review.

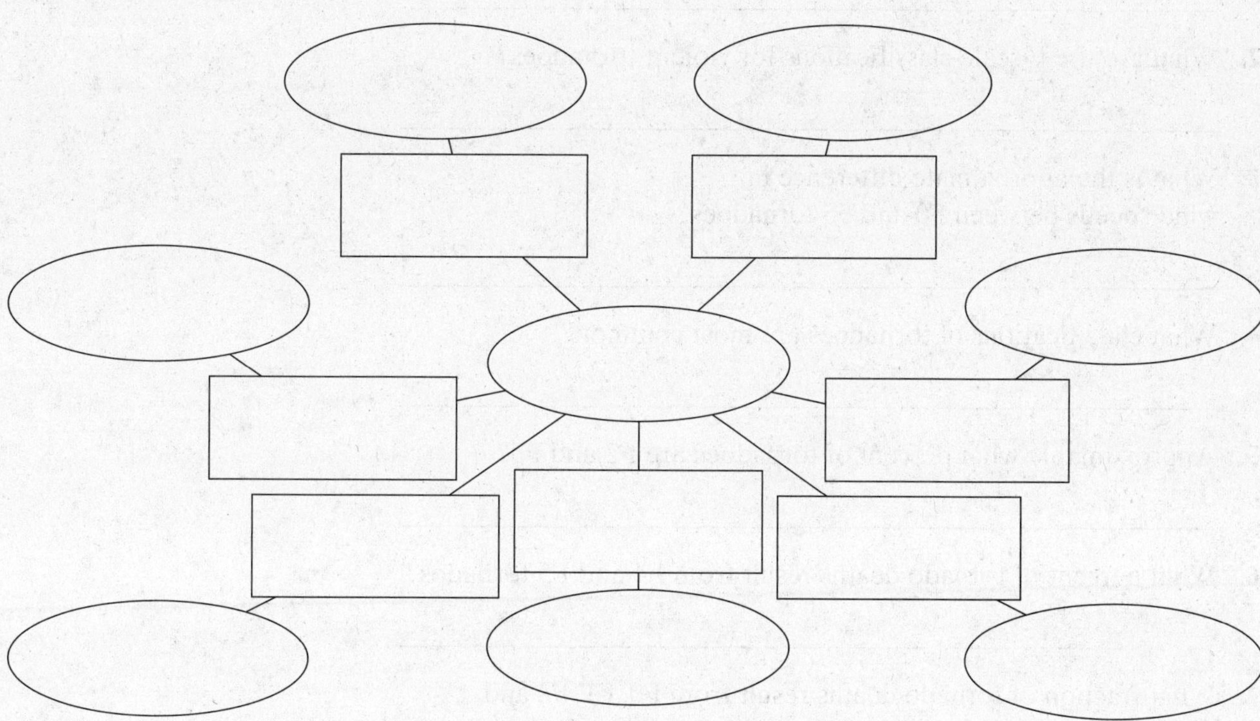

Vocabulary and Study Skills

Name ______________________ Class ______________ Date ______________

4B: Reading Comprehension

For use after Lesson 4-3

Study Skill Reading is an important part of every subject you will take. Practice picking out important information when you read.

Read the paragraph below and answer the questions.

The Fujita Scale used for classifying tornadoes is listed below:

F-Scale Number	Tornado Strength
F0 and F1	weak
F2 and F3	strong
F4 and F5	violent

Scientists estimate that F0 tornadoes have wind speeds of up to 70 miles per hour, while F5 tornadoes reach speeds of 260 to 300 miles per hour. In the United States, 75% of all tornadoes are classified as either F0 or F1. Only about 1% are F4 or F5 tornadoes. However, F4 and F5 tornadoes account for nearly two-thirds of all tornado deaths.

1. What is the strength classification of F2 and F3 tornadoes?

____

2. What are the F-scale classifications for violent tornadoes?

____

3. What is the approximate difference in wind speeds between F0 and F5 tornadoes?

____

4. What classifications of tornadoes are most common?

____

5. Approximately what percent of tornadoes are F2 and F3?

____

6. What percent of tornado deaths result from F4 and F5 tornados?

____

7. What fraction of tornado deaths result from F0, F1, F2 and F3 tornadoes?

____

8. **High-Use Academic Words** In the paragraph, what does it mean for scientists to *estimate* wind speeds?

   a. to approximate
   b. to justify

Name ____________________ Class ____________ Date ____________

4C: Reading/Writing Math Symbols

For use after Lesson 4-4

Study Skill Use abbreviations, formulas, and symbols when you take notes, so you can write mathematical statements quickly and with fewer words.

Write the following statements using the appropriate mathematical symbols.

1. Triangle *ABC* is congruent to triangle *XYZ*. ____________
2. The square root of twenty-five is five.

   ____
3. The ratio of *A* to *B* is equal to the ratio of *M* to *N*.

   ____
4. Triangle *FGH* is similar to triangle *PQR*.

   ____
5. The square root of sixteen and one tenth is approximately equal to four.

   ____

Write the following mathematical statements in words.

6. $H : J = K : L$

   ____
7. $\sqrt{9} = 3$

   ____
8. $\triangle DEF \sim \triangle TUV$

   ____
9. $\triangle EFG \cong \triangle MNP$

   ____
10. $P = 2l + 2w$

    ____

    ____
11. $\frac{4}{6} = \frac{x}{3}$

    ____

Vocabulary and Study Skills

Name ______________________ Class ______________ Date ______________

4D: Visual Vocabulary Practice

For use after Lesson 4-7

Study Skill When interpreting an illustration, notice the information that is given and also notice what is not given. Do not make assumptions.

Concept List

congruent angles	reduction	enlargement
cross products	unit rate	proportions
conversion factors	scale factor	indirect measurement

Write the concept that best describes each exercise. Choose from the concept list above.

1. For the equation $\frac{2}{5y} = \frac{6}{30}$, these are represented by 2×30 and $5y \times 6$.

____

2.

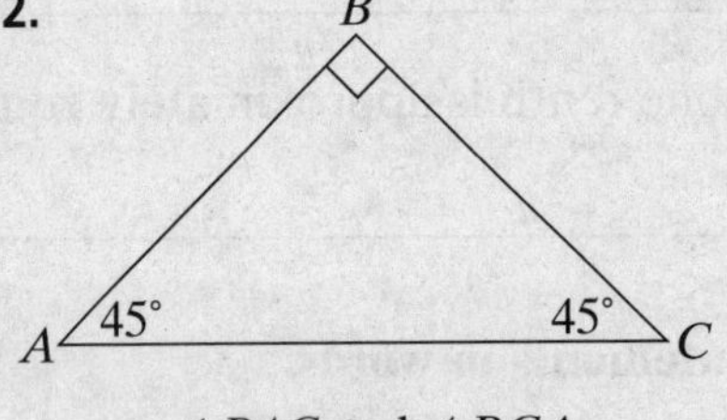

$\angle BAC$ and $\angle BCA$

____

3. James traveled 165 miles in 3 hours. This can also be represented as 55 mi/hr.

____

4. $\frac{16 \text{ oz}}{1 \text{ lb}}$ and $\frac{1 \text{ lb}}{16 \text{ oz}}$

____

5.

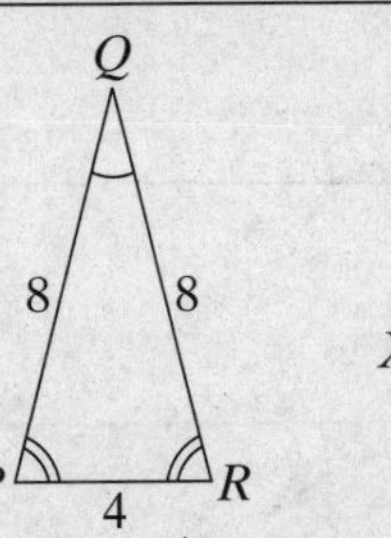

This is $\frac{1}{2}$ for the polygons.

____

6.

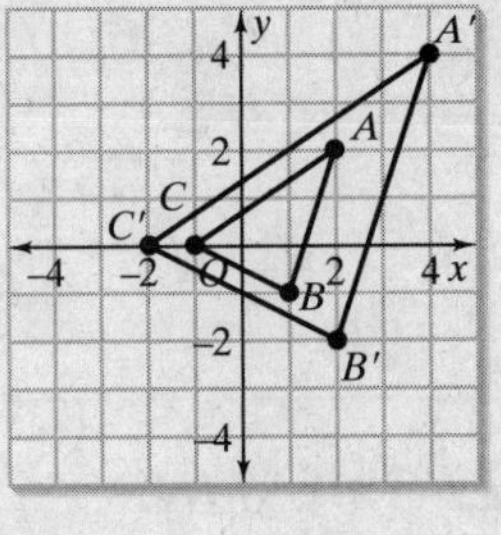

____

7. A dilation with a scale factor of $\frac{3}{4}$.

____

8.

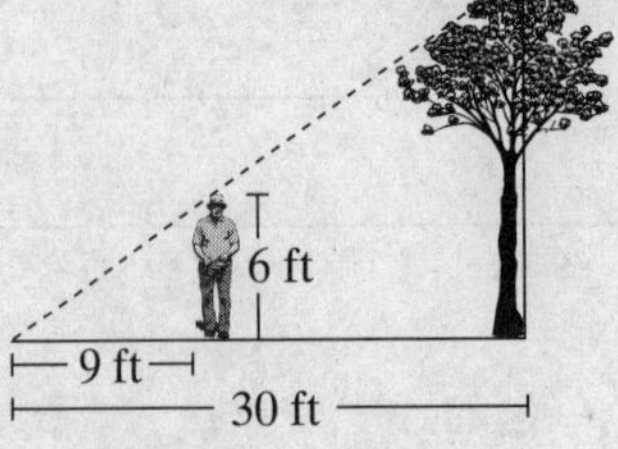

Height of tree = ?

____

9. $\frac{x}{12} = \frac{3}{4}$

____

Name ______________________ Class ______________ Date ____________

4E: Vocabulary Check

For use after Lesson 4-5

Study Skill Strengthen your vocabulary. Use these pages and add cues and summaries by applying the Cornell Notetaking style.

Write the definition for each word or term at the right. To check your work, fold the paper back along the dotted line to see the correct answers.

______________________________ dilation

______________________________ similar figures

______________________________ proportion

______________________________ rate

______________________________ scale factor

Name ______________________ Class ______________ Date ____________

4E: Vocabulary Check (continued)

For use after Lesson 4-5

Write the vocabulary word or term for each definition. To check your work, fold the paper forward along the dotted line to see the correct answers.

a transformation in which the original figure and its image are similar ______________________

figures that have the same shape, but not necessarily the same size ______________________

an equation stating that two ratios are equal ______________________

a ratio that compares two quantities measured in different units ______________________

the ratio of the dimension of the image to the dimensions of the original figure ______________________

Name ____________________ Class ____________ Date ____________

4F: Vocabulary Review Puzzle

For use with the Chapter Review

Study Skill Some concepts are very difficult to grasp on your own. If you pay attention in class, you can ask questions about concepts you do not understand.

Complete the crossword puzzle. For help, use the glossary in your textbook. Use these words to complete this crossword puzzle.

similar	slope
proportion	variable
hypotenuse	absolute value
scale	ratio
range	exponent
enlargement	reduction
rate	

ACROSS

3. ratio of the length of a model to the corresponding length of the actual object
4. the comparison of two quantities by division
5. ratio comparing quantities measured in different units
7. y in the expression $2y - 5$
10. the change in y over the change in x
11. longest side of a right triangle
12. the difference between the greatest and least values in a data set

DOWN

1. a transformation in which the image is larger than the original figure
2. distance a number is from zero
5. a transformation in which the image is smaller than the original figure
6. a term that describes figures that have the same shape but not necessarily the same size
8. 6, in the expression 5^6
9. an equation stating that two ratios are equal

Name ______________________ Class ______________ Date ____________

Practice 5-1

Fractions, Decimals, and Percents

Use mental math to write each decimal as a percent.

1. 0.95 ________
2. 0.06 ________
3. 0.004 ________
4. 0.63 ________
5. 0.005 ________
6. 1.4 ________

Write each fraction as a percent. Round to the nearest tenth of a percent.

7. $\frac{4}{5}$ ________
8. $\frac{7}{10}$ ________
9. $\frac{5}{6}$ ________
10. $\frac{5}{8}$ ________
11. $\frac{1}{15}$ ________
12. $\frac{9}{25}$ ________
13. $\frac{1}{6}$ ________
14. $\frac{11}{12}$ ________
15. $\frac{1}{20}$ ________

Use mental math to write each percent as a decimal.

16. 70% ________
17. 10% ________
18. 800% ________
19. 2.6% ________
20. 234% ________
21. 9% ________

Write each percent as a fraction in simplest form.

22. 10% ________
23. 47% ________
24. $5\frac{1}{2}\%$ ________
25. 15% ________
26. 92% ________
27. $3\frac{1}{4}\%$ ________
28. 85% ________
29. 42% ________
30. 70% ________

Order each set of numbers from least to greatest.

31. $12\%, \frac{1}{8}, 1.2, \frac{1}{12}$

____

32. $0.047, 0.5\%, \frac{1}{20}, 1.5\%$

____

33. $\frac{3}{7}, 3.7\%, 0.37, 0.073$

____

34. $0.001, \frac{1}{100}, 0.01\%, \frac{1}{10}$

____

Solve.

35. There are twelve pairs of cranial nerves connected to the brain. Ten of these pairs are related to sight, smell, taste, and sound. What percent of the pairs are related to sight, smell, taste, and sound? ________

36. If a person weighs 150 lb, then calcium makes up 3 lb of that person's weight. What percent of a person's weight does calcium make up? ________

Name ____________________ Class ______________ Date ____________

5-1 • Guided Problem Solving

GPS Student Page 213, Exercise 28:

Jobs The average employee in the United States works about 248 days per year and receives about 13 days of paid vacation. Write the number of vacation days as a percent of the total number of days worked. Round to the nearest hundredth of a percent.

Understand

1. Place a circle around the number of vacation days and a square around the number of days worked.

2. What are you being asked to find?

   ____

   ____

Plan and Carry Out

3. Set up a ratio: $\dfrac{\text{number of } \_\_\_\_\_\_\_\_}{\text{number of } \_\_\_\_\_\_\_\_}$

4. Substitute the given information in the fraction. __________

5. Write the decimal equivalent for the fraction. __________

6. Which direction do you need to move the decimal point to change a decimal to a percent? __________

7. Write the decimal as a percent. Insert a percent sign. __________

Check

8. Is it reasonable to say that 5% of 248 is about 13?

   ____

Solve Another Problem

9. The Lakewood High School band has 318 members and 42 band members play the flute. Write the number of flute players as a percent of the total number of band members.

   ____

Name ______________________ Class ______________ Date ____________

Practice 5-2

Estimating With Percents

Estimate each percent using decimals.

1. 6% of 140 ______
2. 18.9% of 44 ______
3. 61% of 180 ______
4. 5.1% of 81 ______
5. $16\frac{1}{2}$% of 36 ______
6. 81% of 241 ______
7. 67% of 300 ______
8. 51% of 281 ______
9. 62.9% of 400 ______

Estimate each percent using fractions.

10. 76% of 600 ______
11. 88% of 680 ______
12. 37% of 481 ______
13. 19.1% of 380 ______
14. 41% of 321 ______
15. 33% of 331 ______
16. 83% of 453 ______
17. 76.3% of 841 ______
18. 67.1% of 486 ______

Estimate.

19. Of the 307 species of mammals on the endangered list in 1992, 12.1% of them were found only in the United States. Estimate the number of mammal species in the United States that were on the endangered list.

______

20. In 1990, 19% of the people of Mali lived in urban settings. If the population that year was 9,200,000, estimate the number of people who lived in urban settings.

______

21. Of the 1,267 students at the school, 9.8% live within walking distance of school. Estimate the number of students within walking distance.

______

Name ______________________ Class ______________ Date ______________

5-2 • Guided Problem Solving

GPS Student Page 217, Exercise 33:

Blood Types About 40% of Americans have type A blood. Suppose there are about 301,421,900 Americans. Estimate how many Americans have type A blood.

Understand

1. Circle the number of Americans.
2. What percent have type A blood?

   ____

3. Do you need to find an exact answer or an estimate?

   ____

Plan and Carry Out

4. Convert 40% to a decimal that is easy to work with.

   ____

5. Round the number of Americans to a number that is compatible with your decimal from Step 4.

   ____

6. Multiply the compatible number of Americans by the decimal to determine the number of Americans that have type A blood.

   ____

Check

7. Solve for the exact amount to see if your estimation is reasonable.

   ____

Solve Another Problem

8. Of the 38 students in math class, approximately 82% of them got an A on their math test. Estimate the number of students who got an A.

   ____

Name ____________________ Class ______________ Date ______________

Practice 5-3

Percents and Proportions

Use a proportion to solve each problem.

1. What percent is 21 of 50? ______________
2. What is 45% of 72? ______________
3. 83 is 70% of what number? ______________
4. 45 is what percent of 65? ______________

Use a proportion to solve each problem.

5. 78% of 58 is ______________.
6. 86 is 12% of ______________.
7. 90 is ______________ of 65.
8. 40 is 17% of ______________.
9. 57 is 31% of ______________.
10. 280% of ______________ is 418.
11. What percent of 16 is 40? ______________
12. 65 is 60% of what number? ______________
13. What is 175% of 48? ______________
14. 210 is what percent of 70? ______________
15. What percent of 56 is 7? ______________
16. 68 is 50% of what number? ______________
17. What is 63% of 148? ______________
18. 215 is what percent of 400? ______________

Solve.

19. In 1990, the population of El Paso, Texas, was 515,342. Of this population, 69% were of Hispanic origin. How many people were of Hispanic origin? ______________
20. Bangladesh covers 55,598 mi^2. Of this land, 2,224 mi^2 are meadows and pastures. What percent of the land is meadow and pasture? ______________

Name ______________________ Class ______________ Date ______________

5-3 • Guided Problem Solving

GPS Student Page 222, Exercise 44:

One semester, 27 college students registered for an art history class. After two male students dropped out of the class, 44% of the students in the class were male. What percent of the students in the original class were female? Round to the nearest tenth of a percent.

Understand

1. How many students were in the original class? ______________
2. How many students were in the class after two male students dropped out? ______________
3. At that time, what percent were males? ______________
4. What are you being asked to find?

____

Plan and Carry Out

5. Find the number of males in the class after two dropped out.

____

6. What was the original number of males in the class? ________
7. How many females were in the original class? ________
8. Divide the number of females by the total number of students in the original class.

____

9. Change the decimal to a percent rounded to the nearest tenth.

____

Check

10. How did finding the number of males in the adjusted class help to find the percentage of females in the original class?

____

____

____

Solve Another Problem

11. Beth and her mom picked a bushel of red and yellow delicious apples, totaling 52 apples. They made tarts with 8 yellow apples. After making the tarts, 25% of the remaining apples were yellow. What percent of the original apples were red? Round to the nearest tenth of a percent.

____

Name ______________________ Class ______________ Date ______________

Practice 5-4

Percents and Equations

Use an equation to solve each problem. Round to the nearest tenth.

1. What percent of 80 is 25? ________

2. 8.6 is 5% of what number? ________

3. What is 140% of 85? ________

4. 70 is what percent of 120? ________

5. What percent of 90 is 42? ________

6. 18.4 is what percent of 10? ________

7. 56% of what number is 82? ________

8. Find 93% of 150. ________

9. 30% of what number is 120? ________

10. What percent of 420 is 7? ________

11. 79 is what percent of 250? ________

12. 9.1 is 3% of what number? ________

13. What is 94% of 260? ________

14. 45 is what percent of 18? ________

15. What percent of 280 is 157? ________

16. 20.7 is what percent of 8? ________

17. 114% of what number is 75? ________

18. Find 72% of 18,495. ________

19. 75% of what number is 200? ________

20. What percent of 940 is 15? ________

Solve.

21. In a recent survey, 216 people, or 54% of the sample, said they usually went to a family restaurant when they went out to eat. How many people were surveyed?

____

22. In a school survey, 248 students, or 32% of the sample, said they worked part time during the summer. How many students were surveyed?

____

23. Juliet sold a house for $112,000. What percent commission did she receive if she earned $6,720?

____

24. Jason earns $200 per week plus 8% commission on his sales. How much were his sales last week if Jason earned $328?

____

25. Stella makes 2% royalties on a book she wrote. How much money did her book earn in sales last year if she made $53,000 in royalties?

____

26. Linda earns $40 base pay per week, plus 10% commission on all sales. What were her sales if she made $112 in one week?

____

Name ______________________ Class ______________ Date ______________

5-4 • Guided Problem Solving

GPS Student Page 226, Exercise 17:

Royalties A singer makes 2% royalties on the sales of her album. How much did her album earn in sales if she made $53,000 in royalties?

Understand

1. What information are you given?

____

2. Underline what you are asked to find.

Plan and Carry Out

3. What are you looking for, the whole, or a percent of the whole?

____

4. What equation will you use to solve the problem?

____

5. How do you change 2% to a decimal?

____

6. Write the equation with the values that you know, letting *w* stand for the unknown.

____

7. Solve for *w* to determine how much the album earned.

____

Check

8. Is 53,000 two percent of 2,650,000?

____

Solve Another Problem

9. A home cookware demonstrator earns a 3% commission on her total sales. How much did the demonstrator sell if she made $225 in commission?

____

Name ______________________ Class ______________ Date ______________

Practice 5-5

Percent of Change

Find each percent of increase or decrease. Round your answer to the nearest tenth, if necessary.

1. 15 to 20 ________

2. 18 to 10 ________

3. 10 to 7.5 ________

4. 86 to 120 ________

5. 17 to 34 ________

6. 32 to 24 ________

7. 27 to 38 ________

8. 40 to 10 ________

9. 8 to 10 ________

10. 43 to 86 ________

11. 100 to 23 ________

12. 846 to 240 ________

13. 130 to 275 ________

14. 193 to 270 ________

15. 436 to 118 ________

16. 457 to 318 ________

17. 607 to 812 ________

18. 500 to 118 ________

Solve.

19. In 1995, the price of a laser printer was $1,299. In 2002, the price of the same type of printer had dropped to $499. Find the percent of decrease.

____

20. The amount won in harness racing in 1991 was $1.238 million. In 1992, the amount was $1.38 million. What was the percent of increase?

____

21. In 1980, there were about 3 million people in Chicago. In 1990, the population was about 2.8 million people. Find the percent of decrease in the population of Chicago.

____

22. Caryn was 58 in. tall last year. This year she is 61 in. tall. What is the percent of increase in her height?

____

Name ______________________ Class ______________ Date ______________

5-5 • Guided Problem Solving

GPS Student Page 233, Exercise 30:

Education A middle school increased the length of its school day from 6 h 10 min to 6 h 25 min. Find the percent of increase in the length of the school day. Round to the nearest tenth of a percent.

Understand

1. What is the original length of the school day? ______________
2. What is the new length of the school day? ______________
3. Was the length of the day increased or decreased? ______________
4. What are you being asked to find?

____

____

Plan and Carry Out

5. What is the original length of the school day in minutes?

____

6. What is the new length of the school day in minutes?

____

7. How many minutes has the school day changed? ______________
8. What is the percent change equation? ______________
9. Substitute the values in the equation. ______________
10. Solve to the nearest tenth of a percent. ______________

Check

11. Is your answer reasonable? Is 4.1% of 370 minutes approximately 15 minutes?

____

Solve Another Problem

12. Albert is 3 ft 1 in. tall on his second birthday and grows to 6 ft 4 inches by his 20th birthday. Find the percent of increase in his height to the nearest tenth of a percent.

____

Name ____________ Class ____________ Date ____________

Practice 5-6

Markup and Discount

Find each selling price. Round to the nearest cent.

1. cost: $10.00
   markup rate: 60%
2. cost: $12.50
   markup rate: 50%
3. cost: $15.97
   markup rate: 75%
4. cost: $21.00
   markup rate: 100%
5. cost: $25.86
   markup rate: 70%
6. cost: $32.48
   markup rate: 110%
7. cost: $47.99
   markup rate: 160%
8. cost: $87.90
   markup rate: 80%
9. cost: $95.90
   markup rate: 112%

Find each sale price. Round to the nearest cent.

10. regular price: $10.00
    discount rate: 10%
11. regular price: $12.00
    discount rate: 15%
12. regular price: $18.95
    discount rate: 20%
13. regular price: $20.95
    discount rate: 15%
14. regular price: $32.47
    discount rate: 20%
15. regular price: $39.99
    discount rate: 25%
16. regular price: $42.58
    discount rate: 30%
17. regular price: $53.95
    discount rate: 35%
18. regular price: $82.99
    discount rate: 50%

Find each item's regular price. Round to the nearest cent.

19. selling price: $55
    markup rate: 20%
20. selling price: $25.50
    markup rate: 45%
21. selling price: $79.99
    markup rate: 30%
22. selling price: $19.95
    markup rate: 75%
23. selling price: $95
    markup rate: 25%
24. selling price: $64.49
    markup rate: 10%

Name ____________________ Class ______________ Date ______________

5-6 • Guided Problem Solving

GPS Student Page 238, Exercise 22:

DVDs are on sale for 40% off the regular price of $22.99. Your friend has $45 to spend. How many DVDs can your friend buy at the reduced price?

Understand

1. What is the original price of the DVDs? ____________________
2. What is the percent of discount? ____________________
3. How much does your friend have to spend? ____________________
4. What is it that you are being asked to find?

____

____

Plan and Carry Out

5. What is the sale price of each DVD? ____________________
6. Divide $45 by the sale price.

____

7. To determine how many DVDs can be purchased, why can you not leave the answer as a decimal?

____

8. How many DVDs can be purchased? ____________________

Check

9. If you multiply the number of DVDs by the sale price, what is the total? Is it less than $45? Could you purchase another DVD?

____

Solve Another Problem

10. Ethan goes to a book fair at his school on the last day. The three books that he wants originally costs $4.99 each, but are marked down 35%. If his mom gave him $10 to spend, could he afford to buy all three books?

____

____

____

Name ____________ Class ____________ Date ____________

Practice 5-7

Simple Interest

Find the interest earned on each account. Round answers to nearest cent.

1. $100 at 6% simple interest for 3 years ____________

2. $200 at 7% simple interest for 1 year ____________

3. $142 at $5\frac{1}{4}$% simple interest for 5 years ____________

4. $6,250 at 4% simple interest for 2 years ____________

5. $884 at 5% simple interest for 10 years ____________

6. $75 at $3\frac{1}{2}$% simple interest for 5 years ____________

7. Bonnie deposited $500 in an account with a simple interest rate of $6\frac{1}{4}$%. How much interest will she earn in 4 years?

____

8. John invested $100 in an account with 2% simple interest. Julie invested $75 in an account with 3% simple interest. Who will earn more interest in 5 years?

____

Find the final balance in each account.

9. $200 invested at 2% simple interest for 5 years ____________

10. $200 invested at $4\frac{1}{2}$% simple interest for 5 years ____________

11. $4,500 invested at 6% simple interest for 7 years ____________

12. $1,256 invested at 7% simple interest for 6 years ____________

13. You deposit $100 in an account with $7\frac{1}{2}$% simple interest. What is the account balance after 2 years?

____

14. Simon invested $3,200 in an account with $3\frac{1}{2}$% simple interest. After 3 years, he transferred his balance to an account with 6% simple interest. What is Simon's final balance after 6 years in the second account?

____

Name ________________ Class ________________ Date ________________

5-7 • Guided Problem Solving

GPS Student Page 244, Exercise 12:

Investments A woman invests $500 in a 36-month certificate of deposit (CD) with a simple interest rate of 5.36%. At the end of the 36 months, the woman redeposits her final balance into another 36-month CD with the same simple interest rate. Find the final balance.

Understand

1. How much money does the woman originally invest? ________
2. What is the original length of time and interest rate?

   ____
3. Underline what you are asked to do.

Plan and Carry Out

4. What is the formula for simple interest? ________
5. In the simple interest formula, is time represented in months or years? ________
6. Find the interest of the first investment by using the simple interest formula.

   ____
7. Find the new balance by adding the original investment and the interest earned.

   ____
8. Using this as the amount of money redeposited, find the interest earned during the next 36-month period.

   ____
9. Find the final balance by adding this interest to the amount that was redeposited.

   ____

Check

10. Would your answer be the same if you added the time together as 6 years and found the balance? Why or why not?

    ____

Solve Another Problem

11. Mrs. Smith and Mrs. Jones open bank accounts for their children, each depositing $250.00. Mrs. Smith earns an interest rate of 4.2%. Mrs. Jones earns an interest rate of 7.2% but pays a $1 monthly maintenance fee. Who will have a higher balance after 2 years?

    ____

Name ______________________ Class ____________ Date ____________

Practice 5-8

Ratios and Probability

You spin the spinner at the right. Find each probability.

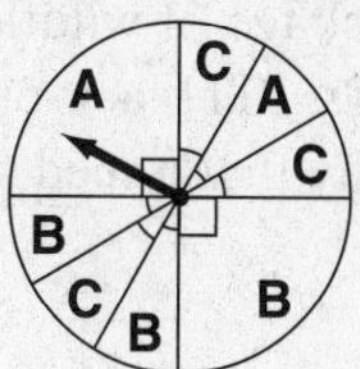

1. $P(\text{A})$ ______
2. $P(\text{B})$ ______
3. $P(\text{C})$ ______
4. $P(\text{A or B})$ ______
5. $P(\text{B or C})$ ______
6. $P(\text{A, B, or C})$ ______

A bag of uninflated balloons contains 5 red, 9 blue, 16 yellow, and 8 green balloons. A balloon is drawn at random. Find each probability.

7. $P(\text{red})$ ______
8. $P(\text{blue})$ ______
9. $P(\text{yellow})$ ______
10. $P(\text{green})$ ______
11. What is the probability of picking a balloon that is not yellow?

    ______
12. What is the probability of picking a balloon that is not red?

    ______

Solve.

13. a. You are a volunteer dog walker at the local animal shelter. Of the 413 dogs housed at the shelter this week, three are basset hounds. If you are assigned to walk a dog at random, what is the probability that you will walk a basset hound?

    ______

    b. On Wednesday morning, one basset hound and 14 other dogs are adopted. Find the probability that one of the remaining dogs is a basset hound.

    ______

14. A box contains purple, green, and red pens. If you randomly select a pen, $P(\text{red}) = 0.36$. Find $P(\text{purple or green})$. If there are 150 pens in the box, how many of the pens are red?

    ______

Name ______________________ Class ______________ Date ______________

5-8 • Guided Problem Solving

GPS Student Page 249, Exercise 27:

Gardening A package of wildflower seeds contains 50 daisy seeds, 80 sunflower seeds, 100 black-eyed Susan seeds, and 20 lupine seeds. Find the probability that a seed selected at random will be a daisy seed.

Understand

1. Place a circle around all the information needed to solve the problem.
2. What are you asked to find?

____

Plan and Carry Out

3. How many seeds are there all together? ______________
4. How many daisy seeds are there? ______________
5. How do you determine probability?

____

6. Calculate the probability.

____

Check

7. If you randomly took out 20 seeds, how many would probably be daisy seeds?

____

Solve Another Problem

8. In a jar of mixed nuts, there are 92 cashews, 125 peanuts, 50 almonds and 33 Brazil nuts. Find the probability that you will randomly choose an almond from the jar.

____

Name ______________________ Class ______________ Date ______________

5A: Graphic Organizer

For use before Lesson 5-1

Vocabulary and Study Skills

Study Skill Develop consistent study habits. Block off the same amount of time each evening for schoolwork. Plan ahead by setting aside extra time when you have a big project or test coming up.

Write your answers.

1. What is the chapter title? ______________________
2. How many lessons are there in this chapter? ______________________
3. What is the topic of the Test-Taking Strategies page? ______________________
4. Complete the graphic organizer below as you work through the chapter.
   - In the center, write the title of the chapter.
   - When you begin a lesson, write the lesson name in a rectangle.
   - When you complete a lesson, write a skill or key concept in a circle linked to that lesson block.
   - When you complete the chapter, use this graphic organizer to help you review.

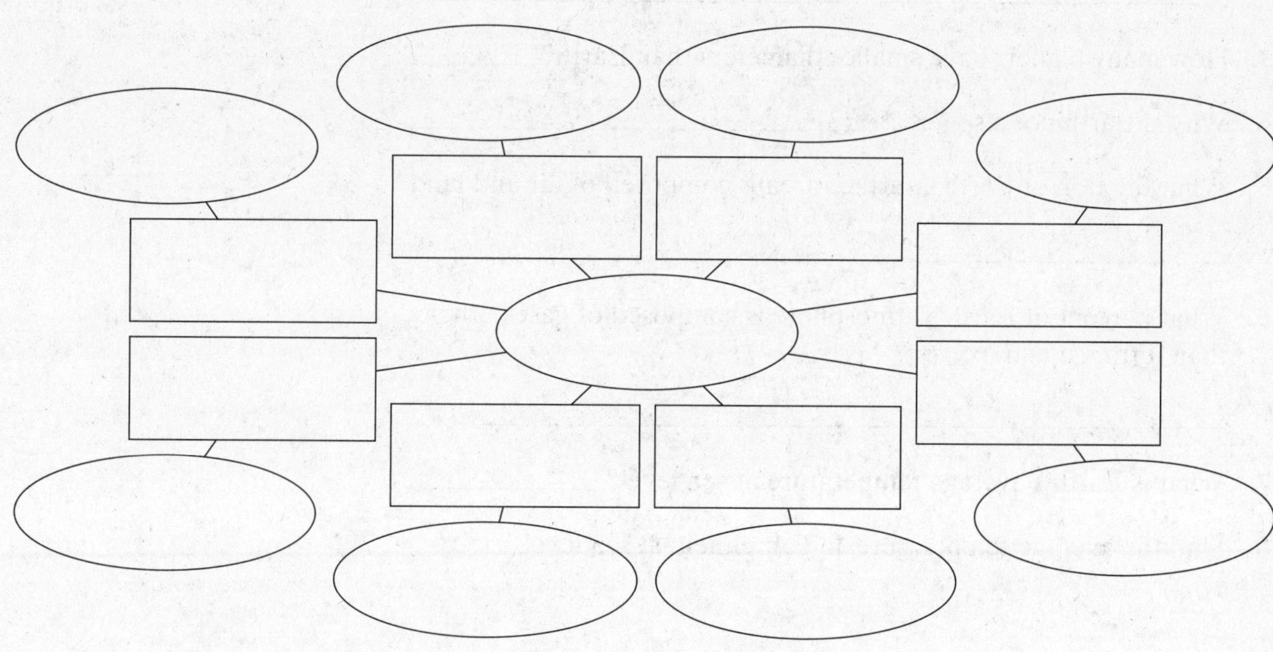

Name ______________________ Class ______________ Date ______________

5B: Reading Comprehension

For use after Lesson 5-2

Study Skill Read problems carefully. Pay special attention to units when working with measurements.

Read the paragraph below and answer the questions.

Earth has an average diameter of 7,926.2 miles. It is not a sphere, since it bulges slightly at the equator. Of the nine major planets in our solar system, Earth is the middle planet in average diameter. The composition of the Earth's surface area is 70% water and 30% air and land. The atmosphere is composed of 78% nitrogen, 21% oxygen, and a mixture of several other gases. The average temperature at sea level is 15°C. The Earth is about 93 million miles from the sun.

1. What is the paragraph about?

   ____

2. What is Earth's radius?

   ____

3. How many planets have smaller diameters than Earth? __________

4. Why is Earth not a sphere? ______________________

5. What fraction of Earth's surface area is composed of air and land?

   ____

6. What percent of Earth's atmosphere is composed of gases other than nitrogen and oxygen?

   ____

7. What is Earth's average temperature at sea level? __________

8. Find the average temperature, in Fahrenheit, at sea level.
   Hint: $F = \frac{9}{5}C + 32$.

   ____

9. **High-Use Academic Words** In Exercise 5, what does the phrase *is composed of* mean?

   a. is needed for
   b. is made up of

Name ______________________ Class ______________ Date ______________

5C: Reading/Writing Math Symbols

For use after Lesson 5-3

Study Skill Use a notebook or a section of a loose-leaf binder for homework assignments.

Write a mathematical statement of expression for each word description.

1. Six and six hundredths percent

____

2. Triangle XYZ is similar to triangle ABC.

____

3. Thirty-nine percent is approximately equal to four tenths.

____

4. Angle G is congruent to angle K.

____

5. One fourth equals twenty-five percent.

____

6. Five elevenths is greater than 45 percent.

____

In the diagram below, $\triangle ABC \cong \triangle A'B'C'$. Use the diagram to write the meaning of each mathematical statement.

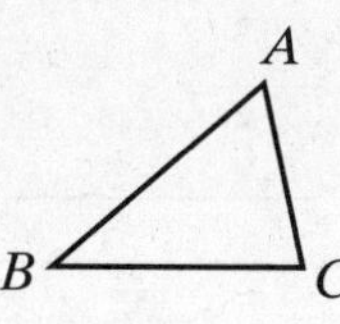

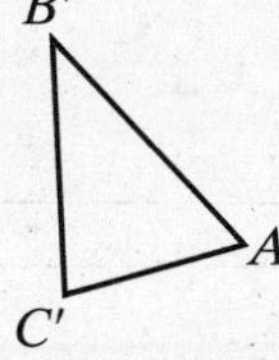

7. $\overline{AC}$ ______________________________

8. $\overrightarrow{CB}$ ______________________________

9. A' ______________________________

10. $\angle B'$ ______________________________

11. $\overline{AC} \cong \overline{A'C'}$ ______________________________

Vocabulary and Study Skills

Name ______________________ Class ______________ Date ______________

5D: Visual Vocabulary Practice

For use after Lesson 5-8

Study Skill Learning mathematics is like learning a foreign language. You have to know the vocabulary before you can speak the language correctly.

Concept List

percent	outcome	balance
interest rate	probability of an event	sample space
sale price	simple interest	markup

Write the concept that best describes each exercise. Choose from the concept list above.

1. Principal + Interest = ____. ______________	**2.** The regular price of a book is \$24.00. Kerri has a 20% off coupon for the book. This is represented by \$24.00 − \$24.00(0.2) = \$24.00 − \$4.80 = \$19.20. ______________	**3.** $P(E) = \frac{1}{2}$ ______________
4. A store buys a CD for \$8 and sells it for \$14. This is \$6. ______________	**5.** If you roll two six-sided number cubes, then rolling a sum of 7 is an example of this. ______________	**6.** Traci deposits \$800 in an account that earns 4% annual interest for 5 years. This is represented by \$800 × 0.04 × 5 = \$160. ______________
7. {heads, tails} ______________	**8.** A checking account is started with \$500. If no deposits or withdrawals are made over the year and the balance at the end of the year is \$540, then this is represented by $\frac{540 - 500}{500} = \frac{40}{500} = \frac{8}{100}$, or 8%. ______________	**9.** x in the equation $\frac{12}{25} = \frac{x}{100}$ ______________

Name ______________________ Class ______________ Date ______________

5E: Vocabulary Check

For use after Lesson 5-7

Study Skill Strengthen your vocabulary. Use these pages and add cues and summaries by applying the Cornell Notetaking style.

Write the definition for each word or term at the right. To check your work, fold the paper back along the dotted line to see the correct answers.

______________________	interest
______________________	percent
______________________	principal
______________________	simple interest
______________________	percent of change

Name ______________________ Class ______________ Date ______________

5E: Vocabulary Check (continued)

For use after Lesson 5-7

Write the vocabulary word or term for each definition. To check your work, fold the paper forward along the dotted line to see the correct answers.

the amount of money paid for the use of money ______________________

a ratio that compares a number to 100 ______________________

the original amount deposited or borrowed ______________________

interest calculated only on the principal ______________________

the percent a quantity increases or decreases from the original amount ______________________

5F: Vocabulary Review

For use with the Chapter Review

Study Skill Take notes while you study. Go back and review your notes before quizzes and tests.

Circle the word that best completes the sentence.

1. A (*percent, sentence*) is a ratio that compares a number to 100.
2. Percent increase is equal to the change in price divided by the (*new, original*) price, times 100.
3. A (*solution, letter*) is a value for a variable that makes an equation true.
4. A(n) (*outlier, range*) is a data value that is much greater than or less than the other values in a set of data.
5. An (*expression, equation*) is a mathematical sentence with an equal sign.
6. The original deposit into a bank account is called the (*rate, principal*).
7. The (*mean, median*) is the number that is the middle value of a data set that is ordered from least to greatest values.
8. The amount a store increases the price of an item is called the (*selling price, markup*).
9. The (*absolute value, opposite*) of a number is its distance from 0 on a number line.
10. A collection of all possible outcomes in an experiment is called the (*event, sample space*).
11. A(n) (*equation, proportion*) states that two ratios are equal.
12. A(n) (*variable, expression*) is a letter that stands for an unknown quantity.

Practice 6-1

Solving Two-Step Equations

Solve each equation.

1. $4r + 6 = 14$ ______
2. $9y - 11 = 7$ ______
3. $\frac{m}{4} + 6 = 3$ ______
4. $\frac{k}{-9} + 6 = -4$ ______
5. $-5b - 6 = -11$ ______
6. $\frac{v}{-7} + 8 = 19$ ______
7. $3.4t + 19.36 = -10.22$ ______
8. $\frac{n}{-1.6} + 7.9 = 8.4$ ______
9. $4.6b + 26.8 = 50.72$ ______
10. $\frac{a}{-8.06} + 7.02 = 18.4$ ______
11. $-2.06d + 18 = -10.84$ ______
12. $\frac{e}{-95} + 6 = 4$ ______

Write and solve an equation to answer each question.

13. Hugo received $100 for his birthday. He then saved $20 per week until he had a total of $460 to buy a printer. Use an equation to show how many weeks it took him to save the money.

______

14. A health club charges a $50 initial fee plus $2 for each visit. Moselle has spent a total of $144 at the health club this year. Use an equation to find how many visits she has made.

______

Solve each equation to find the value of the variable. Write the answer in the puzzle. Do not include any negative signs or any decimal points.

ACROSS

1. $6n - 12 = 2.4$
2. $\frac{n}{3} + 4.6 = 21.6$
4. $x - 3 = 51.29$
6. $2z + 2 = 7.6$

DOWN

1. $\frac{j}{5} - 14 = -9$
2. $3x - 2 = 169$
3. $\frac{x}{4} + 1 = 19$
4. $\frac{x}{3} + 4 = 22$
5. $2x - 2 = 182$

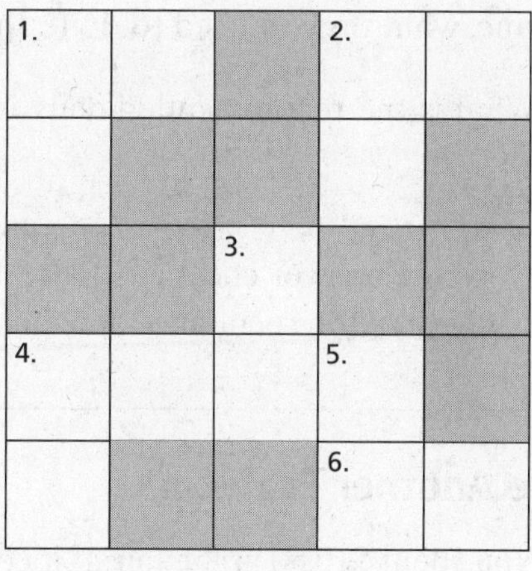

Name ______________________ Class ______________ Date ______________

6-1 • Guided Problem Solving

GPS Student Page 263, Exercise 21:

Nutrition According to the Food and Drug Administration, the recommended daily intake of iron is 18 mg. This is 4 less than twice the recommended daily intake of zinc. What is the recommended daily intake of zinc?

Understand

1. What is the recommended daily intake of iron? ______________________

2. What are you being asked to find? ______________________

   ____

3. Will the recommended daily intake of zinc be more or less than that of iron? ____________

Plan and Carry Out

4. Fill in the names of the minerals to help set up an equation.

   2 times ____________ − 4 = ______________

5. Write an equation, letting z represent the amount of zinc. ______________

6. To solve the equation, what do you do first?

   ____

7. To solve for the recommended amount of zinc, what do you need to do to the equation? ______________

8. What is the recommended daily intake of zinc? __________

Check

9. Does the answer check? Is twice 11 milligrams minus 4 milligrams the recommended daily intake of zinc?

   ____

Solve Another Problem

10. You spent $10.50 at the fair. If it costs $4.50 for admission and you rode 8 rides which all cost the same, how much does one ride ticket cost?

    ____

Name ____________________ Class ____________ Date ____________

Practice 6-2

Simplifying Algebraic Expressions

Combine like terms.

1. $9j + 34j$ ________

2. $23s - 12s$ ________

3. $5t - 12t + 17t$ ________

4. $6q + 14q - 8q$ ________

5. $7t - 12t + 4t$ ________

6. $16w + 7w - 5w$ ________

7. $y + 13y - 9y$ ________

8. $5z - 2z - 13z$ ________

9. $4x + 21x - 6x$ ________

Simplify each expression.

10. $4a + 7 + 2a$ ________

11. $8(k - 9)$ ________

12. $(w + 3)7$ ________

13. $5(b - 6) + 9$ ________

14. $-4 + 3(6 + k)$ ________

15. $12j - (9j + 7)$ ________

16. $-9 + 8(x + 6)$ ________

17. $4(m + 6) - 3$ ________

18. $28k + 36(7 + k)$ ________

19. $3.09(j + 4.6)$ ________

20. $7.9y + 8.4 - 2.04y$ ________

21. $4.3(5.6 + c)$ ________

22. $9.8c + 8d - 4.6c + 2.9d$ ________

23. $18 + 27m - 29 + 36m$ ________

24. $8(j + 12) + 4(k - 19)$ ________

25. $4.2r + 8.1s + 1.09r + 6.32s$ ________

Solve.

26. Tyrone bought 15.3 gal of gasoline priced at g dollars per gallon, 2 qt of oil priced at q dollars per quart, and a wiper blade priced at $3.79. Write an expression that represents the total cost of these items.

____

27. Choose a number. Multiply by 2. Add 6 to the product. Divide by 2. Then subtract 3. What is the answer? Repeat this process using two different numbers. Explain.

____

____

____

Name ______________________ Class ______________ Date ______________

6-2 • Guided Problem Solving

GPS Student Page 269, Exercise 31:

On a shopping trip, Kelly buys 3 barrettes and a headband. Her sister buys 2 barrettes and 2 headbands. Define and use variables to represent the total cost.

Understand

1. Place a circle around the number of barrettes purchased and a square around the number of headbands purchased.
2. How many headbands did Kelly buy? ______________________
3. Underline what you are being asked to do.

Plan and Carry Out

4. Write an expression for the cost of the items Kelly bought on the shopping trip. Let b = cost of a barrette and h = cost of a headband.

____

5. Write an expression for the cost of the items Kelly's sister bought on the shopping trip.

____

6. Combine the like terms to represent the total cost of the items bought.

____

Check

7. Add the numbers in each shape (circle and square) in the original problem to check your answer.

____

Solve Another Problem

8. For a birthday party, you purchase 10 balloons, 8 party hats, and 5 game prizes. At the last minute you find that you will have a few extra guests. You pick up 3 more hats, 2 more balloons, and another game prize. Use variables where b = cost of a balloon, h = cost of a hat, and p = cost of a game prize to represent the total cost.

____

Name ______________________ Class ______________ Date ______________

Practice 6-3

Solving Multi-Step Equations

Solve each equation. Check the solution.

1. $2(2.5b - 9) + 6b = -7$

2. $0.7w + 16 + 4w = 27.28$

3. $24 = -6(m + 1) + 18$

4. $7k - 8 + 2(k + 12) = 52$

5. $4(1.5c + 6) - 2c = -9$

6. $0.5n + 17 + n = 20$

7. $2x - 3 + 4x = 39$

8. $3(3a + 3) + 6 = 81$

9. $20 = -4(f + 6) + 14$

10. $9a - 4 + 3(a - 11) = 23$

11. You want to join the tennis team. You go to the sporting goods store with $100. If the tennis racket you want costs $80 and the tennis balls cost $4 per can, how many cans of tennis balls can you buy?

12. Johnny wants to ship a package to his friend. A shipping company charges $2.49 for the first pound and $1.24 for each additional pound. If it cost Johnny $11.17 to ship the package, how much did his package weigh?

Name ______________________ Class ______________ Date ______________

6-3 • Guided Problem Solving

GPS Student Page 274, Exercise 22:

Jobs An employee earns $7.00 an hour for the first 35 hours worked in a week and $10.50 for any hours over 35. One week's paycheck (before deductions) was for $308.00. How many hours did the employee work?

Understand

1. How much per hour does the employee make for the first 35 hours? ______________
2. How much per hour does the employee make after 35 hours of work? ______________
3. How much was the week's paycheck? ______________
4. What is it you are asked to find?

____

Plan and Carry Out

5. Write an equation for this situation. Multiply the hourly rate by 35 hours. Add the overtime rate multiplied by an unknown, x. Set this sum equal to the total amount of the check.

____

6. Solve for x, the number of overtime hours the employee worked.

____

7. What do you have to do to find the total hours worked?

____

8. How many total hours did the employee work? ______________

Check

9. Does the answer check? Is 35 times $7 plus the overtime hours equal to the total check?

____

Solve Another Problem

10. A college student has a long-distance phone card. The phone-card rate for the first 100 minutes is 12 cents per minute and then goes to 15 cents per minute after that. If the student had a long distance charge of $21, how many total minutes did the student talk?

____

Name ______________________ Class ______________ Date ______________

Practice 6-4

Solving Equations with Variables on Both Sides

Solve each equation. Check the solution.

1. $12y = 2y + 40$

2. $6(c + 4) = 4c - 18$

3. $0.5m + 6.4 = 4.9 - 0.1m$

4. $14b = 16(b + 12)$

5. $7y = y - 42$

6. $9(d - 4) = 5d + 8$

7. $12j = 16(j - 8)$

8. $0.7p + 4.6 = 7.3 - 0.2p$

9. $6(f + 5) = 2f - 8$

10. $4 = -2(4.5p + 25)$

11. Jace owns twice as many DVDs as Louis. Bo has sixty fewer DVDs than five times Louis's collection. If Jace and Bo have the same amount of DVDs, how many DVDs are in Louis's collection?

12. Deborah has two paintings in her portfolio and paints three more each week. Kai has twelve paintings in her portfolio and paints two more each week. After how many weeks will Deborah and Kai have the same number of paintings?

Name ______________________ Class ____________ Date ____________

6-4 • Guided Problem Solving

GPS Student Page 278, Exercise 17:

Efren leaves home at 9 A.M. and walks 4 miles per hour. His brother, Gregory, leaves half an hour later and runs 8.5 miles per hour in the same direction as Efren. Predict the time at which Gregory will catch up to Efren.

Understand

1. What is the distance formula? ____________________
2. What can you say about the distance each boy will have traveled when Gregory catches up to Efren? ____________________

Plan and Carry Out

3. Write an expression for the distance Gregory travels per hour. Let h stand for time in hours. ____________________
4. Write an expression for the distance Efren travels per hour plus the distance he will have traveled when Gregory leaves the house. ____________________
5. Write an equation setting the distance expressions in Steps 3 and 4 equal. ____________________
6. Solve for h. Use your answer to estimate the time at which Gregory will catch up to Efren. ____________________

Check

7. Solve the expressions in Steps 3 and 4 for your value of h. Are the distances equal? ____________________

Solve Another Problem

10. Roshonda begins riding her bike home from school at 3:00 P.M., traveling 12 miles per hour. James leaves school in a bus a quarter of an hour later and travels 35 miles per hour in the same direction. At about what time will James catch up to Roshonda?

____

Name ______________________ Class ______________ Date ______________

Practice 6-5

Solving Inequalities by Adding or Subtracting

Write an inequality for each graph.

1. 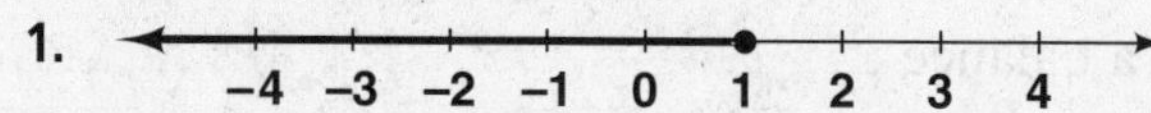

2.

3.

4.

Graph each inequality on a number line.

5. $x \geq -6$

6. $x < -5$

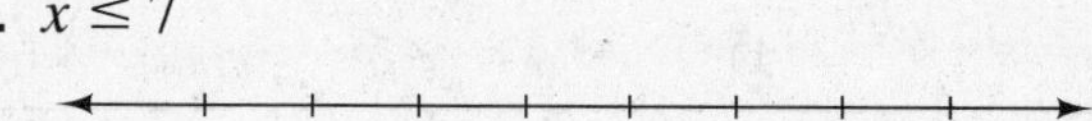

7. $x \leq 0$

8. $x \leq 7$

Solve each inequality. Graph the solutions.

9. $m + 6 > 2$

−8 −7 −6 −5 −4 −3 −2 −1 0

10. $q + 4 \leq 9$

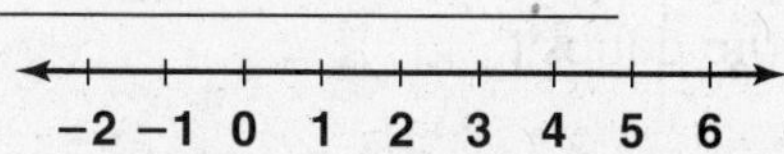

−2 −1 0 1 2 3 4 5 6

11. $w - 6 > -9$

−8 −7 −6 −5 −4 −3 −2 −1 0

12. $y - 3 < -4$

−6 −5 −4 −3 −2 −1 0 1 2

Write and solve an inequality to answer each question.

13. The amount of snow on the ground increased by 8 in. between 7 P.M. and 10 P.M. By 10 P.M., there was less than 2 ft of snow. How much snow was there by 7 P.M.?

14. The school record for points scored in a basketball season by one player is 462. Maria has 235 points so far this season. How many more points does she need to break the record?

Name ______________________ Class ______________ Date ______________

6-5 • Guided Problem Solving

GPS Student Page 285, Exercise 26:

Banking A bank offers free checking for accounts with a balance greater than \$500. You have a balance of \$516.46 and you write a check for \$26.47. Write an inequality to represent how much you would need to deposit to have free checking.

Understand

1. What does your balance have to be in order to get free checking?

____

2. Circle the information you need to know.
3. What do you need to find?

____

____

Plan and Carry Out

4. Write an inequality to represent the given situation, where d represents the deposit.

____

5. Simplify and solve the inequality.

____

6. How much should the deposit be?

____

Check

7. If you deposit \$10.01, will you have free checking? Why?

____

____

Solve Another Problem

8. Most packages contain a nutritional analysis based on an average intake of 2,000 calories. You are trying to follow this guideline and have 580 calories for breakfast and 642 calories for lunch. What number of calories can you have for dinner?

____

Name ______________________ Class ______________ Date ______________

Practice 6-6

Solving Inequalities by Multiplying and Dividing

Solve each inequality and graph the solutions.

1. $-5m < 20$

____

−8 −7 −6 −5 −4 −3 −2 −1 0

2. $\frac{j}{6} \le 0$

____

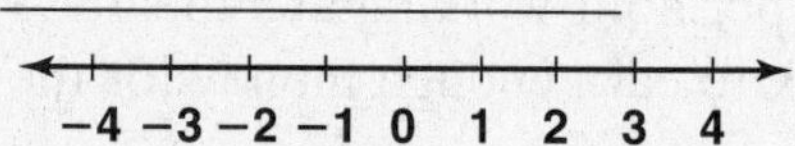

3. $4v > 16$

____

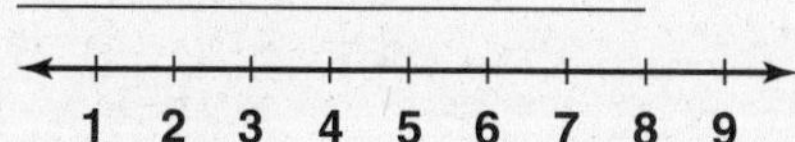

4. $\frac{b}{2} < 4$

____

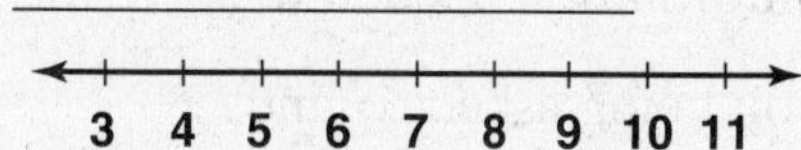

5. $5a > -10$

____

−6 −5 −4 −3 −2 −1 0 1 2

6. $\frac{c}{-3} \ge 6$

____

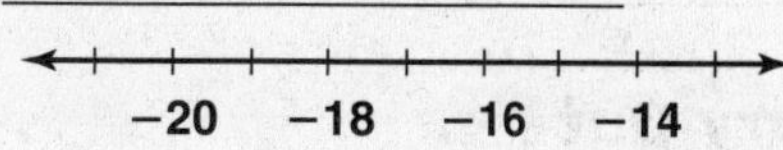

7. $\frac{c}{-6} > 1$

____

−12 −10 −8 −6 −4

8. $-4i \le -16$

____

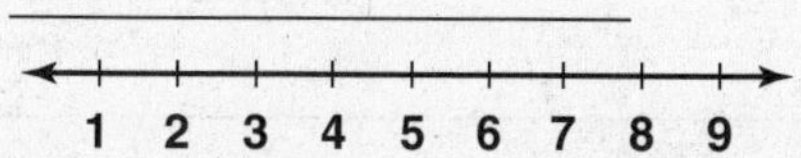

9. $5d < -75$

____

−20 −18 −16 −14 −12

10. $\frac{d}{12} < -1$

____

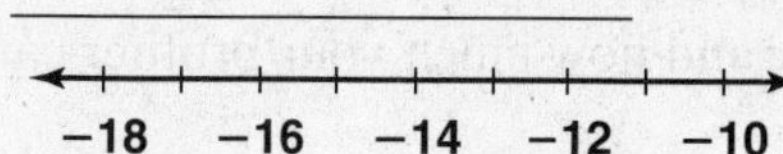

11. $0.5n \ge -2.5$

____

−8 −7 −6 −5 −4 −3 −2 −1 0

12. $\frac{p}{0.2} \le 10$

____

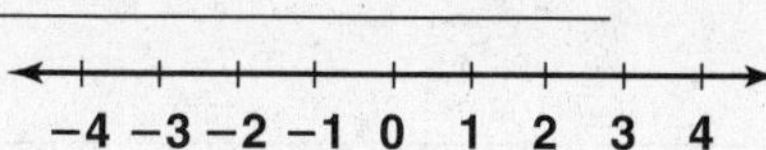

Write an inequality for each problem. Solve the inequality. Then write the solution to the problem.

13. Dom wants to buy 5 baseballs. He has \$20. What is the most each baseball can cost?

____

14. A typing service charges \$5.00 per page. Mrs. Garza does not want to spend more than \$50 for the typing. What is the maximum number of pages she can have typed?

____

15. The tables at a restaurant can each seat 8 people. A dinner at the restaurant will be attended by 125 people. How many tables does the restaurant need in order for every person at the dinner to have a seat?

____

Name ________________ Class ________________ Date ________________

6-6 • Guided Problem Solving

GPS Student Page 292, Exercise 30:

Your brother wants to buy a new multi-disc DVD player for $182.89. He earns $6.85 per hour working at a theater. How many hours will he need to work to earn enough money for the player?

Understand

1. Circle the information needed to solve the problem.
2. What are you being asked to find?

____

____

Plan and Carry Out

3. How would you calculate the amount your brother earns in h hours?

____

____

4. Write an inequality with what you know about the price of the DVD player and how much your brother can earn in h hours.

____

5. What do you need to do to solve for the variable h? Solve the inequality.

____

Check

6. Could your brother work only 26 hours to pay for the DVD player? Could he work 27 hours to pay for the DVD player?

____

____

Solve Another Problem

7. A construction site foreman orders pizza for her crew. There are 9 people on the crew and she expects each person to eat at least 4 slices of pizza. At least how many large pizzas should she order if each pizza is cut into 8 slices? (Let p represent the number of pizzas.)

____

6A: Graphic Organizer

For use before Lesson 6-1

Study Skill It is important that you fully understand the basic concepts in each chapter before moving on to more complex material. Be sure to ask questions when you are not comfortable with the material you have learned.

Write your answers.

1. What is the chapter title? ______________________
2. How many lessons are there in this chapter? ______________________
3. What is the topic of the Test-Taking Strategies page? ______________________
4. Complete the graphic organizer below as you work through the chapter.
   - In the center, write the title of the chapter.
   - When you begin a lesson, write the lesson name in a rectangle.
   - When you complete a lesson, write a skill or key concept in a circle linked to that lesson block.
   - When you complete the chapter, use this graphic organizer to help you review.

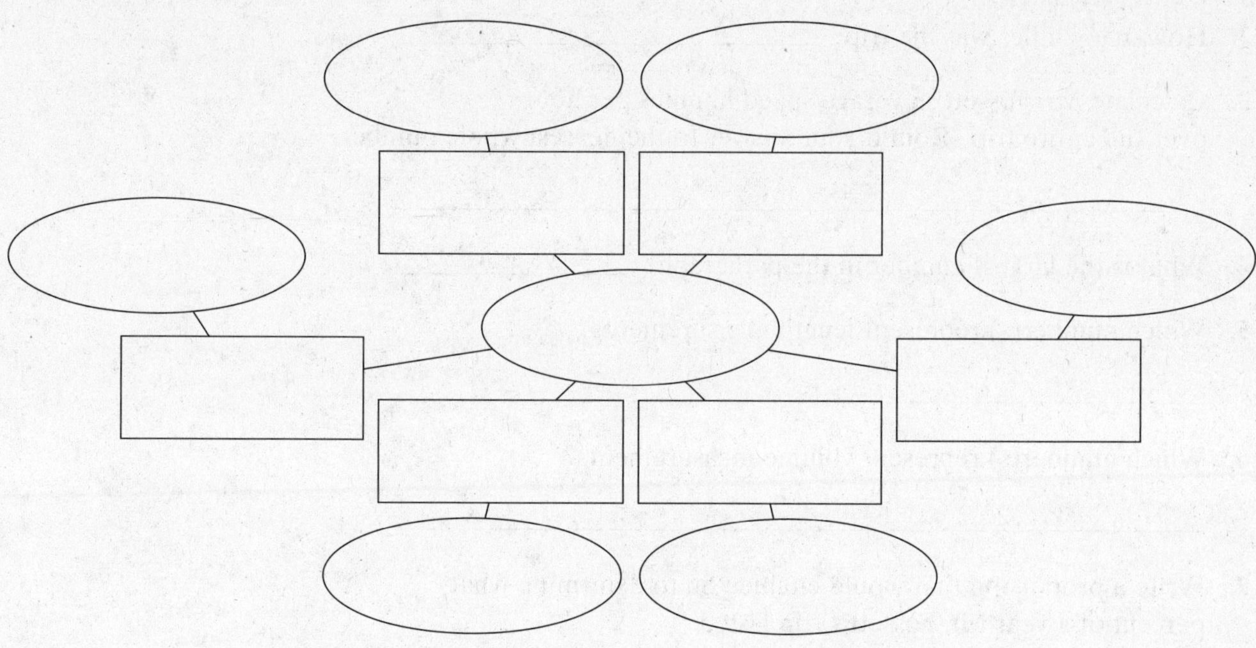

Name ______________________ Class ______________ Date ______________

6B: Reading Comprehension

For use after Lesson 6-2

Study Skill Go to class prepared. Always bring your textbook, notebook or paper, and a pencil, unless your teacher tells you otherwise.

Read the paragraph below and answer the questions.

Steve Fossett, a Chicago millionaire, was the first person to fly solo around the world in a hot air balloon. Mr. Fossett accomplished this feat in July of 2002. The 1.7×10^4 mile trip took him $13\frac{1}{2}$ days to complete. At times, Mr. Fossett's speed reached 200 mi/h. The Spirit of Freedom, Mr. Fossett's balloon, was about the size of six Olympic-size swimming pools, with a volume of about 5.5×10^5 cubic feet.

Mr. Fossett made five previous attempts before he was finally successful. During his earlier attempts, he had some narrow escapes. For example, in 1998, his journey was cut short by a severe thunderstorm during which his balloon fell 2.9×10^4 feet into the shark-infested waters of the Coral Sea. He survived, and finally accomplished his goal on his sixth attempt.

1. How long did Mr. Fossett's trip take? ______________

2. How many miles was the trip? ______________

3. Calculate Mr. Fossett's average speed in miles per hour over the entire trip. Round your answer to the nearest whole number.

   ____

4. What is the largest number in the paragraph? ______________

5. Which number(s) represent length measurements?

   ____

6. Which number(s) represent volume measurements?

   ____

7. Write a proportion that would enable you to determine what percent of a year Mr. Fossett's trip lasted.

   ____

8. **High-Use Academic Words** In Exercise 7, what does it mean to *determine*?

   a. to calculate

   b. to support

Name ______________________ Class ______________ Date ______________

6C: Reading/Writing Math Symbols

For use after Lesson 6-5

Study Skill Explore your textbook so you can use its features to the fullest.

Vocabulary and Study Skills

Match each symbol to its meaning

1. $\approx$	A. is not equal to
2. $=$	B. is congruent to
3. $\cong$	C. is similar to
4. $\neq$	D. is approximately equal to
5. $\geq$	E. is greater than or equal to
6. $\sim$	F. is equal to

Write a mathematical expression or statement for each word description.

7. Ninety one percent is approximately equal to nine tenths.

____

8. Fifteen thousandths times ten to the third power is less than twenty.

____

9. The quantity eight plus a number, cubed

____

10. Five percent is less than sixty thousandths.

____

Write out the following mathematical statements in word form.

11. $0.003 \times 10^2 = 30\%$

____

12. $81\% \approx 4/5$

____

13. $x + 5 \geq -2$

____

Name ______________________ Class ______________ Date ______________

6D: Visual Vocabulary Practice

For use after Lesson 6-4

High -Use Academic Words

Study Skill When making a sketch, make it simple but make it complete.

Concept List

represent	verify	convert
model	explain	pattern
property	calculate	graph

Write the concept that best describes each exercise. Choose from the concept list above.

1. *a* to *b* $a : b$ $\frac{a}{b}$ ______________	**2.** 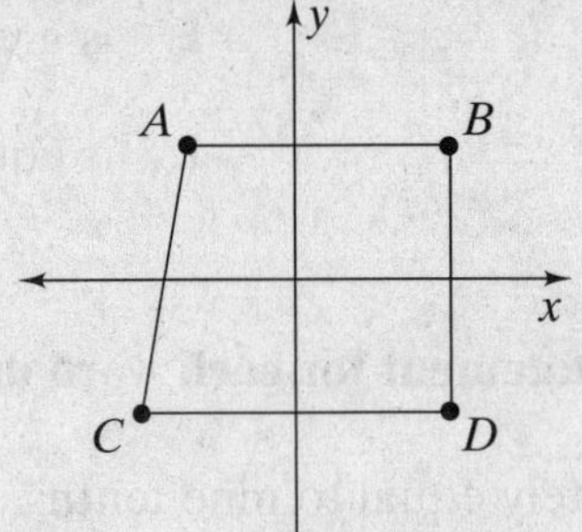 ______________	**3.** The ratios $\frac{5}{7}$ and $\frac{60}{84}$ form a proportion. Check: $60 \div 5 = 12$, and $84 \div 7 = 12$ ______________
4. 1 in. = 2.54 cm ______________	**5.** $P(2) = \frac{1}{6}$ A number cube has six sides and only one side has two dots. Thus the probability of rolling a two is $\frac{1}{6}$. ______________	**6.** $2x - 3 = 4$ 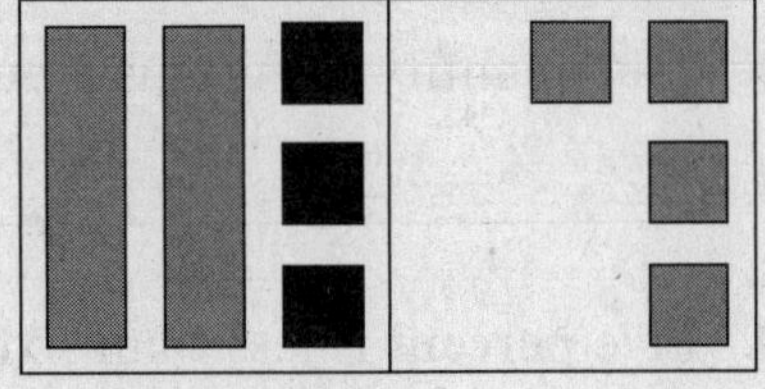 ______________
7. $1 \cdot 11 = 121$ $11 \cdot 111 = 1{,}221$ $11 \cdot 1111 = 12{,}221$ ______________	**8.** The price of potatoes increased by \$0.30/lb this year. If the old price was \$1.50/lb, what is the percent of change? $\frac{0.30}{1.50} = 20\%$ ______________	**9.** $a(b + c) = ab + ac$ ______________

Name ____________________ Class ____________ Date ____________

6E: Vocabulary Check

For use after Lesson 6-6

Study Skill Strengthen your vocabulary. Use these pages and add cues and summaries by applying the Cornell Notetaking style.

Write the definition for each word or term at the right. To check your work, fold the paper back along the dotted line to see the correct answers.

term

like terms

inequality

Subtraction Property of Inequality

Addition Property of Inequality

Name ____________________ Class ______________ Date ______________

6E: Vocabulary Check (continued)

For use after Lesson 6-6

Write the vocabulary word or term for each definition. To check your work, fold the paper back along the dotted line to see the correct answers.

a number, a variable, or the product of a number and a variable ____________________

terms with exactly the same variable factors ____________________

a mathematical sentence that contains $<, >, \leq, \geq$ or $\neq$ ____________________

If you subtract the same number from each side of an inequality, the relationship between the two sides does not change. ____________________

If you add the same number to each side of an inequality, the relationship between the two sides does not change. ____________________

Name ______________________ Class ______________ Date ______________

6F: Vocabulary Review Puzzle

For use with the Chapter Review

Study Skill Turn off the television and radio when studying.

Find each of the words below in the Word Search. Circle the word and cross it off the Word List. Words can be displayed forwards, backwards, up, down, or diagonally.

variable	absolute value	integer	exponent
inequality	equation	additive inverse	inverse
isolate	like terms	solution	

L	F	E	E	T	P	U	O	M	O	I	I	H	H	H	R	D	K	W	V
I	B	T	F	C	C	S	P	R	R	J	N	H	E	I	E	O	B	C	M
K	M	A	G	T	J	L	B	X	P	X	T	X	A	E	L	S	T	F	I
E	A	V	V	E	Z	Y	S	C	I	O	E	B	O	B	O	J	Z	J	N
T	B	L	L	P	A	D	L	S	E	J	G	M	L	L	O	T	D	N	E
E	S	Q	W	C	K	K	C	T	U	O	E	H	U	K	G	N	V	F	Q
R	O	F	C	Y	N	R	L	Z	S	L	R	T	N	S	L	Z	M	X	U
M	L	W	A	D	D	I	T	I	V	E	I	N	V	E	R	S	E	G	A
S	U	G	N	R	E	U	I	V	E	O	U	C	M	V	B	A	I	H	L
W	T	T	R	R	C	M	O	Q	N	D	U	V	S	T	M	E	S	L	I
R	E	M	Q	N	N	S	Y	V	N	L	V	S	I	I	G	X	U	I	T
P	V	E	O	M	G	W	A	B	N	Z	Y	P	M	I	O	P	S	E	Y
D	A	A	V	Z	Y	R	K	A	W	S	D	I	N	K	U	O	A	D	C
O	L	B	G	Q	I	B	I	L	I	C	U	V	Y	Q	L	N	U	O	Z
H	U	J	A	A	K	D	I	Q	U	W	E	I	M	A	L	E	F	N	T
K	E	J	B	R	E	N	L	W	T	R	I	F	T	L	D	N	V	W	P
T	R	L	R	M	Q	H	N	S	S	L	D	E	H	E	R	T	K	F	W
S	E	E	D	E	W	A	R	E	J	I	R	O	N	G	E	E	W	V	Y
W	T	K	H	T	R	F	F	C	A	R	H	F	U	W	J	K	Y	F	V
E	Q	U	A	T	I	O	N	T	Q	N	H	G	H	M	U	N	C	W	C

Name ______________________ Class ______________ Date ______________

Practice 7-1

Pairs of Angles

Name a pair of vertical angles and a pair of adjacent angles in each figure. Find $m\angle 1$.

1\.

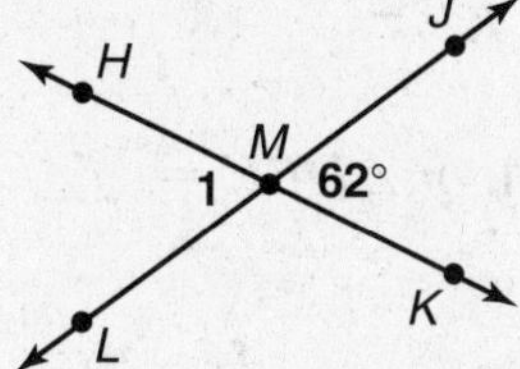

2\.

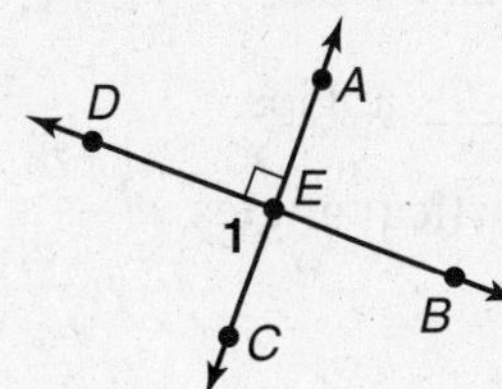

3\.

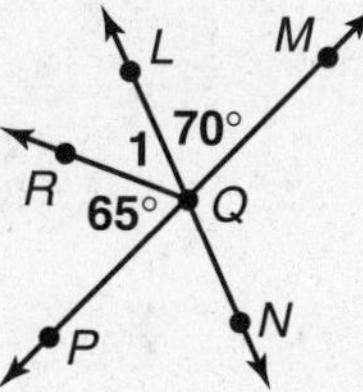

4\.

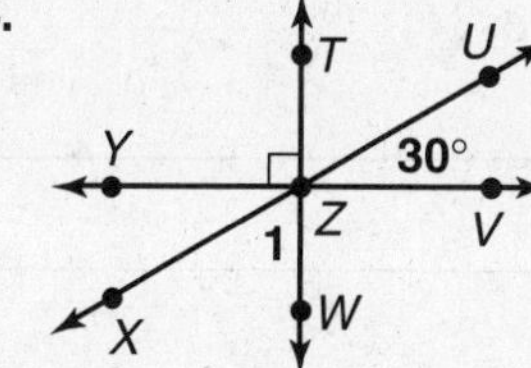

Find the measure of the supplement and the complement of each angle.

5\. 10°

6\. 42.5°

7\. 80°

Use the diagram at the right for Exercises 8–12. Decide whether each statement below is true or false.

8\. $\angle GAF$ and $\angle BAC$ are vertical angles. ______

9\. $\angle EAF$ and $\angle EAD$ are adjacent angles. ______

10\. $\angle CAD$ is a supplement of $\angle DAF$. ______

11\. $\angle CAD$ is a complement of $\angle EAF$. ______

12\. $m\angle DAF = 109°$ ______

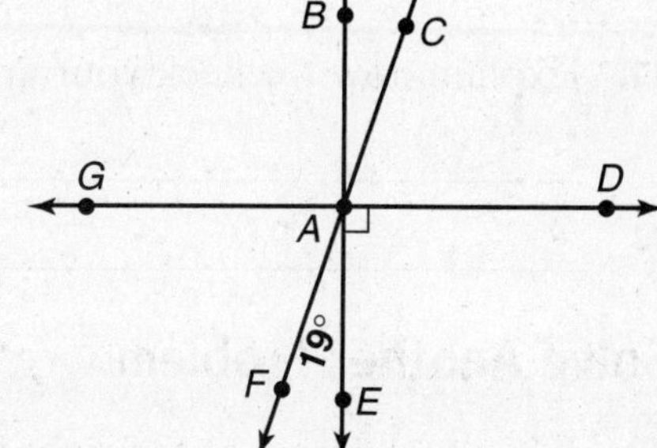

Name ____________________ Class ____________ Date ____________

7-1 • Guided Problem Solving

GPS Student Page 306, Exercises 28–31:

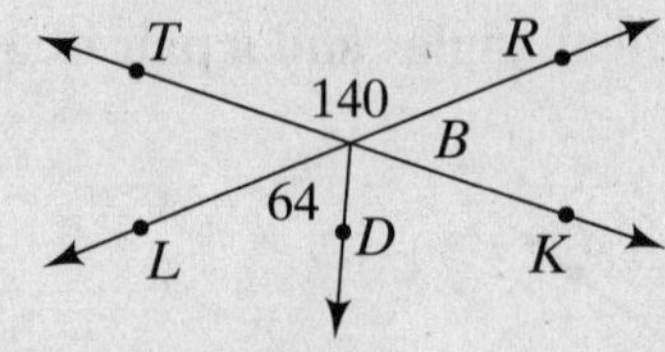

Use the diagram for Exercises 28–31.

28. $\angle LBD$ and $\angle TBL$ are _?_ angles.

29. $\angle RBT$ and $\angle$ _?_ are vertical angles.

30. $m\angle KBL$ = _?_

31. $m\angle DBK$ = _?_

Understand

1. What are you asked to do?

____

2. What is true about the measures of two vertical angles?

____

3. What are adjacent angles?

____

____

Plan and Carry Out

4. Do angles $\angle LBD$ and $\angle TBL$ share a side? If so, what is it? ______________

5. What type of angles are $\angle LBD$ and $\angle TBL$? ______________

6. What pairs of vertical angles are formed by the intersection of $\overleftrightarrow{TK}$ and $\overleftrightarrow{RL}$?

____

7. What is the measure of angle KBL? ________

8. $m\angle LBD + m\angle DBK$ = ________

9. Which angle is adjacent to $\angle LBD$?

____

10. Substitute what you know into the equation in step 8 and solve.

____

Check

11. Explain how to check your answer in Step 10.

____

____

Solve Another Problem

12. Use the diagram at the right to solve.

a. $\angle CFA$ and $\angle DFE$ are _?_ angles.

____

b. $m\angle BFC$ = _?_ °

____

Name ______________________ Class ______________ Date ______________

Practice 7-2

Angles and Parallel Lines

Identify each pair of angles as *vertical, adjacent, corresponding, alternate interior,* or *none of these.*

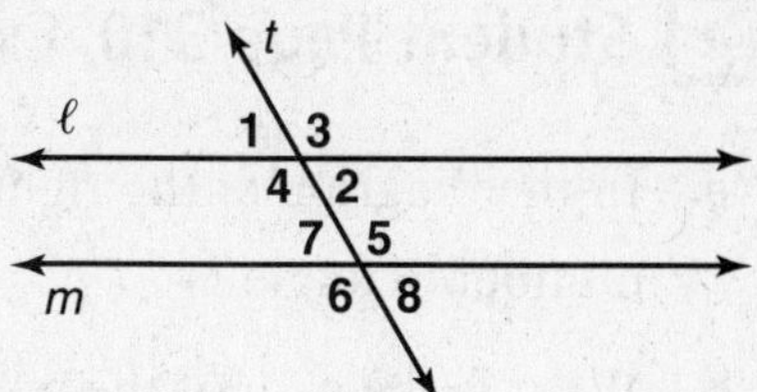

1. $\angle 7, \angle 5$ ______________

2. $\angle 1, \angle 2$ ______________

3. $\angle 1, \angle 7$ ______________

4. $\angle 4, \angle 7$ ______________

Use the diagrams at the right for Exercises 5 and 6.

5. Name four pairs of corresponding angles.

____

6. Name two pairs of alternate interior angles.

____

In each diagram below, $\ell \parallel m$. Find the measure of each numbered angle.

7.

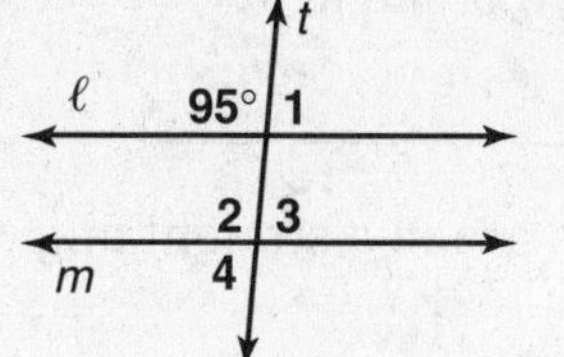

8.

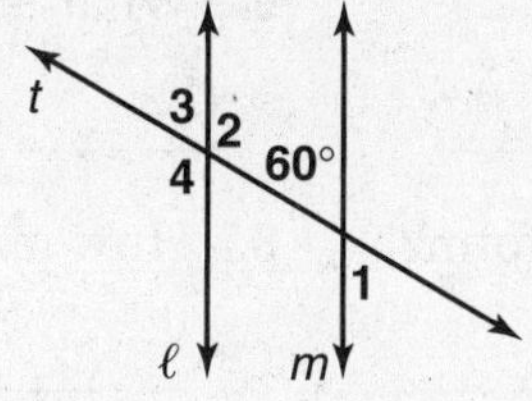

9.

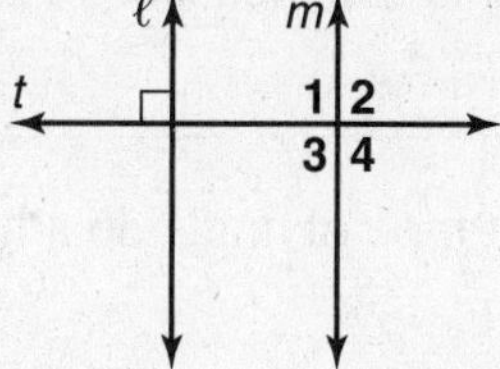

7.	8.	9.
$m\angle 1 =$ ______	$m\angle 1 =$ ______	$m\angle 1 =$ ______
$m\angle 2 =$ ______	$m\angle 2 =$ ______	$m\angle 2 =$ ______
$m\angle 3 =$ ______	$m\angle 3 =$ ______	$m\angle 3 =$ ______
$m\angle 4 =$ ______	$m\angle 4 =$ ______	$m\angle 4 =$ ______

10. Use the figure at the right. Is line ℓ parallel to line m? Explain how you could use a protractor to support your conjecture.

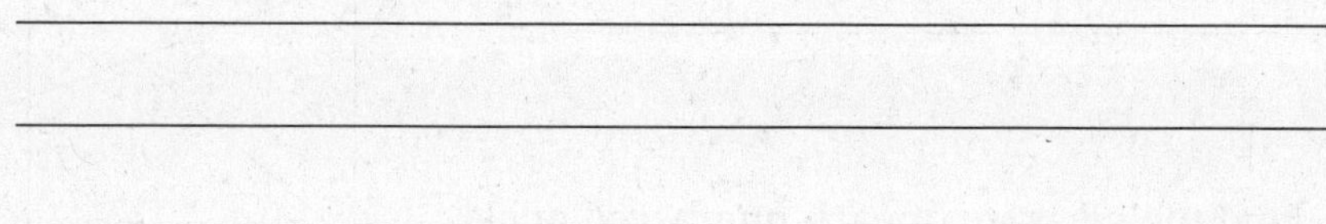

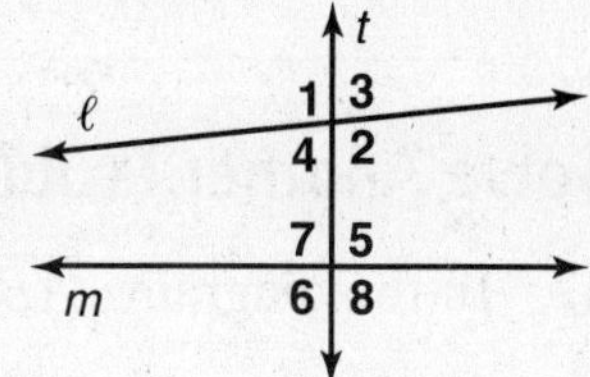

____

____

____

____

Name ____________________ Class ____________________ Date ____________________

7-2 • Guided Problem Solving

GPS Student Page 310, Exercise 31:

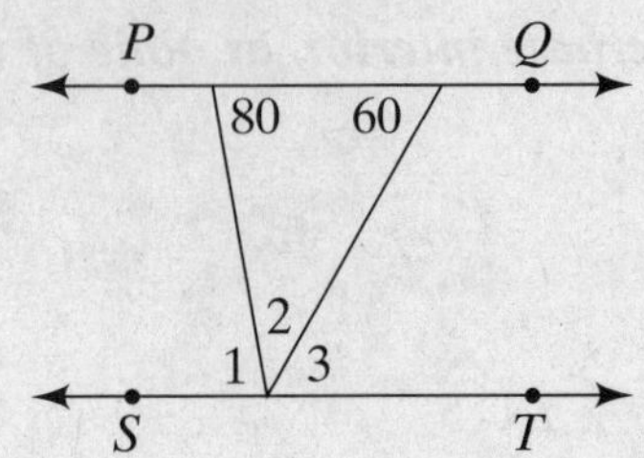

a. In the diagram at the right, $\overleftrightarrow{PQ} \parallel \overleftrightarrow{ST}$. Find the measure of each numbered angle.

b. What is the sum of the angle measures of the triangle?

Understand

1. What are alternate interior angles?

____

____

2. What are you asked to do?

____

Plan and Carry Out

3. Use angle 1 and angle 3 to name two pairs of alternate interior angles.

____

4. What is true of the measure of alternate interior angles?

____

5. What is the measure of angle 1?

____

6. What is the measure of angle 3?

____

7. What type of angle do angles 1, 2 and 3 form?

____

8. How many degrees are in a straight angle?

____

9. Use the information from Steps 5 and 6 to help find the measure of angle 2.

____

10. What is the sum of the angle measures in the triangle?

____

Check

11. Explain your answer from Step 10.

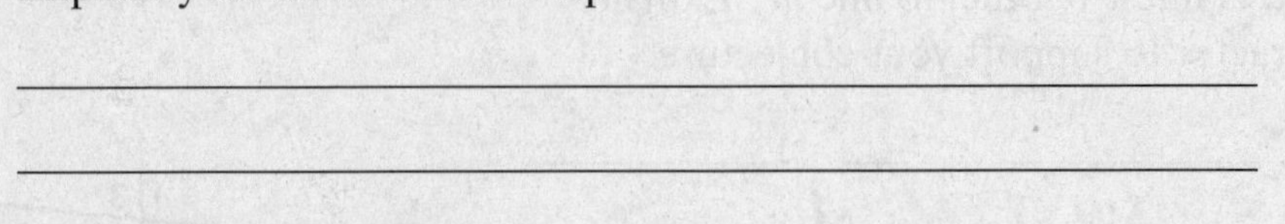

Solve Another Problem

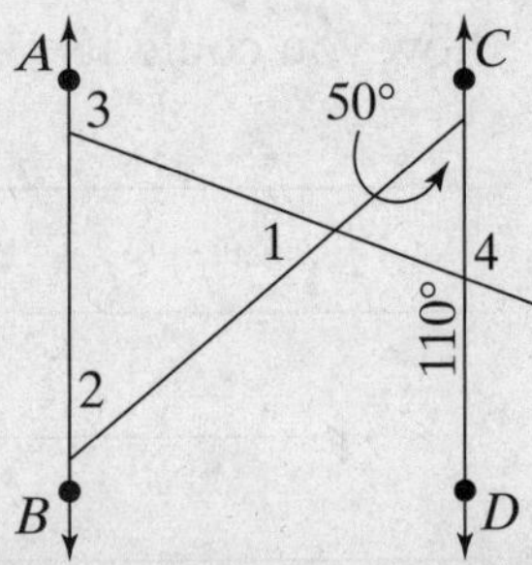

12. In the diagram, $\overleftrightarrow{AB} \parallel \overleftrightarrow{CD}$. Find the measure of each numbered angle.

____

Name ______________________ Class ______________ Date ______________

Practice 7-3

Congruent Polygons

Determine whether each pair of triangles is congruent. Explain.

1.

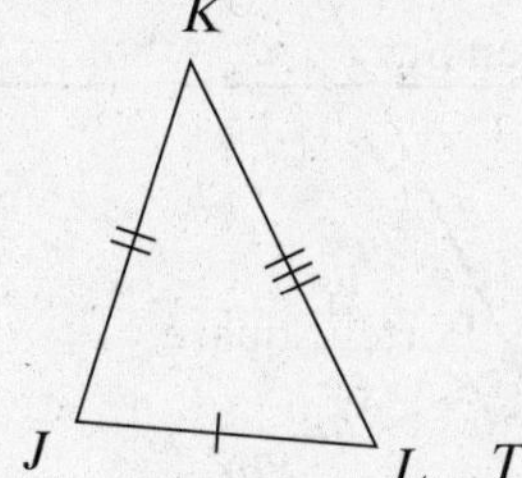

____

2.

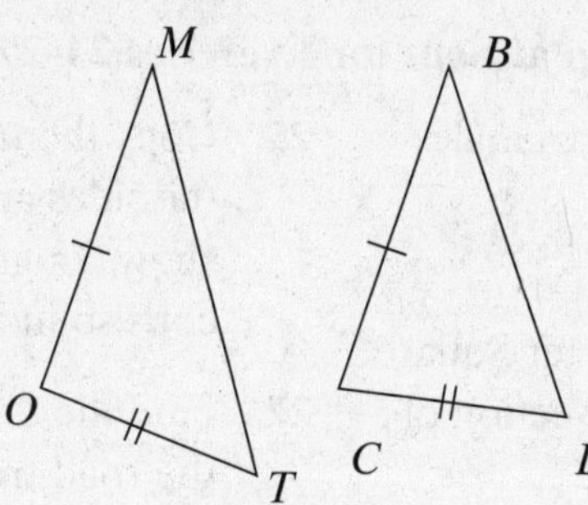

____

3.

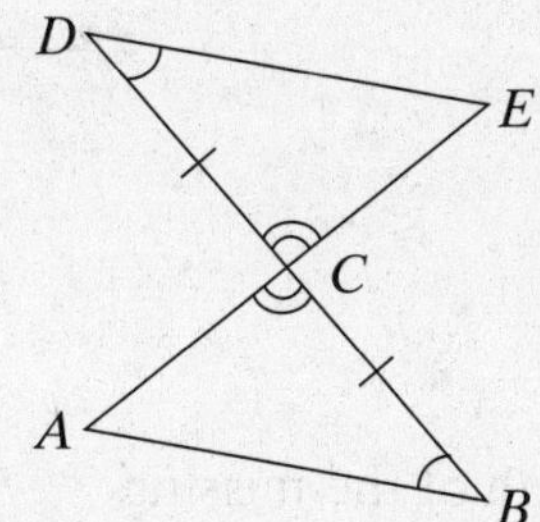

____

4.

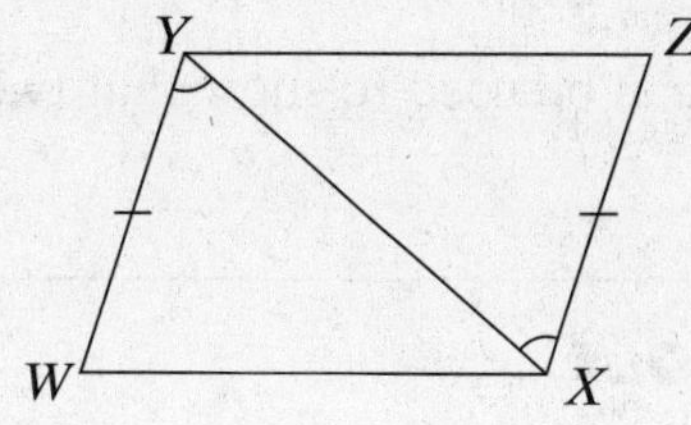

____

Determine if each triangle in Exercises 5–7 is congruent to $\triangle XYZ$ at the right.

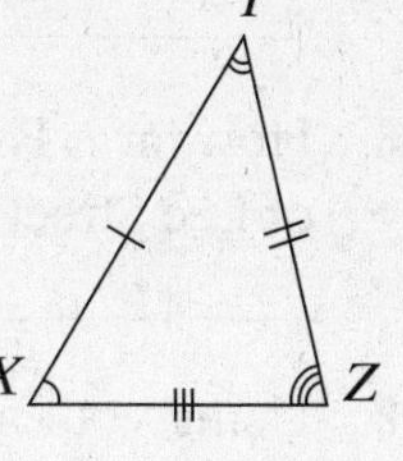

5.

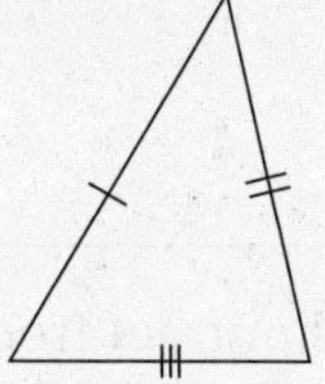

____

6.

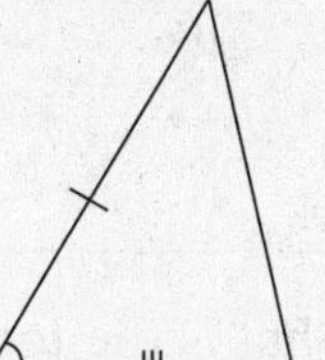

____

7.

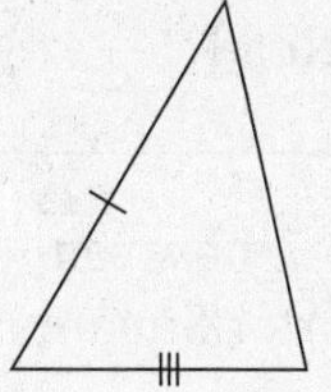

____

For Exercises 8–9, use the triangles at the right.

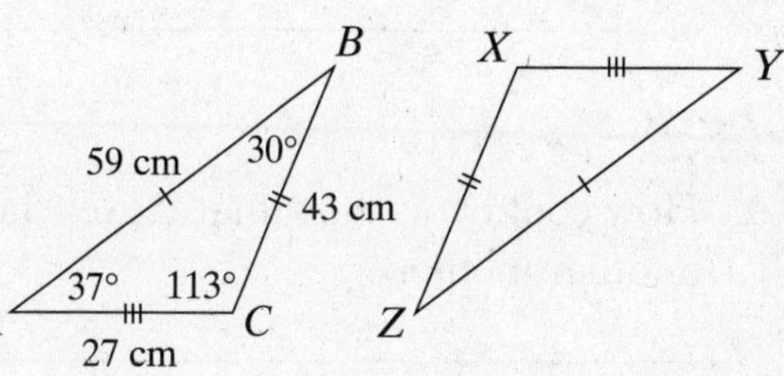

8. $\triangle XYZ \cong$ ______________ by ______________

9. Find the missing measures for $\triangle XYZ$.

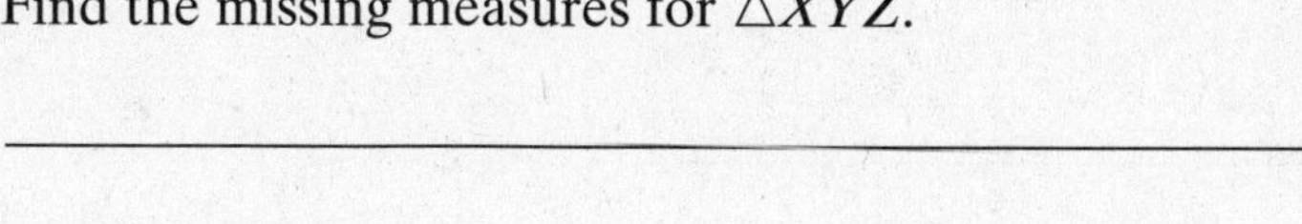

Name ______________________ Class ______________ Date ______________

7-3 • Guided Problem Solving

GPS Student Page 316, Exercises 24–27:

Maps Use the map at right for Exercises 24–27.

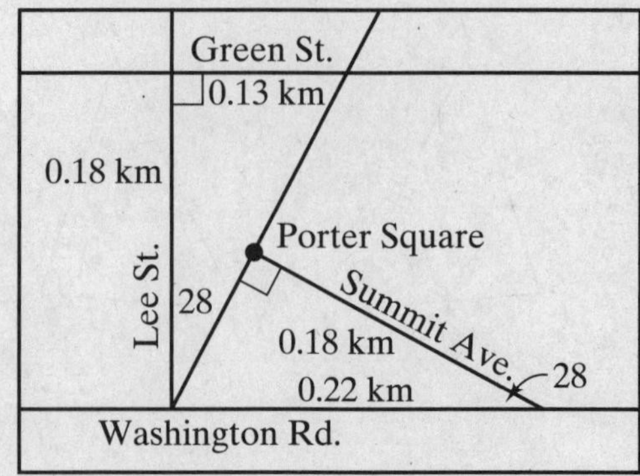

24. Show that the triangles in the map are congruent.

25. Copy the triangles. Mark the sides and angles to show congruent corresponding parts.

26. How far is Porter Square from the intersection of Lee Street and Washington Road?

27. Find the distance along the road from Porter Square to Green Street.

Understand

1. What methods can be used to show that two triangles are congruent?

____

Plan and Carry Out

2. How can you find the length of a missing side?

____

3. What is the total length of the missing hypotenuse?

____

4. Are the two triangles congruent? Why?

____

5. Sketch the two triangles. Mark their corresponding parts.

____

6. How far is Porter Square from the intersection of Lee Street and Washington Road?

____

7. What is the total length of the street from Washington to Green by the way of Porter Square? ______________

8. Using your answer from Step 7, how can you find the distance from Porter Square to Green Street?

____

____

Check

9. How could you show that these triangles are congruent by another method?

____

Solve Another Problem

10. Explain why the pair of triangles shown are congruent. Find the missing measures in the diagram.

____

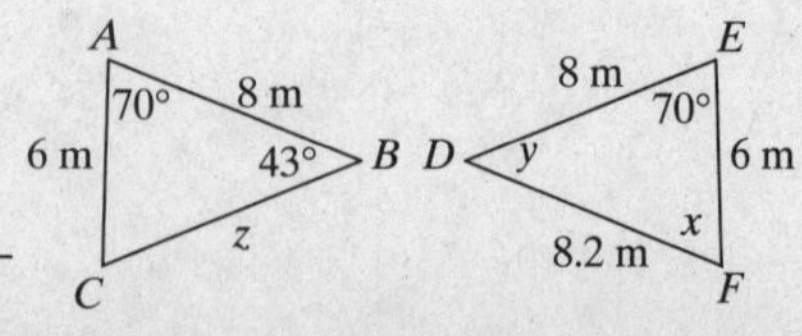

Name ______________________ Class ______________ Date ______________

Practice 7-4

Classifying Triangles and Quadrilaterals

Determine the best name for each quadrilateral. Explain your choice.

1. 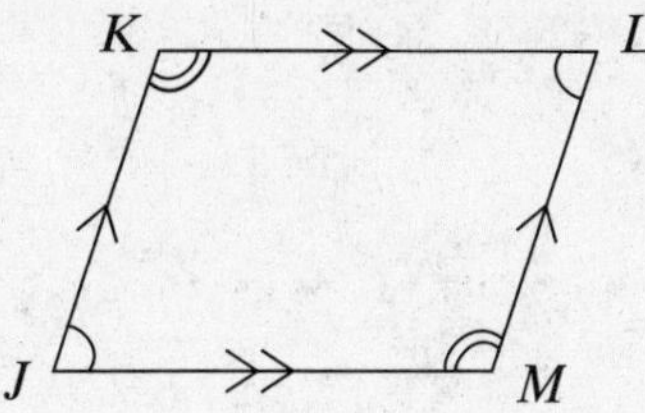

2. 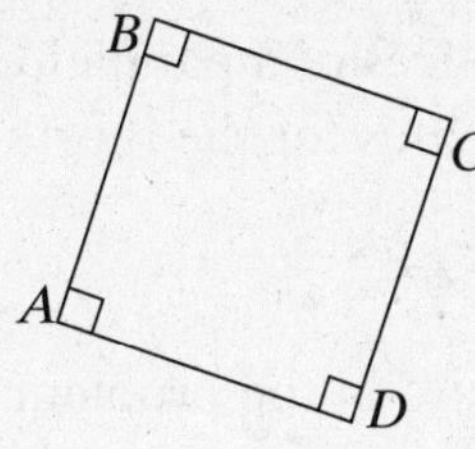

3. 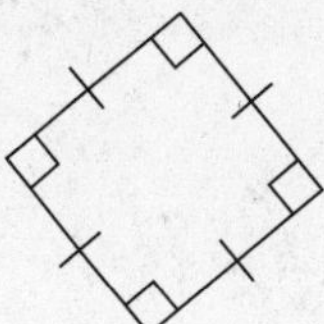

4 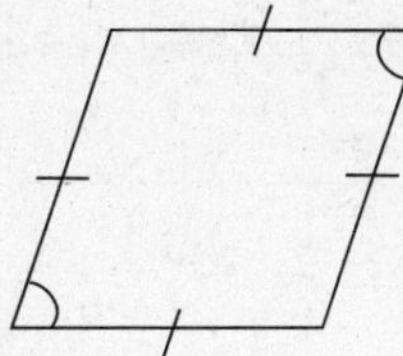

5. 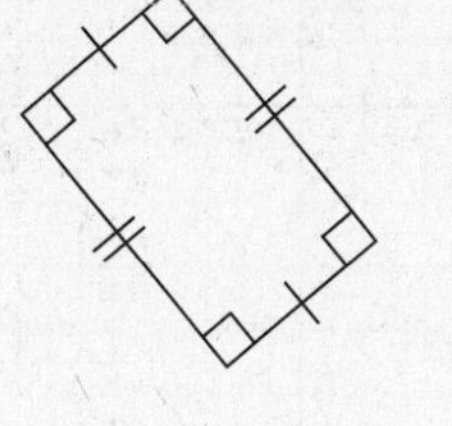

6. $\triangle ABC \cong \triangle CDA$

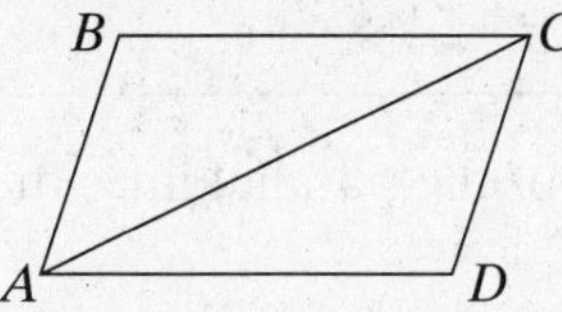

Classify each triangle by its sides and its angles. Explain your choice.

7. 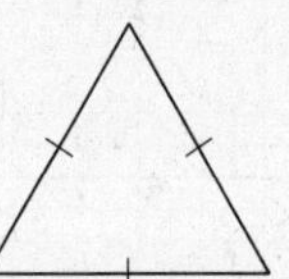

8. 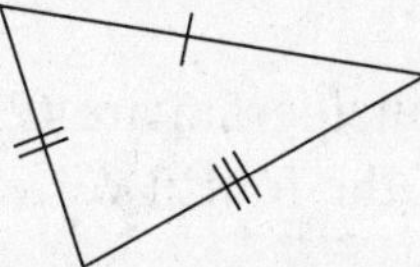

9. 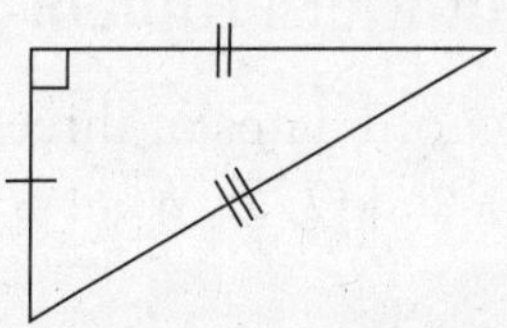

Name ______________________ Class ______________ Date ______________

7-4 • Guided Problem Solving

GPS Student Page 321, Exercise 22:

The coordinates of three vertices of a parallelogram are (3, 5), (8, 5), and (1, −1). Find the coordinates for the fourth vertex.

Understand

1. Name the geometric figure in the problem.

____

2. What do you know about the sides of this figure?

____

3. What do you know about the lengths of the opposite sides of this figure?

____

4. What are you looking for?

____

Plan and Carry Out

5. Plot the given points on the grid at right.

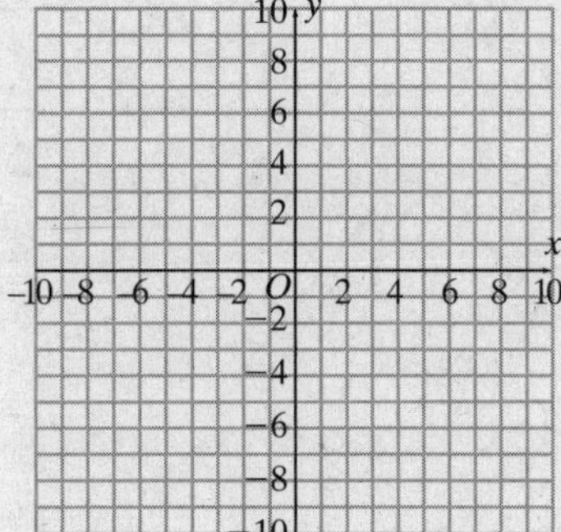

6. Must a parallelogram have right angles? ______________

7. Draw the horizontal line segment. How long is it?

____

8. Keeping the length of the parallel lines the same, where should you place the point?

____

Check

9. Is every point plotted correctly to create a parallelogram?

____

Solve Another Problem

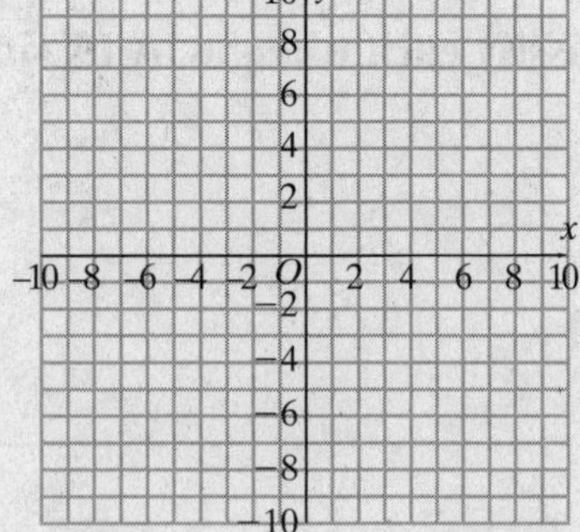

10. The coordinates of three vertices of a parallelogram are (2, 2), (4, 2), and (7, 5). What is the coordinate of the fourth vertex?

____

Name ____________________ Class ____________________ Date ____________________

Practice 7-5

Angles and Polygons

Classify each polygon by its number of sides.

1. 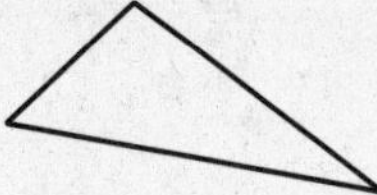

2. 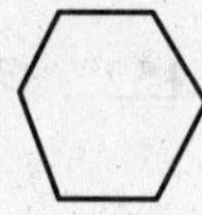

3. 

4. a polygon with 8 sides

5. a polygon with 10 sides

6. Find the measure of each angle of a regular hexagon.

7. The measures of four angles of a pentagon are 143°, 118°, 56°, and 97°. Find the measure of the missing angle.

8. Four of the angles of a hexagon measure 53°, 126°, 89°, and 117°. What is the sum of the measures of the other two angles?

9. Four of the angles of a heptagon measure 109°, 158°, 117°, and 89°. What is the sum of the measures of the other three angles?

10. Complete the chart for the total number of diagonals from all vertices in each polygon. The first three have been done for you.

Polygon	Number of Sides	Number of Diagonals
triangle	3	0
rectangle	4	2
pentagon	5	5
hexagon		
heptagon		
octagon		
nonagon		
decagon		

11. From the table you completed in Exercise 10, what pattern do you see? Explain.

Name ____________________ Class ____________ Date ____________

7-5 • Guided Problem Solving

GPS Student Page 327, Exercise 28:

The measures of six angles of a heptagon are 145°, 115°, 152°, 87°, 90°, and 150°. Find the measure of the seventh angle.

Understand

1. How many sides does a heptagon have? ____________

2. How many interior angles does a heptagon have?

   ____

3. What are you asked to find?

   ____

Plan and Carry Out

4. For a polygon with n sides, the sum of the measures of the interior angles is $(n - 2)180°$. Substitute what you know into the formula to find the sum of the interior angles. Show your work.

   ____

5. Find the total of the measures of the six interior angles given in the problem.

   ____

6. Subtract the total you found in Step 5 from the total number of degrees in a heptagon that you found in Step 4.

   ____

Check

7. Add all seven angles to verify that they total 900°.

   ____

Solve Another Problem

8. A decagon has interior angle measures of 156°, 178°, 124°, 132°, 138°, 142°, 116°, 178°, and 159°. Find the measure of the missing angle.

   ____

Name ______________________ Class ______________ Date ______________

Practice 7-6

Find the area of each parallelogram or trapezoid.

1\.

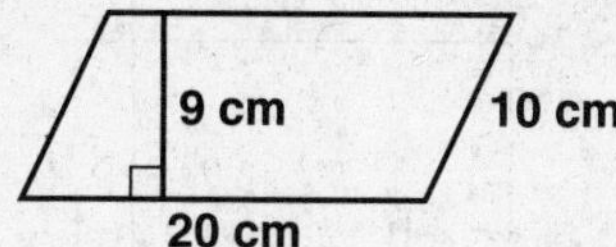

2\.

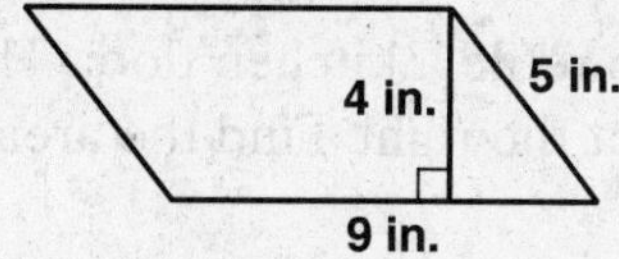

3\.

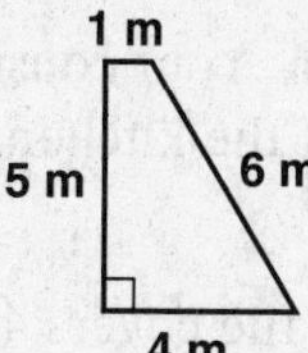

______________ ______________ ______________

4\.

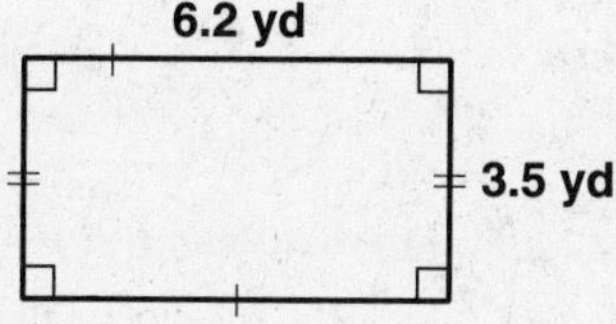

5\.

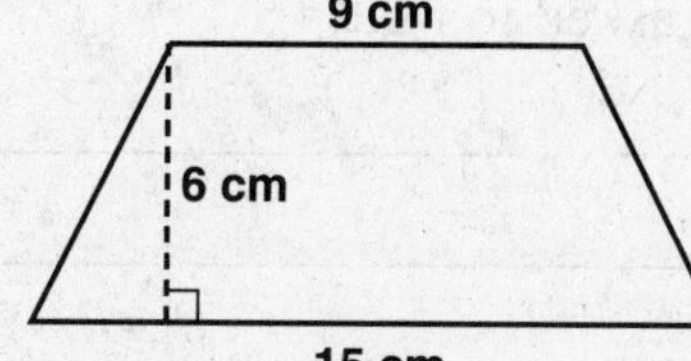

6\.

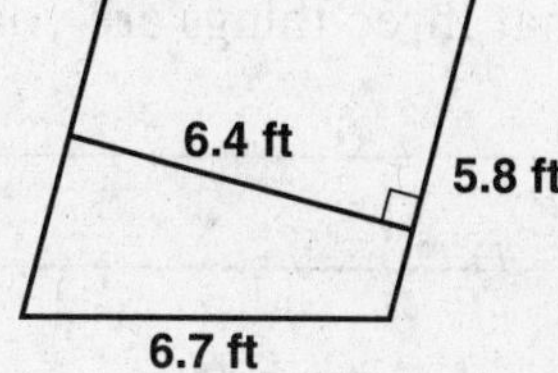

______________ ______________ ______________

7. The area of a parallelogram is 221 yd^2. Its height is 13 yd. What is the length of its corresponding base?

8. The area of a parallelogram is 116 cm^2. Its base is 8 cm. What is the corresponding height?

______________ ______________

Find the area of each triangle.

9\.

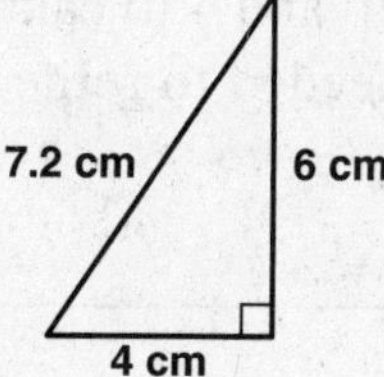

10\.

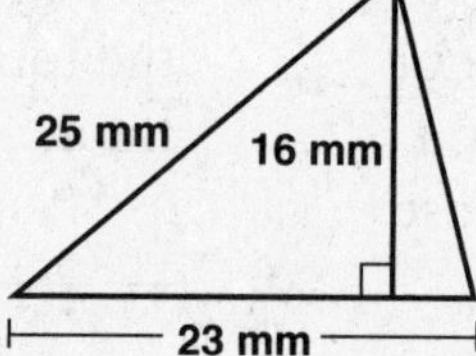

11\.

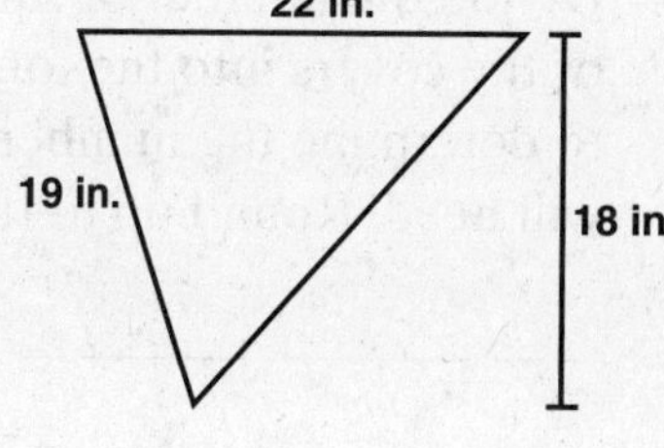

______________ ______________ ______________

Name ______________________ Class ______________ Date ______________

7-6 • Guided Problem Solving

GPS Student Page 332, Exercise 18:

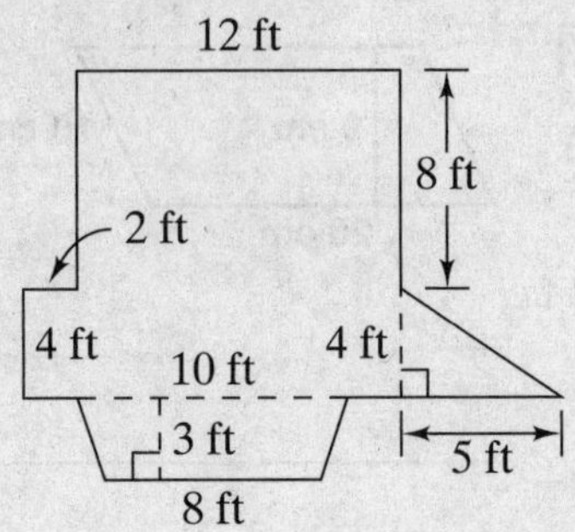

a. Construction Your cousin wants to retile a kitchen floor. The floor plan of the kitchen is shown at the right. Find the area of the floor.

b. One case of tile covers 44 ft^2. How many cases are needed?

c. Each case of tiles costs $39.16. What is the total cost of the tiles?

Understand

1. What three things are you being asked to find?

____

____

Plan and Carry Out

2. What four shapes is the floor plan divided into if one is a square?

____

3 a. Find the area of each shape. Show your work.

____

____

b. Calculate the total area of the kitchen floor. ______________

4. Divide the number of square feet that a case of tile covers into the total area of the floor to determine the number of cases that you will need. Round up to the nearest full case.

____

5. Use the results of Steps 3b and 4 to calculate the total cost of the tile needed to retile the floor.

____

Check

6. If you have a budget of $175 for the tile, are you over or under your budget? ______________

Solve Another Problem

7. If a gallon of paint will cover 300 square feet, how many gallons of paint will you need to paint the wall shown at the right?

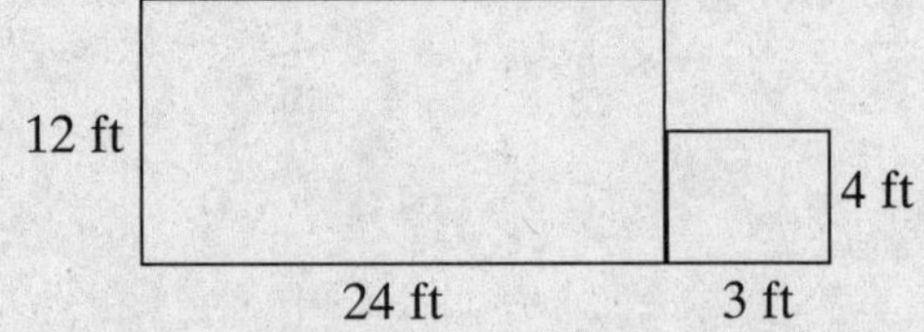

____

Name ______________________ Class ______________ Date ______________

Practice 7-7

Circumference and Area of a Circle

Find the circumference and area of each circle. Round to the nearest hundredth.

1.

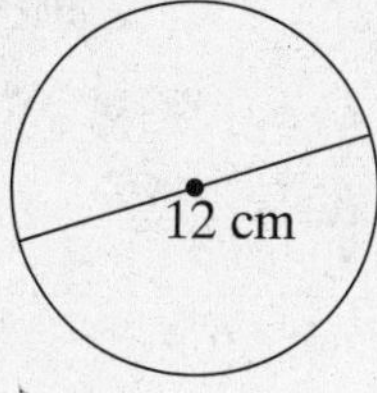

2.

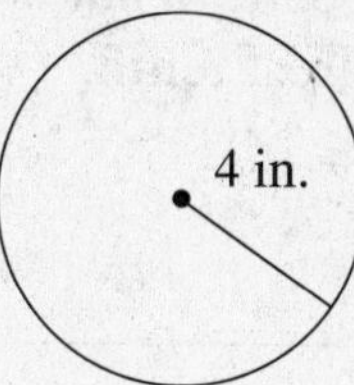

3.

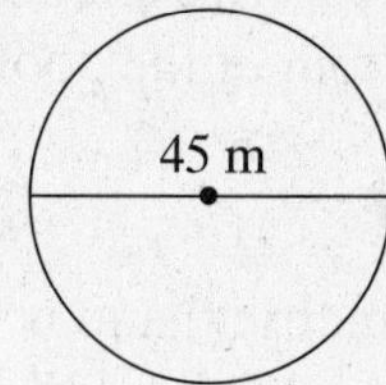

4.

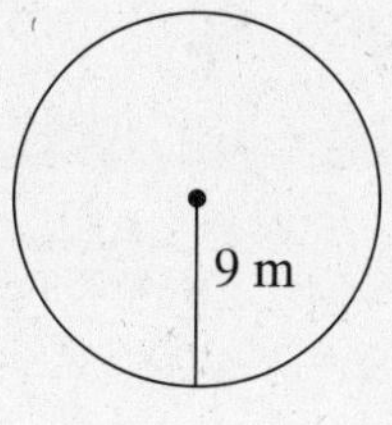

5.

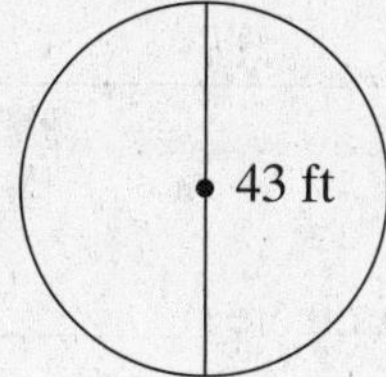

6.

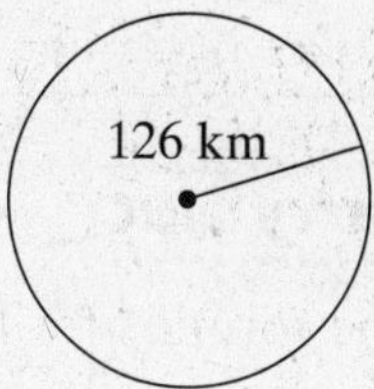

Find the circumference of a circle with the given diameter or radius. Use $\frac{22}{7}$ for π.

7. $d = 70$ cm

8. $r = 14$ cm

9. $d = 35$ in.

Find the radius and the diameter of a circle with the given circumference. Round to the nearest hundredth.

10. $C = 68$ cm

11. $C = 150$ m

12. $C = 218$ in.

13. Use the figure at the right. Find the area of the shaded region. Round your answer to the nearest hundredth.

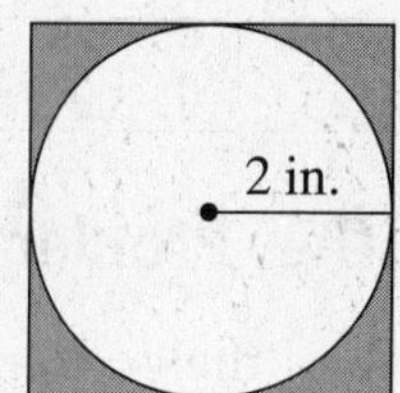

Name ______________________ Class ______________ Date ______________

7-7 • Guided Problem Solving

GPS Student Page 339, Exercise 30:

Recreation The circumference of a pool is about 63 ft. What is the area of the bottom of the pool? Round to the nearest tenth.

Understand

1. What geometric figure is the pool's bottom? ______________
2. What are you asked to find?

   ____
3. What information are you given?

   ____

Plan and Carry Out

4. What is the formula for finding the area of a circle? __________
5. There are two formulas you could use to find circumference, what are they?

   ____
6. Select the formula that contains the radius and solve for the unknown variable using 3.14 for π.

   ____
7. Use you answer from Step 6 to write an equation to find the area of the pool. Solve the equation to find the area of the pool to the nearest tenth.

   ____

Check

8. Find the area of the pool using the other formula for circumference. Show your work.

   ____

   ____

Solve Another Problem

9. The area of the bottom of a circular pool is 452.2 ft^2. What is its circumference, rounded to the nearest tenth?

   ____

   ____

Name ______________________ Class ______________ Date ______________

Practice 7-8

Constructions

Use a compass and straightedge to make each construction.

1. Construct $\angle ABC$ so that it is congruent to the given $\angle STU$.

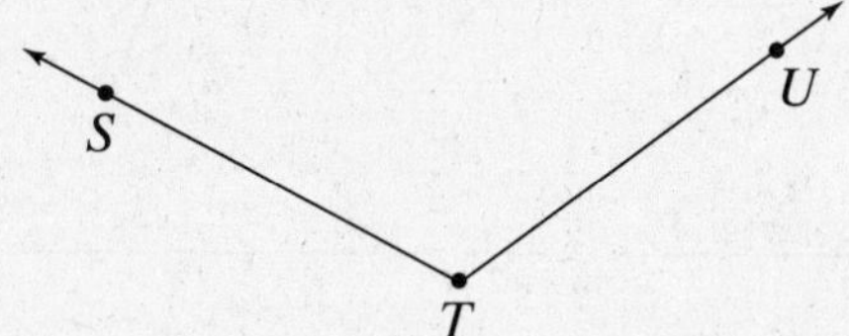

2. Construct $\angle PQR$ so that it is congruent to the given $\angle DEF$.

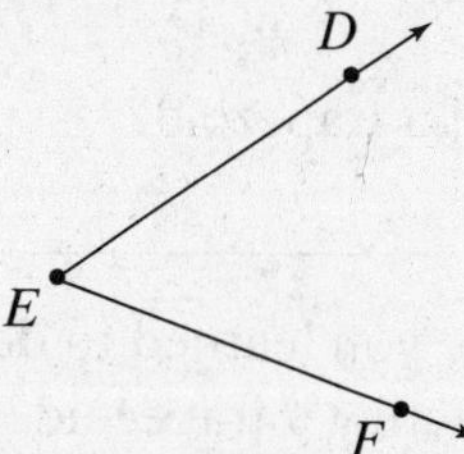

3. Draw an obtuse $\angle G$. Construct an angle congruent to $\angle G$.

4. Use a protractor to draw $\angle XYZ$ with $m\angle XYZ = 36°$. Then use a compass and straightedge to construct $\angle RST$ with the same measure.

Construct a line parallel to the given line.

5.

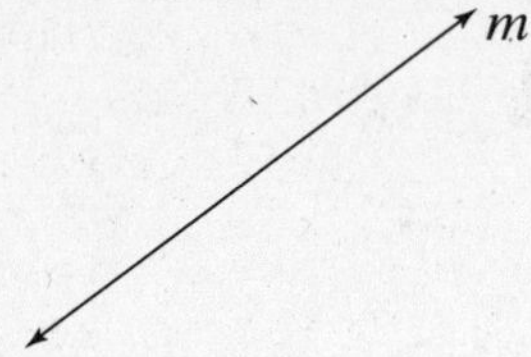

6.

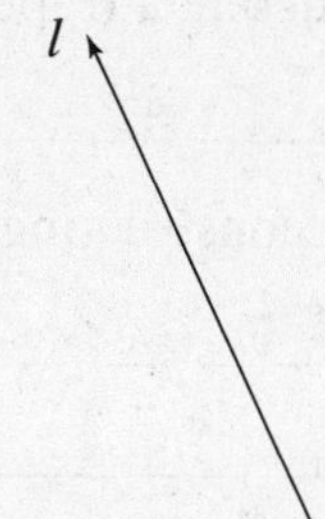

7. Draw a vertical line n. Then construct a line p parallel to n.

8. Draw a horizontal line a. Then construct a line b parallel to a.

Name ______________________ Class ______________ Date ____________

7-8 • Guided Problem Solving

GPS Student Page 343, Exercise 11:

Writing in Math How could you construct a trapezoid?

Understand

1. What is the definition of a trapezoid?

2. What constructions have you learned to do? Which of these could you use in constructing a trapezoid?

Plan and Carry Out

3. How many pairs of sides in a trapezoid are parallel? Do any of the sides of a trapezoid need to be congruent? Explain.

4. Do any of the angles of the trapezoid need to be congruent? Do any of the angles need to be right angles? Explain.

5. Explain the first step in constructing a trapezoid.

6. Explain the rest of the steps in constructing a trapezoid.

Check

7. Follow the steps you wrote in your answers to Steps 5 and 6. Is your figure a trapezoid?

Solve Another Problem

8. How could you construct an isosceles triangle?

7A: Graphic Organizer

For use before Lesson 7-1

Study Skill As your teacher presents new material in the chapter, keep a paper and pencil handy to write down notes and questions. If you miss class, borrow a classmate's notes so you don't fall behind.

Write your answers.

1. What is the chapter title? ______________________
2. How many lessons are there in this chapter? ______________________
3. What is the topic of the Test-Taking Strategies page? ______________________
4. Complete the graphic organizer below as you work through the chapter.
   - In the center, write the title of the chapter.
   - When you begin a lesson, write the lesson name in a rectangle.
   - When you complete a lesson, write a skill or key concept in a circle linked to that lesson block.
   - When you complete the chapter, use this graphic organizer to help you review.

Name ______________________ Class ______________ Date ______________

7B: Reading Comprehension

For use after Lesson 7-2

Study Skill Use tables when you need to organize complex information. The columns and rows allow you to display different types of information in a way that is easy to read. Make sure you use appropriate headings.

Read the paragraph and chart below to answer the questions.

The human skeletal system helps support the body and protects its organs from being damaged. At birth, a human skeleton is made up of 275 different bones. As the body ages, some of the bones fuse together leaving the adult skeleton with 206 bones. There are two major systems of bones in the human body; the axial skeleton which is made up of 80 bones, and the appendicular skeleton which has 126 bones. The following chart lists the types and number of bones located in various parts of the adult body.

Human Bones

Fingers (per hand)	14	Toes (per foot)	14
Each Palm	5	Instep of Each Foot	5
Each Wrist	8	Each Ankle	7
Facial Bones	14	Cranium	8
Lumbar Vertebrae	5	Cervical Vertebrae	7
Thoracic Vertebrae	12	Ribs	12 pairs

1. How many bones fuse together between birth and adulthood?

____

2. What is the total number of bones in the hand and wrist?

____

3. What is the ratio of cervical vertebrae to thoracic vertebrae?

____

4. What percent of bones in the adult skeleton are located in the cranium?

____

5. What is the total number of bones in an adult's toes and fingers?

____

6. What percent of bones in the human skeleton are located in an adult's ankle, instep, and toes?

____

7. Explain the function of the human skeleton.

____

8. **High-Use Academic Words** In question 7, what does the word *explain* mean?

   a. to display using illustrations, tables, or graphs

   b. to give facts and details that make an idea easier to understand

Name ______________________ Class ______________ Date ______________

7C: Reading/Writing Math Symbols

For use after Lesson 7-7

Study Skill Take notes while you study. Use a highlighter to emphasize important material in your notes.

Write the following mathematical expressions or equations in words.

1. $m\angle 1 = 50^\circ$

   ____

2. $\angle JKL$ ______________________________

3. $a \parallel b$ ______________________________

4. $\overline{GH} \cong \overline{LK}$

   ____

5. $\angle R \cong \angle T$

   ____

6. $\overleftrightarrow{AB} \parallel \overleftrightarrow{CD}$

   ____

7. $\overrightarrow{AB}$ ______________________________

8. t^5 ______________________________

9. $\overleftrightarrow{AB} \perp \overleftrightarrow{JK}$

   ____

Write each of the following statements using mathematical symbols.

10. Segment *AB* and segment *SR* are equal in length. ____________

11. angle *STU* ______________________________

12. Segment *BA* is parallel to segment *RK*. ____________

13. The measure of angle *JKL* is 43 degrees. ____________

14. Angle *R* is congruent to angle *Y*. ____________

15. *x* raised to the sixth power ____________

16. arc *TY* ______________________________

17. The sum of the measures of angles *ABC* and *XYZ* is 90 degrees.

    ____

Vocabulary and Study Skills

Name ______________________ Class ______________ Date ______________

7D: Visual Vocabulary Practice

For use after Lesson 7-5

Study Skill Use Venn Diagrams to understand the relationship between words whose meanings overlap such as squares, rectangles, and quadrilaterals or real numbers, integers, and counting numbers.

Concept List

obtuse triangle	transversal	rhombus
supplementary	complementary	regular polygon
corresponding angles	isosceles triangle	alternate interior angles

Write the concept that best describes each exercise. Choose from the concept list above.

1.

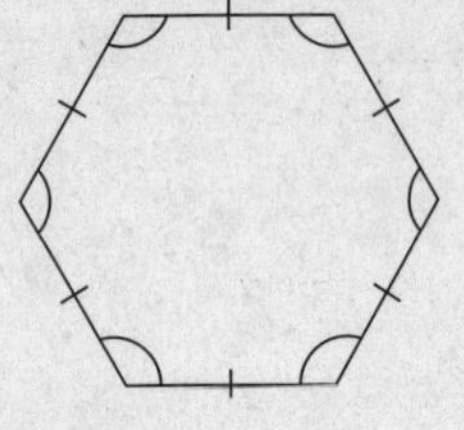

____

2.

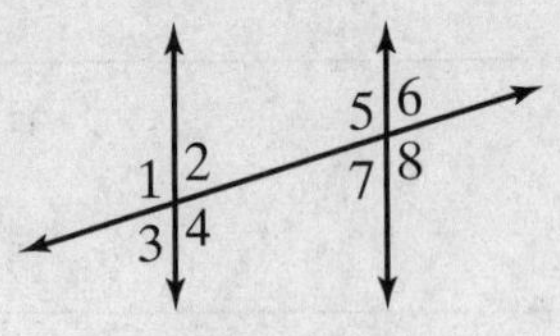

$\angle 2$ and $\angle 7$

____

3.

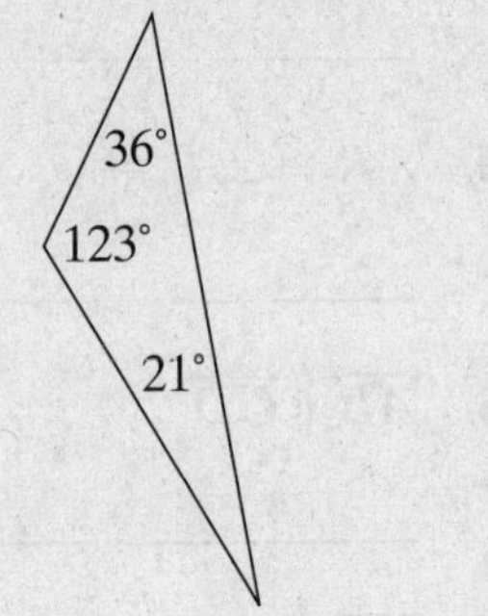

____

4.

$m\angle 1 = 30°$ and $m\angle 2 = 60°$

____

5.

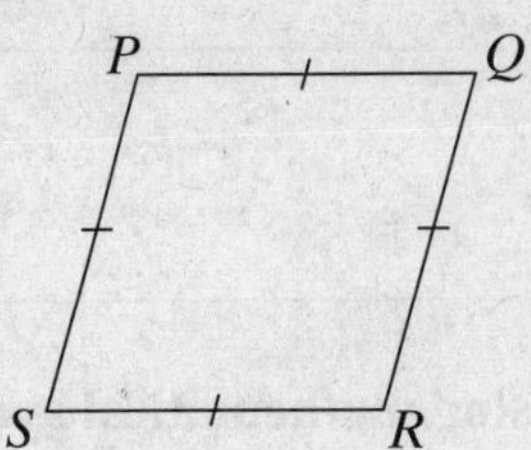

____

6.

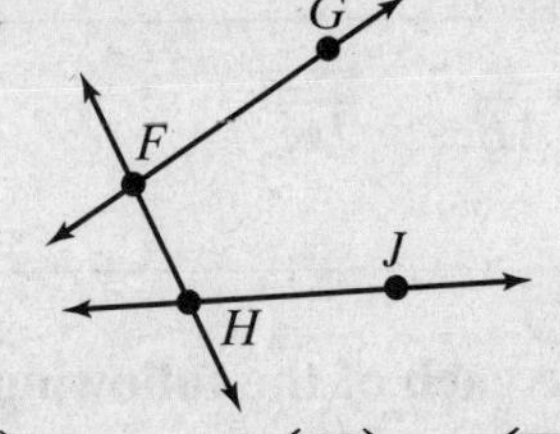

$\overleftrightarrow{FH}$ is one for $\overleftrightarrow{FG}$ and $\overleftrightarrow{HJ}$

____

7.

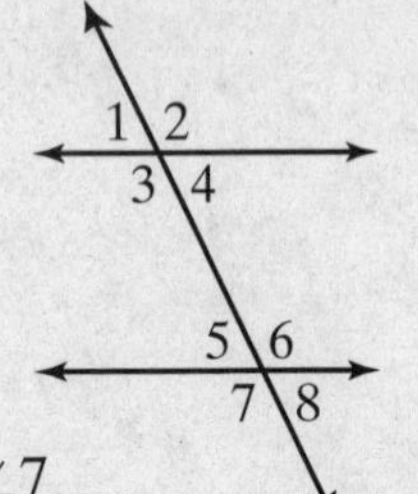

$\angle 3$ and $\angle 7$

____

8.

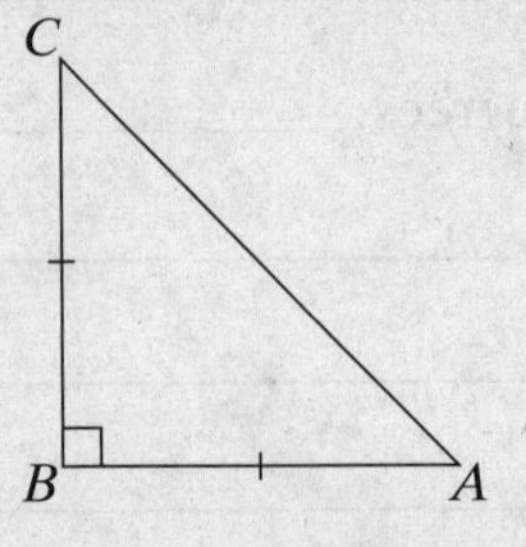

____

9.

$m\angle ABC = 24°$ and
$m\angle XYZ = 156°$

____

Name ______________________ Class ______________ Date ______________

7E: Vocabulary Check

For use after Lesson 7-8

Study Skill Strengthen your vocabulary. Use these pages and add cues and summaries by applying the Cornell Notetaking style.

Write the definition for each word or term at the right. To check your work, fold the paper back along the dotted line to see the correct answers.

______________________________________ scalene triangle

____

____

______________________________________ chord

____

____

______________________________________ trapezoid

____

____

______________________________________ congruent polygons

____

____

______________________________________ perpendicular lines

____

____

Name ______________________ Class ______________ Date ____________

7E: Vocabulary Check (continued)

For use after Lesson 7-8

Write the vocabulary word or term for each definition. To check your work, fold the paper forward along the dotted line to see the correct answers.

a triangle with no congruent sides ______________________

a line segment that has both endpoints on a circle ______________________

a quadrilateral with exactly one pair of parallel sides ______________________

polygons that have the same size and shape ______________________

lines that intersect to form right angles ______________________

Name ______________________ Class ______________ Date ______________

7F: Vocabulary Review Puzzle

For use with the Chapter Review

Study Skill As you read through a new lesson, write new vocabulary words and the definitions on index cards.

Complete the crossword puzzle below. For help, use the glossary in your textbook.

Here are the words you will use to complete this crossword puzzle.

right	square	trapezoid	vertical	supplementary
scalene	acute	isosceles	circumference	complementary
obtuse	adjacent	rectangle	transversal	parallelogram

ACROSS

1. two angles whose sum is 180 degrees
5. a triangle with one angle measuring 90 degrees
6. a triangle with angles each measuring less than 90 degrees
8. a triangle with at least two sides congruent
9. two angles whose sum is 90 degrees
12. a type of angle formed by intersecting lines
13. a parallelogram with four right angles and four congruent sides
14. a quadrilateral with exactly one pair of parallel sides

DOWN

1. a triangle with no congruent sides
2. a quadrilateral with two pairs of opposite sides that are parallel
3. a line that intersects two other lines in different points
4. a parallelogram with four right angles
7. the distance around a circle
10. a triangle with one angle larger than 90 degrees
11. two angles that share a vertex and a side but have no common interior points

Vocabulary and Study Skills

Name ______________________ Class ______________ Date ______________

Practice 8-1

Solids

For each figure, describe the base(s) of the figure, and name the figure.

1. 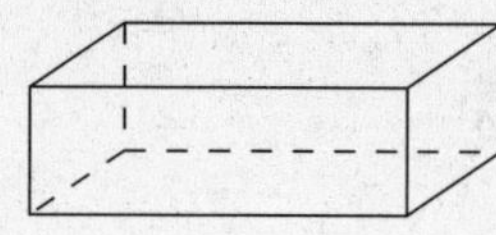

____

____

2. 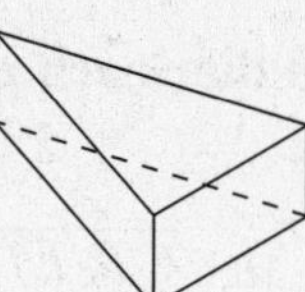

____

____

3. 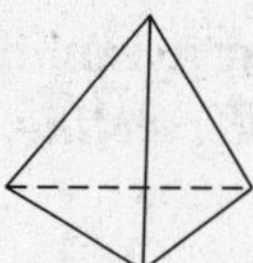

____

____

4. 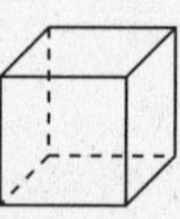

____

____

5. 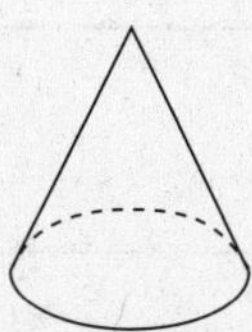

____

____

6. 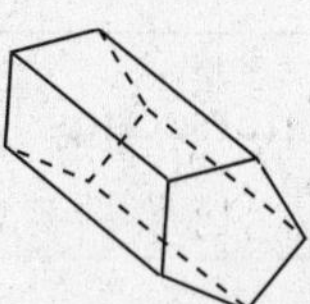

____

____

Name the solid that describes each item.

7. bowling ball ______________

8. DVD player ______________

9. soup can ______________

Complete.

10. A ______________ has exactly two circular bases.

11. A hexagonal prism has ______________ faces.

12. A cube has ______________ edges.

13. A pentagonal pyramid has ______________ faces.

14. A pentagonal pyramid has ______________ edges.

Name the figure described.

15. a space figure with six congruent square faces

____

16. a space figure with parallel bases that are congruent, parallel circles

____

Name ______________________ Class ______________ Date ______________

8-1 • Guided Problem Solving

GPS Student Page 357, Exercises 14–16:

Use the rectangular pyramid at the right. State whether each pair of line segments is *intersecting, parallel,* or *skew*.

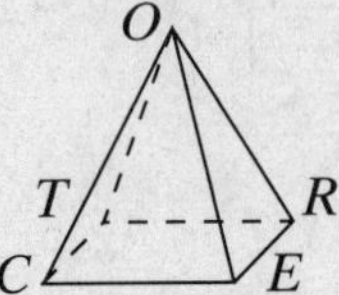

14. $\overline{CO}, \overline{CE}$ **15.** $\overline{OR}, \overline{CE}$ **16.** $\overline{CT}, \overline{ER}$

Understand

1. What figure is formed by the line segments?

____

2. What are intersecting lines?

____

3. What are parallel lines?

____

____

4. What are skew lines?

____

____

Plan and Carry Out

5. Trace $\overline{CO}$ and $\overline{CE}$ on the rectangular pyramid.

6. If you extended these two line segments what would happen to them? ______________

7. Therefore, these line segments are ______________.

8. Repeat Steps 5–7 for segments $\overline{OR}$ and $\overline{CE}$ and for segments $\overline{CT}$ and $\overline{ER}$.

Check

9. If $\overline{CE}$ and $\overline{TR}$ are parallel, what must then be true about the relationship between $\overline{OT}$ and $\overline{TR}$?

____

Solve Another Problem

10. In the rectangular pyramid at the right, state whether line segments $\overline{MN}$ and $\overline{PQ}$ are intersecting, parallel, or skew.

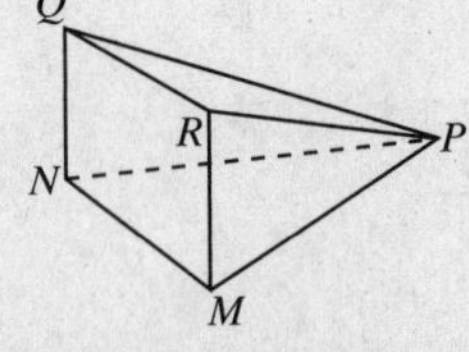

____

Name ______________________ Class ______________ Date ______________

Practice 8-2

Drawing Views of Three-Dimensional Figures

Draw a base plan for each set of stacked cubes.

1. 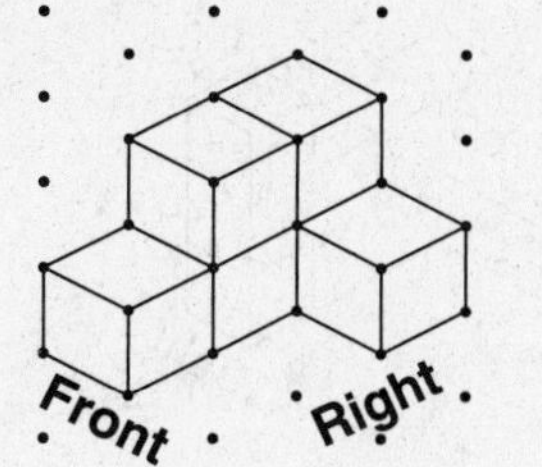

2. 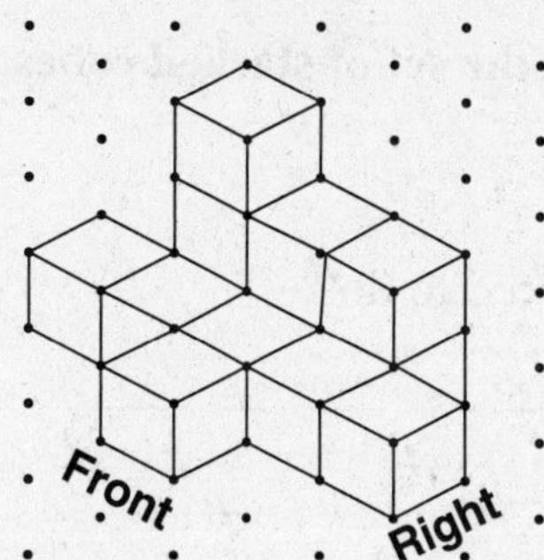

Draw the top, front, and right views of each figure.

3. 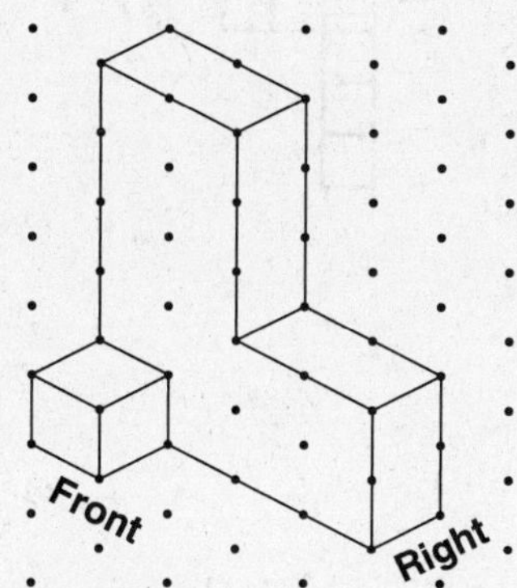

4. 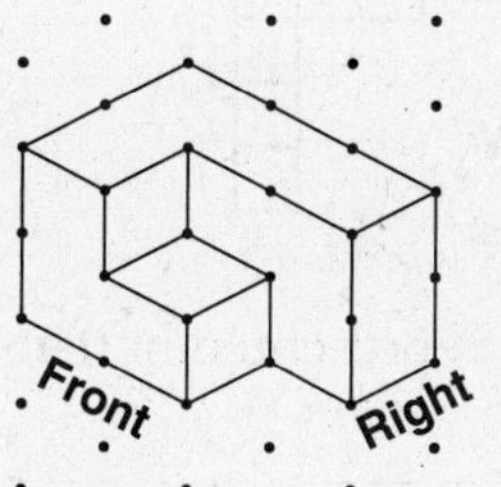

Name ______________________ Class ______________ Date ____________

8-2 • Guided Problem Solving

GPS Student Page 361, Exercise 13:

Draw a base plan for the set of stacked cubes.

Understand

1. What are you asked to do?

____

2. What is a base plan?

____

____

Plan and Carry Out

3. Which type of angles will be in your sketch? ____________

   a. Acute b. Obtuse c. Right

4. Which of these plans represents the base? ____________

   a. 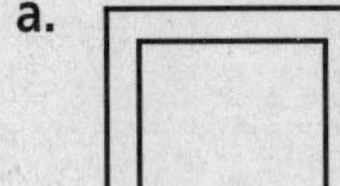 b. 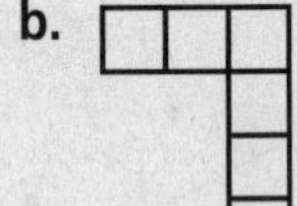 c. 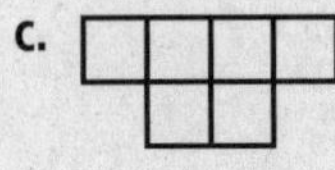 d. 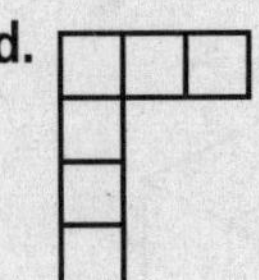

5. What are the heights represented in the stack of cubes?

____

6. Draw the base plan.

Check

7. How can you check that your base plan is accurately sketched?

____

____

Solve Another Problem

8. Draw a base plan for the set of stacked cubes.

Name ______________________ Class ______________ Date ____________

Practice 8-3

Nets and Three-Dimensional Figures

List the shapes that make up the net for each figure, and write the number of times each shape is used.

1. rectangular prism
2. pentagonal pyramid
3. cylinder
4. triangular pyramid
5. cone
6. hexagonal prism

7. Draw a net for a rectangular box that is 9 cm long, 5 cm wide, and 3 cm tall.

8. Draw a net for a cylinder whose height is 8 in. and whose radius is 3 in.

Identify the solid that each net forms.

9.

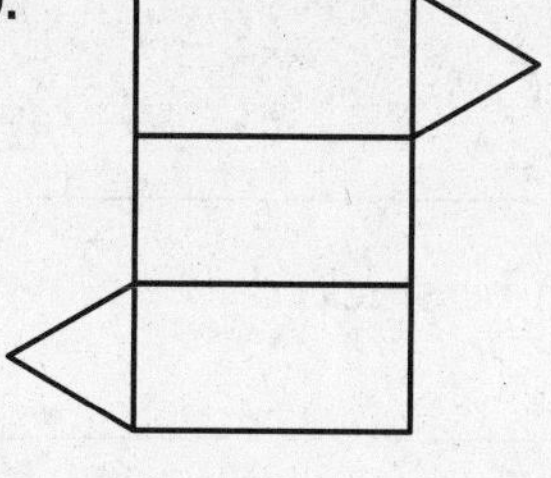

10.

11.

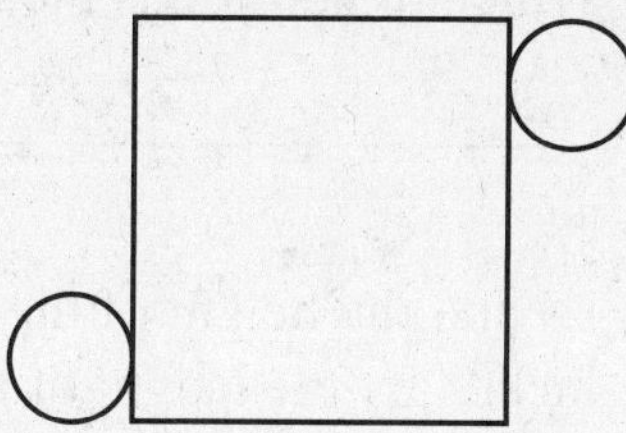

12. What three-dimensional figure can be made from this net?

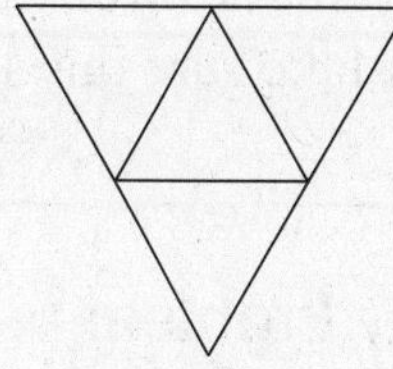

Name ______________________ Class ______________ Date ______________

8-3 • Guided Problem Solving

GPS Student Page 366, Exercise 12:

Moving The net at the right shows the dimensions of a storage box. How many of these boxes can be stacked on top of each other to fit inside a moving van with a cargo space that is 7 feet high?

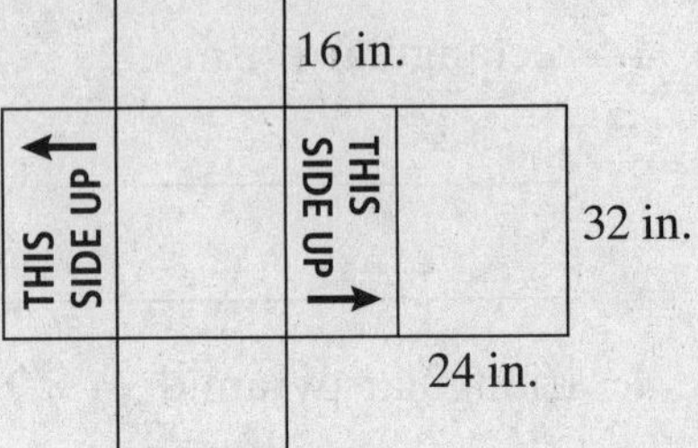

Understand

1. What does the net show?

____

2. Circle the height of the cargo space given in the problem.

3. What are you asked to determine?

____

____

Plan and Carry Out

4. If you fold the box, how do you know which way it will sit?

____

____

5. Which dimension is the height of the box?

____

6. Convert the height of the cargo area to inches.

____

7. Divide the height of the cargo area, in inches, by the height of the box.

____

8. How many boxes can be stacked?

____

Check

9. Copy the picture on to a piece of paper and fold to create the storage box. Check if you used the correct dimension as the height of the box. Make sure that the correct side is facing upward.

____

Solve Another Problem

10. You want to send a vase to your friend. The vase is 10 inches in diameter and stands 17 inches tall. Will the vase fit in the box to the right?

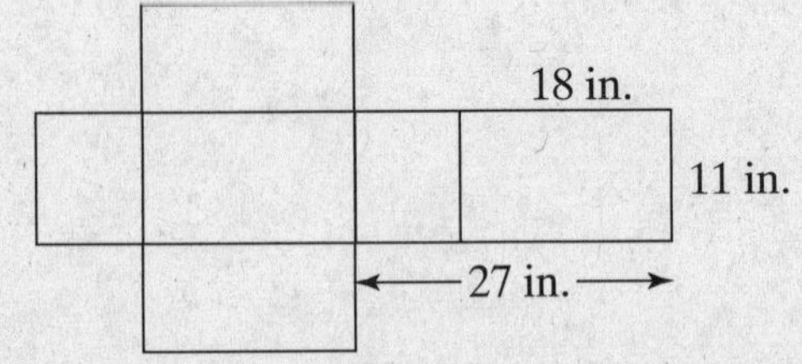

____

Name ______________________ Class ______________ Date ______________

Practice 8-4

Surface Areas of Prisms and Cylinders

Use a net or a formula to find the surface area of each figure to the nearest square unit.

1. 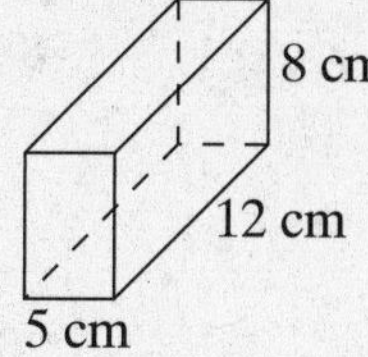

2. 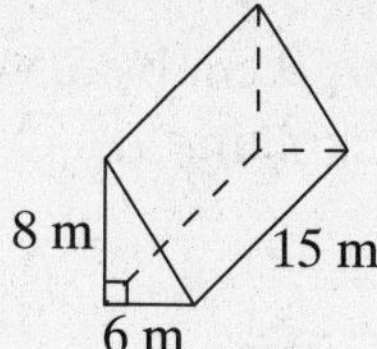

3. 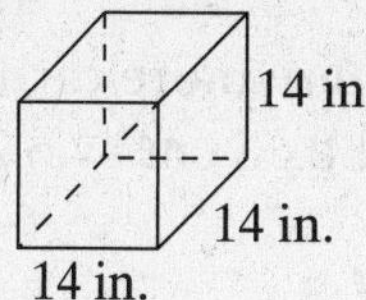

4. 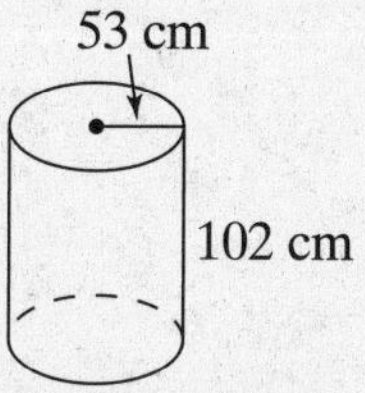

5. 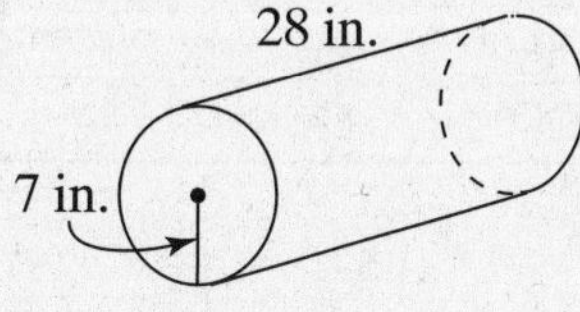

6. 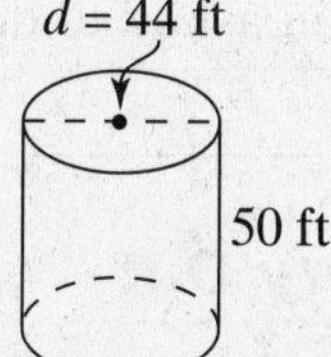

Rachel and Sam are going to paint the exposed surfaces of each figure. Find the area to be painted to the nearest square unit.

7. 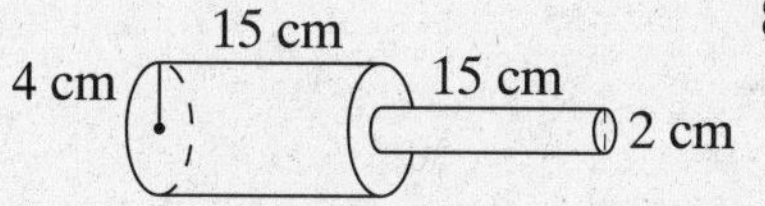

8. 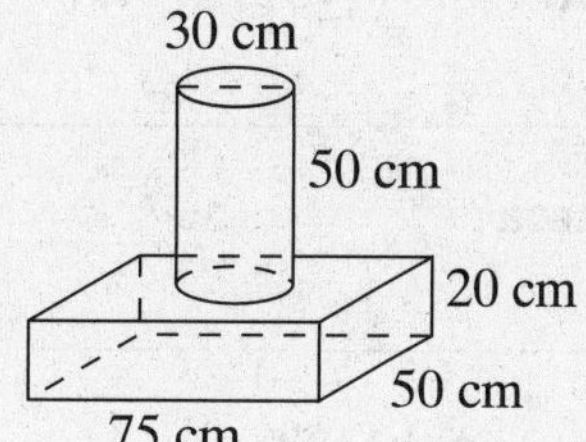

9. 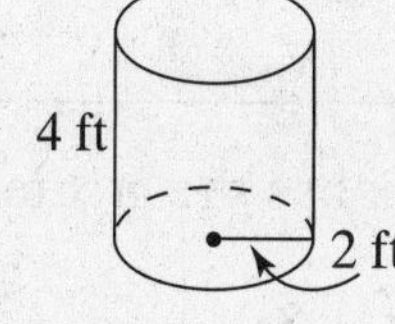

Find the lateral area and surface area of each figure. Round to the nearest square unit.

10. 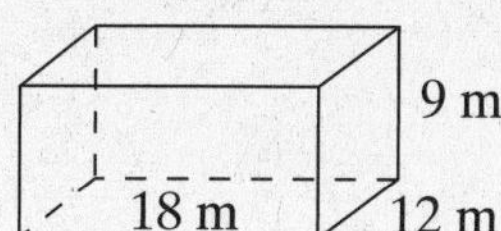

11. 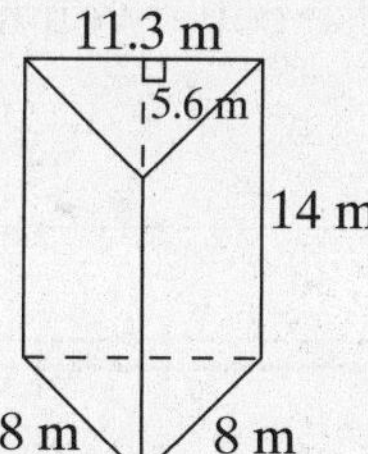

12. 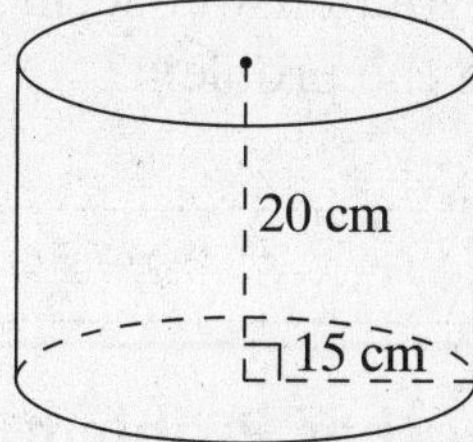

Name ______________________ Class ______________ Date ______________

8-4 • Guided Problem Solving

GPS Student Page 372, Exercise 15:

Which will require more cardboard to make: a box 9 cm by 5.5 cm by 11.75 cm, or a box 8 cm by 6.25 cm by 10.5 cm? Explain.

Understand

1. Circle the dimensions of the first figure, and place a square around the dimensions of the second.

2. What are you asked to determine?

____

Plan and Carry Out

3. How many sides does the box have? ______________

4. Find the surface area of the first box by finding the area of all the sides. Show your work. ______________

5. Find the surface area of the second box by finding the area of the four sides and the area of the two ends. Show your work.

____

6. Which box has the greatest surface area?

____

7. Which box would require more cardboard to make?

____

Check

8. Does your answer seem reasonable? How else could you have solved the problem?

____

____

Solve Another Problem

9. For a school play two stage props need to be painted. The first measures 3 feet by 5.5 feet by 4.5 feet. The second measures 2 feet by 11.5 feet by 1.75 feet. Which will require more paint if all the surfaces are to be painted?

____

____

Name ______________________ Class ______________ Date ______________

Practice 8-5

Surface Areas of Pyramids and Cones

Use a net to find the surface area of each square pyramid to the nearest square unit.

1. 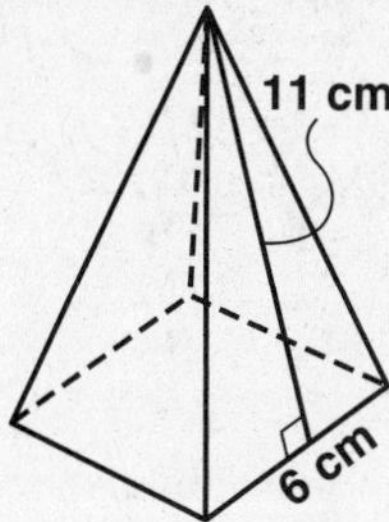

____

2. 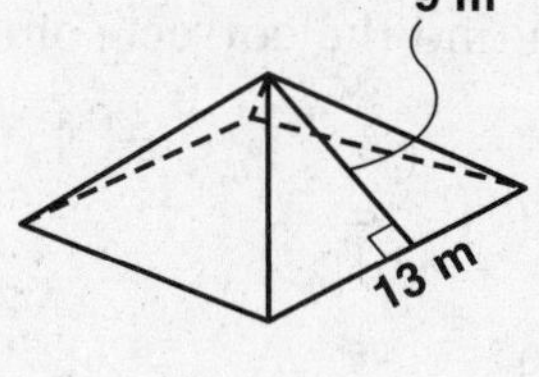

____

3. 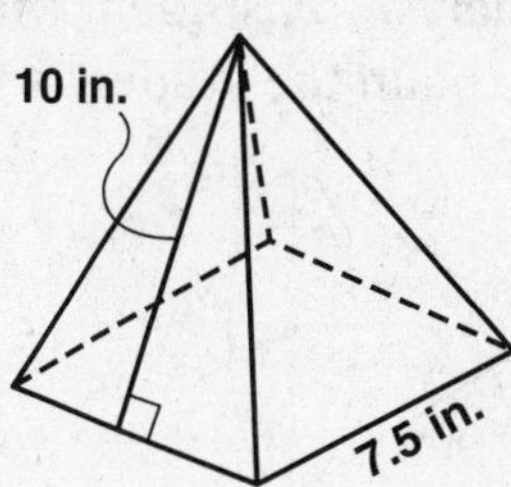

____

Find the lateral area of each pyramid to the nearest whole square unit.

4. 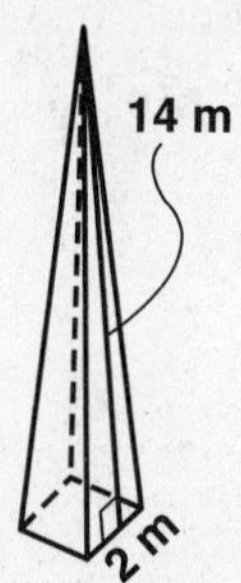

____

5. 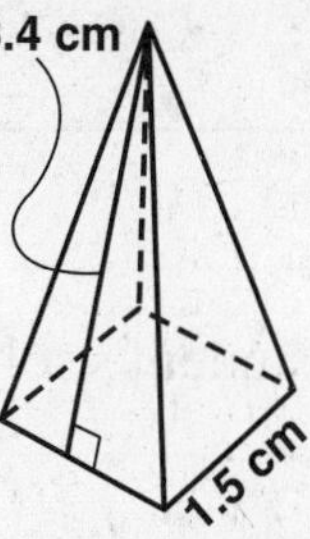

____

Find the surface area of each cone to the nearest square unit.

6. 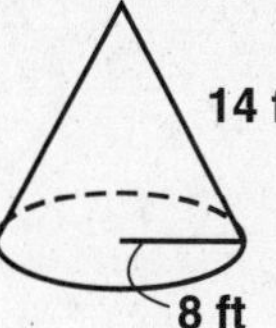

____

7. 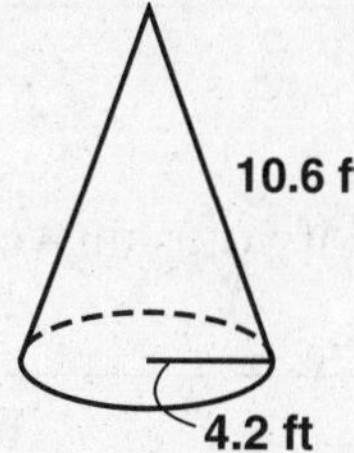

____

Find the lateral area of each cone to the nearest square unit.

8. 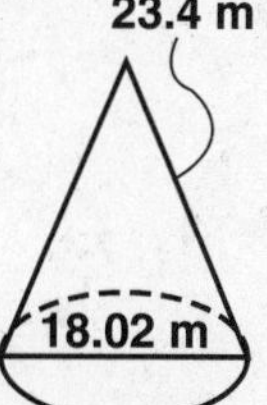

____

9. 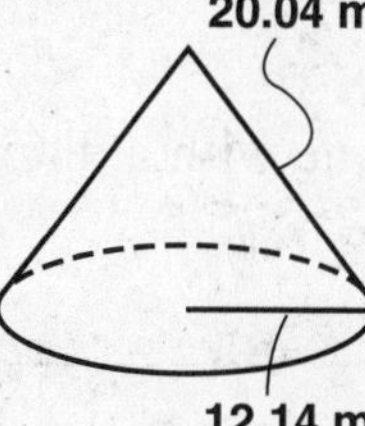

____

Name ______________________ Class ______________ Date ______________

8-5 • Guided Problem Solving

GPS Student Page 378, Exercise 16:

Error Analysis A student tried to find the lateral area of the cone below. Explain the student's mistake. Then find the correct solution.

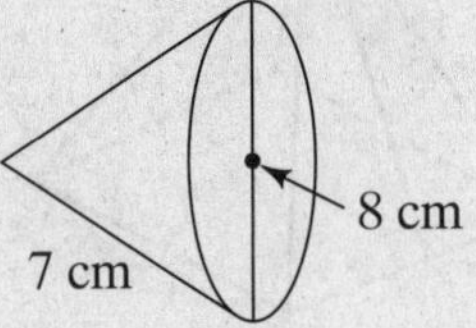

L.A. $= \pi rl$
$= \pi(8)(7)$
$= 56\pi$
≈ 175.93
$\approx 176 \text{ cm}^2$

Understand

1. Is the answer given correct? ______________________
2. What are you asked to find?

____

Plan and Carry Out

3. Look at the first step of the student's solution. What is the mistake?

____

4. What value should he have used? ______________________
5. Solve the problem using the correct dimensions. Show your work.

____

Check

6. How can you estimate to see if your answer is reasonable?

____

____

____

____

Solve Another Problem

7. Find the lateral area of a cone with a diameter of 6 inches and slant height of 8 inches.

____

Name ______________________ Class ____________ Date ____________

Practice 8-6

Volumes of Prisms and Cylinders

Find the volume of each solid to the nearest whole number.

1. 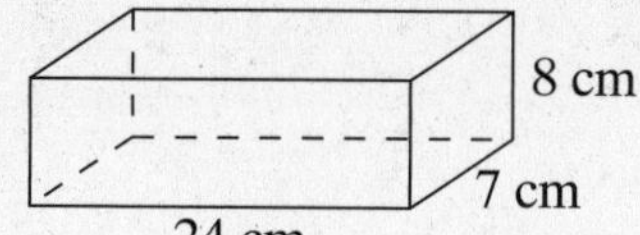

2. 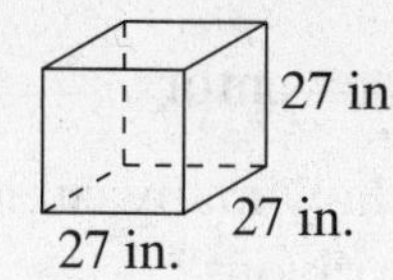

3. 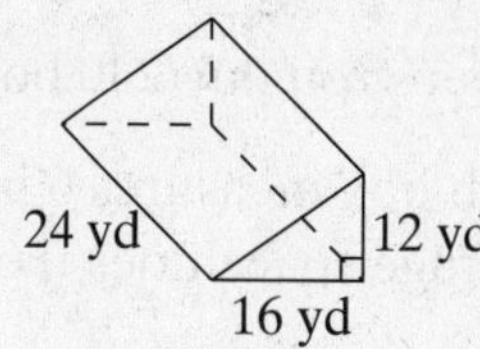

4. 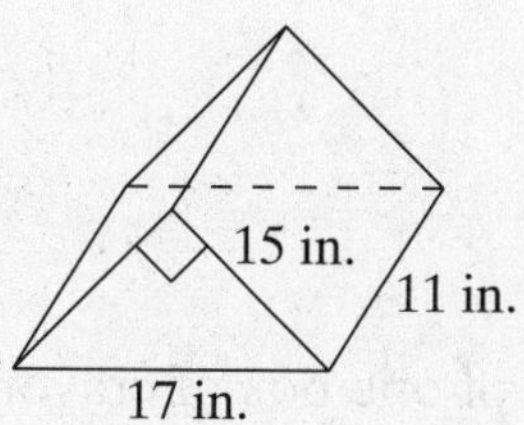

5. 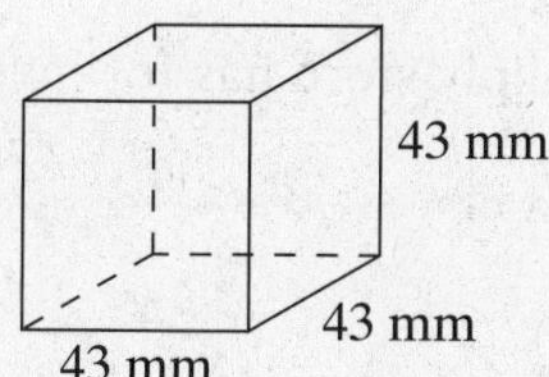

6. 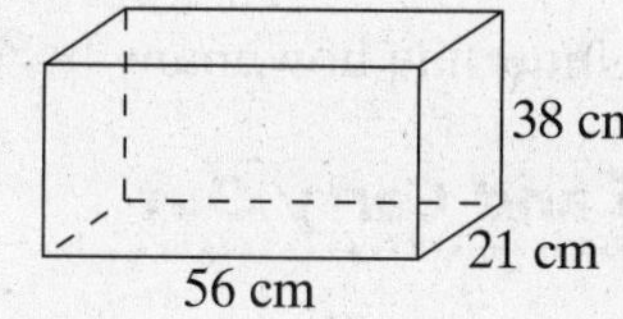

7. 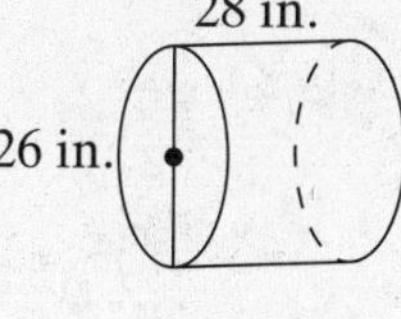

8. 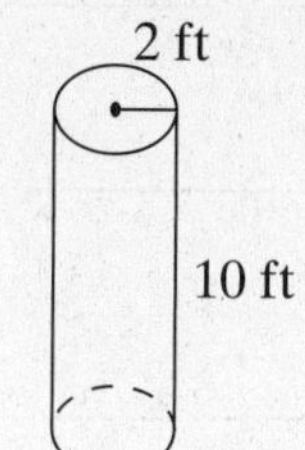

9. 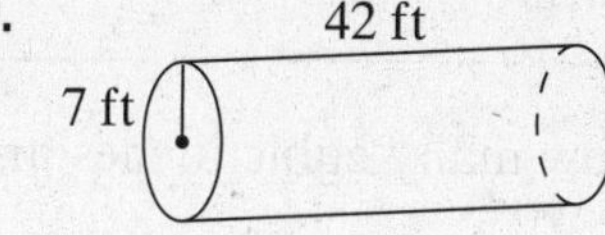

10. Suppose you want to buy concrete for a 36 ft by 24 ft by 9 in. patio. If concrete costs $55/yd^3, how much will the concrete for the patio cost?

11. A cylinder has a volume of about 500 cm^3 and a height of 10 cm. What is the length of the radius to the nearest tenth of a cm?

Name ______________________ Class ______________ Date ______________

8-6 • Guided Problem Solving

GPS Student Page 384, Exercise 20:

A store keeps roughly 240 boxes of crayons in its inventory.

a. If each box measures 6 in. by 2.5 in. by 4 in., how many cubic inches of storage space does the store need for the crayons?

b. One cubic foot is equal to (12 in.)^3, or 1,728 in.^{3}. Find the number of cubic feet necessary for storing 240 boxes of crayons.

Understand

1. Circle the measures of the crayon boxes.
2. Underline how many boxes the art supply store has for inventory.

Plan and Carry Out

3. What formula will you use to find the volume of one box of crayons? ______________

4. What is the volume of one box of crayons? ______________

5. What operation will you use to find the volume of 240 boxes? ______________

6. What is the volume of 240 boxes of crayons? ______________

7. How many cubic inches are in one cubic foot? ______________

8. How can you change cubic inches to cubic feet? ______________

9. How many cubic feet are necessary for storing 240 boxes of crayons? ______________

Check

10. What is a way to check the problem? ______________

Solve Another Problem

11. A video store keeps approximately 350 boxes of storage cases in its inventory.

a. If each storage case measures 1 in. by 5.5 in. by 8.75 in., how many cubic inches of storage space does the store need for the boxes of storage cases? ______________

b. Find the number of cubic feet necessary for storing 350 boxes of cases. ______________

Name ______________ Class ______________ Date ______________

Practice 8-7

Volumes of Pyramids and Cones

Find the volume of each figure to the nearest cubic unit.

1. 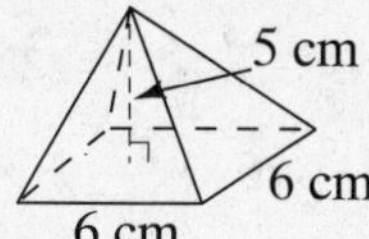

2. 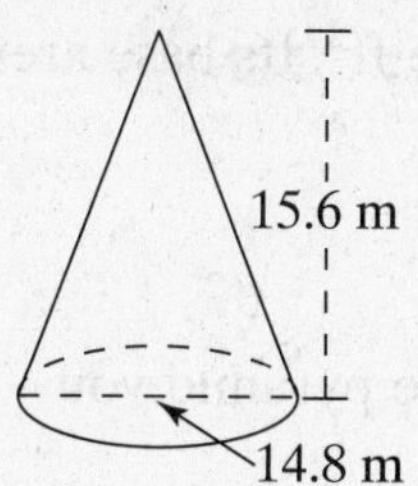

3. 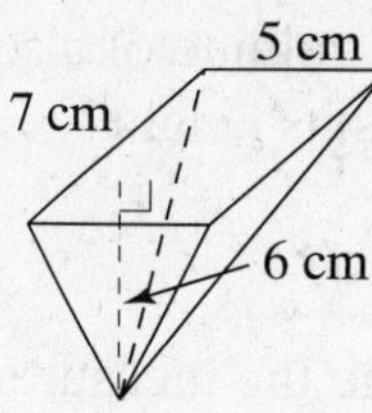

______________ ______________ ______________

4. 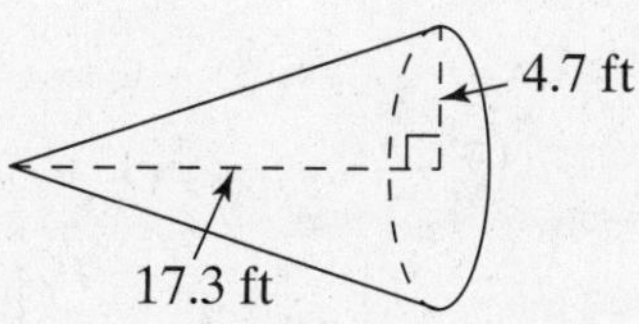

5. 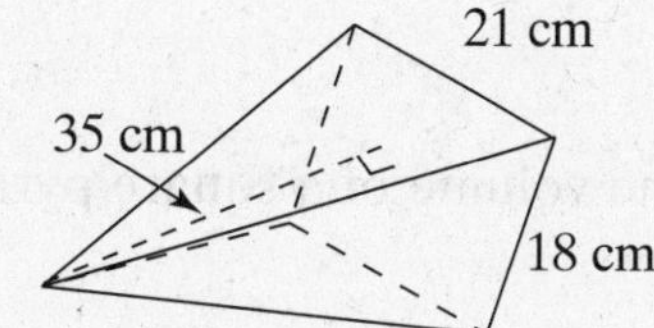

6. 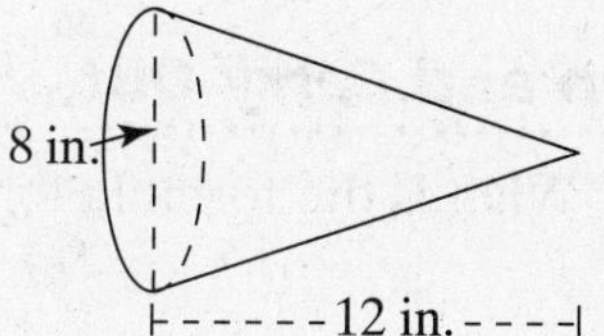

______________ ______________ ______________

Find the missing dimension for each three-dimensional figure to the nearest tenth, given the volume and other dimensions.

7. rectangular pyramid, $l = 8$ m, $w = 4.6$ m, $V = 88$ m^3

____

8. cone, $r = 5$ in., $V = 487$ in.^{3}

____

9. square pyramid, $s = 14$ yd, $V = 489$ yd^3

____

10. square pyramid, $h = 8.9$ cm, $V = 56$ cm^3

____

11. Find the volume of a 4 ft by 2 ft by 3 ft rectangular prism with a cylindrical hole, radius 6 in., through the center.

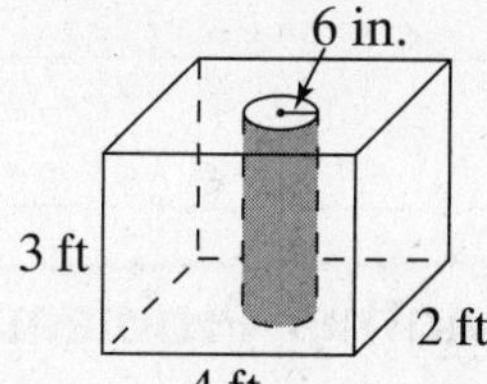

____

12. Margarite has a cylindrical tin of popcorn that is 18 in. tall and has a radius of 4 in. She wants to use the tin for something else and needs to empty the popcorn into a box. The box is 8 in. long, 8 in. wide, and 14 in. tall. Will the popcorn fit in the box? Explain.

____

____

Name ______________________ Class ______________ Date ______________

8-7 • Guided Problem Solving

GPS Student Page 391, Exercise 17:

Algebra The volume of a square pyramid is 15 ft^3. Its base area is 27 ft^2. What is its height?

Understand

1. Underline the measurements of the square pyramid you are given.

2. What are you asked to find?

____

Plan and Carry Out

3. What is the formula for finding the volume of a square pyramid?

____

4. What measurements are you given?

____

5. Substitute what you know into the formula.

____

6. What variable are you solving for? ______________

7. Solve.

____

Check

8. How can you check your answer?

____

____

Solve Another Problem

9. The volume of a cone is 113.04 ft^3. Its base area is 28.26 ft^2. What is its height?

____

____

Name ______________________ Class ______________ Date ______________

Practice 8-8

Spheres

Find each sphere's surface area and volume to the nearest whole number.

1.

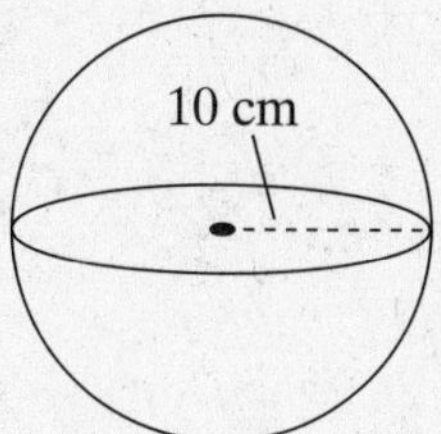

____

____

2.

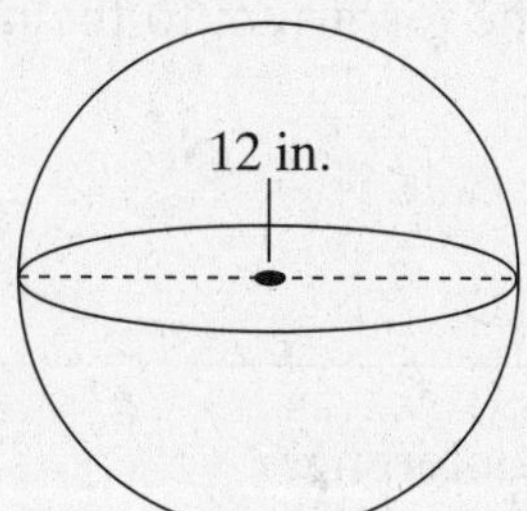

____

____

3.

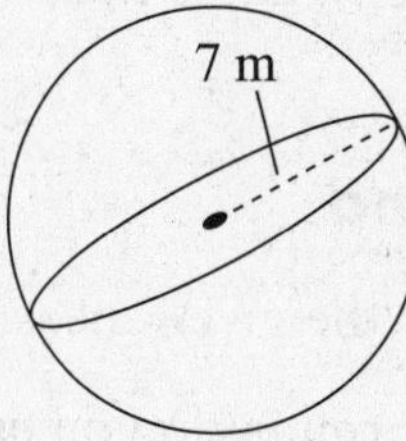

____

____

4.

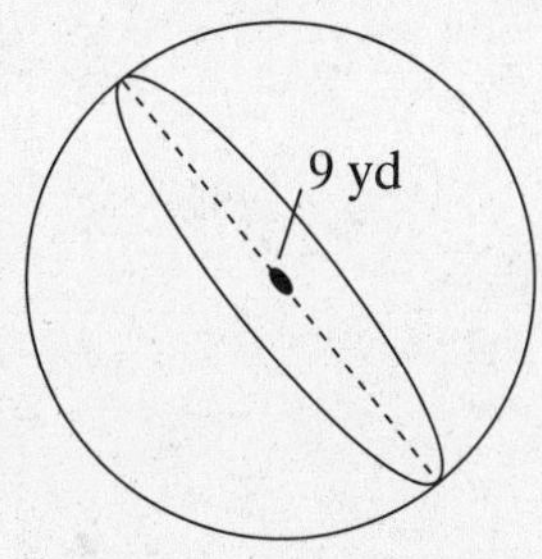

____

____

5.

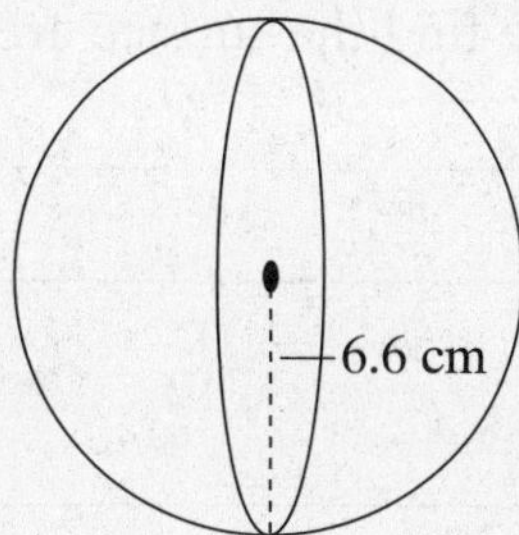

____

____

6.

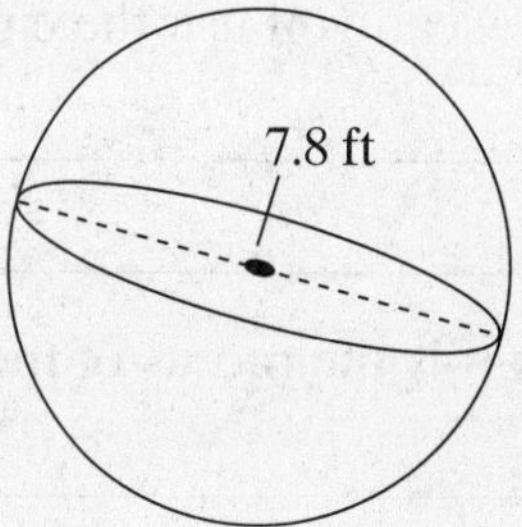

____

____

7. A sphere has a radius of 9 ft. Find its surface area to the nearest whole square unit.

____

8. A geography professor has a spherical globe with a diameter of 14 in. What is the volume of the globe?

____

9. Jenny has four marbles that are all of different sizes and colors. They have diameters of 18 mm, 19 mm, 21 mm, and 24 mm. What is the average surface area of the four marbles?

____

Name ______________________ Class ______________ Date ______________

8-8 • Guided Problem Solving

GPS Student Page 396, Exercise 16:

The circumference of a glass terrarium in the shape of a sphere is about 12.5 in. What is the surface area of the terrarium to the nearest square inch?

Understand

1. What is the given measurement? ______________

2. What formula do you use to find circumference?

____

3. What are you being asked to find?

____

Plan and Carry Out

4. How can you use the circumference to find the surface area?

____

____

5. What is the radius of the terrarium?

____

6. How will you find the surface area of the terrarium?

____

7. What is the surface area of the terrarium to the nearest square inch?

____

Check

8. Does your answer check? Is your answer consistent with the circumference given in the question?

____

Solve Another Problem

9. The volume of a weather balloon is about 33.5 ft^3. What is the surface area of the weather balloon? Round your answer to the nearest whole square unit.

____

____

Name ______________________ Class ______________ Date ______________

Practice 8-9

Exploring Similar Solids

Complete the table for each prism.

	Original Size		Doubled Dimensions		
	Dimensions (m)	S.A. (m^2)	Dimensions (m)	S.A. (m^2)	New S.A. 4 Old S.A.
1.	$2 \times 3 \times 4$				
2.	$5 \times 5 \times 9$				
3.	$7 \times 7 \times 7$				
4.	$8 \times 12 \times 15$				
5.	$15 \times 15 \times 20$				
6.	$32 \times 32 \times 32$				

7. What conclusion can you draw?

____

____

8. A rectangular prism is 8 cm by 10 cm by 15 cm. What are the volume and surface area of the prism?

____

9. In Exercise 8, if each dimension of the prism is halved, what are the new volume and surface area?

____

Use the triangular prism shown at the right for Exercises 10 and 11.

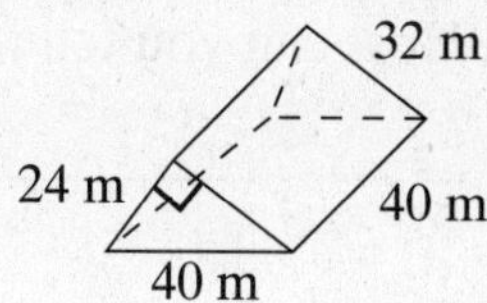

10. Find the volume and surface area.

____

11. If each dimension of the prism is doubled, what are the new volume and surface area?

____

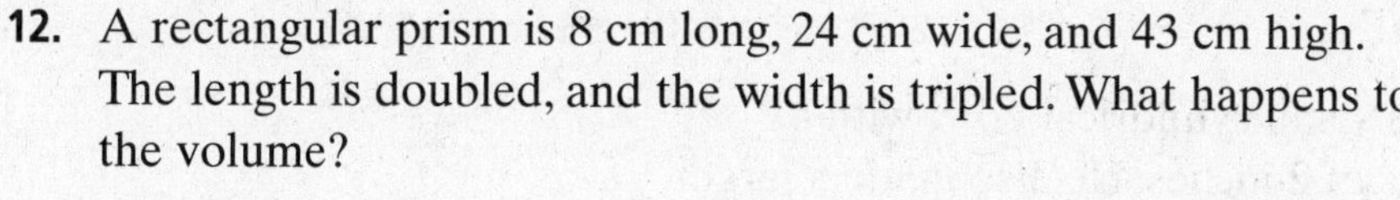

12. A rectangular prism is 8 cm long, 24 cm wide, and 43 cm high. The length is doubled, and the width is tripled. What happens to the volume?

____

Name ______ Class ______ Date ______

8-9 • Guided Problem Solving

GPS Student Page 401, Exercise 14:

Carpentry Gina used 78 square feet of plywood to build a storage bin to hold her gardening supplies. How much plywood will she need to build a similar box for her hand tools if the dimensions of the box are half the dimensions of the bin?

Understand

1. What are you asked to do?

______

______

2. How many square feet of plywood did Gina use? ______

Plan and Carry Out

3. What is the ratio for the surface area of similar solids? ______

4. What are the dimensions of the similar box?

______

______

5. What is the ratio of the surface areas? ______

6. Write a proportion. ______

7. Solve. ______

Check

8. How can you tell if your answer is reasonable?

______

______

______

Solve Another Problem

9. In pottery class, Mark made a small cylindrical bowl with a volume of 75 in.^{3} and a radius of 2 inches. He also made a larger bowl with a similar shape. It has a diameter of 8 inches. Find the volume of the larger bowl.

______

8A: Graphic Organizer

For use before Lesson 8-1

Study Skill Try to read new lessons the night before your teacher presents them in class. Important information is sometimes printed in bold face type or highlighted inside a box with color. Pay special attention to this information.

Write your answers.

1. What is the chapter title? ______________________
2. How many lessons are there in this chapter? ______________________
3. What is the topic of the Test-Taking Strategies page? ______________________
4. Complete the graphic organizer below as you work through the chapter.
   - In the center, write the title of the chapter.
   - When you begin a lesson, write the lesson name in a rectangle.
   - When you complete a lesson, write a skill or key concept in a circle linked to that lesson block.
   - When you complete the chapter, use this graphic organizer to help you review.

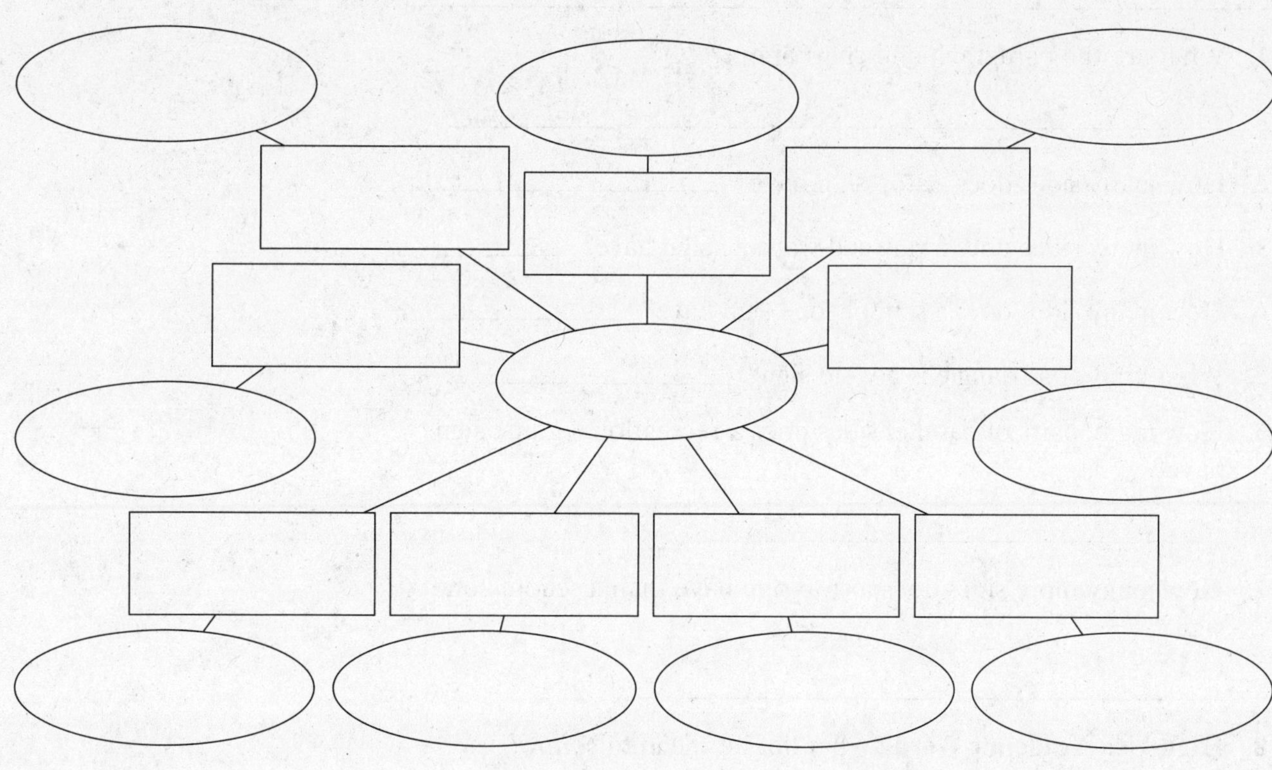

Name ______________________ Class ______________ Date ______________

8B: Reading Comprehension

For use after Lesson 8-3

Study Skill Try to visualize math concepts when possible. Having a mental picture of something might help you remember it better.

Read the paragraph below and answer the questions.

Traffic signs are devices placed beside, above, or at the intersection of roadways. They control the flow of traffic which includes cars, trucks, bicycles, and pedestrians. Signs are necessary for safety and proper control of traffic.

Shape	Use	Notes
octagon	stop signs only	most expensive to produce
equilateral triangle	yield signs	points downward
circle	railroad warning signs	
trapezoid	recreational guide signs	
rectangle	guide signs	horizontal
rectangle	regulatory signs	vertical
pentagon	school zone signs	

1. What are the paragraph and chart about?

   ____

2. How many sides does a stop sign have? ______________
3. How many sides does a railroad warning sign have? __________
4. How many sides does a school zone sign have? __________
5. What kind of a triangle is a yield sign? ______________
6. How many pairs of parallel sides does a recreational guide sign have?

   ____

7. How many more sides does a stop sign have than a school zone sign?

   ____

8. **High-Use Academic Words** What does it mean to *control,* as mentioned in the paragraph?

   a. to direct the action of

   b. to make a choice

Name ______________________ Class ______________ Date ______________

8C: Reading/Writing Math Symbols

For use after Lesson 8-5

Study Skill In mathematics, abbreviations or certain letter combinations take on special meanings. It is important that you recognize these abbreviations and know what they mean.

Below are some common mathematical abbreviations and letter combinations. Write the meaning of each.

1. SAS ______________
2. ASA ______________
3. S.A. ______________
4. L.A. ______________
5. SSS ______________

Write each of the following formulas in words and give a brief description of what the formula is used to find.

6. $A = bh$

____

____

7. $A = \frac{1}{2}bh$

____

____

8. $C = \pi d$

____

____

9. $C = 2\pi r$

____

____

10. $SA = 2\pi r^2 + 2\pi rh$

____

____

____

11. $SA = \pi r^2 + \pi rl$

____

____

____

Vocabulary and Study Skills

Name ______________________ Class ______________ Date ______________

8D: Visual Vocabulary Practice

For use after Lesson 8-6

Study Skill When learning a new concept, try to draw a picture to illustrate it.

Concept List

prism	cone	cylinder
base plan	lateral area	volume
skew lines	surface area	pyramid

Write the concept that best describes each exercise. Choose from the concept list above.

1.

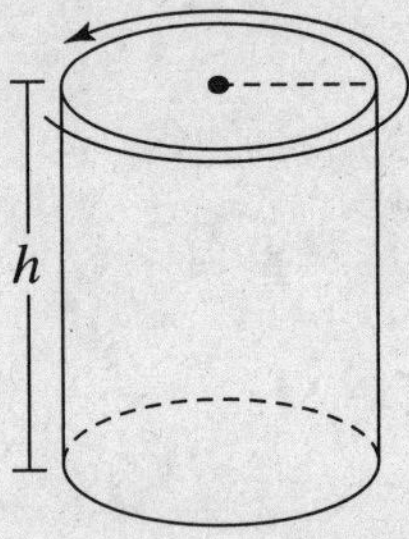

$C \times h$

____

2.

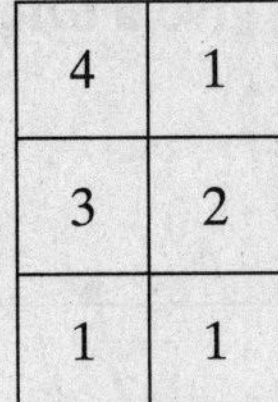

Right

Front

____

3.

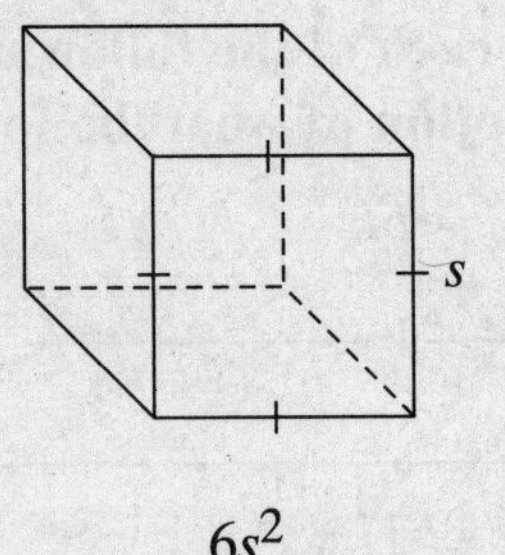

$6s^2$

____

4.

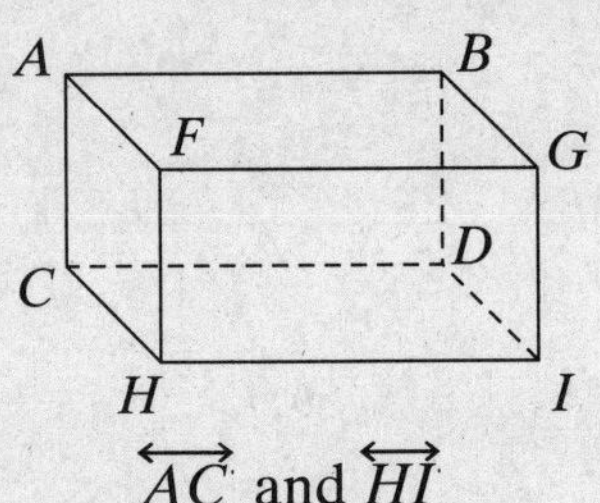

$\overleftrightarrow{AC}$ and $\overleftrightarrow{HI}$

____

5.

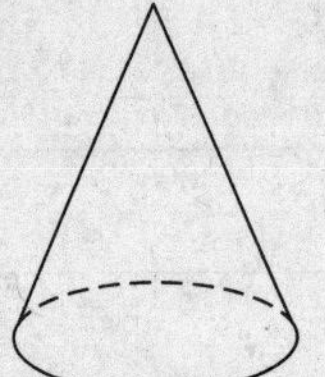

____

6.

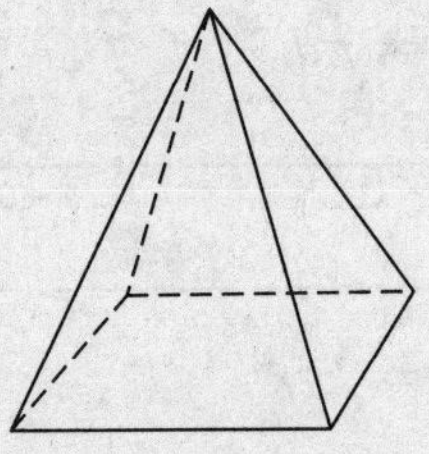

____

7.

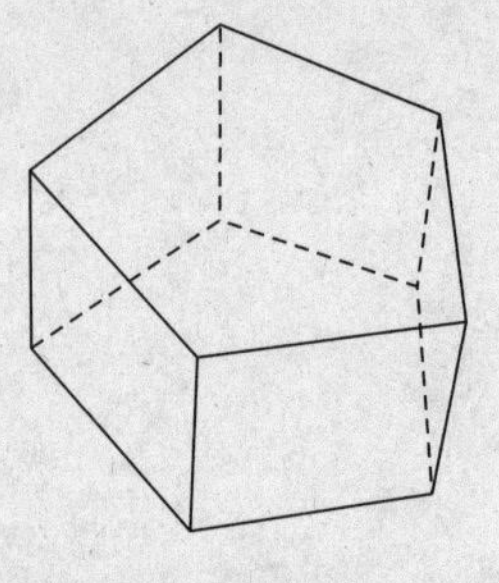

____

8.

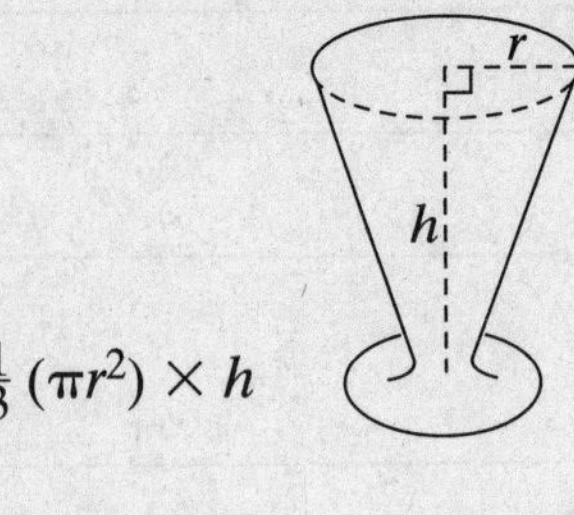

$\frac{1}{3}(\pi r^2) \times h$

____

9.

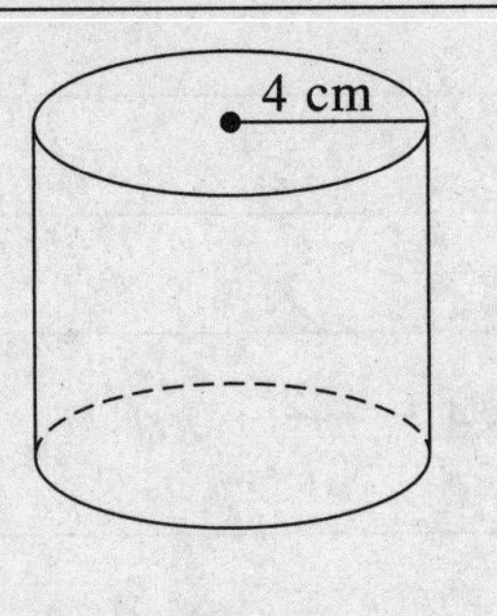

____

Name ______________ Class ______________ Date ______________

8E: Vocabulary Check

For use after Lesson 8-9

Study Skill Strengthen your vocabulary. Use these pages and add cues and summaries by applying the Cornell Notetaking style.

Write the definition for each word or term at the right. To check your work, fold the paper back along the dotted line to see the correct answers.

polyhedron

skew lines

volume

sphere

similar solids

8E: Vocabulary Check (continued)

For use after Lesson 8-9

Write the vocabulary word or term for each definition. To check your work, fold the paper forward along the dotted line to see the correct answers.

a solid with a polygon for each face ______________________

lines that lie in different planes that are neither parallel nor intersecting ______________________

the number of unit cubes, or cubic units, needed to fill a solid ______________________

the set of all points in space that are the same distance from a center point ______________________

two solids that have the same shape and have corresponding dimensions that are proportional ______________________

8F: Vocabulary Review Puzzle

For use with the Chapter Review

Study Skill Take a few minutes to relax before and after studying. Your mind will absorb and retain more information if you alternate studying with brief rest intervals.

Find and circle each of the words below in the puzzle. Words can be displayed forwards, backwards, up, down, or diagonally.

prism	pyramid	cylinder	cone
skew	polyhedron	space figures	obtuse
precision	isometric view	base plan	slant height
scale factor	parallelogram	square	rectangle
rhombus	acute	straight	

```
Q D R S N O U T A L L E S S E T H M
O R H V A W I X L R R U P M R E N B
N U O Q Z E J J E A S Y A P C W U G
O C M O J I I J E N R F P R I S M X
R Y B W R V X N E A O F B H S R Y M
D L U R L C V O M F S C A Z Q V A R
E I S E E I Y I B Z W K S A U S Z G
H N U C S R D E K F F S E K A L N Y
Y D R T U T J G B B Z T P W R A O Y
L E P A T E S T O H V R L D E N I B
O R B N B M T K F E S A A O D T S O
P U R G O O F A Q R H I N N G H I O
I C J L F S Z H K Z X G B S U E C P
C J X E J I C N P H J H U Y O I E V
N F I S X X N X L V E T U C A G R I
P A R A L L E L O G R A M E N H P V
X O N F S C A L E F A C T O R T Y R
A X J S E R U G I F E C A P S J I K
```

Name ____________ Class ____________ Date ____________

Practice 9-1

Finding Mean, Median, and Mode

Find the mean, median, mode, and range of each data set.

1. hours of piano practice ____________

   Hours Mr. Capelli's students practice

   2 1 2 0 1 2 2 1 2 2

2. days of snow per month ____________

   Monthly snow days in Central City

   8 10 5 1 0 0 0 0 0 1 3 12

3. number of students per class ____________

   Class size in Westmont Middle School

   32 26 30 35 25 24 35 30 29 25

4. ratings given by students to a new movie ____________

   Student ratings of a movie

   10 9 10 8 9 7 5 3 8 9 9 10 9 9 7

Is the mean, median, or mode the best measure of central tendency for each type of data? Explain.

5. most popular movie in the past month ____________

6. favorite hobby ____________

7. class size in a school ____________

8. ages of members in a club ____________

Each person has taken four tests and has one more test to take. Find the score that each person must make to change the mean or median as shown.

9. Barry has scores of 93, 84, 86, and 75. He wants to raise the mean to 86. ____________

10. Liz has scores of 87, 75, 82, and 93. She wants to raise the median to 87. ____________

11. Jim has scores of 60, 73, 82, and 75. He wants to raise the mean to 75. ____________

12. Andrea has scores of 84, 73, 92, and 88. She wants the median to be 86. ____________

Name ______________________ Class ______________ Date ______________

9-1 • Guided Problem Solving

GPS Student Page 416, Exercise 24:

Reasoning You have one more math test to take. The scores you have already received are 89, 92, 78, 83, and 83.

a. What score must you get to raise the mean to 87?

b. What score must you get to raise the median by 2 points?

Understand

1. How many tests have been taken? ______________

2. How many more tests are to be taken? ______________

3. What two measures of central tendency will be used? ______________

Plan and Carry Out

4. How do you find the mean? ______________

5. How many points do you have so far? ______________

6. How many tests will you have taken? ______________

7. How many total points do you need to have so that when you divide the total by 6, you get an answer of 87? ______________

8. How many points do you need on the last math test so that you can get that total number of points? ______________

9. List your current tests scores in order from least to greatest. ______________

10. How do you find the median if there are an even number of scores? ______________

11. What do the two middle scores have to total to average 85? ______________

12. One middle score is 83. What does the other have to be? ______________

Check

13. Do your answers check? ______________

Solve Another Problem

14. Your bowling scores for two games are 134 and 142. What score must you get on the last game to raise your mean to 141 and raise the median by 4 points? ______________

Practice 9-2

Displaying Frequencies

Use the Olympic medal data at the right for Exercises 1–3. Use the space below or a separate sheet of paper.

2006 Winter Olympic Gold Medals	
Country	**Medals**
Australia	1
Austria	9
Canada	7
China	2
Croatia	1
Czech Republic	1
Estonia	3
France	3
Germany	11
Italy	5
Japan	1
Netherlands	3
Norway	2
Russia	8
South Korea	6
Sweden	7
Switzerland	5
U.S.A.	9

1. Make a line plot for the data.

1 2 3 4 5 6 7 8 9 10 11

Number of Medals

2. Make a frequency table. Use intervals of equal sizes to group the data.

3. Make a histogram.

Use these ages of bike club members for Exercises 4 and 5. Use the space below or a separate sheet of paper.

19 16 10 14 15 19 13 14 15 16 21 14 12 14 16 13 13

4. Using intervals, display the data in a frequency table.

5. Use the frequency table to draw a histogram.

Name ______________________ Class ______________ Date ______________

9-2 • Guided Problem Solving

GPS Student Page 420, Exercise 10:

Use a line plot to display the frequency of medals won at the 2002 Winter Olympics.

Distribution of Gold Medals at the 2002 Winter Olympics

Country	Medals
Germany	12
Norway	11
United States	10
Canada	6
Russian Federation	6
Finland	4
France	4
Italy	4

Understand

1. What kind of medals are being compared? ______________
2. Which Olympic games results are being displayed in the table?

   ____
3. How many countries are listed in the table? ______________
4. What type of display are you asked to create? ______________

Plan and Carry Out

5. What should be listed below the number line?

   ____
6. Draw this part of the graph.
7. How do you display the frequency?

   ____

   ____
8. Place the number of ✗ marks that corresponds to the number of medals won, according to the chart.
9. Give the graph a title.

   ____

   ____

Check

10. Add the number of marks on your line plot. Does it match the total number of medals distributed according to the table?

    ____

Solve Another Problem

11. The following chart shows the number of goals scored by each soccer team in the 12-year-old recreational league during the championship weekend. Use a line plot to display the frequency of goals.

Team	Goals
Creekside	5
Evergreen	8
Westerville	10
Canton	10
Swanton	12

Name ______________________ Class ______________ Date ______________

Practice 9-3

1. The Venn diagram at the right shows how many members of a group of international travelers speak French (*F*), Spanish (*S*), and Italian (*I*). How many people in the group speak Spanish and French but not Italian?

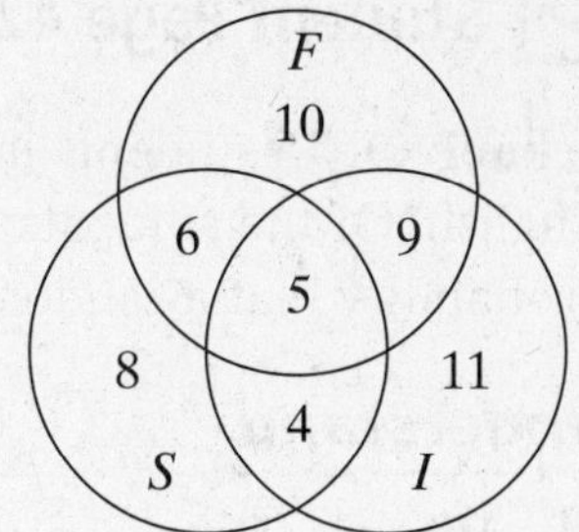

____

Solve each problem by drawing a Venn diagram.

2. A group of 32 students went to the amusement park. All of them rode either the Ferris wheel or the roller coaster. Seventeen rode the Ferris wheel, 23 rode the roller coaster, and 8 did both. How many rode only the Ferris wheel?

____

3. The Exotic Pets Club has 23 members, all of whom have a snake, an iguana, or a tarantula. Four members have all three kinds of pets. Ten members have a snake, 14 have iguanas, and 13 have tarantulas. Two have a snake and an iguana, three have an iguana and a tarantula, and one has a snake and a tarantula. How many members have only a tarantula?

____

4. What are the common factors of 36 and 45? What is the greatest common factor?

	Factors
36	1, 2, 3, 4, 6, 9, 12, 18, 36
45	1, 3, 5, 9, 15, 45

____

5. A photography show at Lucy's Art Gallery contains 27 photos. There are 21 black-and-white photos and 12 portraits. How many are black-and-white portraits?

____

6. A survey on favorite kinds of books shows that 9 people like mysteries, 10 like adventure stories, and 8 enjoy biographies. Three of the people read only mysteries and adventure stories, 4 read only adventure stories and biographies, 4 read only mysteries, and 2 read all three kinds of books. How many people were surveyed?

____

Name ______________________ Class ______________ Date ______________

9-3 • Guided Problem Solving

GPS Student Page 425, Exercise 10:

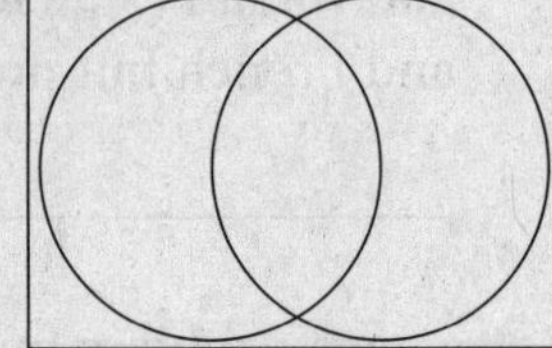

School Of 15 students in summer school, 11 take math and 9 take English. Of the students taking English, 5 also take math. What is the probability that a randomly selected student takes only math?

Understand

1. What is the total number of students? ______________
2. What are you asked to find? ______________
3. How can you use a Venn diagram to help solve this problem?

____

____

Plan and Carry Out

4. In the Venn diagram, label one circle for math and the other circle for English.
5. How many English students are also taking math? Write that number in the diagram.

____

6. What is the total number of students taking English?

____

7. Find the number of students taking English only. Write that number in the diagram.

____

8. What is the total number of students taking math?

____

9. How many students are taking math only? Write that number in the diagram. Use this number to write a probability that a randomly selected student takes only math.

____

Check

10. Find the sum of the numbers in your diagram. Does it equal the total number of students? Compare these numbers with your probability.

____

Solve Another Problem

11. One shelf in the library contains 24 novels. Suppose 16 of the novels were written by women and 19 were written after 1950. Of those 19 novels, 8 were written by men. How many of the novels were written by women before 1950?

____

Name ______________________ Class ______________ Date ______________

Practice 9-4

Reading Graphs Critically

Use the graph below for Exercises 1–5.

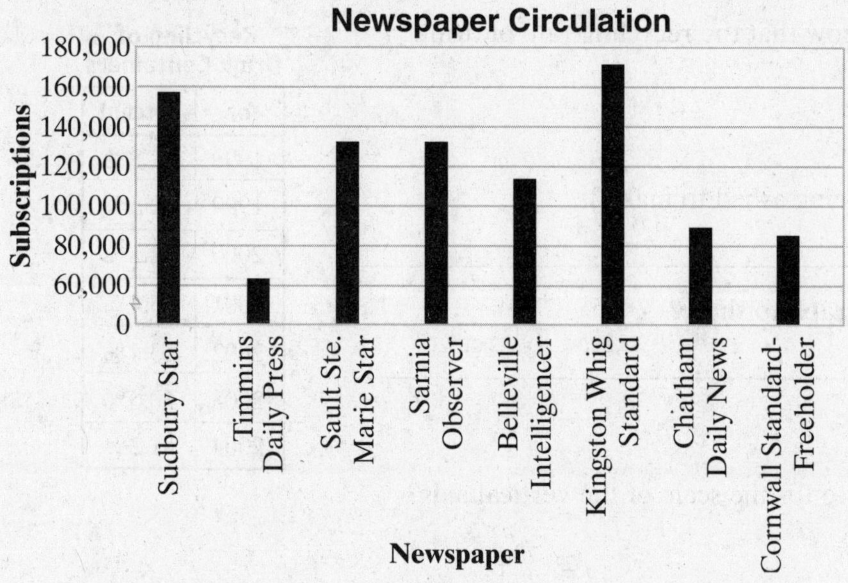

1. Which newspaper appears to have twice the circulation of *The Cornwall Standard-Freeholder*? ______________

2. Which newspaper actually has about twice the circulation of *The Cornwall Standard-Freeholder*? ______________

3. *Belleville Intelligencer* appears to have about how many times the circulation of *Chatham Daily News*? ______________

4. Explain why the graph gives a misleading visual impression of the data.

____

____

5. Redraw the graph to give an accurate impression of the data.

9-4 • Guided Problem Solving

GPS Student Page 431, Exercise 11:

Recycling Make a line graph to show that the recycling rate of drink containers stayed about the same.

Recycling of Drink Containers

Year	Percent
1998	62.8%
1999	62.5%
2000	62.1%
2001	55.4%
2002	53.4%
2003	50.0%
2004	51.2%

Understand

1. What kind of graph are you being asked to make?

____

2. What do you want your line graph to show?

____

Plan and Carry Out

3. Which would be a better choice for the scale of the vertical axis?

a.

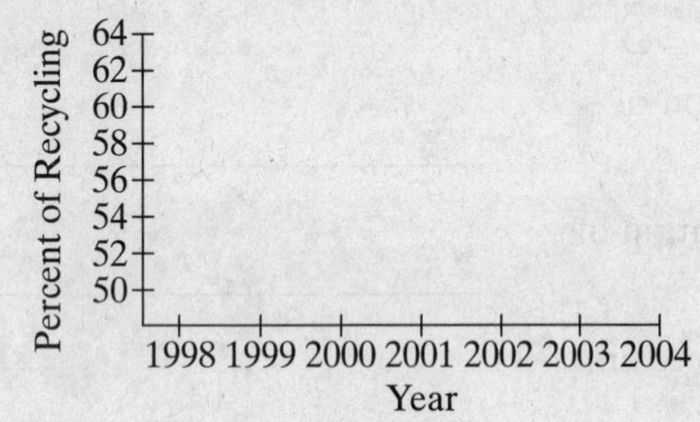

b.

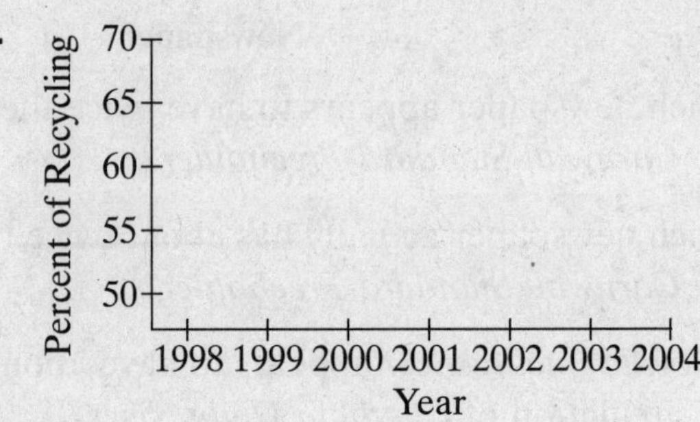

____

4. Plot the points from the table on the graph you chose in Step 3.

Check

5. Does your graph match the change in recycling of drink containers? ____________

Solve Another Problem

6. Make a line graph to show that Kendra's salary has increased over the years.

Kendra's Salary

Year	Salary
1998	$26,000
1999	$28,000
2000	$32,000
2001	$34,000
2002	$37,000

Name ______________________ Class ______________ Date ______________

Practice 9-5

Stem-and-Leaf Plots

The stem-and-leaf plot at the right shows the bowling scores for 20 bowlers. Use the plot for Exercises 1–3.

Stem	Leaves
10	0 2 2 4 4 4
11	1 3 5 5 5 9
12	4 5 9 9
13	0 6 8 8

Key: 13 | 8 means 138.

1. What numbers make up the stems?

____

2. What are the leaves for the stem 12?

____

3. Find the median and mode.

____

Make a stem-and-leaf plot for each set of data. Then find the median and mode.

4. 8 19 27 36 35 24 6 15 16 24 38 23 20

____

5. 8.6 9.1 7.4 6.3 8.2 9.0 7.5 7.9 6.3 8.1 7.1 8.2 7.0 9.6 9.9

____

6. 436 521 470 586 692 634 417 675 526 719 817

____

The back-to-back stem-and-leaf plot at the right shows the high and low temperatures for a week in a certain city. Use this plot for Exercises 7–9.

Low		High
8 7	5	
4 3	6	5 9 9
2 1 0	7	2 5 6
	8	0

63 ← 3 | 6 | 5 → 65

7. Find the mean for the high temperatures.

____

8. Find the median for the low temperatures.

____

9. Find the mode for the high temperatures.

____

Name ______________________ Class ______________ Date ______________

9-5 • Guided Problem Solving

GPS Student Page 435, Exercise 6:

Make a stem-and-leaf plot for the data below. Find the median and the mode.

18 19 27 8 19 20 19 6 18 27 16 13 12 7 8 18 19 11 10 19 18 18 8 17 16 12

Understand

1. What are you being asked to do?

____

2. What are you being asked to find?

____

Plan and Carry Out

3. What are the least and greatest values in the set of data?

____

4. What will the stems be? ______________________

5. Make a stem-and-leaf plot for the data. Include a key.

6. How many data values are there? ______________

7. Average the two middle values to find the median.

____

8. Find the mode(s) by looking at the stem-and-leaf plot.

____

Check

9. Order the numbers to find the median. Is your answer correct?

____

Solve Another Problem

10. The Cougars' practice times, in minutes, for the past two weeks are listed below. Make a stem-and-leaf plot of the data. Then find the median and the mode.
    51 69 65 66 78 79 65 56 59 79 66 79 71 67

____

Name ______________________ Class ______________ Date ______________

Practice 9-6

Box-and-Whisker Plots

Use the box-and-whisker plot to find each value.

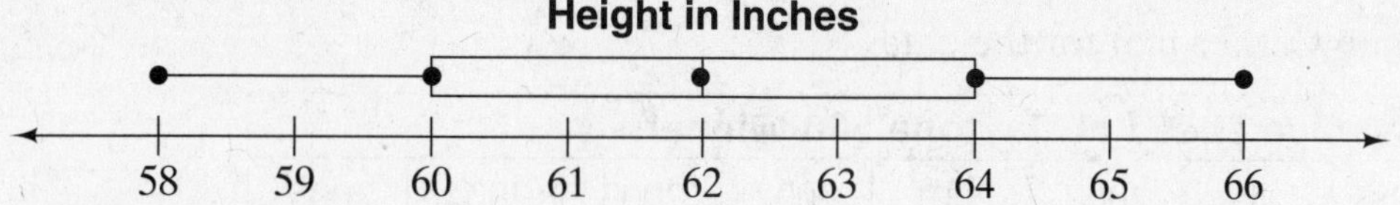

1. the median height ____________
2. the lower quartile ____________
3. the upper quartile ____________
4. the greatest height ____________
5. the shortest height ____________
6. the range of heights ____________

Make a box-and-whisker plot for each set of data.

7. 8 10 11 7 12 6 10 5 9 7 10

8. 20 21 25 18 25 15 27 26 24 23 20 20

9. **Cargo Airlines in the U.S. (1991)**

Airline	Freight ton-miles (1,000,000s)
Federal Express	3,622
Northwest	1,684
United	1,214
American	884
Delta	668
Continental	564
Pan American	377
Trans World	369
United Parcel Service	210

10. **Immigration to the U.S. (1981–1990)**

Country	Number (1,000s)
Mexico	1,656
Philippines	549
China	347
Korea	334
Vietnam	281
Dominican Republic	252
India	251
El Salvador	214
Jamaica	208
United Kingdom	159

Name ________________________ Class ______________ Date ______________

9-6 • Guided Problem Solving

GPS Student Page 441, Exercise 14:

Racing Make a box-and-whisker plot for the data.

Average Speed of Daytona 500 Winners								
Year	1998	1999	2000	2001	2002	2003	2004	2005
Speed (mi/h)	173	162	156	162	143	134	156	135

Understand

1. What three values will you need to make the box?

____

2. What two values will you need to make the whiskers?

____

Plan and Carry Out

3. Order the speeds from least to greatest and find the median.

____

4. Find the upper and lower quartiles by finding the medians of the upper and lower halves.

____

5. Use the number line at right. Use the median and the lower and upper quartiles to draw the box. Draw the whiskers from the box to the least and greatest values.

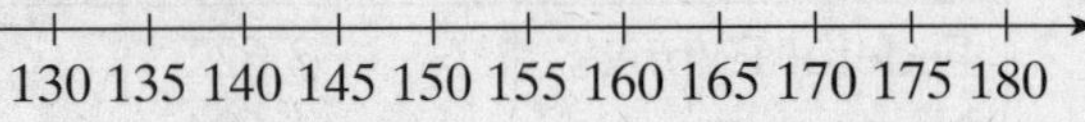

Check

6. Are all of the data displayed or it is it summarized? ______________

Solve Another Problem

7. A biology class consists of sophomores and a few freshmen. Make a box-and-whisker plot from the grades in the table.

Test Scores								
Freshmen	89	78	91	87	92	89		
Sophomores	72	95	86	87	98	76	85	93

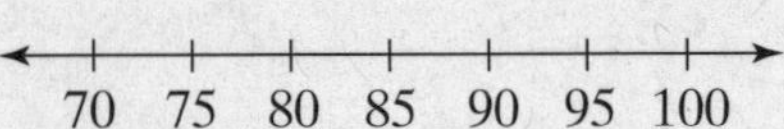

Name ______________________________ Class ____________________ Date ____________________

Practice 9-7

Making Predictions from Scatter Plots

Tell whether a scatter plot made for each set of data would describe a *positive trend*, a *negative trend*, or *no trend*.

1. amount of education and annual salary

   ____

2. weight and speed in a foot race

   ____

3. test score and shoe size

   ____

4. Make a scatter plot showing the number of homeowners on one axis and vacation homeowners on the other axis. If there is a trend, draw a trend line.

Residents of Maintown

Year	Homeowners	Vacation Homeowners
1997–98	2,050	973
1996–97	1,987	967
1995–96	1,948	1,041
1994–95	1,897	1,043
1993–94	1,862	1,125
1992–93	1,832	1,126

5. Make a scatter plot for the data. If there is a trend, draw a trend line.

Arm Span vs. Height

Person #	Arm Span	Height
1	156	162
2	157	160
3	159	162
4	160	155
5	161	160
6	161	162
7	162	170
8	165	166
9	170	170
10	170	167
11	173	185
12	173	176

6. Wynetta found the graph shown at the right. The title of the graph was missing. What could the graph be describing?

   ____

   ____

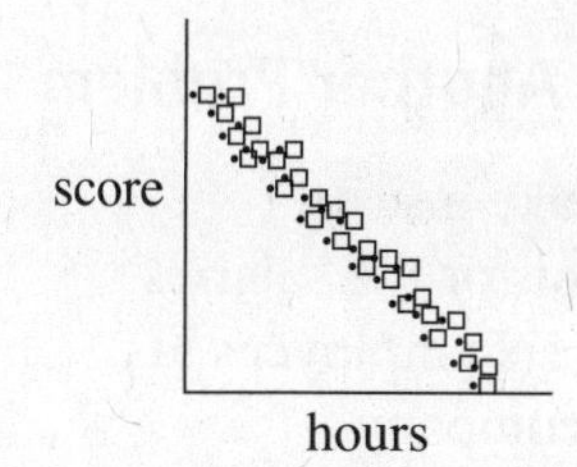

Name ________________ Class ________________ Date ________________

9-7 • Guided Problem Solving

GPS Student Page 447, Exercise 13:

a. **Baseball** Make a scatter plot for the data at the right.

b. Draw a trend line.

c. How many hits would a player be expected to have with 500 at-bats?

d. How many at-bats would a player with 250 hits have?

Name	At Bats	Hits
T. Hunter	564	147
I. Rodriguez	442	136
C. Beltran	617	189
G. Anderson	672	194
R. Sierra	344	100
B. Daubach	407	107
J. Liefer	254	65

Understand

1. How are you asked to display the data?

____

2. What is a trend line?

____

Plan and Carry Out

3. Plot the data on the graph at right. Choose a scale to accurately represent the data.

4. What kind of trend does the scatter plot show? ________________

5. Draw a trend line in the graph from Step 5. Make sure there are as many points above the line as there are below it.

6. Using the trend line, how many hits would a player be expected to have with 500 at-bats? ________________

7. How many at-bats would a player have with 250 hits? ________________

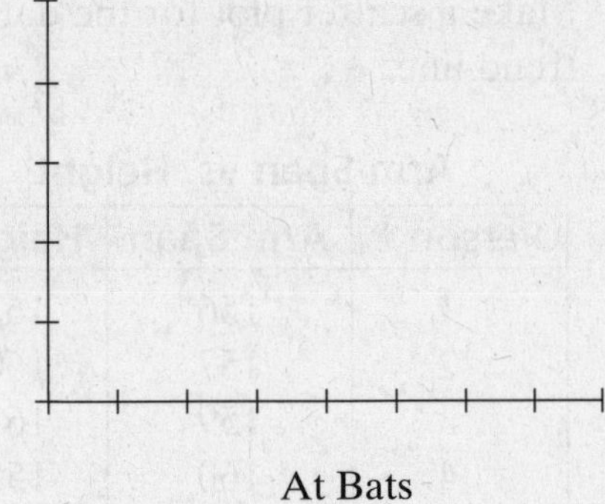

Check

8. Does the scatter plot show how at-bats and hits are related? ________________

Solve Another Problem

9. Make a scatter plot for the salaries of six employees at a company.

Years at Company	Salary
2	$56,000
4	$62,000
8	$64,000
12	$70,000
18	$76,000
20	$84,000

Name ______________________ Class ______________ Date ______________

Practice 9-8

Circle Graphs

Use the circle graph at the right for Exercises 1 and 2.

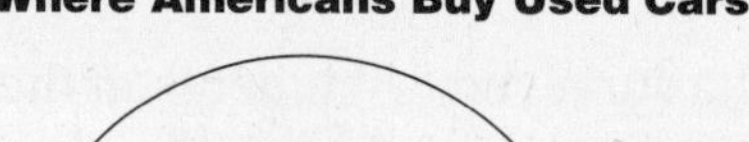

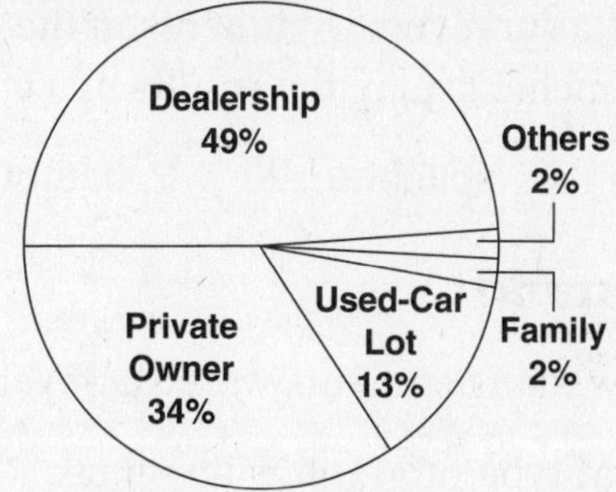

1. From which group are about $\frac{1}{3}$ of used cars purchased?

   ____

2. If 49,778 people bought used cars one month, estimate how many bought them from a dealership.

   ____

Make a circle graph for each set of data.

3.

Activity	Percent of Day
Sleep	25%
School	25%
Job	17%
Entertainment	17%
Meals	8%
Homework	8%

4.

Favorite Pet	Percent
Dogs	30%
Cats	25%
Fish	12%
Birds	11%
Other	22%

5.

Type of Milk	Percent
Skim	27%
Lowfat	37%
Whole	36%

6.

Activity	Percent
Visiting w/Friends	26%
Talk on Phone	26%
Play Sports	19%
Earn Money	19%
Use Computers	10%

Name ______________________ Class ______________ Date ______________

9-8 • Guided Problem Solving

GPS Student Page 453, Exercise 11:

Food Ella surveyed 81 students in the cafeteria about their favorite school lunch. Display the results in a circle graph.

pizza: 35 spaghetti: 20 hamburger: 18 grilled cheese: 8

Understand

1. How many students were surveyed? ______________
2. What type of graph will you use to display the results of the survey? ______________
3. What must the total percent of the data equal? ______________

Plan and Carry Out

4. How many sectors will the circle have? ______________
5. How will you find the percentage of students that chose each lunch?

____

____

6. What proportion would you use to find the measures of the central angles?

____

7. Find the percentage of students that chose each lunch as their favorite and the measure the central angle for each sector of the circle.

____

____

8. Use a protractor to draw the sectors of the circle and label each sector.

Favorite School Lunch

Check

9. Do your angles total 360°?

Solve Another Problem

10. Henry surveyed 70 band members to see what instrument they played. Display the results in a circle graph.

flute: 16 drum: 7 horn: 42 cymbals: 5

Name ______________________ Class ______________ Date ______________

Practice 9-9

Choosing an Appropriate Graph

Use the graph to the right for Exercises 1 and 2.

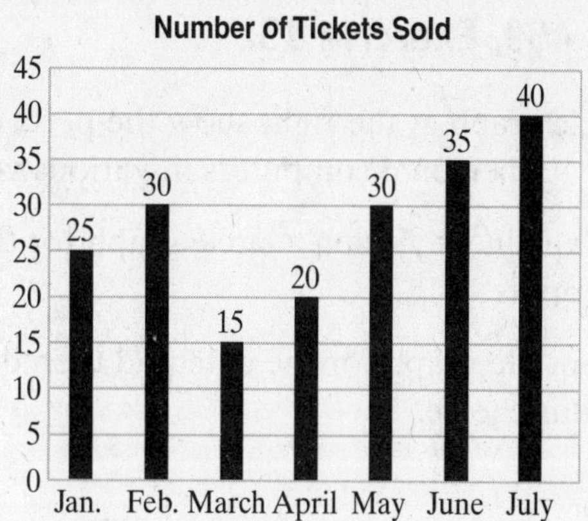

1. The bar graph shows the number of tickets a movie house sold each month last year. The owners want to look at last year's sales trend. Which type of graph would be more appropriate for the data?

   ____

2. Draw the graph.

Decide which type of graph would be the most appropriate for the data. Explain your choice.

3. sizes of U.S. farms from 1950 to 2000

   ____

4. lengths of rivers

   ____

5. height versus weight of students in a class

   ____

6. the way a family budgets its income

   ____

Name ______________________ Class ______________ Date ______________

9-9 • Guided Problem Solving

GPS Student Page 459, Exercise 15:

The table and the circle graph at the right show the percent of homes in the United States with personal computers in various years.

a. Error Analysis Explain why using a circle graph for this set of data is not appropriate.

b. Choose an appropriate graph for the data and then draw the graph. Explain your choice.

Percent of Homes in the United States With Personal Computers

Year	Percent
1994	33
1996	40
1998	44
2000	56
2002	61
2004	68

Percent of Homes in the United States With Personal Computers

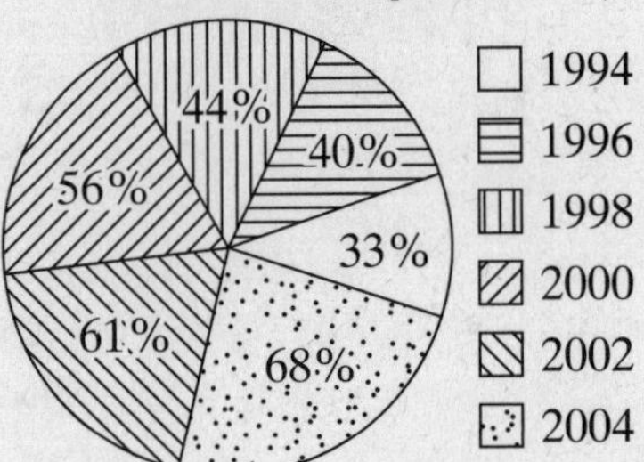

Understand

1. What are you asked to explain?

____

____

2. What are you asked to draw?

____

Plan and Carry Out

3. What does a circle graph not show for the data given?

____

4. Would a line graph or a histogram be a better choice to display the given data? Why?

____

____

5. Draw your graph.

Check

6. Does your graph show the change in percents between the years 1994 and 2004? ______

Solve Another Problem

7. A deli owner wants to know what percentages of sales are from the following lunchmeats. Draw an appropriate graph for the data.

Lunchmeats	%
Ham	32
Salami	14
Turkey	26
Roast beef	18
Pastrami	10

Name ______________________ Class ______________ Date ______________

9A: Graphic Organizer

For use before Lesson 9-1

Study Skill Pay attention in class and concentrate when reading assignments so information does not slip out of your "short-term" memory.

Write your answers.

1. What is the chapter title? ______________________
2. How many lessons are there in this chapter? ______________________
3. What is the topic of the Test-Taking Strategies page? ______________________
4. Complete the graphic organizer below as you work through the chapter.
   - In the center, write the title of the chapter.
   - When you begin a lesson, write the lesson name in a rectangle.
   - When you complete a lesson, write a skill or key concept in a circle linked to that lesson block.
   - When you complete the chapter, use this graphic organizer to help you review.

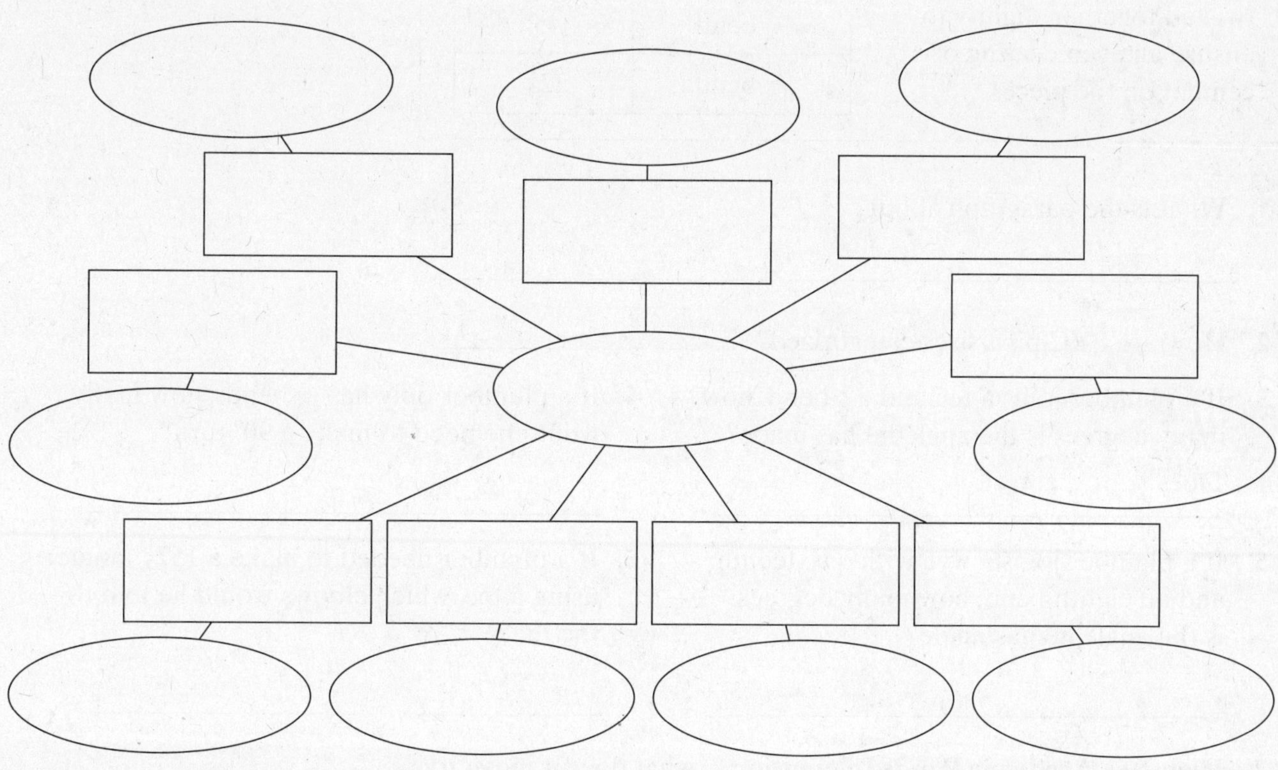

Name ______________________ Class ______________ Date ____________

9B: Reading Comprehension

For use after Lesson 9-2

Study Skill Participating in class discussions might help you remember new material better. Sometimes, explaining or questioning a new concept can help you understand.

Read the paragraph below and answer the questions.

Plumbers often use a non-metallic pipe called PVC pipe for sink and toilet drain lines. The four most common diameters of PVC pipe are $1\frac{1}{2}$ in., 2 in., 3in., and 4 in. When plumbers need to combine pipes with diameters of difference sizes, they use a bushing or reducer coupling. Elbows or "bends" help make turns when connecting pipes. There are three different sizes of elbows and two common fittings that are used. A "wye" is a straight fitting with a 45° elbow attached to one end, and a "tee" is a straight fitting with a 90° elbow attached to one end. Pipes are connected by cleaning and priming the ends and then fitting them together. Liquid cement is applied to each piece and the pieces are twisted together slightly to ensure an even coating of cement on the pieces.

Elbows	
$\frac{1}{4}$ bend	90°
$\frac{1}{8}$ bend	45°
$\frac{1}{16}$ bend	$22\frac{1}{2}°$

1. What is the paragraph about?

____

2. How are PVC pipe sizes categorized? ______________

3. If a plumber joins a tee and a $\frac{1}{8}$ bend, how many degrees is the angle he has made?

____

4. If a plumber only has $\frac{1}{16}$ bends, how many would he need to make a 90° turn?

____

5. If a plumber joins a wye with a sixteenth and an eighth bend, how many degrees is the angle he has made?

____

6. If a plumber needed to make a $157\frac{1}{2}°$ angle using a tee, which elbows would he join to the tee?

____

7. **High-Use Academic Words** In question 2, what does it mean to *categorize?*

a. to classify

b. to expand

9C: Reading/Writing Math Symbols

For use after Lesson 9-3

Study Skill Read aloud or recite when you are studying at home. Reciting a rule or formula can help you to remember it and recall it for later use.

Write each of the following mathematical symbols or formulas in words.

1. $\cong$ ____________________
2. $>$ ____________________
3. $|x|$ ____________________
4. $\geq$ ____________________
5. $=$ ____________________
6. -4 ____________________
7. $\times$ ____________________
8. $\div$ ____________________
9. $\%$ ____________________
10. $\angle$ ____________________
11. $\neq$ ____________________
12. $\sqrt{}$ ____________________
13. $\mathrm{R} : \mathrm{L} = \mathrm{S} : \mathrm{T}$ ____________________

    ____
14. $\triangle ABC \sim \triangle DEF$ ____________________

    ____
15. $\overset{\frown}{BC}$ ____________________
16. $V = lwh$ ____________________

    ____
17. $A = bh$ ____________________
18. $C = \pi d$ ____________________

    ____

Name ______________________ Class ______________ Date ______________

9D: Visual Vocabulary Practice

For use after Lesson 9-7

High-Use Academic Words

Study Skill When you feel you're getting frustrated, take a break.

Concept List

acronym	symbolize	predict
classify	abbreviate	equal
analyze	deduce	dimensions

Write the concept that best describes each exercise. Choose from the concept list above.

1. Graph: Profits (in millions of dollars) vs. Year; axis marks O, 2, 4, 6. In year five, profits will increase. ____________	**2.** $60\% = 0.6 = \frac{3}{5}$ ____________	**3.** Find the range and mean on the data set and identify any outliers. ____________
4. qt for quarts ____________	**5.** A transversal t intersects parallel lines m and n such that t is perpendicular to m. t is perpendicular to n. ____________	**6.** $l \times w \times h$ ____________
7. angle ∠ parallel ‖ perpendicular ⊥ ____________	**8.** Write SAS for Side Angle Side. ____________	**9.** Prisms and pyramids are polyhedrons; cylinders and cones are not. ____________

Name ______________________ Class ______________ Date ______________

9E: Vocabulary Check

For use after Lesson 9-8

Study Skill Strengthen your vocabulary. Use these pages and add cues and summaries by applying the Cornell Notetaking style.

Write the definition for each word or term at the right. To check your work, fold the paper back along the dotted line to see the correct answers.

______________________________	central angle
______________________________	mode
______________________________	mean
______________________________	negative trend
______________________________	outlier

Vocabulary and Study Skills

9E: Vocabulary Check (continued)

For use after Lesson 9-8

Write the vocabulary word or term for each definition. To check your work, fold the paper forward along the dotted line to see the correct answers.

Definition	Answer
an angle whose vertex is the center of a circle	______________________
the item in a data set that occurs with the greatest frequency	______________________
the sum of the data divided by the number of data items	______________________
when one set of values tends to increase while the other set tends to decrease	______________________
an item in a data set that is much higher or much lower that the other items in a data set	______________________

9F: Vocabulary Review

For use with the Chapter Review

Study Skill Taking short breaks can help you stay focused. Every 30 minutes, take a 5-minute break, then return to studying.

I. Match the term in Column A with its definition in Column B.

Column A	Column B
1. negative trend	A. type of graph used to show changes over time
2. bar graph	B. a type of graph used to show trends
3. rhombus	C. two angles whose sum is 90 degrees
4. hypotenuse	D. the longest side of a right triangle
5. stem-and-leaf plot	E. shows data items in order
6. complementary	F. as one set of values increases, the other set tends to decrease
7. line graph	G. two angles whose sum is 180 degrees
8. supplementary	H. a quadrilateral with four congruent sides

II. Match the term in Column A with its definition in Column B.

Column A	Column B
1. slope	A. divides the data into four equal parts
2. regular polygon	B. lines that intersect to form right angles
3. trapezoid	C. a quadrilateral with exactly one pair of parallel sides
4. quartiles	D. as one set of values increases, the other set tends to increase
5. positive trend	E. a figure with all sides congruent and all angles congruent
6. perpendicular	F. a ratio that describes the steepness of a line
7. circle graph	G. the difference between the greatest and least values in a data set
8. range	H. a graph that shows parts of a whole

Name ______________________ Class ______________ Date ______________

Practice 10-1

Theoretical and Experimental Probability

A dart is thrown at the game board shown. Notice that the diameters are at right angles and that some of the slices are congruent. Find each probability.

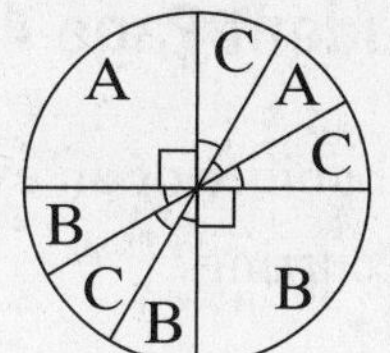

1. $P(A)$ ______
2. $P(B)$ ______
3. $P(C)$ ______
4. $P(\text{not } A)$ ______
5. $P(\text{not } B)$ ______
6. $P(\text{not } C)$ ______

The odds in favor of winning a game are 5 to 9.

7. Find the probability of winning the game. ______
8. Find the probability of *not* winning the game. ______

A box of marbles contains 10 red, 12 blue, 15 yellow, and 8 green marbles. A marble is drawn at random. Find each probability.

9. $P(\text{red})$ ______
10. $P(\text{blue})$ ______
11. What are the odds in favor of picking a blue marble? ______
12. What are the odds in favor of picking a green marble? ______
13. What is the probability of picking a marble that is not yellow? ______
14. What is the probability of picking a marble that is not red? ______

Solve.

15. a. You buy a ticket for the weekly drawing by a community charity. Last week you bought one ticket. Find the probability and odds of winning if 1,200 tickets were bought that week. ______

    b. Find the probability and odds of you winning if you bought three tickets and there were 1,200 tickets bought that week. ______

16. A cheese tray contains slices of Swiss cheese and cheddar cheese. If you randomly pick a slice of cheese, $P(\text{Swiss}) = 0.45$. Find $P(\text{cheddar})$. If there are 200 slices of cheese, how many slices of Swiss cheese are on the cheese tray?

______

Name ______________________ Class ______________ Date ______________

10-1 • Guided Problem Solving

GPS Student Page 472, Exercise 12:

The probability of an event is $\frac{1}{4}$. What are the odds in favor of the event occurring?

Understand

1. What does the probability of an event being $\frac{1}{4}$ mean?

____

____

2. What are you being asked to determine?

____

Plan and Carry Out

3. How many outcomes are there? ______________
4. What does the first number of a ratio mean when finding the odds in favor of an event?

____

5. What does the second number of a ratio mean when finding the odds in favor of an event?

____

6. Write the odds in favor of the event occurring. ______________

Check

7. How can you determine the probability when given the odds?

____

____

Solve Another Problem

8. The probability of an event is $\frac{3}{8}$. What are the odds in favor of the event occurring?

____

Name ______________________ Class ______________ Date ______________

Practice 10-2

Making Predictions

A cube has 3 green sides, 2 red sides, and 1 orange side. Find the probability of each toss result.

1. *P*(green)________
2. *P*(red)________
3. *P*(orange)________

Using the probability data from exercises 1–3, predict how many times the given outcome will occur for each number of tosses.

4. 600 tosses; red ____________
5. 144 tosses; green ____________
6. 86 tosses; orange ____________
7. 45 tosses; red ____________

Suppose 300 students were surveyed to find which method of transportation they most frequently use to get to school. Based on the data at the right, predict how many students in a school of 800 frequently use each method of transportation.

Most Frequent Student Transportation

Transportation to School	Number of Students
Bus	160
Automobile or Motorcycle	80
Bicycle	20
Walk	40

8. bus ____________
9. automobile or motorcycle ____________
10. bicycle ____________
11. walk ____________
12. A certain shoe manufacturer examined 250 pairs of shoes and found 41 pairs with defects. In a shipment of 6,000 pairs of shoes, how many are likely to have defects?

____

13. A store owner notes that 1 out of 4 customers do not make a purchase. How many customers need to come into the store in order for the owner to make 70 sales?

____

14. A large jar contains pennies, nickels, dimes, and quarters. If you pick a coin at random *P*(quarter) = 0.28. If there are 500 coins in the jar, how many quarters are in the jar?

____

Name ______________________ Class ______________ Date ______________

10-2 • Guided Problem Solving

GPS Student Page 477, Exercise 20:

Transportation The probability that a flight on a certain airline will be on time is $\frac{4}{5}$. At an airport, the airline has 125 flights leaving each day. Predict how many of these flights will be on time.

Understand

1. What are you being asked to do?

____

2. What does the probability of an event being $\frac{4}{5}$ mean?

____

____

Plan and Carry Out

3. Does 125 represent favorable outcomes or all outcomes?

____

4. Set up a proportion.

____

5. Find the cross products.

____

6. Simplify.

____

Check

7. Is your answer $\frac{4}{5}$ of 125?

____

Solve Another Problem

8. Mike won 7 out of 8 votes in the club election. There were 64 votes cast. How many votes did Mike win?

____

Name ____________________ Class ____________________ Date ____________________

Practice 10-3

Conducting a Survey

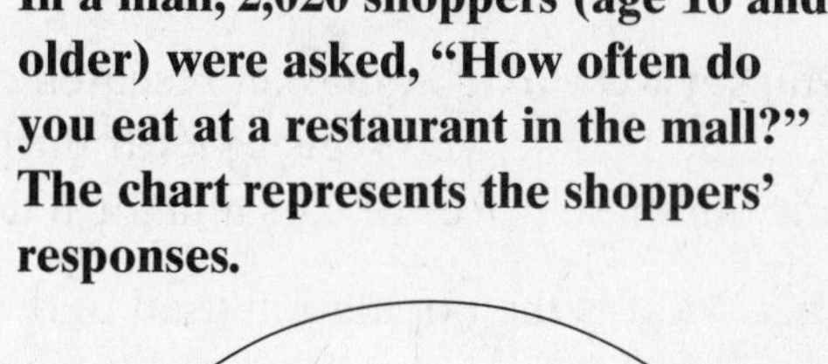

In a mall, 2,020 shoppers (age 16 and older) were asked, "How often do you eat at a restaurant in the mall?" The chart represents the shoppers' responses.

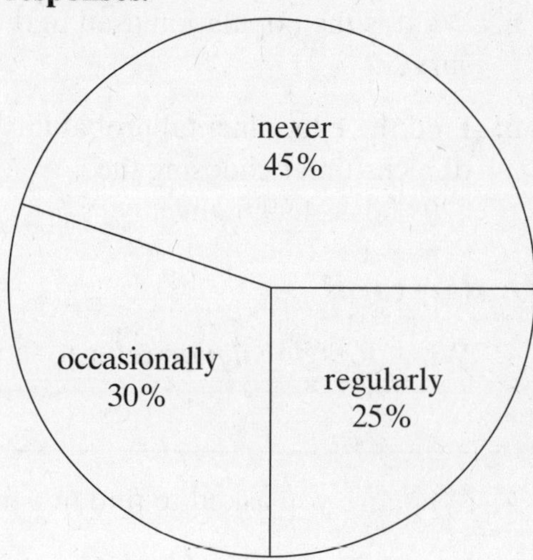

1. What population does the sample represent?

2. How many people responded in each of the categories?

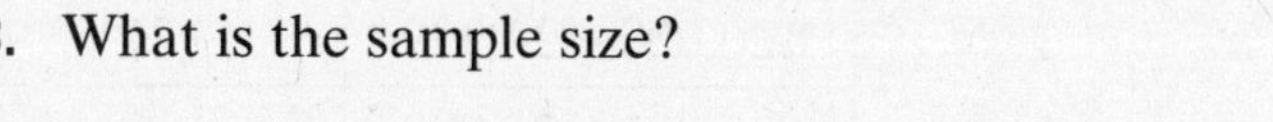

3. What is the sample size?

4. Can you tell if the sample is random? Explain.

Explain why the survey questions in exercises 5 and 6 are biased.

5. Would you rather buy the TV dinner with a picture of a luscious gourmet meal on it, or one in a plain package?

6. Do you want your kids to receive a faulty education by having their school day shortened?

7. A researcher wants to find out what brand of tomato sauce is most popular with people who work full time. He samples shoppers at a supermarket between 10 A.M. and 2 P.M. Is this a good sample? Explain.

8. You decide to run for student council. What factors are important to consider if you decide to survey your fellow students?

Name ______________________ Class ______________ Date ____________

10-3 • Guided Problem Solving

GPS Student Page 483, Exercise 15:

Market Research A market research company interviews randomly selected people who register a car during the year to recommend fair purchase prices of cars at a local dealership.

a. What is the population used in the survey?

b. Find the experimental probability of a customer choosing the $20,000–$24,999 range.

Recommended Purchase Price

Price Range	Frequency
$10,000–$14,999	15
$15,000–$19,999	8
$20,000–$24,999	12
$25,000–$29,999	6

Understand

1. What does *population* refer to in part (a)?

____

2. What are you asked to find in part (b)?

____

Plan and Carry Out

3. Who is interviewed?

____

4. What is the population used for the survey?

____

5. What is the ratio for experimental probability?

____

6. Use the frequencies from the chart to find the experimental probability.

____

Check

7. For a sample to be random, each item has an equal opportunity to be picked. Did this market research use a random sample? Explain.

____

Solve Another Problem

8. Jane conducts a survey of women's fitness club members aged 35–44. What is the population used for her survey?

____

Name ______ Class ______ Date ______

Practice 10-4

A drawer contains 3 black socks and 2 white socks. A sock is drawn at random and then replaced. Find each probability.

1. P(2 blacks) ______
2. P(black, then white) ______
3. P(white, then black) ______
4. P(2 whites) ______

Each letter from the word MASSACHUSETTS is written on a separate slip of paper. The 13 slips of paper are placed in a sack and two slips are drawn at random. The first pick is not replaced.

5. Find the probability that the first letter drawn is M and the second letter is S. ______

6. Find the probability that the first letter drawn is S and the second letter is A. ______

7. Find the probability that the first letter drawn is S and the second letter is also S. ______

Solve.

8. On a TV game show, you can win a car by drawing a 1 and a 15 from a stack of cards numbered 1–15. The first card you draw is not replaced. What is your probability of winning?

______

9. You roll a number cube eight times, and each time you roll a 4. What is the theoretical probability that on the ninth roll, you will roll a 6? Is rolling a 6 dependent or independent of rolling a 4 eight times?

______

10. There are 4 brown shoes and 10 black shoes on the floor. Your puppy carries away two shoes and puts one shoe in the trash can and one shoe in the laundry basket.

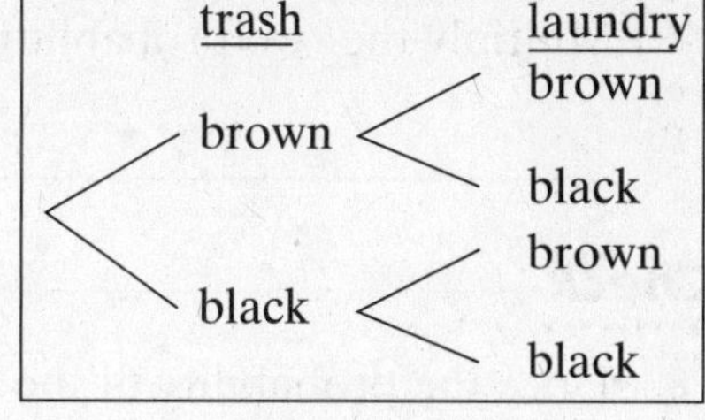

a. What is the probability that there will be a black shoe in the trash and a brown shoe in the laundry basket?

______

b. What is the probability that there will be a brown shoe in both the trash and the laundry basket?

______

11. Use the data at the right to find P(right-handed female, then left-handed male) if two people are chosen at random.

______

	Male	Female
Right-handed	86	83
Left-handed	14	17
Total	100	100

Name ______________________ Class ______________ Date ______________

10-4 • Guided Problem Solving

GPS Student Page 489, Exercise 23:

School Carnival For a carnival game, a cube is rolled. Each of its six faces has a different color. To win, you must select the color rolled. You play the game twice. Find the probability of winning both times.

Understand

1. What are you being asked to do? ______________________

____

2. Are the events dependent or independent?

____

Plan and Carry Out

3. How many faces are on the cube?

____

4. How many colors are on the cube?

5. What is the probability of winning the first time?

____

6. What is the probability of winning the second time?

____

7. Multiply the two probabilities.

____

Check

8. Does the probability of the first roll affect the probability of the second roll?

____

Solve Another Problem

9. In your pocket you have five nickels and three quarters. You randomly take out one coin and then put it back into your pocket. Then you take out a second coin at random. What is the probability of picking a quarter and a nickel?

____

Name ________________ Class ________________ Date ________________

Practice 10-5

Permutations

Simplify each expression.

1. 6!
2. 12!
3. 9!
4. ${}_9P_5$
5. ${}_8P_2$
6. ${}_{10}P_8$

Use the counting principle to find the number of permutations.

7. In how many ways can all the letters of the word WORK be arranged? ________________

8. In how many ways can you arrange seven friends in a row for a photo? ________________

9. A disk jockey can play eight songs in one time slot. In how many different orders can the eight songs be played?

10. Melody has nine bowling trophies to arrange in a horizontal line on a shelf. How many arrangements are possible?

11. At a track meet, 42 students entered the 100-m race. In how many ways can first, second, and third places be awarded?

12. In how many ways can a president, a vice-president, and a treasurer be chosen from a group of 15 people running for office?

13. A car dealer has 38 used cars to sell. Each day two cars are chosen for advertising specials. One car appears in a television commercial and the other appears in a newspaper advertisement. In how many ways can the two cars be chosen?

14. A bicycle rack outside a classroom has room for six bicycles. In the class, 10 students sometimes ride their bicycles to school. How many different arrangements of bicycles are possible for any given day?

15. A certain type of luggage has room for three initials. How many different 3-letter arrangements of letters, with no repetition of the same letter, are possible?

16. A roller coaster has room for 10 people. The people sit single file, one after the other. How many different arrangements are possible for 10 passengers on the roller coaster?

Name ______________________ Class ______________ Date ______________

10-5 • Guided Problem Solving

GPS Student Page 494, Exercise 27:

Dog Shows Twenty-five dogs entered the dog show. The show awards prizes for first, second, and third places. How many different arrangements of three winners are possible?

Understand

1. How many dogs are entered in the show?

   ____

2. How many prizes are given out? ______________________

3. What are you being asked to find?

   ____

   ____

Plan and Carry Out

4. How many different dogs could win first place? ____________

5. After the first place is awarded, how many dogs have the possibility of winning second place?

   ____

6. After the first and second places are awarded, how many dogs are left that could win third place?

   ____

7. Use the counting principle to find the number of possible arrangements.

   ____

Check

8. Write the problem using permutation notation. Then, solve the problem.

   ____

Solve Another Problem

9. A storage company asks you to choose five different digits from 0 to 9 as your personal identification number (PIN) to enter the property after hours. How many possible five-digit numbers can you choose from?

   ____

Name ______________________ Class ______________ Date ______________

Practice 10-6

Combinations

Simplify each expression.

1. ${}_9C_1$ ________ **2.** ${}_8C_4$ ________ **3.** ${}_{11}C_4$ ________

4. ${}_4C_4$ ________ **5.** ${}_9C_3$ ________ **6.** ${}_{12}C_6$ ________

7. 3 videos from 10 ________

8. 2 letters from the word LOVE ________

9. 4 books from 8 ________

Solve.

10. Ten students from a class have volunteered to be on a committee to organize a dance. In how many ways can six be chosen for the committee?

____

11. Twenty-three people try out for extra parts in a play. In how many ways can eight people be chosen to be extras?

____

12. A team of nine players is to be chosen from 15 available players. In how many ways can this be done?

____

13. At a party there are 12 people present. A group of 4 is going to pick up the pizza. How many combinations of 4 can pick up the pizza?

____

14. In math class there are 24 students. The teacher picks 4 students to serve on the bulletin board committee. How many different committees of 4 are possible?

____

15. Five friends, Billi, Joe, Eduardo, Mari, and Xavier, want one photograph taken of each possible pair of friends. Using B, J, E, M, and X, list all of the pairs that need to be photographed.

____

16. A team of 3 people is chosen from 8 available players. Describe the number of possible teams using combination notation.

____

Name ____________________ Class ____________ Date ____________

10-6 • Guided Problem Solving

GPS Student Page 499, Exercise 24:

Travel A group of six tourists arrives at an airport gate 15 minutes before flight time, but only two seats are available.

a. How many different groups of two can get on the airplane?

b. How many different groups of four *cannot* get on the airplane?

Understand

1. How many people arrive at the airport?

____

2. How many seats are left on the plane?

____

3. Does the order of the people in the groups matter? ____________________

Plan and Carry Out

4. Write the formula for combination notation.

____

5. Use the formula to determine how many groups of two can get on the plane.

____

6. Use the formula to determine how many groups of four will not be able to get on the plane.

____

Check

7. Why are the answers the same?

____

____

____

____

____

Solve Another Problem

8. In a courthouse, 18 people report for jury duty. There will only be 12 people seated on the jury for the trial. How many different 12-person juries can be chosen?

____

Name ______________________ Class ______________ Date ______________

10A: Graphic Organizer

For use before Lesson 10-1

Study Skill As you learn new material, it might help to work with other students. They might work problems differently which could make the material easier for you to understand.

Write your answers.

1. What is the chapter title? ______________________
2. How many lessons are there in this chapter? ______________________
3. What is the topic of the Test-Taking Strategies page?

   ____

4. Complete the graphic organizer below as you work through the chapter.
   - In the center, write the title of the chapter.
   - When you begin a lesson, write the lesson name in a rectangle.
   - When you complete a lesson, write a skill or key concept in a circle linked to that lesson block.
   - When you complete the chapter, use this graphic organizer to help you review.

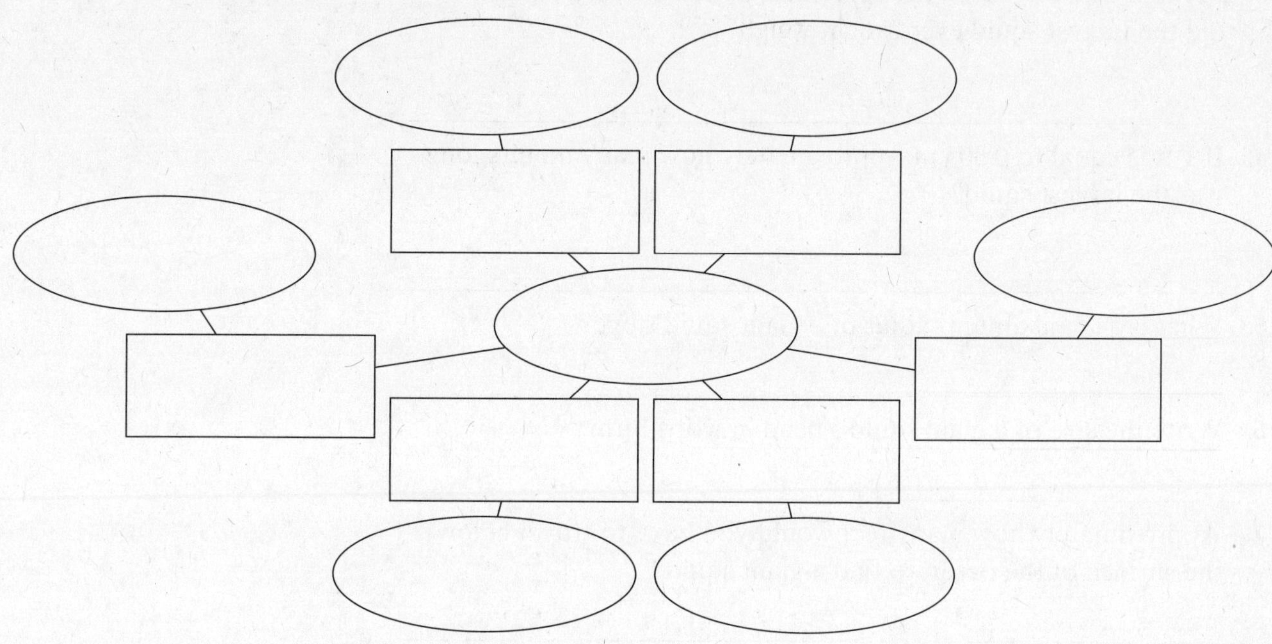

Vocabulary and Study Skills

Name ______________________ Class ______________ Date ____________

10B: Reading Comprehension

For use after Lesson 10-3

Study Skill When working math problems, be sure your answers make sense. Check the answers with the other facts in the problem. For example, probability can never be negative or greater than one.

Read the paragraph and answer the questions.

> The giant squid has eight arms like an octopus. It also has two large tentacles that are much longer than its arms. The squid uses its arms to catch prey. Giant squid live in seas and oceans at depths of a mile or more. The giant squid's head is enormous, about 3.3 feet in length. Squid also have the largest eyes of any animal, measuring up to 10 inches in diameter. The largest squid ever caught was 66 feet long and weighed 880 pounds.

1. How can you differentiate between squid and octopi?

____

____

2. What is the ratio of tentacles to arms for a giant squid?

____

3. If 1 lb is equal to 0.454 kg, approximately how many kilograms did the largest squid ever caught weigh?

____

4. If 1 ft is equal to 0.305 m, approximately how many meters long was the largest squid?

____

5. What is the maximum radius of a giant squid's eye?

____

6. Write the size of a giant squid's head in word form.

____

7. Approximately how many feet would you have to travel below the surface of the ocean to find a giant squid?

____

8. **High-Use Academic Words** In Exercise 1, what does it mean to *differentiate?*

   a. to see or state the differences

   b. to fit together the parts of

Name ______________________ Class ______________ Date ______________

10C: Reading/Writing Math Symbols

For use after Lesson 10-6

Study Skill Explore your textbook so you can use its features to the fullest.

Match each expression in Column A to its meaning in Column B.

Column A	Column B
1. %	**A.** the probability of an event occurring
2. *P*(heads, then tails)	**B.** 1 – *P*(heads)
3. 8!	**C.** percent
4. *P*(not heads)	**D.** eight factorial
5. *P*(event)	**E.** *P*(heads) · *P*(tails)

Write each statement using appropriate mathematical symbols.

6. five factorial multiplied by three factorial

____

7. the probability of event X not occurring

____

8. the number of possible seating arrangements for a table of 6

____

9. the probability of rolling a 5 and then a 2 on a number cube

____

10. the number of ways 36 items can be chosen 4 at a time where order does matter

____

11. the number of ways 7 cards can be chosen from a 52-card deck where order does not matter

____

Name ________________________ Class ________________ Date ______________

10D: Visual Vocabulary Practice

For use after Lesson 10-5

Study Skill When you come across something you don't understand, view it as an opportunity to increase your brain power.

Concept List

combinations	permutations	population
counting principle	random sample	experimental probability
dependent events	independent events	theoretical probability

Write the concept that best describes each exercise. Choose from the concept list above.

1. G A M E S

$P(\text{M, then S}) =$

$\frac{1}{5} \times \frac{1}{4} = \frac{1}{20}$

____

2. The number of different ways 5 kids can sit in 3 bean bags is $5 \times 4 \times 3 = 60$.

____

3. Coin Flips

Heads	44
Tails	56

$P(\text{heads}) = 0.44$

____

4. Ways to choose 2 CDs from 5 CDs are:

(1, 2)(1, 3)(1, 4)(1, 5)
~~(2, 1)~~(2, 3)(2, 4)(2, 5)
~~(3, 1)~~~~(3, 2)~~(3, 4)(3, 5)
~~(4, 1)~~~~(4, 2)~~~~(4, 3)~~(4, 5)
~~(5, 1)~~~~(5, 2)~~~~(5, 3)~~~~(5, 4)~~

____

5. Marco recorded the number of books purchased by every 10th customer at a bookstore until he had 200 customers in this study. The 200 customers represent this.

____

6. Sandwich choices

Meat	Cheese
Ham	Swiss
Turkey	Cheddar
	Provolone

The total number of possible outcomes is $2 \times 3 = 6$.

____

7.

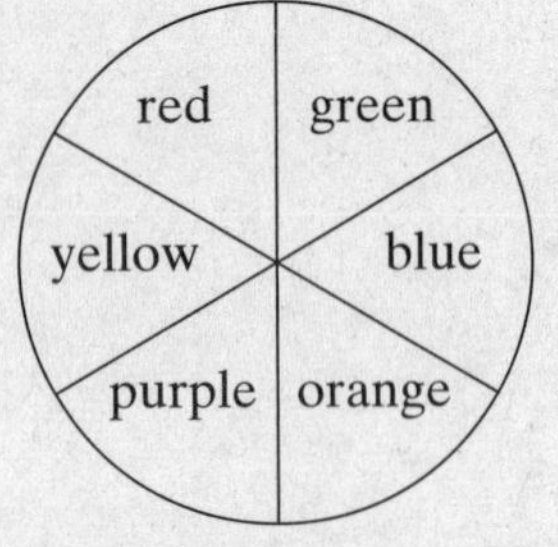

$P(\text{purple, then red}) =$

$\frac{1}{6} \times \frac{1}{6} = \frac{1}{36}$

____

8. A student conducted a study about the percent of the voting-age students at her college who actually vote. The voting-age students at her college represent this for the study.

____

9.

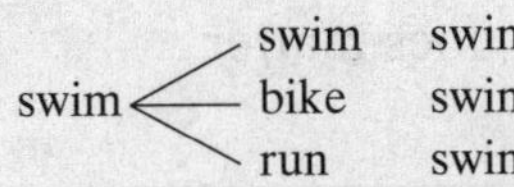

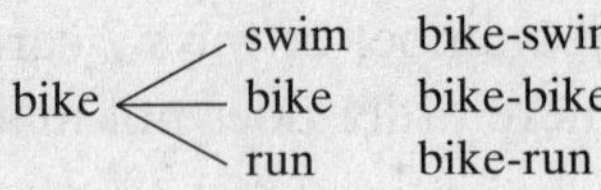

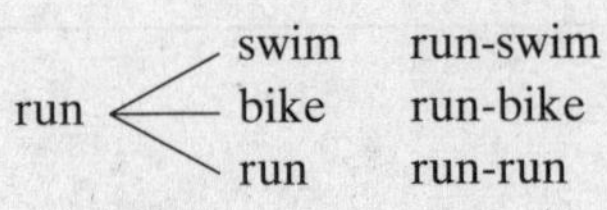

$P(\text{same sport}) = \frac{3}{9} = \frac{1}{3}$

____

Name ______________________ Class ______________ Date ______________

10E: Vocabulary Check

For use after Lesson 10-6

Study Skill Strengthen your vocabulary. Use these pages and add cues and summaries by applying the Cornell Notetaking style.

Write the definition for each word or term at the right. To check your work, fold the paper back along the dotted line to see the correct answers.

______________________	combination
______________________	permutation
______________________	factorial
______________________	biased questions
______________________	independent events

Name ______________________ Class ______________ Date ______________

10E: Vocabulary Check (continued)

For use after Lesson 10-6

Write the vocabulary word or term for each definition. To check your work, fold the paper forward along the dotted line to see the correct answers.

a group of items in which the order of the items is not considered ______________________

an arrangement of objects in a particular order ______________________

the product of all positive integers less than or equal to a number ______________________

unfair questions in a survey that make assumptions that may not be true, or make one answer seem better than another ______________________

two events where the occurrence of one event does not affect the probability of the occurrence of the other ______________________

10F: Vocabulary Review

For use with the Chapter Review

Study Skill Take short breaks between assignments. You will be able to concentrate on a new assignment more easily if you take a brief "time out" before starting.

Circle the term that best completes each sentence.

1. A(n) (*event, sample*) is one or more possible outcomes.
2. A (*combination, permutation*) is an arrangement of items in which the order does not matter.
3. The (*combination, complement*) of an event is the opposite of the event.
4. You can use a (*sample, population*) to gather information and make predictions.
5. Spinning a spinner and then tossing a coin is an example of two (*independent, dependent*) events.
6. A (*combination, permutation*) is an arrangement of a set of objects in a particular order.
7. The product of all positive integers less than or equal to a number is a (*factorial, complement*).
8. You can find (*experimental probability, theoretical probability*) without using trials.
9. Questions that may influence the answers are (*dependent, biased*).
10. When the outcome of one event affects the outcome of a second event, the events are (*independent, dependent*).

Name ______________________ Class ____________ Date ____________

Practice 11-1

Sequences

Write the rule for each sequence and find the next three terms.

1. 3, 8, 13, 18, ___, ___, ___

2. 7, 14, 28, 56, ___, ___, ___

3. 32, 8, 2, $\frac{1}{2}$, ___, ___, ___

4. 14, 11, 8, 5, ___, ___, ___

5. 35, 23, 11, −1, ___, ___, ___

6. 3000, 300, 30, 3, ___, ___, ___

Find the next three terms in each sequence. Identify each as *arithmetic, geometric,* or *neither.* For each arithmetic or geometric sequence, find the common difference or ratio.

7. 7.1, 7.5, 7.9, 8.3, ___, ___, ___

8. 5, 6, 8, 11, 15, 20, ___, ___, ___

9. 8000, 4000, 2000, 1000, ___, ___, ___

10. 92, 89, 86, 83, ___, ___, ___

11. 3, 9, 27, 81, ___, ___, ___

12. 540, 270, 90, 22.5, ___, ___, ___

Tell whether each situation produces an *arithmetic sequence, geometric sequence,* or *neither.*

13. The temperature rises at the rate of 0.75°F per hour. ____________

14. A toadstool doubles in size each week. ____________

15. A person receives a 6% raise each year. ____________

Find the first four terms of the sequence represented by each expression.

16. $-5n$

17. $4 + 3(n-2)$

Name ______________________ Class ______________ Date ______________

11-1 • Guided Problem Solving

GPS Student Page 516, Exercise 39:

a. **Geometry** Find the volumes of cubes with side lengths of 2, 3, 4, and 5.

b. These volumes form a sequence. How do you find each term?

c. Write an expression for the sequence.

Understand

1. What is a sequence?

____

____

____

2. What are you asked to find?

____

Plan and Carry Out

3. How do you find the volume of a cube?

____

4. Complete the table for the volumes of cubes.

Side Length	2	3	4	5	6	7	8
Volume							

5. How do you find each term? ______________

6. Write an expression for the volume of a cube.

____

____

7. Write an expression for the sequence.

____

____

Check

8. How can you determine if your sequence is reasonable?

____

Solve Another Problem

9. Find the areas of squares with side lengths 2, 3, 4, and 5.

Write an expression for the sequence. ______________

Name ______________________ Class ______________ Date ____________

Practice 11-2

Relating Graphs to Events

Each graph represents a situation. Match a graph with the appropriate situation.

a.

Time

b.

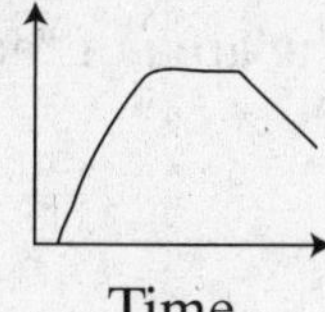

Time

c.

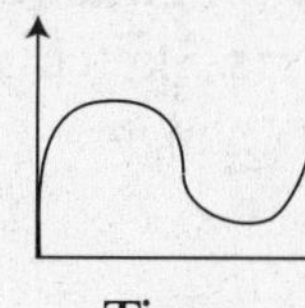

Time

d.

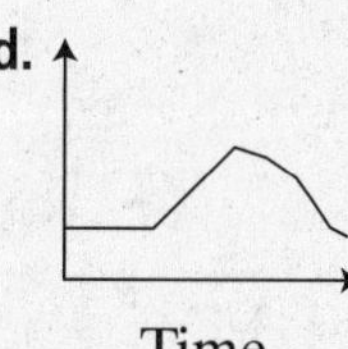

Time

e.

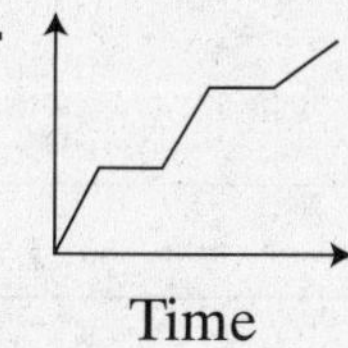

Time

f.

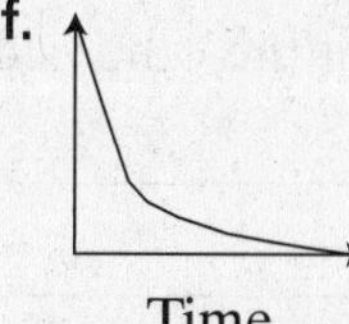

Time

1. the amount of an unpaid library fine ______________
2. the height above ground of a skydiver during a dive ______________
3. one's adrenaline flow when receiving a fright ______________
4. the temperature of the air during a 24-h period beginning at 9:00 A.M. ______________
5. oven temperature for baking cookies ______________
6. elevator ride up with stops ______________

Sketch and label a graph of each relationship.

7. the height of a football after it has been kicked

8. the distance traveled by a car that was traveling at 50 mph, but is now stopped by road construction

9. The function table at the right shows the distance in feet that an object falls over time.

Time (s)	Distance (ft)
1	16
2	64
3	144
4	256

Name ______________________ Class ______________ Date ______________

11-2 • Guided Problem Solving

GPS Student Page 521, Exercise 19:

Geometry As the length of the side of a square increases, the area of the square increases. Sketch a graph that shows the area of the square as the side length changes.

Understand

1. As the length of one side of a square increases, what happens to the lengths of the other sides?

____

____

Plan and Carry Out

2. What is the formula for the area of a square in terms of one side length? ______________

3. Complete the chart.

Side Length	1	2	3	4	5
Area					

4. Draw a graph with the *x*-axis labeled "side length" and the *y*-axis labeled "area." Plot each of the values from Step 3, and draw a line connecting the points.

Check

5. Another way to find the area of a square is to multiply the length times the width. Are your calculations correct? ______________

Solve Another Problem

6. As the length of one side of a square increases, the perimeter of the square increases. Sketch a graph that shows the perimeter of a square as its side length increases in increments of one.

Name ______________________ Class ______________ Date ______________

Practice 11-3

Functions

Complete the table of input/output pairs for each function.

1. $y = 3x$

Input x	Output y
4	
8	
12	
16	

2. $z = 15n$

Input n	Output z
1	
2	
3	
	60

3. $d = 30 - s$

Input s	Output d
0	
5	
	20
	15

4. $h = 120 \div g$

Input g	Output h
2	
6	
	10
15	

5. $r = 2t - 1$

Input t	Output r
3	
9	
20	
	99

6. $p = 2v - 12$

Input v	Output p
	6
	40
43	
75	

Does each situation represent a function? Explain.

7. Input: the distance that needs to be biked
Output: the time it takes if you bike at 5 mph

____

8. Input: the time of day you go to the grocery store
Output: the cost of the groceries

____

Use the function rule $f(x) = 5x + 1$. Find each output.

9. $f(3)$ ______________

10. $f(-6)$ ______________

11. $f(8)$ ______________

12. $f(1.5)$ ______________

13. $f(25)$ ______________

14. $f(30)$ ______________

Use the function rule $f(n) = 4n^2 - 1$. Find each output.

15. $f(0)$ ______________

16. $f(1)$ ______________

17. $f(-1)$ ______________

18. $f(-2)$ ______________

19. $f(3)$ ______________

20. $f(2.5)$ ______________

Name ______________________ Class ______________ Date ______________

11-3 • Guided Problem Solving

GPS Student Page 526, Exercise 20:

Fruit smoothies cost $1.50 each plus $.50 for each fruit mixed into the smoothie. Use function notation to find the cost of a smoothie with 4 different fruits mixed in.

Understand

1. Which two quantities are related?

____

2. Circle what you are asked to find.

Plan and Carry Out

3. What two operations are needed to determine the cost?

____

4. Let *n* be the number of fruits mixed into the smoothie. Write an expression for the total cost of a smoothie with *n* fruits mixed in.

____

5. Use the expression you found in Step 4 to write a function.

____

6. Use the function to find the cost of a smoothie with 4 fruits mixed in.

____

Check

7. How could you find the answer another way?

____

____

Solve Another Problem

8. You spent $4.50 for admission to the fair. Each ride ticket costs $.75. Use function notation to find the cost of 6 ride tickets.

____

Name ______________________ Class ______________ Date ______________

Practice 11-4

Understanding Slope

Find the slope of each line.

1.

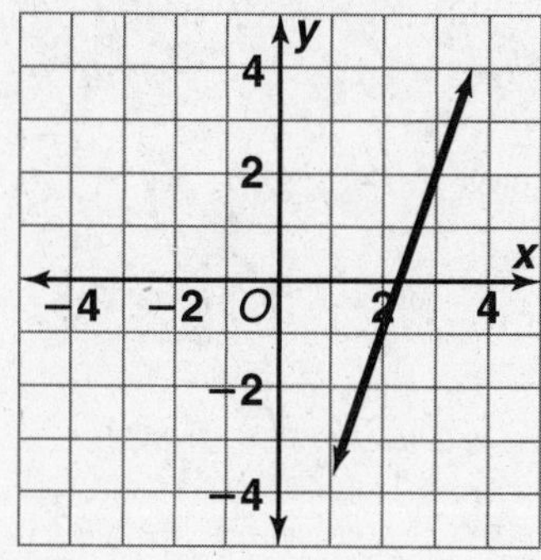

____

2.

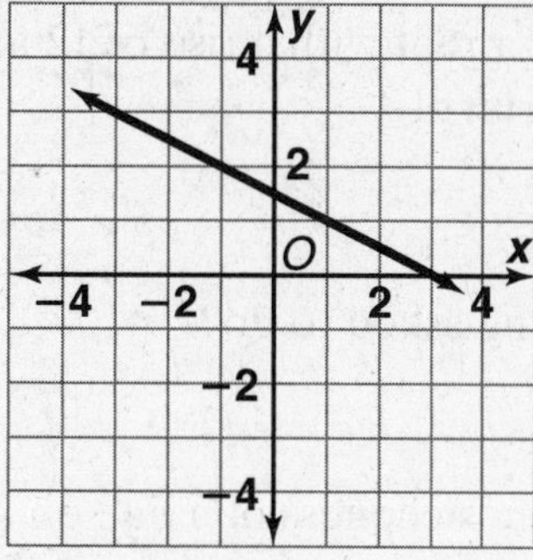

____

3.

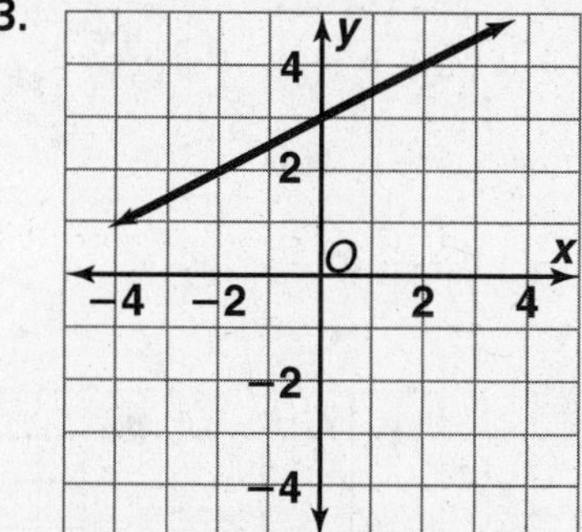

____

4.

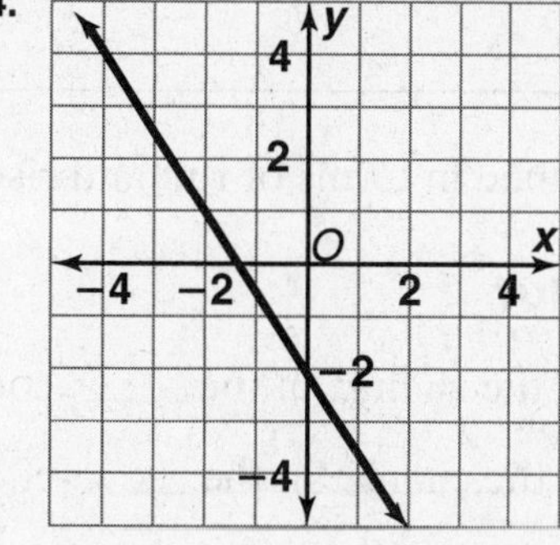

____

The points from each table lie on a line. Use the table to find the slope of each line. Then graph the line.

5.

x	0	1	2	3	4
y	−3	−1	1	3	5

slope = ________

6.

x	0	1	2	3	4
y	5	3	1	−1	−3

slope = ________

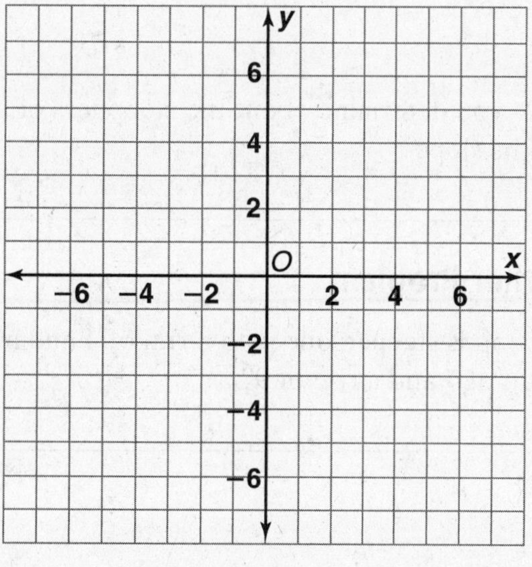

Name ______________________ Class ______________ Date ______________

11-4 • Guided Problem Solving

GPS Student Page 531, Exercise 12:

Which roof is steeper: a roof with a rise of 12 and a run of 7 or a roof with a rise of 8 and a run of 4?

Understand

1. What are you being asked to do?

____

2. What describes the steepness of a line on a coordinate plane?

____

3. What is a good way to visualize this problem?

____

____

4. How is slope defined in terms of run and rise? ______________

Plan and Carry Out

5. The rise involves the change in the ____ -coordinates.
6. The run involves the change in the ____ -coordinates.
7. Graph each slope on the coordinate plane.
8. Which roof is steeper?

____

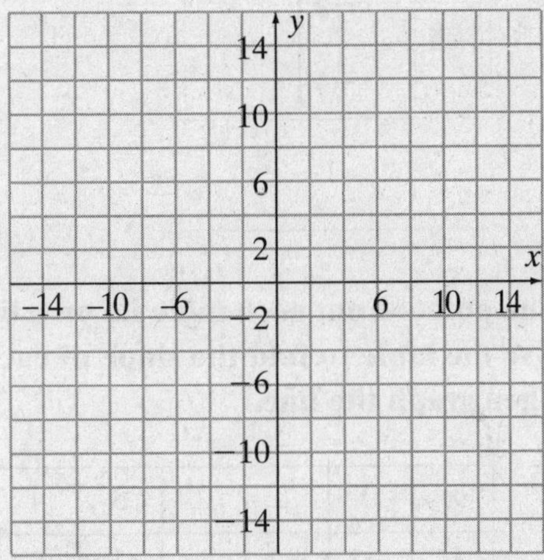

Check

9. What can you determine about the steepness of a line in terms of its slope?

____

Solve Another Problem

10. Which ramp is steeper: one with a run of 4 and a rise of 6, or one with a run of 7 and a rise of 9?

____

Name ______________________ Class ______________ Date ______________

Practice 11-5

Graphing Linear Functions

Complete the table and determine whether the data are *discrete* or *continuous*. Then graph the function. Show only the portion that makes sense for each situation.

1. On a trip Alex averages 300 mi/day. The distance he covers (y) is a function of the number of days (x).

Days				
Miles				

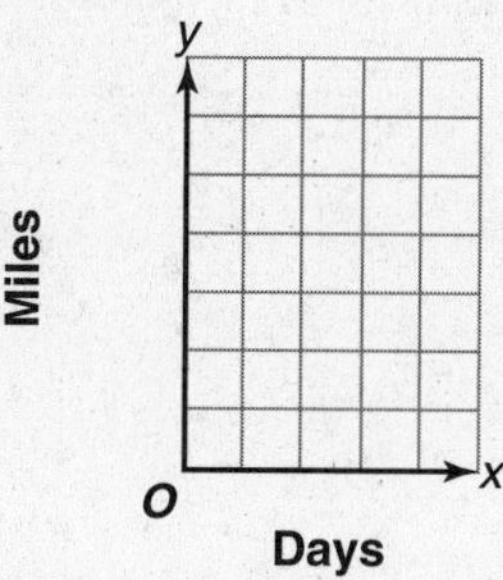

2. You have $10.00 in a savings account. Each Friday you deposit $2.50 more. The number of weeks you save (x) increases your savings (y).

Weeks				
Savings				

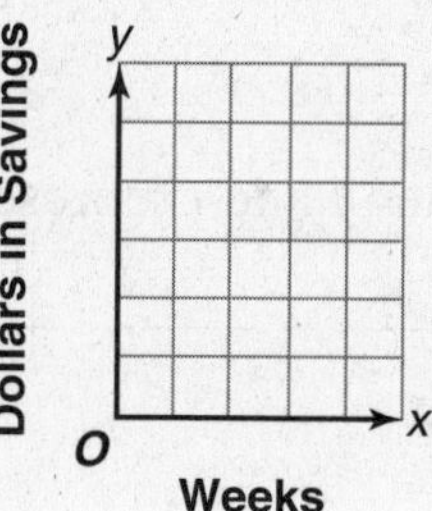

Graph each linear function.

3. $f(x) = -x + 4$

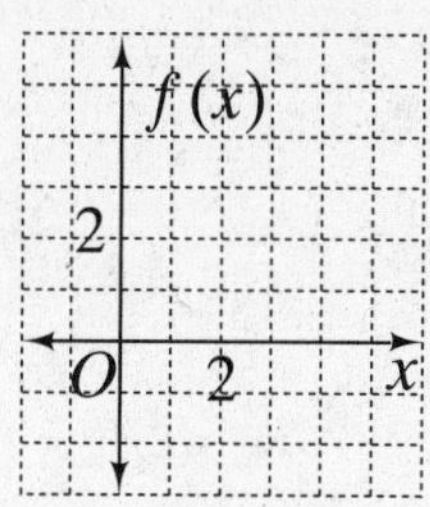

4. $f(x) = \frac{2}{3}x + 1$

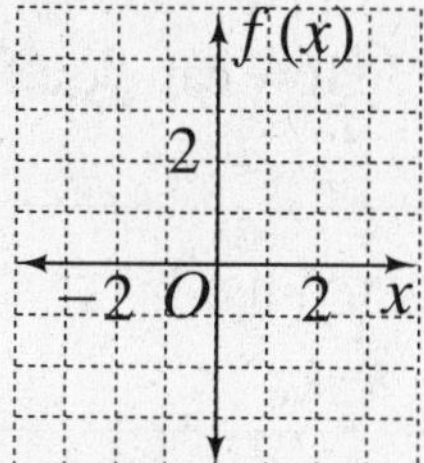

5. $f(x) = -2x + 1$

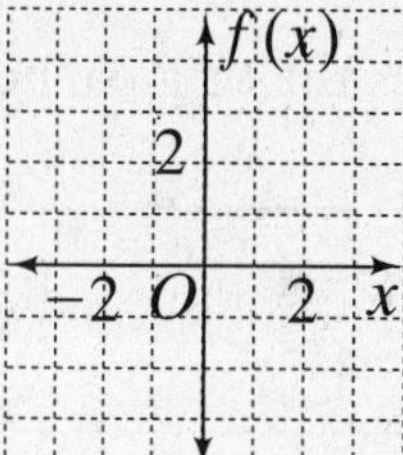

6. $y = -\frac{1}{2}x + 3$

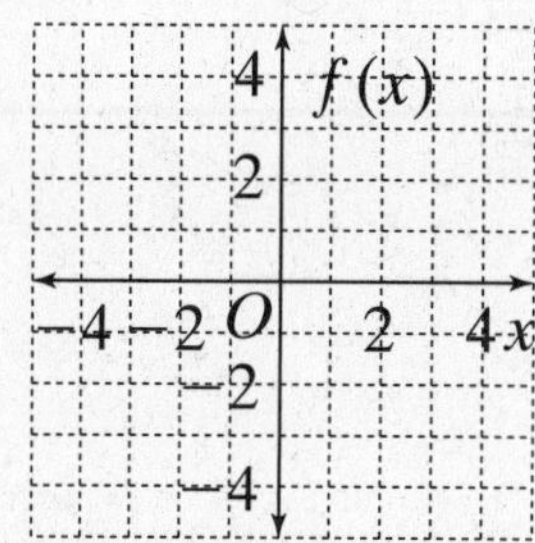

7. $y = -2 - 3x$

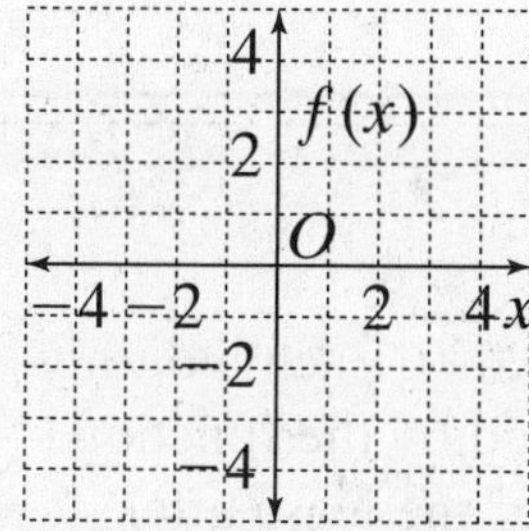

8. $y = 5 - 0.2x$

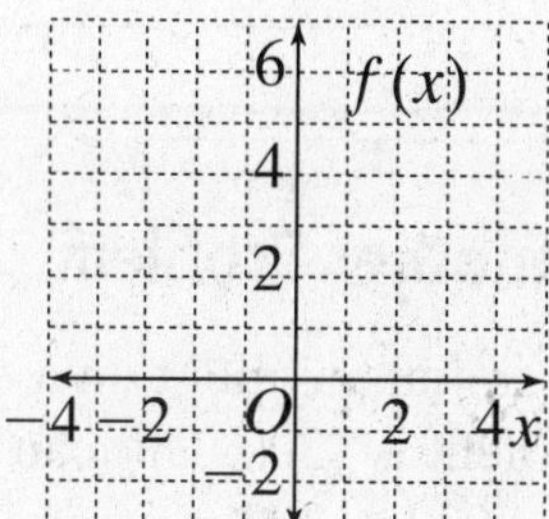

Name ______________________ Class ______________ Date ______________

11-5 • Guided Problem Solving

GPS Student Page 537, Exercise 17:

Science The height of a burning candle depends on how long the candle has been burning. For one type of candle, the function $h = 8 - \frac{1}{2}t$ gives the candle's height h (in centimeters) as a function of the time t the candle has burned (in hours).

a. Graph the function.

b. What was the original height of the candle?

c. What is the greatest amount of time the candle can burn?

Understand

1. What do the variables h and t represent?

____

Plan and Carry Out

2. Graph the function on a separate sheet of paper.

3. What does the x-axis represent?

____

____

4. What does the y-axis represent?

____

____

5. What was the original height of the candle? How can you tell?

____

6. How long can the candle burn? How can you tell?

____

Check

7. How can you check your answer?

____

____

Solve Another Problem

8. The initial payment on a car lease is \$3,000. Each monthly payment is \$300. This can be represented by the function $c = 3{,}000 + 300m$, where c is the cost of the lease after m months. Graph the function on a separate sheet of paper. How many months will it be until the cost of the lease is \$4,800?

____

Name ______________________ Class ______________ Date ______________

Practice 11-6

Writing Rules for Linear Functions

Write a linear function rule for each situation. Identify the *x* and *y* variables.

1. Amy sells tote bags at a craft fair for a day. She pays $50 to rent a booth. The materials and labor cost on each tote bag is $3.50. Her expenses for the day depend on how many tote bags she sells.

____

2. Ms. Watson receives a base pay of $150 plus a commission of $45 on each appliance that she sells. Her total pay depends on how many appliances she sells.

____

Does the data in each table represent a linear function? If so, write the function rule.

3.

x	0	1	2	3	4
y	2	5	8	11	14

____

4.

x	0	1	2	3	4
y	0	2	5	2	0

____

5.

x	−2	0	4	6	8
y	−1	−3	−7	−9	−11

____

6.

x	−3	−2	−1	0	1
y	−1	1	2	2	2

____

Use the slope and *y*-intercept to write a linear function rule for each graph.

7. 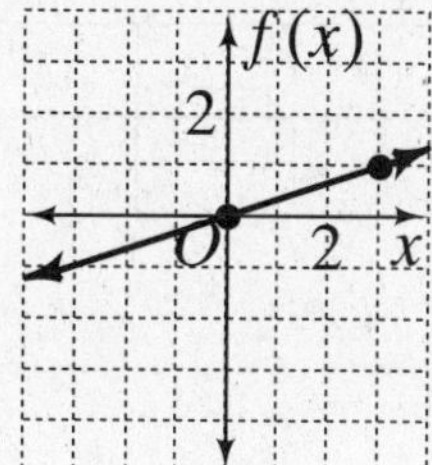

____

8. 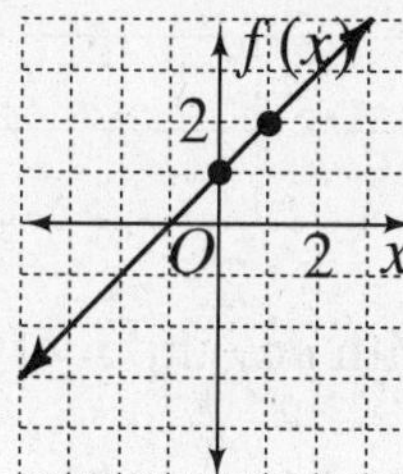

____

9. 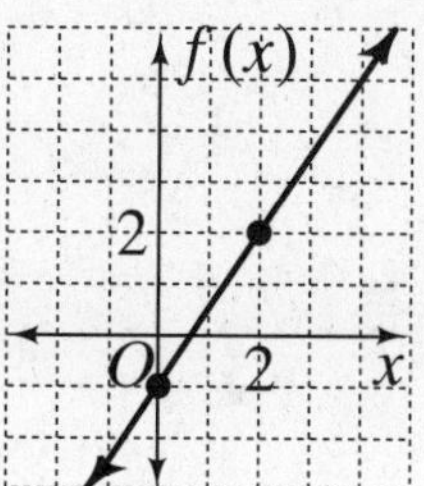

____

10. 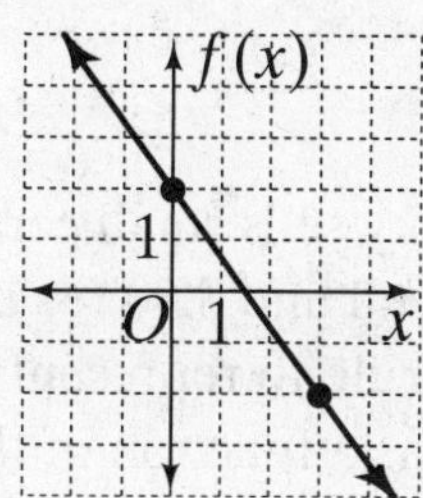

____

Name ______________________ Class ______________ Date ______________

11-6 • Guided Problem Solving

GPS Student Page 543, Exercise 11:

Art At a fair, an artist draws caricatures. He pays the fair $30 for space to set up his table and $2 for each drawing that he sells.

a. Write a function rule to represent the artist's total payment to the fair as a function of the number of drawings he sells.

b. **Reasoning** What input is paired with the output $54? What does this input represent? Express the input-output pair in the form $f(\square) = \square$.

Understand

1. What is a caricature?

____

____

Plan and Carry Out

2. How much does the artist pay the fair for space rental and each drawing he sells?

____

3. Which expression shows the amount of money the artist will pay the fair if *c* represents the number of caricatures he sells?

____

4. Complete the table below.

Number of Caricatures	1	2	3	4	5	6	7	8	9	10	11	12
Total Payment to Fair												

5. What input is paired with an output of $54? _______________

Check

6. How could you have found the input value another way?

____

Solve Another Problem

7. At the craft show, Becky sells small ceramic, painted balls. She pays $25 for booth rental and $.50 for each ceramic ball that she sells. Write a function rule to represent her total payment to the craft show organizers as a function of the number of ceramic balls she sells.

____

Name ______________________ Class ______________ Date ______________

Practice 11-7

Quadratic and Other Nonlinear Functions

Write a quadratic function rule for the data in each table.

1.

x	0	1	2	3	4
f(x)	3	4	7	12	19

____

2.

x	−2	−1	0	1	2
f(x)	−8	−2	0	−2	−8

____

3.

x	−1	0	1	2	3
f(x)	4	0	4	16	36

____

4.

x	−10	−5	0	5	10
f(x)	95	20	−5	20	95

____

Complete the table for each function. Then graph the function.

5. $f(x) = x^2 + 1$

x	$x^2 + 1 = f(x)$
−3	
−2	
−1	
0	
1	
2	
3	

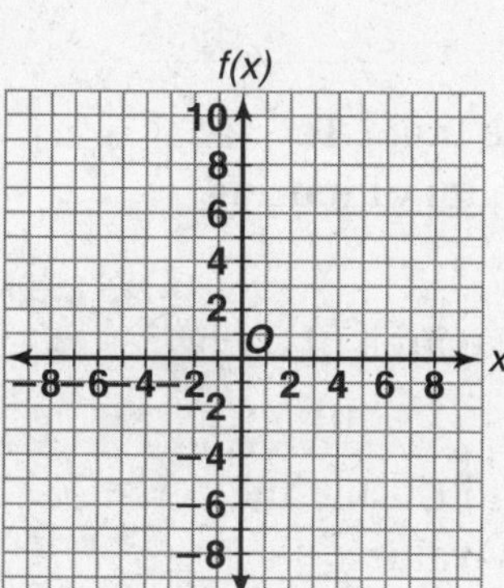

6. $f(x) = 4 - x^2$

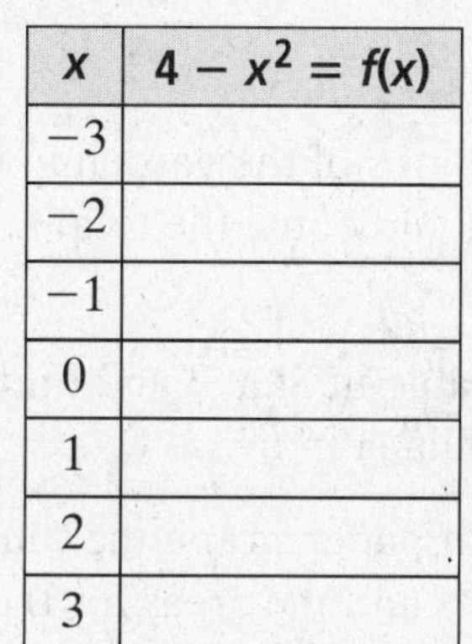

x	$4 - x^2 = f(x)$
−3	
−2	
−1	
0	
1	
2	
3	

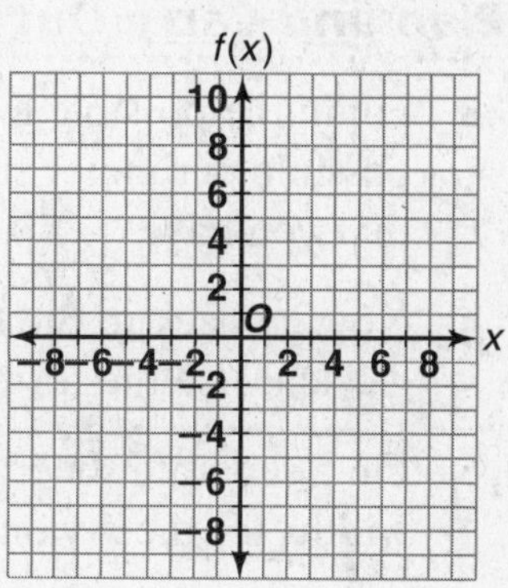

7. $f(x) = \frac{20}{x}$

x	f(x)
2	
4	
5	
10	

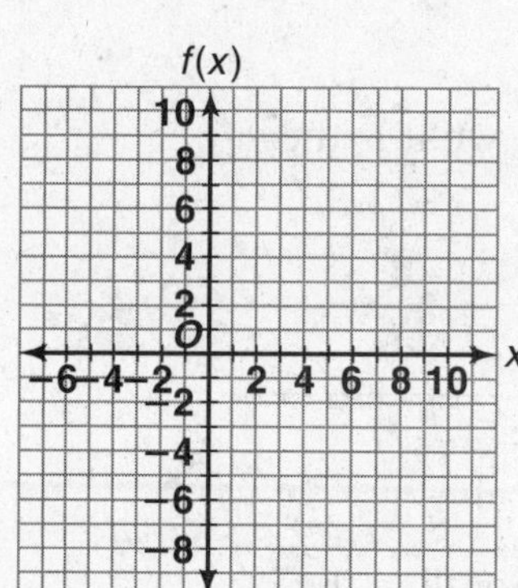

8. $f(x) = 2^x - 1$

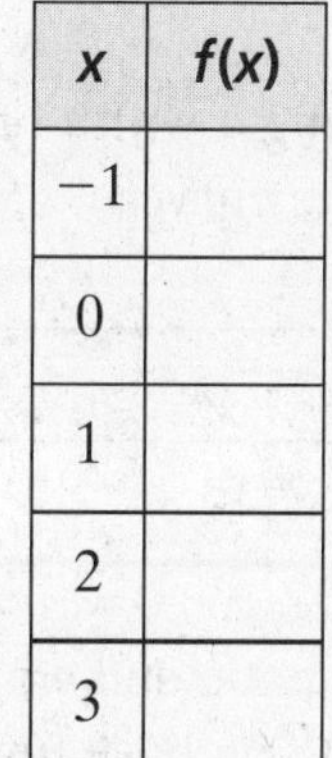

x	f(x)
−1	
0	
1	
2	
3	

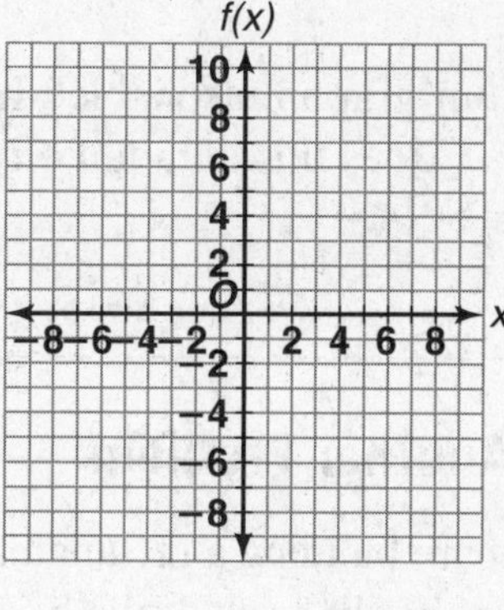

Does the point (2, 2) lie on the graph of each function?

9. $f(x) = 2x - 2$ ______________

10. $f(x) = \left(\frac{1}{2}\right)^x$ ______________

11. $f(x) = x^2 - x$ ______________

12. $f(x) = \frac{4}{x}$ ______________

Name ______________________ Class ______________ Date ______________

11-7 • Guided Problem Solving

GPS Student Page 548, Exercise 19:

Gardening Suppose you have 12 yards of fencing to enclose a rectangular garden plot. Complete the table at the right to show area as a function of the garden's width. Then graph the function.

Width w	Length l	Area A
1	5	
2	4	
3		
4		
5		

Understand

1. What is the greatest perimeter the garden can have?

____

2. What two things are you being asked to do?

____

____

Plan and Carry Out

3. Fill in the possible lengths of the garden in the table. The possible perimeter should equal the total amount of fencing that you have.
4. Now go back to the table in Step 3 and find the area of each garden. Use the formula $A = lw$.
5. On a separate sheet of paper, graph the function, using the widths for the x-values and the areas for the y-values.

Check

6. Is your graph reasonable? Using a width of 3.5 yards, what is the area? Does this data fall on the curve?

____

____

Solve Another Problem

7. You are building a rectangular patio and would like to outline the perimeter in brick. If the bricks you have total 40 feet in length, what would the area of the patio be for the following widths: 6 ft, 8 ft, 10 ft, 12 ft, and 14 ft?

____

11A: Graphic Organizer

For use before Lesson 11-1

Study Skill Your textbook includes a Skills Handbook with extra problems and questions. Working these exercises is a good way to review material and prepare for the next chapter.

Write your answers.

1. What is the chapter title? ________________
2. How many lessons are there in this chapter? ________________
3. What is the topic of the Test-Taking Strategies page?

____

4. Complete the graphic organizer below as you work through the chapter.
   - In the center, write the title of the chapter.
   - When you begin a lesson, write the lesson name in a rectangle.
   - When you complete a lesson, write a skill or key concept in a circle linked to that lesson block.
   - When you complete the chapter, use this graphic organizer to help you review.

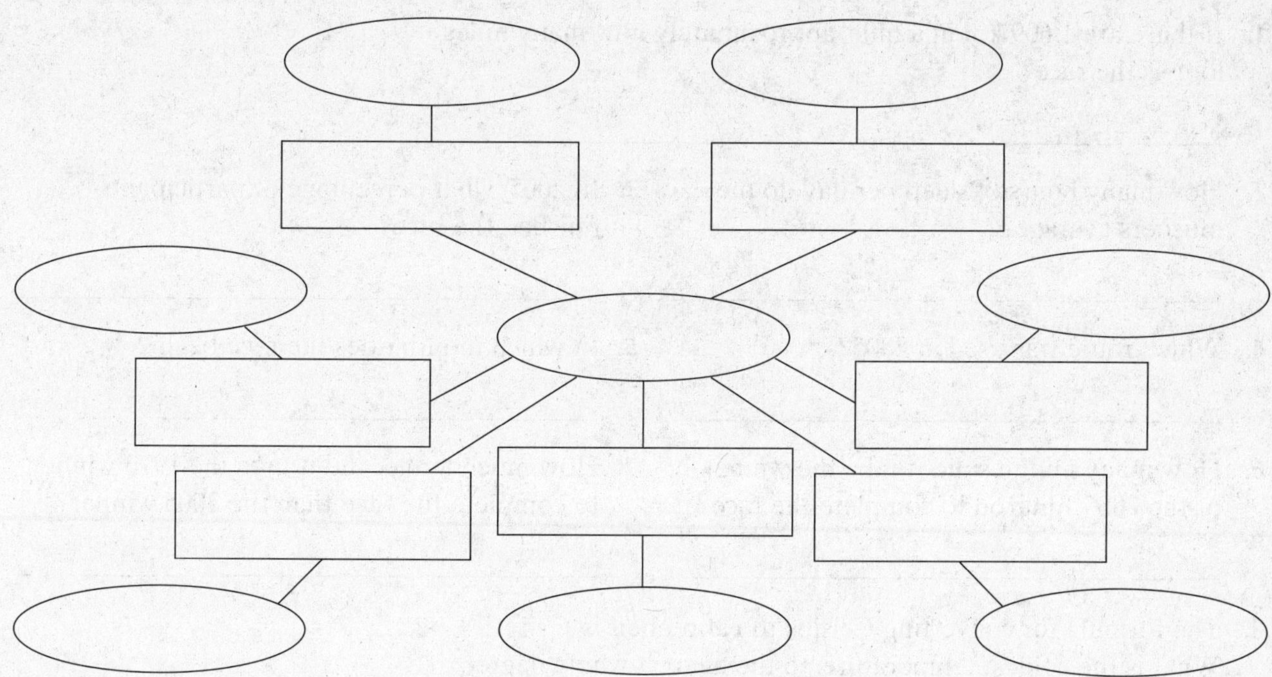

Name ______________________ Class ______________ Date ______________

11B: Reading Comprehension

For use after Lesson 11-2

Study Skill Pay attention to detail when you read. Try to pick out the important points as you go along.

Read the paragraph below and answer the questions.

The Iditarod is an annual dog sledding competition that begins the first Saturday in March. This event, which covers about 1,850 km, begins in Anchorage and ends in Nome, Alaska. There are two possible routes: a northern route that is used in even-numbered years and a southern route that is used in odd-numbered ones. The weather is often unpredictable, with wind chill temperatures as low as −73°C. The drivers ("mushers") average approximately two hours of sleep each day. In 2005, there were 79 participants who started the race, but only 63 finished. Mushers are required to carry everything they need for the journey in their sleds. A fully loaded sled weighs approximately 150 lb. The first Iditarod was held in 1973 and it took the winner 20 days to complete. In 2005, the winner completed the course in 9 days, 18 hours, and 39 minutes.

1. If there are 1.609 km in a mile, approximately how many miles long is the race?

   ____

2. How many hours of sleep per day do the mushers average?

   ____

3. In 2005, what percentage of participants finished the race?

   ____

4. Which route was used in 2005?

   ____

5. In which month does the race begin?

   ____

6. How many minutes did it take the winner of the 2005 Iditarod to complete the race?

   ____

7. How much longer did it take the 1973 winner to complete the race than the 2005 winner?

   ____

8. The formula for converting Celsius to Fahrenheit is $F = \frac{9}{5}C + 32$. What is the coldest temperature, to the nearest whole degree Fahrenheit, that the racers must endure?

   ____

9. **High-Use Academic Words** What is a *detail,* as mentioned in the study skill?

   a. a small part or feature

   b. a short statement of the main part

Name ______________________ Class ______________ Date ______________

11C: Reading/Writing Math Symbols

For use after Lesson 11-3

Study Skill Work in a well-lit, quiet spot with the proper materials.

Write the meaning of the following mathematical expressions or equations.

1. $P(B)$ ______________________
2. $P(\text{not } A)$ ______________________
3. $\angle S \cong \angle R$ ______________________
4. $n!$ ______________________
5. ${}_8C_3$ ______________________
6. $y < 15$ ______________________
7. $(-16 + 4^2) = 0$ ______________________
8. $12 - x$ ______________________
9. $\sqrt{64} = 8$ ______________________
10. $|-41| = 41$ ______________________
11. $\frac{3}{4} = 75\%$ ______________________
12. $f(x) = x + 3$ ______________________
13. $\triangle ABC \cong \triangle DEF$ ______________________
14. $\pi \approx 3.14$ ______________________
15. $3:4 = 9:12$ ______________________
16. $\sqrt{48} \approx 7$ ______________________
17. $A = bh$ ______________________

Name ________________ Class ________________ Date ________________

11D: Visual Vocabulary Practice

For use after Lesson 11-7

Study Skill Mathematics builds on itself, so build a strong foundation.

Concept List

geometric sequence	parabola	arithmetic sequence
common ratio	slope of a line	slope-intercept form
term	quadratic function	y-intercept

Write the concept that best describes each exercise. Choose from the concept list above.

1. 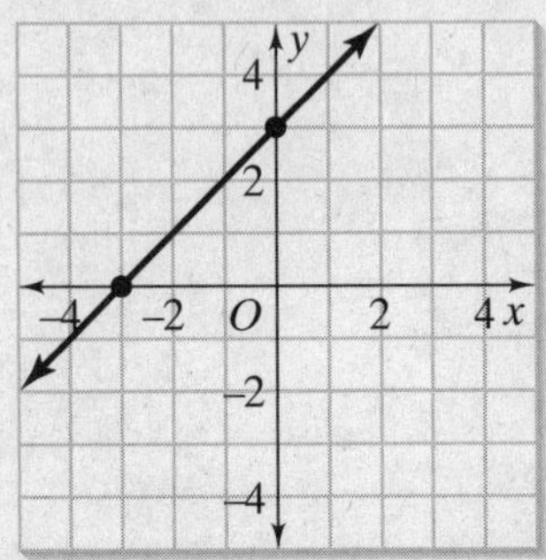 3 for the line in the graph ________	2. 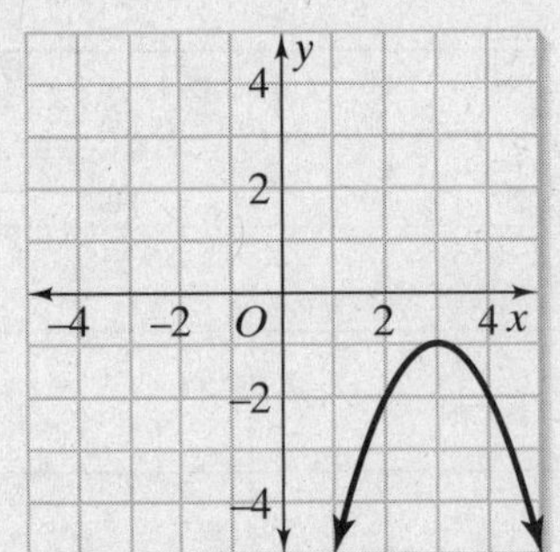 ________	3. 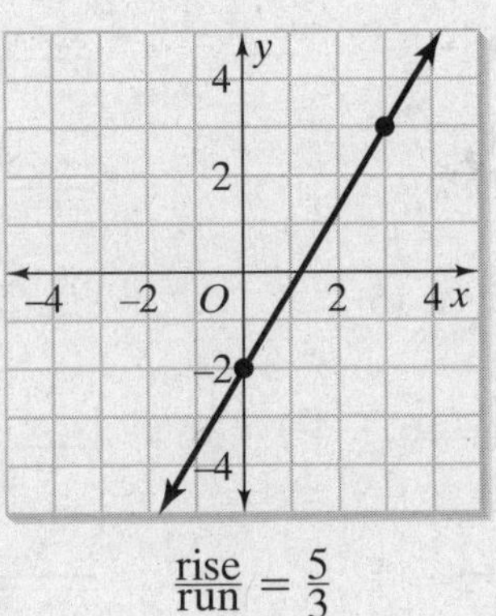 $\frac{\text{rise}}{\text{run}} = \frac{5}{3}$ ________
4. $h(x) = \frac{1}{4}x^2 - 8$ ________	5. $2, 1, \frac{1}{2}, \frac{1}{4}, \frac{1}{8}, \ldots$ ________	6. In the sequence $1, -3, 9, -27, \ldots$, this is -3. ________
7. $1, \frac{1}{2}, 0, -\frac{1}{2}, -1, \ldots$ ________	8. $y = mx + b$ ________	9. In the sequence 2, 5, 8, 11, . . ., the next one is 14. ________

Name ______________________ Class ______________ Date ______________

11E: Vocabulary Check

For use after Lesson 11-5

Study Skill Strengthen your vocabulary. Use these pages and add cues and summaries by applying the Cornell Notetaking style.

Write the definition for each word or term at the right. To check your work, fold the paper back along the dotted line to see the correct answers.

______________________	discrete data
______________________	continuous data
______________________	sequence
______________________	slope
______________________	function

Name ______________________ Class ______________ Date ______________

11E: Vocabulary Check (continued)

For use after Lesson 11-5

Write the vocabulary word or term for each definition. To check your work, fold the paper forward along the dotted line to see the correct answers.

data that involve a count of items ______________________

data where the numbers between any two data values have meaning ______________________

a set of numbers that follow a pattern ______________________

a ratio that describes the steepness of lines in the coordinate plane ______________________

a relationship that assigns exactly one output value for each input value ______________________

Name ______________________ Class ______________ Date ______________

11F: Vocabulary Review Puzzle

For use with the Chapter Review

Study Skill Read problems carefully. Pay special attention to units when working with measurements.

Complete the crossword puzzle below. For help, use the Glossary in your textbook.

Here are the words you will use to complete this crossword puzzle:

geometric	circumference	equilateral	right	scalene
combination	permutation	arithmetic	coefficient	mean
parabola	perpendicular	function	linear	solution

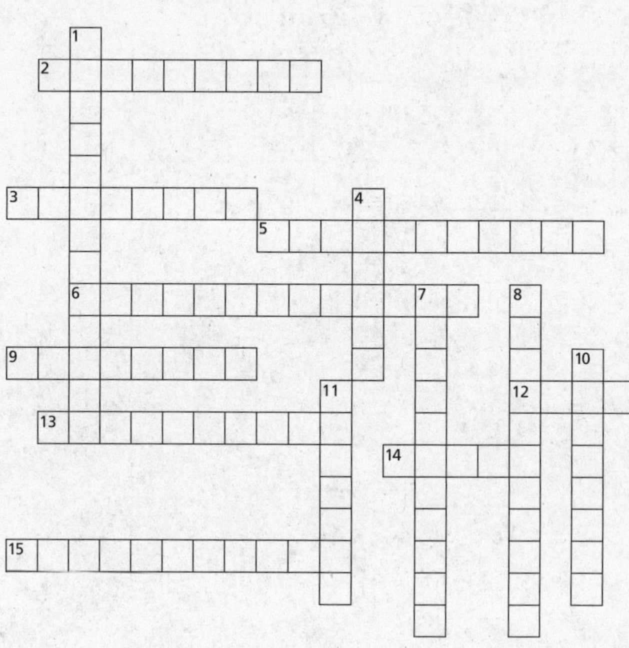

ACROSS

2. sequence in which each term is found by multiplying the previous term by a fixed number
3. relationship that assigns exactly one output value to each input value
5. triangle with three congruent sides
6. distance around a circle
9. value that makes an equation true
12. sum of the values in a data set divided by the number of items in the data set
13. sequence in which each term is found by adding a fixed number to the previous term
14. angle measuring exactly 90°
15. arrangement of items in which the order of the items is not considered

DOWN

1. two lines that intersect and form a right angle
4. type of function whose points lie in a line
7. number that is multiplied by a variable
8. arrangement of objects in a particular order
10. shape of the graph of a quadratic function
11. triangle with no congruent sides

Name ______________________ Class ______________ Date ______________

Practice 12-1

Exploring Polynomials

In exercises 1–5:

 represents x^2,  represents x, ☐ represents 1,

 represents $-x^2$, ▮ represents $-x$, ■ represents -1.

Write a variable expression for each model.

1. 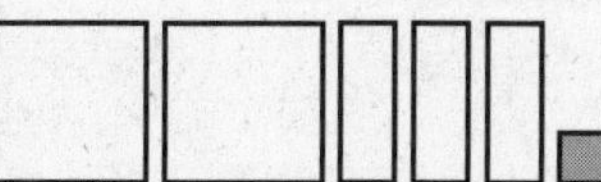

____

2. 

____

3. 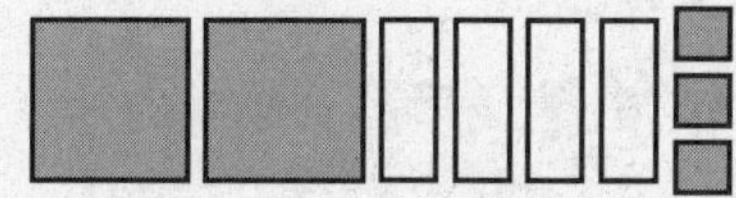

____

Write and simplify the polynomials represented by each model.

4. 

____

5. 

____

Simplify each polynomial.

6. $2x^2 - x^2 + 7x - 2x + 5$

7. $3x^2 + 2x - 8x + 6$

8. $x^2 - 4x^2 + x + 5x - 8 + 3$

9. $x^2 + 6x + x^2 - 4x + 1 - 5$

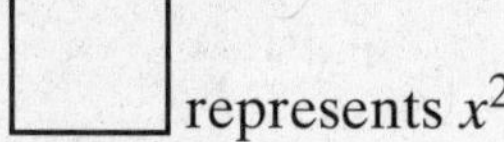
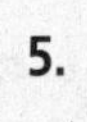

Name ______________________ Class ______________ Date ______________

12-1 • Guided Problem Solving

GPS Student Page 564, Exercise 18:

Science A ball is projected upward at a speed of 48 feet per second. Its height in feet, after t seconds, is given by the polynomial $48t - 16t^2$. Evaluate the polynomial to find the height after 3 seconds.

Understand

1. Circle the polynomial that you are to evaluate.
2. What are you asked to evaluate the polynomial for?

   ____

Plan and Carry Out

3. Rewrite the polynomial, substituting the given height for t.

   ____

4. What operation will you do first?

   ____

5. Write the expression, performing the operation in Step 4.

   ____

6. Which operation will you do next?

   ____

7. Perform the operations in Step 7 to find your answer.

   ____

Check

8. Is your answer reasonable? How far has the ball traveled before it hits the ground?

   ____

Solve Another Problem

9. A quarterback throws a football 64 ft per second. Its height in feet, after t seconds, is given by the polynomial $32t - 16t^2$. Could this pass be caught in the air after 2 seconds? Explain.

   ____

Name ________________ Class ________________ Date ________________

Practice 12-2

Adding and Subtracting Polynomials

Name the coefficients in each polynomial.

1. $x^2 - 3x + 5$ ________________

2. $b^2 - 4b + 3$ ________________

3. $-2a^2 + 4a - 6$ ________________

4. $x^3 - 2x^2 + 4x$ ________________

5. $14y^3 + 4y + 0$ ________________

6. $-11s^2 - 9s + 2$ ________________

Find each sum.

7. $(5x - 4) + (6x + 2)$ ________________

8. $(7x^2 + 3x - 5) + (-4x^2 - x + 4)$ ________________

9. $(2x^2 + 8) + (3x^2 - 9)$ ________________

10. $(5x^2 - 3x + 3) + (4x - 5)$ ________________

Write the perimeter of each figure as a polynomial. Simplify.

11.

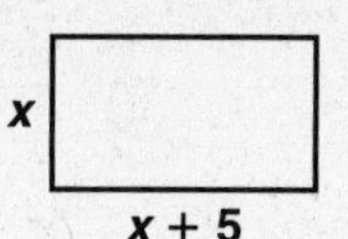

____

12.

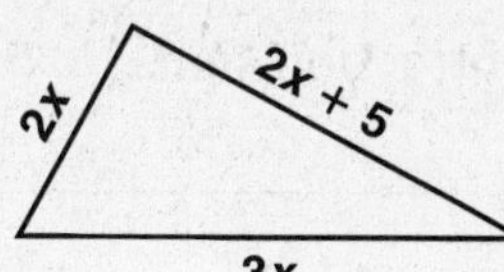

____

13.

x + 6

3x – 5

____

Find each difference.

14. $(4x^2 + 1) - (x^2 + 3)$ ________________

15. $(3x^2 + 7x - 5) - (x^2 - 4x - 1)$ ________________

16. $(6x^2 + 8x + 1) - (4x^2 - 8x + 7)$ ________________

Name ____________________ Class ____________________ Date ____________________

12-2 • Guided Problem Solving

GPS Student Page 569, Exercise 25:

Pools A homeowner is planning a deck but has not decided on the final dimensions. The rectangular structure will have an area of $12x^2 + 4x$ square feet. The homeowner plans to have a pool with an area of $6x^2 - 12x$ square feet in the deck. Subtract the polynomials to find the area of the deck around the pool.

Understand

1. Circle the information you need to solve the problem.
2. Underline what you are asked to do.

Plan and Carry Out

3. What is the proposed area of the deck? ____________________
4. What is the proposed area of the pool? ____________________
5. What do you need to remember when subtracting polynomials?

____

____

6. Write the two expressions, using the subtraction sign.

____

7. Add the opposite of each term in the second polynomial.

____

8. Group like terms. ____________________
9. Simplify. ____________________

Check

10. How can you check to see if your answer is reasonable?

____

____

____

Solve Another Problem

11. The area of a large rectangular barn is $16x^2 + 6x$. A rectangular workshop is part of the barn and has an area of $4x^2 - 5x$. Subtract the polynomials to find the area of the remaining barn floor.

____

Name ______ Class ______ Date ______

Practice 12-3

Exponents and Multiplication

Write each expression using a single exponent.

1. $3^2 \cdot 3^5$ ______
2. $1^3 \cdot 1^4$ ______
3. $a^1 \cdot a^2$ ______
4. $(-y)^3 \cdot (-y)^2$ ______
5. $(3x) \cdot (3x)$ ______
6. $4.5^8 \cdot 4.5^2$ ______
7. $3^3 \cdot 3 \cdot 3^4$ ______
8. $x^2y \cdot xy^2$ ______
9. $5x^2 \cdot x^6 \cdot x^3$ ______

Find each product. Write the answers in scientific notation.

10. $(3 \times 10^4)(5 \times 10^6)$ ______
11. $(7 \times 10^2)(6 \times 10^4)$ ______
12. $(4 \times 10^5)(7 \times 10^8)$ ______
13. $(9.1 \times 10^6)(3 \times 10^9)$ ______
14. $(8.4 \times 10^9)(5 \times 10^7)$ ______
15. $(5 \times 10^3)(4 \times 10^6)$ ______
16. $(7.2 \times 10^8)(2 \times 10^3)$ ______
17. $(1.4 \times 10^5)(4 \times 10^{11})$ ______

Replace each __?__ with =, <, or >.

18. 3^8 __?__ $3 \cdot 3^7$ ______
19. 49 __?__ $7^2 \cdot 7^2$ ______
20. $5^3 \cdot 5^4$ __?__ 25^2 ______
21. Double the number 4.6×10^{15}. Write the answer in scientific notation. ______
22. Triple the number 2.3×10^3. Write the answer in scientific notation. ______

Name ______________________ Class ______________ Date ______________

12-3 • Guided Problem Solving

GPS Student Page 574, Exercise 40:

Geography The Sahara is a desert of about 3.5 million square miles. There are about 2.79×10^7 square feet in a square mile. About how many square feet does the Sahara cover? Write your answer in scientific notation.

Understand

1. What are you being asked to do?

____

____

2. What form will your answer be in? ______________

Plan and Carry Out

3. Write 3.5 million in standard form. ______________
4. Write 3.5 million in scientific notation. ______________
5. To convert from square miles to square feet, what operation will you use?

____

6. Write the conversion for square feet to square miles.

____

7. Convert the square miles of the Sahara to square feet.

____

Check

8. Use another method to solve the problem. Does your answer check?

____

____

____

Solve Another Problem

9. The human body contains about 3.2×10^4 microliters of blood per pound of body weight. How many microliters of blood would a 185-pound man have circulating in his body? Write your answer in scientific notation.

____

Name ____________ Class ____________ Date ____________

Practice 12-4

Multiplying Polynomials

Find the area of each figure.

1. 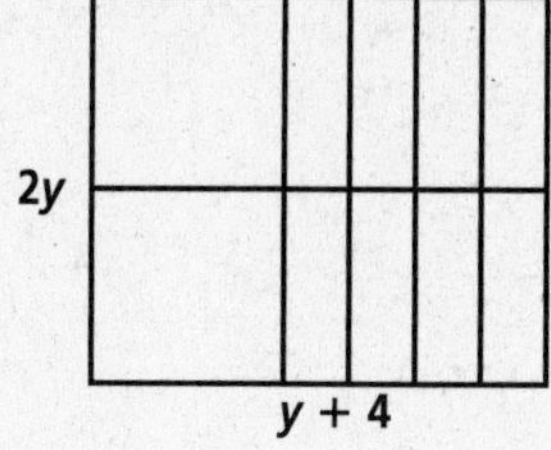

2. 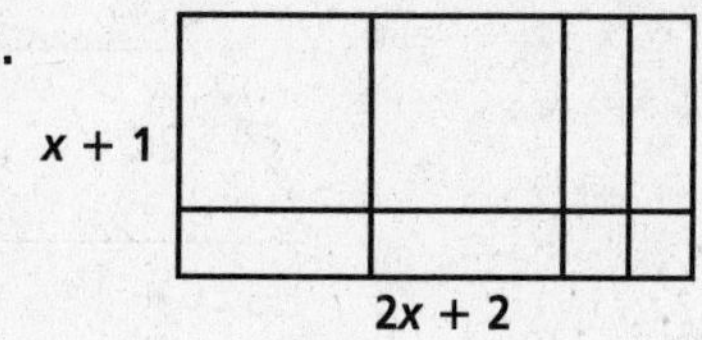

3. 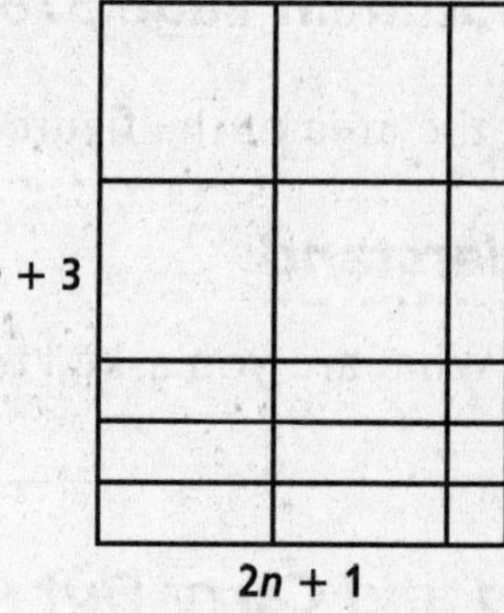

Simplify each expression.

4. $x^2 \cdot x^2$

5. $7x \cdot 2x$

6. $(-3t)t$

7. $5m^2 \cdot 2m^2$

8. $(-x)(7x^2)$

9. $(3x^2)(-2x^3)$

Use the Distributive Property to simplify each expression.

10. $x(x + 2)$

11. $3b(b - 5)$

12. $2x^2(x + 9)$

13. $2(a^2 + 8a + 1)$

14. $2x^2(4x + 1)$

15. $3l(l^2 + 4l - 6)$

Find the area of each figure.

16. 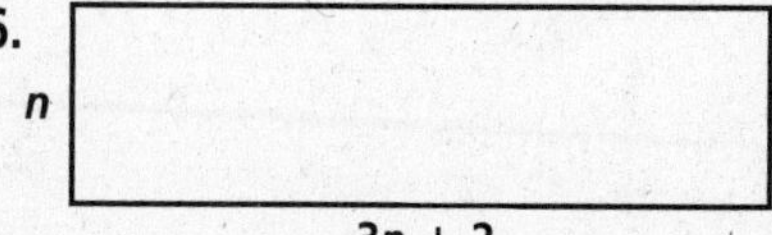

17. 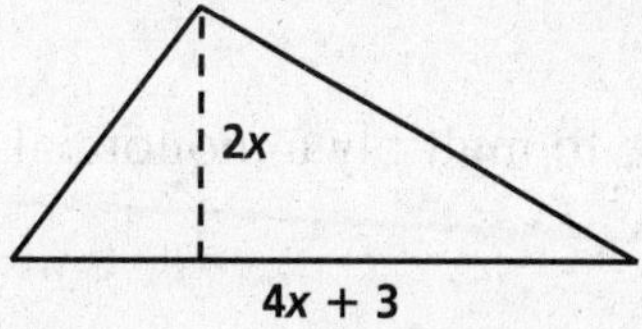

18. 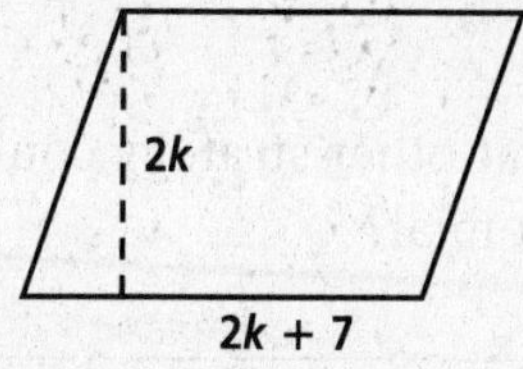

Simplify each expression.

19. $4x(-x^2 + 2x - 9)$

20. $-6x(-2x^2 - 3x + 1)$

Name ____________________ Class ____________ Date ____________

12-4 • Guided Problem Solving

GPS Student Page 579, Exercise 25:

Find the area of the figure.

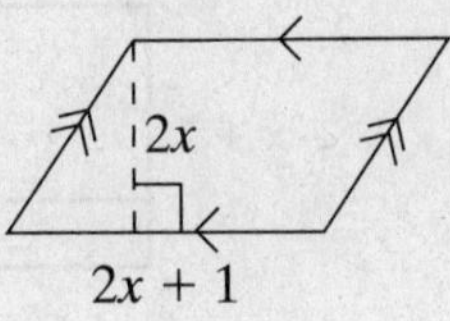

Understand

1. What are you asked to do?

____

Plan and Carry Out

2. What shape is the figure?

____

3. What is the formula for finding the area of the figure?

____

4. What is the length of the base in the figure?

____

5. What is the height of the figure?

____

6. Substitute the base and height into the formula.

____

7. How do you multiply a monomial and a binomial?

____

8. Simplify the formula in Step 6.

____

Check

9. What other strategy could you use to multiply a monomial by a binomial?

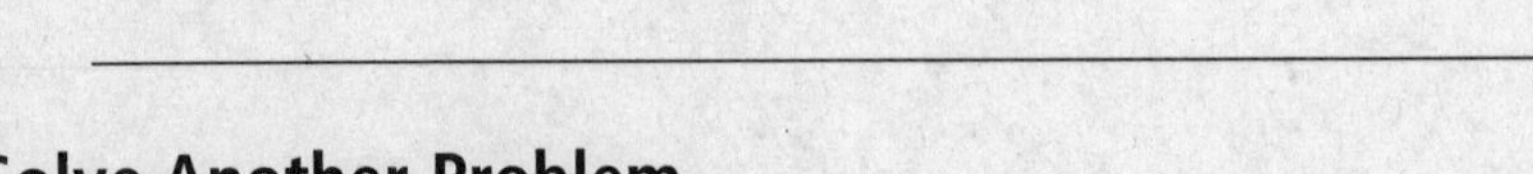

Solve Another Problem

10. Find the area of the figure. ____________________

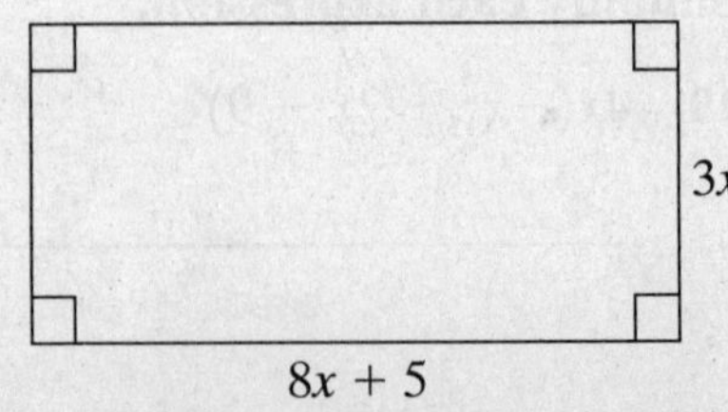

Name ______ Class ______ Date ______

Practice 12-5

Exponents and Division

Simplify each expression.

1. 8^{-2}
2. $(-3)^0$
3. 5^{-1}
4. 18^0
5. 2^{-5}
6. 3^{-3}
7. 2^{-3}
8. 5^{-2}
9. $\frac{4^4}{4}$
10. $8^6 \div 8^8$
11. $\frac{(-3)^6}{(-3)^8}$
12. $\frac{8^4}{8^0}$
13. $1^{15} \div 1^{18}$
14. $7 \div 7^4$
15. $\frac{(-4)^8}{(-4)^4}$
16. $\frac{10^9}{10^{12}}$
17. $\frac{b^{12}}{b^4}$
18. $\frac{g^9}{g^{15}}$
19. $x^{16} \div x^7$
20. $v^{20} \div v^{25}$

Complete each equation.

21. $\frac{1}{3^5} = 3^{?}$
22. $\frac{1}{(-2)^7} = -2^{?}$
23. $\frac{1}{x^2} = x^{?}$
24. $\frac{1}{-125} = (-5)^{?}$
25. $\frac{1}{1,000} = 10^{?}$
26. $\frac{5^{10}}{?} = 5^5$
27. $\frac{z^{?}}{z^8} = z^{-3}$
28. $\frac{q^5}{?} = q^{-7}$

Is each statement true or false? Explain your reasoning.

29. $(-1)^3 = 1^{-3}$
30. $3^{-1} \cdot 3^{-1} = 3^1$
31. $2^2 \cdot 2^{-2} = 1$
32. $7^2 \cdot (-7)^3 = (-7)^{-6}$

Name ______________________ Class ______________ Date ______________

12-5 • Guided Problem Solving

GPS Student Page 584, Exercise 24:

Astronomy The Sun's diameter is 1.39×10^6 kilometers. Earth's diameter is 1.28×10^4 kilometers. How many times greater is the Sun's diameter than Earth's diameter?

Understand

1. Which diameter is larger? ______________________
2. What are you being asked to find?

____

____

Plan and Carry Out

3. The diameters are in scientific notation, and the numbers 1.28 and 1.39 are close in value, so what do you need to compare?

____

4. When dividing powers with the same base, what do you do to the exponents?

____

5. Subtract the exponents and write the power in standard form.

____

6. How many times greater is the Sun's diameter than Earth's?

____

Check

7. What other strategy could you use to find the answer?

____

____

____

Solve Another Problem

8. When you donate a pint of blood, you lose about 2.3×10^{12} red blood cells. If your body can produce about 2×10^6 red blood cells per second, about how many seconds would it take for your body to replenish the red blood cells lost through donation? Write your answer in standard form.

____

Name ______________________ Class ______________ Date ____________

12A: Graphic Organizer

For use before Lesson 12-1

Study Skill Your textbook includes a Skills Handbook with extra problems and questions. Working these exercises is a good way to review material and prepare for the next chapter.

Write your answers.

1. What is the chapter title? ______________________
2. How many lessons are there in this chapter? ______________________
3. What is the topic of the Test-Taking Strategies page?

____

4. Complete the graphic organizer below as you work through the chapter.
   - In the center, write the title of the chapter.
   - When you begin a lesson, write the lesson name in a rectangle.
   - When you complete a lesson, write a skill or key concept in a circle linked to that lesson block.
   - When you complete the chapter, use this graphic organizer to help you review.

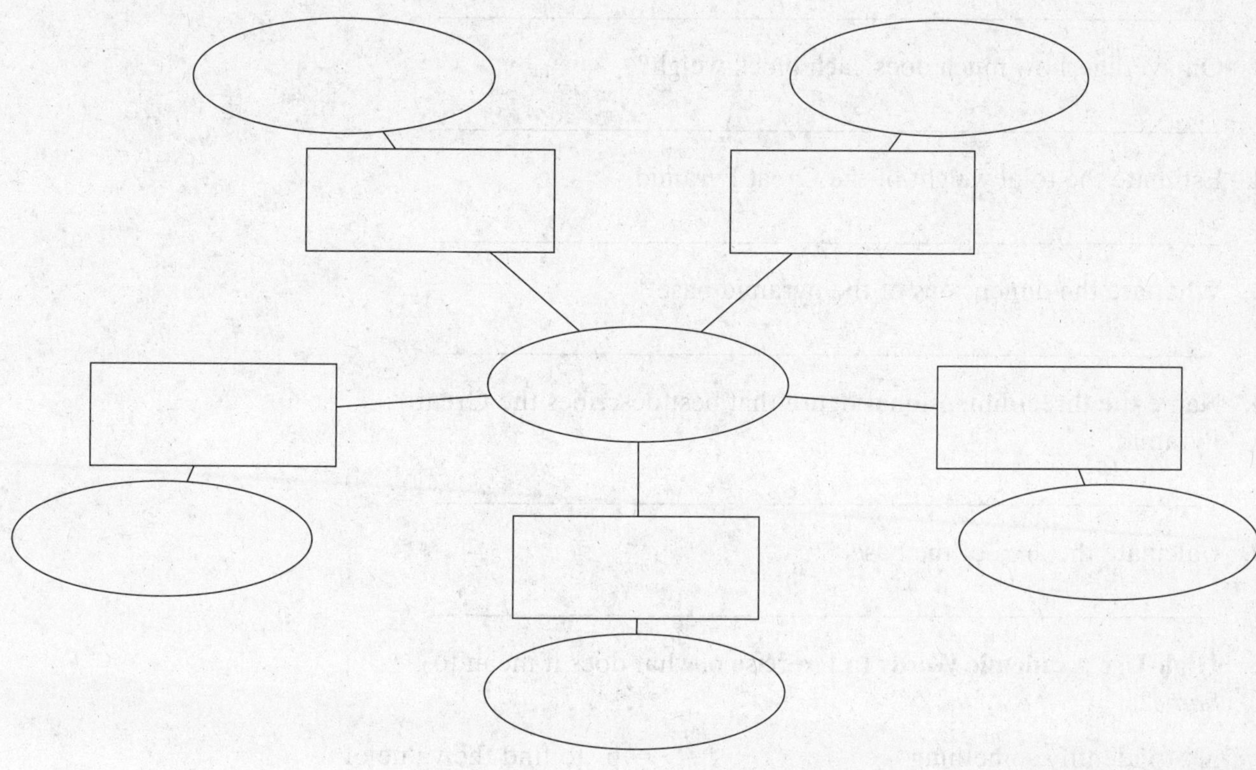

Vocabulary and Study Skills

Name ______________________ Class ______________ Date ______________

12B: Reading Comprehension

For use after Lesson 12-2

Study Skill Attitude is everything.

Read the paragraph below and answer the questions that follow.

The Great Pyramid of Giza, one of the Seven Wonders of the World, is located just outside the city of Cairo, Egypt. It was built between 2589 and 2566 B.C. by the pharaoh Khufu. The walls are set at an incline of approximately 52 degrees. The square base is 745 feet on each side and the height is 449 feet. The pyramid is oriented to face the four cardinal directions: north, south, east, and west. It is composed of more than 2.3 million stone blocks that weigh about 2.5 tons each on average. The heaviest stones weigh almost 9 tons.

1. How long did it take to build the Great Pyramid?

   ____

2. About how many stone blocks were used? Give your answer in scientific notation.

   ____

3. On average, how much does each block weigh?

   ____

4. Estimate the total weight of the Great Pyramid.

   ____

5. What are the dimensions of the pyramid base?

   ____

6. Name the three-dimensional figure that best describes the Great Pyramid.

   ____

7. Calculate the area of the base.

   ____

8. **High-Use Academic Words** In Exercise 6, what does it mean to *name*?

   a. to identify something

   b. to find the value of

Name ______________________ Class ______________ Date ______________

12C: Reading/Writing Math Symbols

For use after Lesson 12-5

Study Skill Appreciate your efforts even when you have yet to see them pay off.

Match each expression in Column A to its meaning in Column B.

Column A	Column B
1. $6^{(4-2)}$	**A.** $1 - P(6)$
2. $6!$	**B.** 1
3. 6^{-2}	**C.** a^4
4. 0.06×10^4	**D.** 600
5. $P(\text{not } 6)$	**E.** $\frac{1}{6^2}$
6. $(-6a)^0$	**F.** $6 \times 5 \times 4 \times 3 \times 2 \times 1$
7. $\frac{a^6}{a^2}$	**G.** 6^2

Write each statement using appropriate mathematical symbols.

8. five raised to the *n* plus three power

____

9. The square root of 168 is approximately thirteen.

____

10. *y* is equal to three times *x* plus eleven.

____

11. eight and sixty-five hundredths, multiplied by ten raised to the ninth power

____

12. the quantity seven plus *z*, squared

____

13. the number of ways 3 objects can be chosen from 25 where order does matter

____

14. Line segment *XY* is congruent to line segment *AB*.

____

Name ______________________ Class ______________ Date ______________

12D: Visual Vocabulary Practice

For use after Lesson 12-5

Study Skill Making sense of mathematical symbols is like reading a foreign language that uses different letters.

Concept List

binomial	constant	sequence
coefficient	monomial	polynomial
common difference	like terms	linear function

Write the concept that best describes each exercise. Choose from the concept list above.

1. $3x^6 - 3x^4 + 3x^2 - 3$ __________	**2.** -1 for the variable b in the expression $2a - b + c - 2$ __________	**3.** $f(x) = -2x + 11$ __________
4. In the sequence $-10, -9, -8, -7, \ldots,$ this is 1. __________	**5.** $2y$ and $-8y$ in the expression $2y + 3y^2 - 8y - 5$ __________	**6.** -4 in the expression $-\frac{4}{5}x^5 - 6x^4 + 4x - 4$ __________
7. $\frac{z^3}{3}$ __________	**8.** $\frac{5}{6}a^4 + 14$ __________	**9.** $2, -4, 8, -10, 20, \ldots$ __________

12E: Vocabulary Check

For use after Lesson 12-4

Study Skill Strengthen your vocabulary. Use these pages and add cues and summaries by applying the Cornell Notetaking style.

Write the definition for each word or term at the right. To check your work, fold the paper back along the dotted line to see the correct answers.

______________________________ polynomial

______________________________ binomial

______________________________ coefficient

______________________________ constant

______________________________ monomial

12E: Vocabulary Check (continued)

For use after Lesson 12-4

Write the vocabulary word or term for each definition. To check your work, fold the paper forward along the dotted line to see the correct answers.

one term or the sum or difference of two or more terms ______

a polynomial that has two terms ______

the numerical factor in any term of a polynomial ______

any term in a polynomial that does not contain a variable ______

a polynomial that only has one term ______

Name ______________________ Class ______________ Date ______________

12F: Vocabulary Review Puzzle

For use with the Chapter Review

Study Skill Read problems carefully. Pay special attention to exponents when working with polynomials.

Complete the crossword puzzle below. For help, use the Glossary in your textbook.

Here are the words you will use to complete this crossword puzzle:

distributive	constant
binomial	polynomial
variable	exponent
coefficient	scientific notation
like terms	monomial

ACROSS

2. may be one term or the sum or difference of two or more terms
5. the numerical factor in any term of a polynomial
8. a polynomial with two terms
9. terms with exactly the same variable factors
10. tells how many times a number, or base, is used as a factor

DOWN

1. a way to write a number as two factors, the second of which is always a power of ten
3. $a(b + c) = ab + ac$ is an example of the ______ Property.
4. $4m$, for example
6. a term in a polynomial that does not contain a variable
7. a letter that stands for a number

Vocabulary and Study Skills